Visions
AND DIVISIONS

mela

multi-ethnic literatures of the americas

AMRITJIT SINGH, CARLA L. PETERSON, C. LOK CHUA, SERIES EDITORS

The MELA Series aims to expand and deepen our sense of American literatures as multicultural and multilingual and works to establish a broader understanding of "America" as a complex site for the creation of national, transnational, and global narratives. Volumes in the series focus on the recovery, consolidation, and reevaluation of literary expression in the United States, Canada, and the Caribbean as shaped by the experience of race, ethnicity, national origin, region, class, gender, and language.

Visions
AND DIVISIONS

AMERICAN IMMIGRATION LITERATURE,
1870–1930

EDITED AND WITH AN INTRODUCTION BY
Tim Prchal and Tony Trigilio

RUTGERS UNIVERSITY PRESS
NEW BRUNSWICK, NEW JERSEY, AND LONDON

Library of Congress Cataloging-in-Publication Data

Visions and divisions : American immigration literature, 1870–1930 / edited and with an introduction by Tim Prchal and Tony Trigilio.

    p. cm. — (Multi-ethnic literatures of the Americas)

  Includes bibliographical references.

  ISBN 978-0-8135-4233-1 (hardcover : alk. paper) – ISBN 978-0-8135-4234-8 (pbk. : alk. paper)

1. Immigrants' writings, American. 2. Immigrants' writings, American–History and criticism. 3. Emigration and immigration–Literary collections. 4. American literature–Minority authors. 5. Immigrants–Literary collections. 6. Ethnic groups–Literary collections. 7. United States–Intellectual life. I. Prchal, Tim, 1958- II. Trigilio, Tony, 1966-

  PS508.I45V57 2008

  810.8'09220691–dc22

2007019968

A British Cataloging-in-Publication record for this book is available from the British Library.

This collection copyright © 2008 by Rutgers, The State University

Introduction and scholarly apparatus © 2008 by Tim Prchal and Tony Trigilio

Text design by Adam B. Bohannon

Visit our Web site: http://rutgerspress.rutgers.edu

Manufactured in the United States of America

CONTENTS

ACKNOWLEDGMENTS

This project involved countless hours of flipping through many musty pages in search of forgotten poems, short stories, essays, and anything else that dealt with immigration and the four "visions" that organize this anthology. In some cases, reading historical analyses of, say, images of the Chinese in American literature led us to useful texts. Toward the end of the process, the editors of the MELA series suggested ways to enhance the diversity of the authors represented, and we certainly thank them for that. As we prepared the manuscript, Jennefer Sixkiller, Elsa Foley, and Cora Jacobs assisted with scanning and often retyping cramped and smudged lines on copies of the original texts, a task for which a free copy of the finished volume is hardly fair recompense.

We wish to express our gratitude to Leslie Mitchner of Rutgers University Press for her encouragement and for her guidance in preparation of the final manuscript. Special thanks to Columbia College Chicago for a Curriculum Diversity Grant that enabled research at the Immigration History Research Center at the University of Minnesota.

Of course, we must salute our immigrant ancestors, who came to the United States during the era to which this volume is devoted. Carrying their surnames—be they deficient or ample in vowels by Anglo-American standards—frequently reminds us of our immigrant heritage. Our desire to understand something of the America that they came to sustained the development of this book from first to last. Prominent among them, for Tim, are Frantisek Prchal, who married Anna Kotrchova's daughter Marie, and Rosalia Placha, who married Frantisek Svec. All had left Bohemia in the late nineteenth century to settle in Chicago. This book's legacy, for Tony, traces back to Frank Trigilio, Sr., who left Sicily and worked the mines of Appalachia, the farmlands of New Jersey and Pennsylvania, and the jazz clubs of the northeastern coast; to Mary Lipari, Frank's wife, whose own journey took her from Sicily, to Tunisia, to New Jersey, to Pennsylvania; and to Giuseppina DiNicola, who came here from Abruzzo, Italy, and raised eight children by herself after the death of her husband, Nicholas Iacobucci, who used to read the Italian newspapers aloud in Erie, Pennsylvania's Little Italy to his fellow Abruzzese immigrants who came to the United States before literacy test legislation took hold.

Angel Island poems from *Island: Poetry and History of Chinese Immigrants on Angel Island, 1910–1940* edited by Him Mark Lai, Genny Lim, and Judy Yung, copyright 1980 by University of Washington Press. Reprinted by permission of the publisher.

Kahlil Gibran, "Dead Are My People" from *A Treasury of Kahlil Gibran* translated by A.R. Ferris, copyright 1951 by The Citadel Press. All rights reserved. Reprinted by arrangement with Citadel Press/Kensington Publishing Corp. www.kensingtonbooks.com.

Gold Mountain poems from *Songs of Gold Mountain: Cantonese Rhymes from San Francisco Chinatown* edited by Marlon K. Hom, copyright 1987 by The Regents of the University of California. Reprinted by permission of The University of California Press.

Dmytro Zakharchuk, "Introduction" and "Foreign Country" from Dmytro Zakharchuk Papers, Box 1, Folder 1, Immigration History Resource Center, University of Minnesota. Reprinted by permission of the Immigration History Resource Center.

CHRONOLOGY

1751   In a pamphlet titled "Observations Concerning the Increase of Mankind," Ben Franklin expresses his worry that German immigrants resisting becoming Anglicized will Germanize the nation. He also calls for a ban on the world's black and "tawny" peoples, which includes almost everybody, even European groups such as the French and the Swedes. Only the English and Saxons are white, he concludes, and only they can enhance the "lovely White and Red" national coloration.

1782   Perhaps the earliest formal articulation of the melting pot vision of America appears in Hector St. John de Crèvecoeur's *Letters from an American Farmer*.

1787   In *Notes on the State of Virginia*, Thomas Jefferson warns of the "heterogeneous, incoherent, distracted mass" that could result from admitting immigrants from nations governed under absolute monarchies.

1790   The federal government requires two years of residency for naturalization.

1808   Congress bans importation of slaves.

1819   Congress initiates numeration of immigrants.

1849   The discovery of gold in California ignites a wave of Chinese immigration.

1854   In *People v. Hall*, the California Supreme Court rules that the testimony of a Chinese man who had witnessed a murder by a white man is inadmissible because of prevailing public opinion that the Chinese are "inferior" and therefore have no right "to swear away the life of a citizen" or "of participating with us in administering the affairs of our Government."

1857   The *Dred Scott* decision by the U.S. Supreme Court declares that blacks are not U.S. citizens.

1862   The Homestead Act makes land just west of the Mississippi River cheap, enticing immigrants to that region.

1864   Congress makes the importation of contract laborers legal.

1868   The Fourteenth Amendment of the Constitution grants citizenship to African Americans.

1870   The Fifteenth Amendment of the Constitution grants African American males the right to vote.

1875   Congress passes legislation to bar prostitutes and convicts from immigrating, the first restriction law.

1882   The Chinese Exclusion Act terminates immigration of Chinese laborers. Congress adds "lunatics, idiots, and persons likely to become public charges" to the list of banned immigrants.

1885   Congress terminates the admission of any contract laborers.

1887   Publication of Lee Yan Phou's *When I Was a Boy in China*, considered the first book written in English by a Chinese immigrant. The volume is designed to improve American readers' images of China and its people.

1891   The federal government takes over immigration processing.

1892   The Ellis Island immigration facility is opened.

1900   Congress establishes a civil government in Puerto Rico and grants U.S. citizenship to the inhabitants there.

1906   Upton Sinclair's *The Jungle* is published, one of the earliest American novels featuring a "new immigrant" from Lithuania.

1907   The United States and Japan form a "Gentlemen's Agreement" in which Japan ends issuance of passports to laborers and the United States agrees not to prohibit Japanese immigration.

1908   Israel Zangwill's play *The Melting Pot* premieres in Washington, D.C.

1910   The Angel Island immigration facility is opened.

1911   The Dillingham Commission identifies Mexican laborers as the best solution to the Southwest labor shortage. Mexicans are exempted from immigrant "head taxes" set earlier.

1912   *Mrs. Spring Fragrance*, Sui Sin Far's collection of short stories about Chinese immigrants, is published. Also published is Mary Antin's *The Promised Land*, an often-cited account of the author's transformation from a Russian Jew to an American citizen. Poet and novelist Claude McKay comes to the United States from Jamaica, becoming one of the many important writers associated with the Harlem Renaissance.

1916   Jamaican-born Marcus Garvey arrives in the United States and begins to spur resistance to discrimination against African Americans.

1917   Congress initiates a literacy test for immigrants over sixteen years of age. Those fleeing religious persecution are exempt. An Asiatic "barred zone" is established, preventing immigration from almost all of Asia. Also, the novel *The Rise of David Levinsky* is published, wherein Abraham Cahan challenges the value of assimilation by telling the story of a Russian Jew who immigrates to America.

1918   *My Ántonia*, by Willa Cather, is published. Featuring Bohemian immigrants adjusting to life in Nebraska, this novel has been described as realistically dramatizing the ideals of cultural pluralism.

1920   Anzia Yezierska's *Hungry Hearts* is published. This collection of short stories reflects the author's own experience as a Jewish immigrant from Poland. Yezierska went on to write *Salome of the Tenements* (1922), *Children of Loneliness* (1923), *The Bread Givers* (1925), and other works.

1921   Congress institutes an "emergency" quota system to curb immigration from southern and eastern Europe.

1922   Japanese immigrant Takao Ozawa petitions to be naturalized on the premise that Japanese people are white. Supreme Court judge George Sutherland rules that "white" is synonymous with "Caucasian," making Ozawa ineligible for citizenship.

1923   Though previously immigrants from India had been awarded citizenship, the case of *United States v. Bhagat Singh Thind* rules that "Hindus" (a term applied to anyone from India) are ineligible for naturalization because, despite valid claims to being "Caucasian," they are not commonly considered "white." As in the 1922 *Ozawa* case, George Sutherland presided.

1924   The Johnson-Reed Act changes the quota to reduce the southern and eastern European influx even more. All persons ineligible for citizenship (essentially meaning Asians) are now barred from immigrating. In contrast, President Calvin Coolidge signs a bill granting Native Americans full citizenship.

1929   Congress makes annual immigration quotas permanent.

1934   Henry Roth's *Call It Sleep* is published. This acclaimed, modernist novel is about a Jewish boy from eastern Europe who suffers the psychological damage of the New York ghetto in the early twentieth century.

1942   Congress allows for importation of agricultural workers from within North, Central, and South America. The Bracero program allows Mexican laborers to work in the United States.

1943   Congress repeals the Chinese Exclusion Act of 1882, establishes quotas for Chinese immigrants, and makes them eligible for U.S. citizenship.

1945   The War Bride Act and the G.I. Fiancées Act allow immigration of foreign-born wives, husbands, children, and betrothed of U.S. armed forces personnel.

1948   The Displaced Persons Act allows admission of persons fleeing persecution; 205,000 refugees enter within two years.

1952   The McCarren-Walter Immigration and Nationality Act ends racial basis for naturalization eligibility. The act reaffirms and even strengthens the administration of the national origins quota system.

1965   The Immigration Act of 1965 abolishes the unequal national origins quota system, replacing it with another that allows twenty thousand immigrants from any given country. (Preference is awarded to family members of immigrants and to skilled workers.) An overall limit of 170,000 from outside the Western Hemisphere is set, while immigration from the Western Hemisphere is restricted to 120,000.

INTRODUCTION:
THE LITERATURE
OF THE NEW CHILL

The sight of immigrants arriving at Ellis Island must have made Henry James shiver. In *The American Scene,* his travelogue of the nation in the early twentieth century, he says that "any sensitive citizen" who witnesses the stream of newcomers being processed for admission will take on "the outward sign of the new chill in his heart." The chill comes from confronting the "affirmed claim of the alien, however immeasurably alien," to partake of "one's supreme relation," namely, "one's relation to one's country." Farther inland, James's sensitivity to the alien quality of immigrants has the same effect. He recounts pausing to watch some recently arrived Italians at work. While coming upon such a scene in Europe would have evoked "the play of mutual recognition, founded on old familiarities and heredities," on American soil, it produces "a chill, straight away, for the heart." The foreboding sensation occurs yet again when James has some trouble asking an Armenian immigrant for directions, and he explains the chill as stemming from the feeling that "there is no claim to brotherhood with aliens in the first grossness of their alienism."[1] James could have seen these people as members of the huddled masses yearning to breathe free or, perhaps, as Americans-in-the-making. Since his own perspective was that of someone who had returned to the United States after twenty years abroad, he could even have seen them as expatriates like himself. Instead, in James's mind, they were a chilling prospect for the United States.

By 1907, when *The American Scene* was first published, James's literary contemporaries and predecessors had devoted only scattered attention to immigrants. That same year, an anonymous editor for *Scribner's* contended that immigrant characters play an insignificant role in American literature and that even Jurgis Rudkus, the protagonist of Upton Sinclair's *The Jungle,* "dwindles into insignificance as the story is unfolded." However, in 1912, an editor for *Current Literature* introduces a story spotlighting such characters by announcing, "A distinct school of American fiction is gradually growing up among those who already discern the rare opportunities thus presented in the attempts of people from many lands to readjust themselves here to their new environment and to one another." By 1923, Henry Seidel Canby could bemoan the "habit" of looking to immigrants for literary inspiration: "A born writer cannot see a booted Russian peasant woman in a subway car without desiring to write a story about her."[2] Willa Cather's *My Ántonia* joins Sinclair's *The Jungle* as works from this "distinct school" that have reached canonical status. While Sinclair and Cather exemplify native-born authors portraying immigrant experience, the movement also included immigrant authors as diverse as Anzia Yezierska, Sui Sin Far, and Claude McKay.

That a significant wave of literature by and about immigrants would appear at this time is not surprising when one considers what was occurring during the late nineteenth and early twentieth centuries. Roger Daniels reports that "in the thirty-five years after 1890 more than twenty million immigrants entered the United States,"[3] an unprecedented swell that would only be rivaled at the end of the twentieth century. The celebrated opening of Israel Zangwill's play *The Melting Pot* came in 1908, its title popularizing the phrase still used to salute the United States as a place where the world's peoples come together. This was also the era when a profoundly new concept of tolerance and diversity crystallized. It came to be called cultural pluralism, the precursor of what is commonly called multiculturalism today. However, these positive events are best seen as counterbalances to far more hostile ones. The cherished image of the United States as a refuge for the world's oppressed and a land of opportunity for all was crumbling as a series of immigration restriction laws were passed. While individuals were barred because they were deemed "criminals," "mental defectives," or "anarchists," more sweeping restrictions were being based on nationality. The Chinese were targeted first, followed by the Japanese. Next on the official list of undesirables were newcomers from the remaining Asian nations (except the Philippines, a U.S. territory at the time), from Arab nations, and from southern and eastern European nations, the latter comprising the vast majority of immigrants. It should come as no surprise, then, that a significant body of literature arose addressing these transformations and conflicts regarding immigration.

These texts introduced or solidified many of the basic ideas found in the immigration literature of a century later. Introducing their anthology of immigrant literature written mostly after 1965, Louis Mendoza and S. Shankar say that the "body of work from before World War II, composed during a period of immigration that was arguably the most intense, sketches out many of the paradigmatic themes of immigrant literature." Among these themes are identity formation, assimilation, and alienation.[4] Our own anthology is designed to highlight that important earlier body of work. We hope to illustrate its widely varied expressions of personal experience and sociopolitical position; its range of genres, from fiction and autobiography to poetry and song lyrics; and its diversity of authors, some still renowned and some "recovered" as well as some immigrants and some native-born.

We do this by organizing our selections into four topics of debate that pervaded the nation during the late nineteenth and early twentieth centuries, an approach we hope will facilitate reading the selections within their historical context. At the foundation of each of these topics is a particular vision of national identity, especially in regard to what made the United States great and how race and ethnicity figured into that greatness. The first section explores literature related to the restriction/open door controversy, and the dates of what might be called the "rise of restrictionism" roughly mark the historical borders of the material in our anthology. The liberal, if not laissez-faire, national policy of unregulated immigration that had been in place since the Revolution was bolstered by a conviction that immigrants would readily assimilate to or even enhance U.S. society. This society, it was hoped, would remain unified by being fundamentally homogeneous. In fact, the open door policy was abandoned when fears arose that certain types of immigrants were inassimilable because of racial or ethnic pride and/or the overwhelming masses in which they were arriving. At other times, natives argued more bluntly that some groups of newcomers would degrade the general populace with their alleged innate inferiority.

The next three sections are devoted to debates that centered on immigrants after they had been admitted and on the consequent relationship between immigrants and their host culture. Writing in 1920, Isaac B. Berkson called these "theories of adjustment," but while restriction addressed national identity by radically revising it, each of these theories envisions a particular national identity to which immigrants were to adjust. Our second section includes works that address assimilation to what many saw as a nation fortified by its British heritage. "According to this position," Berkson writes, "America is pictured as already populated with a fairly homogeneous type, which both in race and culture has Anglo-Saxon affiliations." Adjusting to this image of the nation requires that "all newcomers from foreign lands must as quickly as possible divest themselves of their old characteristics, and through intermarriage and complete taking over of the language, customs, hopes, aspirations of the American type obliterate all ethnic distinctions."[5] The abandonment of any and all traits deemed not Anglo-Saxon is key here, as is the assumption that U.S. culture was, for the most part, steadfast and static.

The melting pot view, the subject of our third section, shifts the idea of wholesale replacement of immigrant characteristics toward sharing some of those characteristics with the host culture. While still aiming for a homogeneous end, U.S. society is now ever-evolving so long as foreigners arrive and contribute something new. Instead of assimilating to Anglo-Saxon ways, says Berkson, "not one race is singled out as the standard.... A better understanding of the foreign groups, a spirit of humane toleration, and a notion of the dynamic nature of society pervade the Melting Pot idea." Still, there is a heavy cost to contributing to the pot. Berkson goes on to say that "always the community which has made the contribution itself perishes as it gives forth the products of its own life. The 'Melting Pot' theory is adequate only for those groups which are willing to give up their identity completely in becoming incorporated into the life of America."[6] Considering that nineteenth-century neologism *miscegenation*, a term invented to stir anxiety about racial commingling, can help us discern how many Americans of the period would recoil at the ramifications of calling their country a melting pot. The homogenization of races, while certainly eradicating problems of racial discrimination, also meant losing the pride, the distinction, and any privileges of belonging to one race in tension with others.

Imagining the United States either as a product of its Anglo-Saxon roots or as an amalgamation of characteristics from many nations is typically traced back to before the Civil War. The next vision of the nation emerged in the early twentieth century, at least in a formal way, and it took a while to name it. Berkson terms it "the 'Federation of Nationalities' theory." However, Randolph Bourne's 1916 essay suggests "trans-nationality." Horace Kallen hit on the more permanent "cultural pluralism" only after he revised his 1915 essay "Democracy Versus the Melting-Pot," which we have placed beside Bourne's at the start of our fourth section. This view refutes the previous two by striking at their assumption that homogeneity is desirable in a democratic society. Instead, the greatness of the nation lies in ethnic and racial heterogeneity—in granting immigrants the freedom to remain true to their backgrounds—and so the distinct characteristics immigrants bring with them should be preserved and respected instead of abandoned or shared. In its time, it was an odd idea, one that failed to have much force until decades later in debates over multiculturalism.

While the United States argued over whether or not to restrict immigrants—and which ones to restrict—it also debated whether or not the society to which they should acclimate was Anglo-Saxon or an amalgamation of diverse characteristics. Many questioned, too, whether or not immigrants should bother to acclimate in the first place. Needless to say, these discussions grew confusing at times. Our organizing the anthology's selections into four discreet categories often involved a good deal of head scratching. For example, Margherita Arlina Hamm's "Kalaun, the Elephant Trainer" shines a positive light on the son's assimilation but casts a dark shadow on the father, who retains his own customs and is tolerant of others maintaining theirs. Surely, the author endorses assimilation while condemning cultural pluralism. Since the father is the focal character, though, we decided it is more a tragedy about cultural pluralism than a success story about assimilation. We do not mean to suggest that the writers included here treated restriction, assimilation, the melting pot, or cultural pluralism as disentangled topics. Quite the contrary, we encourage our readers to find connections between the anthology's sections and selections.

We also encourage readers to find connections between the issues underlying these works and other branches of ethnic literature and ethnic studies. For example, our section on assimilation has particular relevance to pressures being put on American Indians during the period. The year 1924 was a pivotal one for immigrant and indigenous peoples. First, it saw the passage of the Johnson Act, the most stringent immigration restriction law based on "national origins." A week later came the passage of the Indian Citizenship Act, which automatically made citizens out of all non-citizen Indians within U.S. borders. Walter Benn Michaels explains that the Citizenship Act was "the triumphant end" of a string of legislation that required Indians to, in a sense, earn citizenship by demonstrating the behaviors of so-called civilized life or by fighting on the side of the United States in World War I. As Michaels portrays it, these laws were failed attempts to assimilate the indigenous peoples. Furthermore, though the Johnson Act was designed to exclude while the Citizenship Act was designed to include, he sees them as having more in common than one might think: "The perceived impossibility of assimilating large numbers of Eastern European immigrants had led to the erection in the Johnson Act of barriers to citizenship; the actual failure to assimilate Indians led through the Citizenship Act to citizenship."[7] The push to assimilate was felt so deeply that official changes in who qualifies for U.S. citizenship were taking effect. Similarly, the works in our assimilation section have interesting parallels with contemporary works by American Indian authors, such as "School Days of an Indian Girl," by Zitkala-Sa, and "The Problem of Old Harjo," by John M. Oskison.

The immigration history examined here is also interwoven with dynamic changes and turmoil for African Americans. For instance, World War I created a lull in immigration that "created jobs and encouraged what has been called the 'great migration' of many blacks from the South to the North," according to Daniels, who notes that about 750,000 people are estimated to have traveled in this migration.[8] Charles Chesnutt's story "Uncle Wellington's Wives," included in our section on the melting pot, dramatizes an earlier phase of this northward movement. It also echoes what Michaels sees happening in Chesnutt's novel *The House Behind the Cedars*, which, he says, "begins in a world of black, white, and mulatto, [but] ends in black and white." Like Rowena in the novel, Uncle Wellington ultimately chooses to be part of the African American world after he fails to materialize his dream of an idyllic life beyond racial distinctions, to which miscegenation is central. As Michaels says, "the discovery that there are no mulattoes marks the literal definitive defeat of the melting pot."[9] Some of the writers addressing the immigrant's place in the melting pot arrive at similar conclusions.

The Reconstruction and Progressive eras, which coincide with the historical frame of this anthology, were especially important in terms of clarifying the place of African Americans in U.S. society and finding ways to improve it. Black leaders such as Booker T. Washington, W. E. B. Du Bois, and Marcus Garvey raised general awareness of the individual and social trails faced by African Americans. An immigrant from Jamaica, Garvey serves as a reminder that, although immigration figures from the Western Hemisphere were small in comparison to those from Europe, its immigrants certainly made a significant mark. To illustrate the unique perspectives that came from being a black immigrant in the United States in this period, we have included the works by poet Claude McKay and essayist Eric Walrond, both immigrants from the Caribbean.

Alternatively, many of our selections can be useful for those interested in the construction—or, rather, the deconstruction—of whiteness. The Johnson Act of 1924 marks the climax of what Matthew Frey Jacobson calls "the most fractious period in the political history of whiteness in the United States, the period that had begun with the massive influx of undesirable 'white persons' from Ireland and Germany in the 1840s." It is a period in which the white race was split into a variety of races: Anglo-Saxon, Celtic, Teutonic, Slavic, Latin, Semite, and so forth. Indeed, this was an era when stereotypes associated with people from any given nation—ranging from musical talent to a predilection toward certain types of crime—were thought to be so deeply hereditary that "race" and "nationality" were virtually synonymous. Of particular importance to the millions of immigrants arriving from southern and eastern Europe was a theory that divided that continent into three regional races: the Mediterranean race in the south, the Nordic race in the north, and the Alpine race wedged in between them from the east. Allegedly rooted in biological differences, proponents claimed the theory to be verifiable by measuring representative skulls of the three groups. As weird as this might seem in the early twenty-first century, a leading proponent of the theory, Madison Grant, held remarkable influence a century ago. According to Jacobson, Grant's ideas "not only influenced debates over immigration and restriction, but also influenced and reflected popular understanding of peoplehood and diversity."[10] In fact, Grant's declaration that the Nordics were racially superior to the Mediterraneans and Alpines—and yet were threatened by mixing with them in America's melting pot—earned him a fan letter from no less that Adolf Hitler. In this kind of divisive climate, James's chilly reaction to recently arrived European immigrants becomes more fathomable.

Since the white races rather quickly reconsolidated, this legacy of white racial divisions is often neglected. "Modern scholars are most comfortable discussing Poles, Greeks, or Italians as 'ethnic' or 'national' groups," says Jacobson, "and thus they tend to disparage and dismiss the lexicon of white races that characterized an earlier era."[11] A glance at what came to be called "the new immigration" from southern and eastern European and Arab nations will help readers grasp the cultural milieu originally surrounding the selections dealing with such immigrants. Toward end of the nineteenth century, several U.S. citizens descended from Britain, the Netherlands, France, Germany, Ireland, and Scandinavia—"old immigrant" stock, in other words—began to worry about a rising number of "new immigrants" from places such as Russia, Poland, Hungary, Romania, Greece, Turkey, and Syria. For example, in 1907, economics professor John R. Commons interpreted statistics on immigration from Europe and Asiatic Turkey between 1882 and 1906. The overall totals were climbing from 647,082 to 1,024,719, but Commons had special concerns about the fact that northern and western Europe was losing the numerical advantage. Those arriving from this region had fallen from 87 to 21.7 percent during those years while the "new immigrants" had risen from 13 to 78 percent. He portrays this as an alteration not just in kind but also in quality of immigrant stock: "A line drawn across the continent of Europe from northeast to southwest . . . separates countries not only of distinct races but also of distinct civilizations." The line, as Commons draws it, separates Protestantism from Catholicism; representative and popular governments from "absolute monarchies"; universal education from illiteracy; manufacturing, "progressive agriculture, and skilled labor from primitive hand industries, backward agriculture, and unskilled labor." He surmises that, when immigration from "countries so nearly allied to our own" shifts to "countries so remote in the main attributes of Western civilization, the change is one that should challenge the attention of every citizen."[12]

While these divisions between white groups were deep, they were probably not quite as deep as those between whites in general and groups that, like "white," endure as racial classifications in our own time. Nonetheless, the divisions of the late nineteenth and early twentieth centuries were bridged by the visions of national identity as Americans joined sides in opposing restriction or supporting it, resisted assimilation or promoted it, and so forth. Of course, these visions created new divisions, so along with the connections listed above, we encourage readers to be mindful of the disconnections expressed in the works that follow. With the benefit of hindsight, this literature can shed light on the agreements and disagreements that emerge when immigration is discussed in the United States today.

Notes

1. Henry James, *The American Scene* (Bloomington: Indiana University Press, 1968), 85, 118–120.

2. "The Point of View," *Scribner's* (November 1907): 635; introduction to "The Thing Called Play—A Story," by Lucille Baldwin Van Slyke, *Current Literature* (May 1912): 602; Henry Seidel Canby, "Americans in Fiction," *Century* (July 1923): 366.

3. Roger Daniels, *Not Like Us: Immigrants and Minorities in America, 1890–1924* (Chicago: Ivan R. Dee, 1997), viii.

4. Louis Mendoza and S. Shankar, "Introduction: The New Literature of Immigration," in *Crossing into America*, ed. Louis Mendoza and S. Shankar (New York: New Press, 2003), xx.

5. Isaac B. Berkson, *Theories of Americanization: A Critical Study With Special Reference to the Jewish Group* (New York: Teacher's College, Columbia University, 1920), 55.

6. Ibid., 75–76.

7. Walter Benn Michaels, *Our America: Nativism, Modernism, and Pluralism* (Durham: Duke University Press, 1995), 31.

8. Daniels, *Not Like Us*, 85.

9. Michaels, *Our America*, 54, 64.

10. Matthew Frye Jacobson, *Whiteness of a Different Color: European Immigrants and the Alchemy of Race* (Cambridge, Mass.: Harvard University Press, 1998), 90, 82.

11. Ibid., 68.

12. John R. Commons, *Races and Immigrants in America* (1907; rpt. New York: Augustus M. Kelley Publishers, 1967), 69–71.

A NOTE ON THE TEXT

The original texts for this anthology come from late nineteenth- and early twentieth-century periodicals, books, sheet music, and archived manuscripts. In a few cases, the texts were found in much more recent anthologies that include poems and song lyrics from that same era. Spelling and punctuation have been edited to conform to modern standards, and obvious typographical errors have been corrected, all without editorial notation.

Visions
AND DIVISIONS

PART I

The Restriction/Open Door Debate

With credentials as a professor of political economy at Yale, the president of MIT, and the superintendent of the U.S. Census, Francis A. Walker was smart enough to know what he was up against when, in 1896, he rallied for greater immigration restrictions. Published in the esteemed *Atlantic Monthly*, his proposal was to extend restrictions far beyond those relatively few newcomers already being barred for physical or mental disabilities, criminal records, or pauperism and "to exclude perhaps hundreds of thousands, the great majority of whom would be subject to no individual objections." Walker admitted that his proposal was likely to evoke "a high degree of incredulity, arising from the traditions of our country. From the beginning, it has been the policy of the United States, both officially and according to the prevailing sentiment of our people, to tolerate, to welcome, and to encourage immigration, without qualification and without discrimination." Immigration, he added, had been viewed as "a source of both strength and wealth."[1] Walker was not only calling for a change in immigration policy but was also asking for a fundamental change in national identity: should the Golden Door leading to the land of opportunity and to liberty for the world's oppressed be barricaded? In other words, should the vision of the nation embodied in Emma Lazarus's famous "The Great Colossus," found in this part, be abandoned?

At the close of the nineteenth century, then, arguing for restriction required not just changing people's minds but changing how people imagined the United States and its relationship to immigration. An editor at *The Century* magazine had noticed this back in 1887, when there was a "rising and already very general demand for some restriction of immigration." The editor explained: "The hardships of the proposition lie mainly in the visions, which the imagination unconsciously conjures up, of United States marshals lining the shores of the great republic, ready to treat as criminal the desire of any immigrant to enter her jurisdiction."[2] Seemingly in response, restrictionists used words to paint lurid pictures of the nation being invaded by mobs of dangerous foreigners. Walker, for instance, said, "There may be those who can contemplate the addition to our population of vast numbers of persons having no inherited instincts of self-government and respect for law; knowing no restraint upon their own passions but the club of the policeman or the bayonet of the soldier; forming communities, by the tens of thousands, in which only foreign tongues are spoken, and into which can steal no influence from our free institutions and from popular discussion. But I confess to being far less optimistic."[3]

A similar lack of optimism is reflected in Thomas Bailey Aldrich's "Unguarded Gates," placed right after Lazarus's poem. It seems Walker and Aldrich knew that, in order to promote restriction, they must fight negative visions of restriction with worse visions of immigrants. The lack of evidence supporting such generalizations about "vast numbers of persons" did not go unnoticed. A year after Walker's essay appeared, Simon Greenleaf Croswell had this to say about the restriction debate: "Inferences, deductions, conjectures, and a host of less persuasive probabilities have been brought forward and paraded in each line of battle; but of facts, such facts, I mean as bear directly and strongly upon the problems involved, there has been little use made."[4] A review of the facts led Croswell to stand opposed to barring immigration. Of course, an interpretation of data often reflects the interpreter more than the data, but as the nineteenth century became the twentieth, advocates for restriction continued to portray immigrants in the worst possible light with little concern for any facts at all. For example, Madison Grant's *The Passing of the Great Race* stands as one of the most scathing attacks on virtually all immigrants except those belonging the allegedly superior Nordic race of northern Europe. The book first appeared in 1916, but when the fourth edition was published in 1921, Grant added a Documentary Supplement to quell what he called "a persistent demand for 'authorities.'" Curiously—and suspiciously—he added that an early draft of the supplement had supported "substantially every statement in the book, but much was afterward omitted because it would seem that some things could be taken without proof."[5] The phrase "taken without proof" tells us much about the restrictionists, and it reveals something about where the general U.S. population was heading. After all, Grant's book was popular enough without "authorities" to have made it to a fourth edition.

If the restrictionist movement lacked proof, it did have precedent on its side. On the one hand, in 1875, the first national restriction law was passed to prevent the admission of women for the purpose of prostitution and to bar any criminal who, in essence, had swapped punishment for exile to the United States. As the century mark came and went, the categories of exclusion grew from certain types of criminal records to an assortment of mental deficiencies and physical diseases, and from religious practices involving polygamy to political views promoting anarchy. On the other hand, much broader nationality-based legislation had been established with the Chinese Exclusion Act of 1882, the text of which opens this part. The article in *The Century* mentioned above described this piece of legislation as "a precedent and a tempting suggestion" to greater restrictions.[6] The rationales justifying the anti-Chinese law were reiterated to support restrictions against an increasing number of people of various nationalities, so a review of how Chinese exclusion came to be will be instructive.

Though the Chinese had sailed to the New World centuries earlier, the discovery of gold in California in 1849 sparked a wave of immigration from that country. The 325 Chinese immigrants already in California in 1850 were joined by 450 more that year, 2,716 arrived the next year, and 20,026 the year after that. That number had more than tripled by 1870. Though they widely dispersed, about three-fourths of the Chinese population was in California, and this state became the epicenter of restrictionist tremors felt on the national level. Chinese newcomers quickly became seen as competition by white miners, and a series of state laws were enacted to protect native-born workers. For example, California instituted a license tax on foreign miners, the Chinese prominent among them. As the gold waned, the Chinese moved on to other occupations, playing an important role in the development of railroads, manufacturing, and agriculture. However, this only spread their reputation as competition for white laborers. Ronald Takaki points out that the Chinese were victims of the same "dangerous mob" imagery mentioned above: "As an industrial army of aliens from the East, they threatened to displace and force white workers into poverty."[7] One of the rationales for restriction established during these years, then, was protecting labor, a fact revealed in the lyrics of "Twelve Hundred More" and in Mark Twain's satire, "John Chinaman in New York."

Another was to protect the country from the consequences of increasing racial diversity and to guard against the degradation nativists feared would result from sharing the nation with races they deemed inferior. Takaki refers to Hinton Helper, a North Carolinian whose book about his travels to California warned against the effects of racial diversity. Helper wrote that "the greater the diversity of colors and qualities of men, the greater will be the strife and conflict of feeling. . . . Our population was already too heterogeneous before the Chinese came." Writing when slavery was splitting the nation, he speculated that "the copper of the Pacific" would become as divisive an issue as "the ebony of the Atlantic." The connection between Chinese immigrants and African Americans went farther after the Civil War, when newspapers from San Francisco to New York applied stereotypes from one to the other. "Like blacks," Takaki explains, "the Chinese were described as heathen, morally inferior, savage, childlike, and lustful." Fears about miscegenation between black and white were also transferred, and one California official proclaimed that the offspring of white and Chinese would be "a hybrid of the most despicable, a mongrel of the most detestable that has ever afflicted the earth."[8]

These stereotypes and aspersions added fuel to the inflammatory language concerning the labor threat allegedly posed by admitting Chinese immigrants. In this way, frightening images, more than facts, led to the passage of the Chinese Exclusion Act of 1882. Though the Chinese made up one-quarter of California's workforce, they posed little threat on a national level because they made up only 0.002 percent of the U.S. population in 1880. Nonetheless, the Exclusion Act had very real results. While it was designed to ban only laborers and admit merchants, officials, teachers, students, and tourists, the Exclusion Act resulted in a drastic fall in number of the Chinese in the United States: 105,465 in 1880, to 89,863 in 1900, to 61,639 in 1920.[9] Glimpses of how restriction affected the lives of these people are found in this part's offerings of the hopeful poems by Chinese residents of San Francisco; the bleak poems written on the walls of the Angel Island immigration station, where many newcomers were detained for lengthy periods after the Exclusion Act had been instituted; and the often bitter autobiography of New Yorker Lee Chew.

By setting a precedent for nationality-based restriction, the Exclusion Act became a first step toward reducing the numbers of other Asian groups as well as several European and Arab groups in decades to come. The Japanese and Koreans, whose numbers started to climb not too long after restrictions against the Chinese had been established, faced similar agitation. Again, the West Coast was the focal point. However, Japan had proven itself to be a formidable world power when it triumphed in war against China in 1895 and against Russia in 1905. (Negotiations in the latter conflict made Korea a protectorate of Japan.) Regardless, in 1906, the San Francisco Board of Education ordered its Japanese and Korean students to attend a segregated school. According to Hans P. Vought, this "Oriental school," to which Chinese students were already assigned, was "in a burned-out section of the city, too far away to allow many students to attend." Such discrimination infuriated the Japanese government, and President Theodore Roosevelt "decided that the only solution to the problem which would placate West Coast voters and avoid war was to apply the same class-based restriction to the Japanese that was already in effect for the Chinese, but to do it through an informal 'Gentlemen's Agreement.'" Again, the working-class immigrant was banned, but now the onus was on the Japanese to grant passports only to "students, merchants, professionals, and laborers returning to property acquired before 1906 or to their spouses." As a result, Japanese immigration fell from 12,999 in 1907 to 8,340 the following year, and only 1,596 the year after.[10] The "Gentlemen's Agreement" was phased in during 1907 and 1908.

In 1917, restrictions to limit Asian immigration spread much farther and, in fact, reached beyond Asia and well into Europe. An "Asiatic barred zone" was established, affecting newcomers from Arabia to Polynesia and blanketing such diverse regions as Afghanistan, India, and Indonesia. As Bill Ong Hing argues, this legislation, along with the laws barring the Chinese, Japanese and Koreans, is among "the most stark examples of the use of immigration policies to define America. Asians simply did not fall within that definition." While labor competition in the western states was the impetus of hostilities, "time and again the resulting cry for exclusion from the mouths of white Americans was about doing something to protect 'our citizens.' And certainly the concept of 'our citizens' did not include Asian immigrants." However, 1917 also saw the introduction of a literacy test to filter out supposedly unsuitable immigrants. Hing explains that this exam "was directed at southern and eastern Europeans who dominated the numbers of immigrants to the United States around the turn of the century, and particularly in the first decade of the twentieth century. At the time, southern and eastern Europeans did not fit the image of *true Americans*."[11]

Indeed, from the start of European colonization through most of the nineteenth century, the dominant sources of immigration were northern and western European regions: Britain, the Netherlands, France, Ireland, Germany, and Scandinavia. Many native-born citizens descended from these countries considered themselves to be "real Americans," to use a common phrase of the day. This was especially strongly felt when the percentage of immigrants coming from these areas fell drastically below the percentage from countries such as Italy and Greece, Russia and Poland, Hungary and Romania. Four-and-a-half million southern and eastern Europeans arrived by 1910, and over a million more by 1920, according to Hing. Arab groups, such as Syrians, were often grouped with those from southern and eastern Europe.[12]

A prominent restrictionist, Roy L. Garis, reported that the immigrants from northern and western Europe—the so-called old immigrants—were "similar in blood and in political ideas, social training, and economic background," and they "merged with the native stock fairly easily and rapidly." However, he described the "new immigrants" from the rest of Europe in terms of a "racial" change, one calling for such words as "ominous," "menace," and "danger." He reused the image of a threatening mob, this time to suggest that the unity of the United States was jeopardized. Garis even proclaimed, "According to every test made in recent years and from a practical study of the problem, it is evident beyond doubt that the immigrant from Northern and Western Europe is far superior to the one from Southern and Eastern Europe."[13] Again, letting generalities trump specificity, documentation, or "authorities," Garis painted a frightening picture of undesirable foreigners to promote restriction. Fiction gave more specific faces to these demeaning stereotypes. For instance, Caspar Day's "Veronika and the Angelinos" interwove a lesson about motherly devotion with a virtual checklist of negative stereotypes—from drunkenness and dirt-iness to criminality to clannishness—being ascribed to Lithuanian and Italian immigrants during the era. Also, Honoré Willsie's odd combination of essay and fiction explained the dubious theory of "race suicide," an idea propounded by Walker and others to substanti-ate the claim that the fecundity of new immigrants spelled trouble for the native, "old im-migrant" stock.

While the fact that the literacy test passed Congress was significant, it proved to have little effect in deterring the southern and eastern European influx. World War I greatly re-duced the flood of "new immigrants," but it also aroused fears about their national alle-giances, as dramatized in the lyrics of "Don't Bite the Hand That's Feeding You." After the war, the influx from southern and eastern Europe rebounded. In 1921, an emergency quota system was implemented. First, it culled from the 1910 Census the totals of each national origin among the foreign-born population living in the United States. Next, it admitted only 3 percent of each nationality's total. "Since most of those living in the United States in 1910 were northern and western European," Hing explains, "the quota for southern and eastern Europeans was smaller (about 45,000 less). The latter groups filled their quotas easily, but northern and western European countries did not fill their quotas under this law." Despite the inability to fulfill the quota for "old immigrants," an even stricter law was introduced in 1924. Under the direction of Garis, the 3 percent was dropped to 2, and the 1890 Census was used, a Census taken when the "new immigrants" had barely started ar-riving. Hing explains that the 1924 law allotted "85 percent of the total 150,000 [immi-grants admitted] to countries from northern and western Europe, while southern and eastern countries received only 15 percent of the total." Meanwhile, natives of the Western Hemisphere were not subject to restriction, and all aliens ineligible for citizenship—namely, Asians—were barred completely.[14] The "national origins" quota system begun in the 1920s served as standard policy until 1965. Even when the Chinese Exclusion Act was repealed during World War II, a stringent quota controlled the numbers admitted. Yet again, a debate that relied very much on images not founded in fact had a very tangible impact on who could and could not immigrate to the United States.

Just as unfounded yet effective imagery was employed to advance restriction, the vivid images of fiction and poetry were used to uphold an open door vision of the nation. These works also mirror the persuasive strategies found in contemporary expository essays. Louis MacBrayne's story "The Promised Land," for example, enacted the very conflict be-tween preconceptions and in-person experience that Robert Watchhorn, commissioner of immigration at the Port of New York, noted in 1907. In an essay against greater restric-tions, he said, "There are those who vehemently protest against the landing of aliens on these shores *en masse,* so long as their protests are made in abstract form, but who, Pilate-like, say on being brought face to face with the units of the mass, 'I find no fault in him.'"[15] MacBrayne dramatized this shift in perspective with his characters Senator and Mrs. Baddington, whose commitment to restriction crumbles as they get to know immi-grants on a more personal level. Similarly, the readers of James B. Connolly's "The Americanization of Roll-Down Joe" got to know the title character and, thereby, were led to see how such immigrants could revitalize the nation. As one character puts it, "While the descendants of the old settlers are leanin' back in easy chairs, brains and bodies all used up, . . . it's the new people are coming along and gettin' things goin' again." "Americanization" in this work's title implied (among other things) naturalization, and as such, Connolly addressed the issue of who should be allowed citizenship and the power of voting, a key concern in the restriction debate.

Both MacBrayne and Connolly followed in the tradition of *Uncle Tom's Cabin* by employing the power of sentimental fiction to sway public opinion regarding the nation's racial/ethnic politics. To advance the open door position, Italian immigrant Onorio Ruotolo, in "Mother America," and Syrian immigrant Ajan Syrian, in "Alma Mater," similarly drew on the emotional force of Lazarus's "The New Colossus" by reminding readers of its imagery and the ideals those images represent. Syrian especially showed how incorporating that very public imagery could express one immigrant's personal appreciation of having been admitted to the country, thereby promoting continuance of a liberal immigration policy. Altogether, the works in this part illustrate the political, social, and personal dimensions of the United States reenvisioning its relationship with immigrants and the experience of swinging the Golden Door farther and farther shut.

Notes

1. Francis A. Walker, "Restriction of Immigration," *The Atlantic Monthly* 77 (June 1896): 822–823.
2. "Shall Immigration be Restricted?" *The Century* 34 (October 1887): 954.
3. Walker, "Restriction of Immigration," 829.
4. Simon Greenleaf Croswell, "Should Immigration Be Restricted?" *North American Review* 164 (May 1897): 526. O. P. Austin similarly used statistics to defend an anti-restriction argument in "Is the New Immigration Dangerous to the Country," *North American Review* 178 (April 1904): 558–570.
5. Madison Grant, *The Passing of the Great Race, or the Racial Basis of European History*, 4th ed. (New York: Scribner's, 1921), xxvii.
6. "Shall Immigration be Restricted?" 954.
7. Ronald Takaki, *Strangers from a Different Shore*, rev. ed. (Boston: Little, Brown, 1998), 79, 82, 103.
8. Ibid., 100–101.
9. Ibid., 79, 110–112.
10. Hans P. Vought, *The Bully Pulpit and the Melting Pot: American Presidents and the Immigrant, 1897–1933* (Macon, Ga.: Mercer University Press, 2004), 49–50, 53.
11. Bill Ong Hing, *Defining America through Immigration Policy* (Philadelphia: Temple University Press, 2004), 50–51.
12. Ibid., 62. Regarding the inclusion of Arab groups with the southern and eastern European groups, see John R. Commons, *Races and Immigrants in America* (New York: Macmillan, 1907), 99–101.
13. Roy L. Garis, "America's Immigration Policy," *North American Review* 220 (September 1924): 73–75.
14. Hing, *Defining America*, 68–69.
15. Robert Watchorn, "The Gateway of the Nation," *Outlook* 87 (December 28, 1907): 899.

Text of the Chinese Exclusion Act

Forty-Seventh Congress. Session I. 1882

Chapter 126.—An act to execute certain treaty stipulations relating to Chinese.

Preamble. Whereas, in the opinion of the Government of the United States the coming of Chinese laborers to this country endangers the good order of certain localities within the territory thereof:

Therefore,

Be it enacted by the Senate and House of Representatives of the United States of America in Congress assembled,

That from and after the expiration of ninety days next after the passage of this act, and until the expiration of ten years next after the passage of this act, the coming of Chinese laborers to the United States be, and the same is hereby, suspended; and during such suspension it shall not be lawful for any Chinese laborer to come, or, having so come after the expiration of said ninety days, to remain within the United States.

SEC. 2. That the master of any vessel who shall knowingly bring within the United States on such vessel, and land or permit to be landed, any Chinese laborer, from any foreign port or place, shall be deemed guilty of a misdemeanor, and on conviction thereof shall be punished by a fine of not more than five hundred dollars for each and every such Chinese laborer so brought, and may be also imprisoned for a term not exceeding one year.

SEC. 3. That the two foregoing sections shall not apply to Chinese laborers who were in the United States on the seventeenth day of November, eighteen hundred and eighty, or who shall have come into the same before the expiration of ninety days next after the passage of this act, and who shall produce to such master before going onboard such vessel, and shall produce to the collector of the port in the United States at which such vessel shall arrive, the evidence hereinafter in this act required of his being one of the laborers in this section mentioned; nor shall the two foregoing sections apply to the case of any master whose vessel, being bound to a port not within the United States by reason of being in distress or in stress of weather, or touching at any port of the United States on its voyage to any foreign port of place: Provided, That all Chinese laborers brought on such vessel shall depart with the vessel on leaving port.

SEC. 4. That for the purpose of properly identifying Chinese laborers who were in the United States on the seventeenth day of November, eighteen hundred and eighty, or who shall have come into the same before the expiration of ninety days next after the passage of this act, and in order to furnish them with the proper evidence of their right to go from and come to the United States of their free will and accord, as provided by the treaty between the United States and China dated November seventeenth, eighteen hundred and eighty, the collector of customs of the district from which any such Chinese laborer shall depart from the United States shall, in person or by deputy, go on board each vessel having on board any such Chinese laborer and cleared or about to sail from his district for a foreign port, and on such vessel make a list of all such Chinese laborers, which shall be entered in registry-books to be kept for that purpose, in which shall be stated the name, age, occupation, last place of residence, physical marks or peculiarities, and all facts necessary for the identification of each of such Chinese laborers, which books shall be safely kept in the custom-house; and every such Chinese laborer so departing from the United States shall be entitled to, and shall receive, free of any charge or cost upon application therefor, from the collector or his deputy, at the time such list is taken, a certificate, signed by the collector or his deputy and attested by his seal of office, in such form as the Secretary of the Treasury shall prescribe, which certificate shall contain a statement of the name, age, occupation, last place of residence, personal description, and fact of identification of the Chinese laborer to whom the certificate is issued, corresponding with the said list and registry in all particulars. In case any Chinese laborer after having received such certificate shall leave such vessel before her departure he shall deliver his certificate to the master of the vessel, and if such Chinese laborer shall fail to return to such vessel before her departure from port the certificate shall be delivered by the master to the collector of customs for cancellation. The certificate herein provided for shall entitle the Chinese laborer to whom the same is issued to return to and re-enter the United States upon producing and delivering the same to the collector of customs of the district at which such Chinese laborer shall seek to re-enter; and upon delivery of such certificate by such Chinese laborer to the collector of customs at the time of re-entry in the United States, said collector shall cause the same to be filed in the custom house and duly canceled.

SEC. 5. That any Chinese laborer mentioned in section four of this act being in the United States, and desiring to depart from the United States by land, shall have the right to demand and receive, free of charge or cost, a certificate of identification similar to that provided for in section four of this act to be issued to such Chinese laborers as may desire to leave the United States by water; and it is hereby made the duty of the collector of customs of the district next adjoining the foreign country to which said Chinese laborer desires to go to issue such certificate, free of charge or cost, upon application by such Chinese laborer, and to enter the same upon registry-books to be kept by him for the purpose, as provided for in section four of this act.

SEC. 6. That in order to the faithful execution of articles one and two of the treaty in this act before mentioned, every Chinese person other than a laborer who may be entitled by said treaty and this act to come within the

United States, and who shall be about to come to the United States, shall be identified as so entitled by the Chinese Government in each case, such identity to be evidenced by a certificate issued under the authority of said government, which certificate shall be in the English language or (if not in the English language) accompanied by a translation into English, stating such right to come, and which certificate shall state the name, title, or official rank, if any, the age, height, and all physical peculiarities, former and present occupation or profession, and place of residence in China of the person to whom the certificate is issued and that such person is entitled conformably to the treaty in this act mentioned to come within the United States. Such certificate shall be prima-facie evidence of the fact set forth therein, and shall be produced to the collector of customs, or his deputy, of the port in the district in the United States at which the person named therein shall arrive.

SEC. 7. That any person who shall knowingly and falsely alter or substitute any name for the name written in such certificate or forge any such certificate, or knowingly utter any forged or fraudulent certificate, or falsely personate any person named in any such certificate, shall be deemed guilty of a misdemeanor; and upon conviction thereof shall be fined in a sum not exceeding one thousand dollars, and imprisoned in a penitentiary for a term of not more than five years.

SEC. 8. That the master of any vessel arriving in the United States from any foreign port or place shall, at the same time he delivers a manifest of the cargo, and if there be no cargo, then at the time of making a report of the entry of vessel pursuant to the law, in addition to the other matter required to be reported, and before landing, or permitting to land, any Chinese passengers, deliver and report to the collector of customs of the district in which such vessels shall have arrived a separate list of all Chinese passengers taken on board his vessel at any foreign port or place, and all such passengers on board the vessel at that time. Such list shall show the names of such passengers (and if accredited officers of the Chinese Government traveling on the business of that government, or their servants, with a note of such facts), and the name and other particulars, as shown by their respective certificates; and such list shall be sworn to by the master in the manner required by law in relation to the manifest of the cargo. Any willful refusal or neglect of any such master to comply with the provisions of this section shall incur the same penalties and forfeiture as are provided for a refusal or neglect to report and deliver a manifest of cargo.

SEC. 9. That before any Chinese passengers are landed from any such vessel, the collector, or his deputy, shall proceed to examine such passengers, comparing the certificates with the list and with the passengers; and no passenger shall be allowed to land in the United States from such vessel in violation of law.

SEC. 10. That every vessel whose master shall knowingly violate any of the provisions of this act shall be deemed forfeited to the United States, and shall be liable to seizure and condemnation on any district of the United States into which such vessel may enter or in which she may be found.

SEC. 11. That any person who shall knowingly bring into or cause to be brought into the United States by land, or who shall knowingly aid or abet the same, or aid or abet the landing in the United States from any vessel of any Chinese person not lawfully entitled to enter the United States, shall be deemed guilty of a misdemeanor, and shall, on conviction thereof, be fined in a sum not exceeding one thousand dollars, and imprisoned for a term not exceeding one year.

SEC. 12. That no Chinese person shall be permitted to enter the United States by land without producing to the proper officer of customs the certificate in this act required of Chinese persons seeking to land from a vessel. And any Chinese person found unlawfully within the United States shall be caused to be removed therefrom to the country from whence he came, by direction of the United States, after being brought before some justice, judge, or commissioner of a court of the United States and found to be one not lawfully entitled to be or remain in the United States.

SEC. 13. That this act shall not apply to diplomatic and other officers of the Chinese Government traveling upon the business of that government, whose credentials shall be taken as equivalent to the certificate in this act mentioned, and shall exempt them and their body and household servants from the provisions of this act as to other Chinese persons.

SEC. 14. That hereafter no State court or court of the United States shall admit Chinese to citizenship; and all laws in conflict with this act are hereby repealed.

SEC. 15. That the words "Chinese laborers", whenever used in this act, shall be construed to mean both skilled and unskilled laborers and Chinese employed in mining.

APPROVED, MAY 6, 1882.

The New Colossus

Emma Lazarus

Not like the brazen giant of Greek fame,*
With conquering limbs astride from land to land;
Here at our sea-washed, sunset gates shall stand
A mighty woman with a torch, whose flame
Is the imprisoned lightning, and her name
Mother of Exiles. From her beacon hand
Glows world-wide welcome; her mild eyes command
The air-bridged harbor that twin cities frame.
"Keep ancient lands, your storied pomp!" cries she
With silent lips. "Give me your tired, your poor,
Your huddled masses yearning to breathe free,
The wretched refuse of your teeming shore.
Send these, the homeless, tempest-tost to me,
I lift my lamp beside the golden door!"

(1883)

brazen giant of Greek fame: Lazarus's sonnet casts the Statue of Liberty as a contemporary, maternal revision of the Colossus of Rhodes, one of the Seven Wonders of the Ancient World. The Colossus, a statue of the Greek god Helios, was the tallest statue of the ancient world. Finished in 280 BC, the statue was destroyed in an earthquake in 224 BC.

Unguarded Gates

Thomas Bailey Aldrich

Wide open and unguarded stand our gates,
Named of the four winds, North, South, East, and West;
Portals that lead to an enchanted land
Of cities, forests, fields of living gold,
Vast prairies, lordly summits touched with snow,
Majestic rivers sweeping proudly past
The Arab's date-palm and the Norseman's pine—
A realm wherein fruits of every zone,
Airs of all climes, for lo! throughout the year
The red rose blossoms somewhere—a rich land,
A later Eden planted in the wilds,
With not an inch of earth within its bound
But if a slave's foot press it sets him free.
Here, it is written, Toil shall have its wage,
And Honor honor, and the humblest man
Stand level with the highest in the law.
Of such a land have men in dungeons dreamed,
And with the vision brightening in their eyes
Gone smiling to the fagot and the sword.

Wide open and unguarded stand our gates,
And through them presses a wild motley throng—
Men from the Volga and the Tartar steppes,
Featureless figures of the Hoang-Ho,
Malayan, Scythian, Teuton, Kelt, and Slav,
Flying the Old World's poverty and scorn;
These bringing with them unknown gods and rites,
Those, tiger passions, here to stretch their claws.
In street and alley what strange tongues are loud,
Accents of menace alien to our air,
Voices that once the Tower of Babel knew!
O Liberty, white Goddess! is it well
To leave the gates unguarded? On thy breast
Fold Sorrow's children, soothe the hurts of fate,
Lift the down-trodden, but with hand of steel
Stay those who to thy sacred portals come
To waste the gifts of freedom. Have a care

Lest from thy brow the clustered stars be torn
And trampled in the dust. For so of old
The thronging Goth and Vandal trampled Rome,
And where the temples of the Caesars stood
The lean wolf unmolested made her lair.

(1892)

Twelve Hundred More

Anonymous

O workingmen dear, and did you hear
The news that's goin' round?
Another China steamer
Has been landed here in town.
Today I read the papers,
And it grieved my heart full sore
To see upon the title page,
O, just "Twelve Hundred More!"

O, California's coming down,
As you can plainly see:
They're hiring all the Chinamen
And discharging you and me;
But strife will be in every town
Throughout the Pacific shore,
And the cry of old and young shall be,
"O, damn 'Twelve Hundred More!'"

They run their steamer in at night
Upon our lovely bay;
If 'twas a free and honest trade,
They'd land it in the day,
They come here by the hundreds—
The country is overrun—
And go to work at any price—
By them the labor's done.

If you meet a workman in the street
And look into his face,
You'll see the signs of sorrow there—
Oh, damn this long-tailed race!
And men today are languishing
Upon a prison floor,
Because they've been supplanted by
This vile "Twelve Hundred More!"

Twelve hundred honest laboring men
Thrown out of work today
By the landing of these Chinamen
In San Francisco Bay.
Twelve hundred pure and virtuous girls,
In the papers I have read,
Must barter away their virtue
To get a crust of bread.

This state of things can never last
In this, our golden land,
For soon you'll hear the avenging cry,
"Drive out the China man!"
And then we'll have the stirring times
We had in days of yore,
And the devil take those dirty words
They call "Twelve Hundred More!"

(1870s)

John Chinaman in New York

Mark Twain

A correspondent (whose signature, "Lang Bemis," is more or less familiar to the public) contributes the following:

As I passed along by one of those monster American tea stores in New York, I found a Chinaman sitting before it acting in the capacity of a sign. Everybody that passed by gave him a steady stare as long as their heads would twist over their shoulders without dislocating their necks, and a group had stopped to stare deliberately.

Is it not a shame that we, who prate so much about civilization and humanity, are content to degrade a fellow-being to such an office as this? Is it not time for reflection when we find ourselves willing to see in such a being matter for frivolous curiosity instead of regret and grave reflection? Here was a poor creature whom hard fortune had exiled from his natural home beyond the seas, and whose troubles ought to have touched these idle strangers that thronged about him; but did it? Apparently not. Men calling themselves the superior race, the race of culture and of gentle blood, scanned his quaint Chinese hat, with peaked roof and ball on top, and his long queue dangling down his back; his short silken blouse, curiously frogged and figured (and, like the rest of his raiment, rusty, dilapidated, and awkwardly put on); his blue cotton, tight-legged pants, tied close around the ankles; and his clumsy blunt-toed shoes with thick cork soles; and having so scanned him from head to foot, cracked some unseemly joke about his outlandish attire or his melancholy face, and passed on. In my heart I pitied the friendless Mongol. I wondered what was passing behind his sad face, and what distant scene his vacant eye was dreaming of. Were his thoughts with his heart, ten thousand miles away, beyond the billowy wastes of the Pacific? among the rice-fields and the plumy palms of China? under the shadows of remembered mountain peaks, or in groves of bloomy shrubs and strange forest trees unknown to climes like ours? and now and then, rippling among his visions and his dreams, did he hear familiar laughter and half-forgotten voices, and did he catch fitful glimpses of the friendly faces of a bygone time? A cruel fate it is, I said, that is befallen this bronzed wanderer. In order that the group of idlers might be touched at least by the words of the poor fellow, since the appeal of his pauper dress and his dreary exile was lost upon them, I touched him on the shoulder and said:

"Cheer up—don't be downhearted. It is not America that treats you in this way—it is merely one citizen, whose greed of gain has eaten the humanity out of his heart. America has a broader hospitality for the exiled and oppressed. America and Americans are always ready to help the unfortunate. Money shall be raised—you shall go back to China—you shall see your friends again. What wages do they pay you here?"

"Divil a cint but four dollars a week and find meself; but it's aisy, barrin' the bloody furrin clothes that's so expinsive."

The exile remains at his post. The New York tea merchants who need picturesque signs are not likely to run out of Chinamen.

(1870)

Poems of Angel Island

Anonymous

These six poems are translations of works found etched into the walls of the immigration facility on Angel Island. The unknown writers were detained there after crossing the Pacific with the hope of being admitted to the United States. Many were not.

[Instead of remaining a citizen of China]

Instead of remaining a citizen of China, I willingly became an ox.
I intended to come to America to earn a living.
The Western styled buildings are lofty; but I have not the luck to live in them.
How was anyone to know that my dwelling place would be a prison?

[Being idle in the wooden building]

Being idle in the wooden building,* I opened a window.
The morning breeze and bright moon lingered together.
I reminisce the native village far away, cut off by clouds and mountains.
On the little island the wailing of cold, wild geese can be faintly heard.
The hero who has lost his way can talk meaninglessly of the sword.
The poet at the end of the road can only ascend a tower.
One should know that when the country is weak, the people's spirit dies.
Why else do we come to this place to be imprisoned?

[Four days before the Qiqiao Festival]

Four days before the Qiqiao Festival,†
I boarded the steamship for America.
Time flew like a shooting arrow.
Already, a cool autumn has passed.
Counting on my fingers, several months have elapsed.
Still I am at the beginning of the road.

---

*wooden building: The name Chinese immigrants gave to the Angel Island Immigration Station.
†Qiqiao Festival: Chinese festival celebrated on the seventh day of the seventh lunar month, also known as "Chinese Valentine's Day." Derived from romantic folk legend in which the Cowherd and the Spinning Girl fell in love and, as a result, neglected their work. The gods were angry that the lovers abandoned their work and separated them. They were allowed to meet only on the seventh day of the seventh moon every year.

I have yet to be interrogated.
My heart is nervous with anticipation.

[The young children do not yet know worry]

The young children do not yet know worry.
Arriving at the Golden Mountain,* they were imprisoned in the wooden
  building.
Not understanding the sad and miserable situation before their eyes,
They must play all day like calves.

Crude Poem Inspired by the Landscape

The ocean encircles a long peak.
Rough terrain surrounds this prison.
There are few birds flying over the cold hills.
The wild goose messenger cannot find its way.
I have been detained and obstacles have been put in my way for half a year.
Melancholy and hate gather on my face.
Now that I must return to my country,
I have toiled like the *jingwei* bird† in vain.

[For one month I was imprisoned]

For one month I was imprisoned; my slippers never moved forward.
I came on the *Manchuria* and will return on the *Mongolia*.
But if I could make the trip to Nanyang, I would.
Why should America be the only place to seek a living.

Translated by Him Mark Lai and Genny Lim

Golden Mountain: Chinese immigrants' name for the United States.
†jingwei *bird*: Chinese legend of Nu Wa, Emperor Yan's third daughter, who drowned when her boat overturned in the ocean. Her grief transforms her into a bird, the name *jingwei* imitating her cries of despair. She
vows to fill the sea that took her life, and in vain each day she brings pebbles and twigs to choke its waters.

Songs of Gold Mountain

Anonymous

These poems were written by Chinese immigrants who, unlike those detained at Angel Island, were admitted to the United States and resided in San Francisco.

[At a moment of tremendous opportunity]

At a moment of tremendous opportunity,
They all come—happiness, prosperity, longevity, and peace.
Treasures from mother nature are rewards for one's good deeds;
Once wealth and nobility arrive, the success story is complete.
With fast-expanding wealth.
I'll turn around and go back to Canton by sea.
No need to wait for luck in the pick-six exacta;
I'll just take nature's endless bounty as it flows.

[Spring returns to the continent]

Spring returns to the continent.
Soothing is the misty scenery.
Flowers by the hundreds in red, by the thousands in purple, all noble and rich;
Everywhere, towers and terraces, all decorated with brilliant lanterns.
It's a delight to the heart.
I sightsee in the Golden City.
Eyes darting around, spirit dashing about, what genuine joy—
Entertaining myself, I have forgotten about going home.

Translated by Marlon K. Hom

The Biography of a Chinaman

Lee Chew

The village where I was born is situated in the province of Canton, on one of the banks of the Si Kiang River. It is called a village, although it is really as big as a city, for there are about 5,000 men in it over eighteen years of age—women and children and even youths are not counted in our villages.

All in the village belonged to the tribe of Lee. They did not intermarry with one another, but the men went to other villages for their wives and brought them home to their fathers' houses, and men from other villages—Wus and Wings and Sings and Fongs, etc.—chose wives from among our girls.

When I was a baby I was kept in our house all the time with my mother, but when I was a boy of seven I had to sleep at nights with other boys of the village—about thirty of them in one house. The girls are separated the same way—thirty or forty of them sleeping together in one house away from their parents—and the widows have houses where they work and sleep, though they go to their fathers' houses to eat.

My father's house is built of fine blue brick, better than the brick in the houses here in the United States. It is only one story high, roofed with red tiles and surrounded by a stone wall which also encloses the yard. There are four rooms in the house, one large living room which serves for a parlor and three private rooms, one occupied by my grandfather, who is very old and very honorable; another by my father and mother, and the third by my oldest brother and his wife and two little children. There are no windows, but the door is left open all day.

All the men of the village have farms, but they don't live on them as the farmers do here; they live in the village, but go out during the daytime and work their farms, coming home before dark. My father has a farm of about ten acres, on which he grows a great abundance of things—sweet potatoes, rice, beans, peas, yams, sugar cane, pineapples, bananas, lychee nuts and palms. The palm leaves are useful and can be sold. Men make fans of the lower part of each leaf near the stem, and waterproof coats and hats, and awnings for boats, of the parts that are left when the fans are cut out.

So many different things can be grown on one small farm, because we bring plenty of water in a canal from the mountains thirty miles away, and every

The editor of *The Independent,* in which this piece first appeared, says this in its introduction: "Mr. Lee Chew is a representative Chinese businessman who expresses with much force views that are generally held by his countrymen throughout America. The interview that follows is strictly as he gave it, except as to detail of arrangement and mere verbiage. Mr. Lee was assisted by the well-known Chinese interpreter, Mr. Joseph M. Singleton, of 24 Pell Street."

farmer takes as much as he wants for his fields by means of drains. He can give each crop the right amount of water.

Our people all working together make these things, the mandarin has nothing to do with it, and we pay no taxes, except a small one on the land. We have our own Government, consisting of the elders of our tribe—the honorable men. When a man gets to be sixty years of age he begins to have honor and to become a leader, and then the older he grows the more he is honored. We had some men who were nearly one hundred years, but very few of them.

In spite of the fact that any man may correct them for a fault, Chinese boys have good times and plenty of play. We played games like tag, and other games like shinny and a sort of football called yin.

We had dogs to play with—plenty of dogs and good dogs—that understand Chinese as well as American dogs understand American language. We hunted with them, and we also went fishing and had as good a time as American boys, perhaps better, as we were almost always together in our house, which was a sort of boys' club house, so we had many playmates. Whatever we did we did all together, and our rivals were the boys of other clubhouses, with whom we sometimes competed in the games. But all our play outdoors was in the daylight, because there were many graveyards about and after dark, so it was said, black ghosts with flaming mouths and eyes and long claws and teeth would come from these and tear to pieces and devour any one whom they might meet.

It was not all play for us boys, however. We had to go to school, where we learned to read and write and to recite the precepts of Kong-foo-tsze* and the other Sages, and stories about the great Emperors of China, who ruled with the wisdom of gods and gave to the whole world the light of high civilization and the culture of our literature, which is the admiration of all nations.

I went to my parents' house for meals, approaching my grandfather with awe, my father and mother with veneration and my elder brother with respect. I never spoke unless spoken to, but I listened and heard much concerning the red-haired, green-eyed foreign devils with the hairy faces, who had lately come out of the sea and clustered on our shores. They were wild and fierce and wicked, and paid no regard to the moral precepts of Kong-foo-tsze and the Sages; neither did they worship their ancestors, but pretended to be wiser than their fathers and grandfathers. They loved to beat people and to rob and murder. In the streets of Hong Kong many of them could be seen reeling drunk. Their speech was a savage roar, like the voice of the tiger or the buffalo, and they wanted to take the land away from the Chinese. Their men and women lived together like animals, without any marriage or faithfulness, and even were shameless enough to walk the streets arm in arm in daylight. So the old men said.

---

*Kong-foo-tsze: Confucius (551–479 BC), Chinese moral philosopher who founded Confucianism.

All this was very shocking and disgusting, as our women seldom were on the street, except in the evenings, when they went with the water jars to the three wells that supplied all the people. Then if they met a man they stood still, with their faces turned to the wall, while he looked the other way when he passed them. A man who spoke to a woman on the street in a Chinese village would be beaten, perhaps killed.

My grandfather told how the English foreign devils had made wicked war on the Emperor, and by means of their enchantments and spells had defeated his armies and forced him to admit their opium, so that the Chinese might smoke and become weakened and the foreign devils might rob them of their land.

My grandfather said that it was well known that the Chinese were always the greatest and wisest among men. They had invented and discovered everything that was good. Therefore the things which the foreign devils had and the Chinese had not must be evil. Some of these things were very wonderful, enabling the red-haired savages to talk with one another, though they might be thousands of miles apart. They had suns that made darkness like day, their ships carried earthquakes and volcanoes to fight for them, and thousands of demons that lived in iron and steel houses spun their cotton and silk, pushed their boats, pulled their cars, printed their newspapers and did other work for them. They were constantly showing disrespect for their ancestors by getting new things to take the place of the old.

I heard about the American foreign devils, that they were false, having made a treaty by which it was agreed that they could freely come to China, and the Chinese as freely go to their country. After this treaty was made China opened its doors to them and then they broke the treaty that they had asked for by shutting the Chinese out of their country.

When I was ten years of age I worked on my father's farm, digging, hoeing, manuring, gathering and carrying the crop. We had no horses, as nobody under the rank of an official is allowed to have a horse in China, and horses do not work on farms there, which is the reason why the roads there are so bad. The people cannot use roads as they are used here, and so they do not make them.

I worked on my father's farm till I was about sixteen years of age, when a man of our tribe came back from America and took ground as large as four city blocks and made a paradise of it. He put a large stone wall around and led some streams through and built a palace and summer house and about twenty other structures, with beautiful bridges over the streams and walks and roads. Trees and flowers, singing birds, waterfowl and curious animals were within the walls.

The man had gone away from our village a poor boy. Now he returned with unlimited wealth, which he had obtained in the country of the American wizards. After many amazing adventures he had become a merchant in a city called Mott Street, so it was said.*

---

*Mott Street: In lower Manhattan, known unofficially as the "Main Street" of New York City's Chinatown.

When his palace and grounds were completed he gave a dinner to all the people who assembled to be his guests. One hundred pigs roasted whole were served on the tables, with chickens, ducks, geese and such an abundance of dainties that our villagers even now lick their fingers when they think of it. He had the best actors from Hong Kong performing, and every musician for miles around was playing and singing. At night the blaze of the lanterns could be seen for many miles.

Having made his wealth among the barbarians this man had faithfully returned to pour it out among his tribesmen, and he is living in our village now very happy, and a pillar of strength to the poor.

The wealth of this man filled my mind with the idea that I, too, would like to go to the country of the wizards and gain some of their wealth, and after a long time my father consented, and gave me his blessing, and my mother took leave of me with tears, while my grandfather laid his hand upon my head and told me to remember and live up to the admonitions of the Sages, to avoid gambling, bad women and men of evil minds, and so to govern my conduct that when I died my ancestors might rejoice to welcome me as a guest on high.

My father gave me $100, and I went to Hong Kong with five other boys from our place and we got steerage passage on a steamer, paying $50 each. Everything was new to me. All my life I had been used to sleeping on a board bed with a wooden pillow, and I found the steamer's bunk very uncomfortable, because it was so soft. The food was different from that which I had been used to, and I did not like it at all. I was afraid of the stews, for the thought of what they might be made of by the wicked wizards of the ship made me ill. Of the great power of these people I saw many signs. The engines that moved the ship were wonderful monsters, strong enough to lift mountains. When I got to San Francisco, which was before the passage of the Exclusion act, I was half starved, because I was afraid to eat the provisions of the barbarians, but a few days' living in the Chinese quarter made me happy again. A man got me work as a house servant in an American family, and my start was the same as that of almost all the Chinese in this country.

The Chinese laundryman does not learn his trade in China; there are no laundries in China. The women there do the washing in tubs and have no washboards or flat irons. All the Chinese laundrymen here were taught in the first place by American women just as I was taught.

When I went to work for that American family I could not speak a word of English, and I did not know anything about housework. The family consisted of husband, wife and two children. They were very good to me and paid me $3.50 a week, of which I could save $3.

I did not know how to do anything, and I did not understand what the lady said to me, but she showed me how to cook, wash, iron, sweep, dust, make beds, wash dishes, clean windows, paint and brass, polish the knives and forks, etc., by doing the things herself and then overseeing my efforts to imitate her. She would take my hands and show them how to do things. She and her husband and children laughed at me a great deal, but it was all good natured. I was not confined to the house in the way servants are confined here, but when my work was done in the morning I was allowed to go out till lunch time. People in California are more generous than they are here.

In six months I had learned how to do the work of our house quite well, and I was getting $5 a week and board, and putting away about $4.25 a week. I had also learned some English, and by going to a Sunday school I learned more English and something about Jesus, who was a great Sage, and whose precepts are like those of Kong-foo-tsze.

It was twenty years ago when I came to this country, and I worked for two years as a servant, getting at the last $35 a month. I sent money home to comfort my parents, but though I dressed well and lived well and had pleasure, going quite often to the Chinese theater and to dinner parties in Chinatown, I saved $50 in the first six months, $90 in the second, $120 in the third and $150 in the fourth. So I had $410 at the end of two years, and I was now ready to start in business.

When I first opened a laundry it was in company with a partner, who had been in the business for some years. We went to a town about 500 miles inland, where a railroad was building. We got a board shanty and worked for the men employed by the railroads. Our rent cost us $10 a month and food nearly $5 a week each, for all food was dear and we wanted the best of everything—we lived principally on rice, chickens, ducks and pork, and did our own cooking. The Chinese take naturally to cooking. It cost us about $50 for our furniture and apparatus, and we made close upon $60 a week, which we divided between us. We had to put up with many insults and some frauds, as men would come in and claim parcels that did not belong to them, saying they had lost their tickets, and would fight if they did not get what they asked for. Sometimes we were taken before Magistrates and fined for losing shirts that we had never seen. On the other hand, we were making money, and even after sending home $3 a week I was able to save about $15. When the railroad construction gang moved on we went with them. The men were rough and prejudiced against us, but not more so than in the big Eastern cities. It is only lately in New York that the Chinese have been able to discontinue putting wire screens in front of their windows, and at the present time the street boys are still breaking the windows of Chinese laundries all over the city, while the police seem to think it a joke.

We were three years with the railroad, and then went to the mines, where we made plenty of money in gold dust, but had a hard time, for many of the miners were wild men who carried revolvers and after drinking would come into our place to shoot and steal shirts, for which we had to pay. One of these men hit his head hard against a flat iron and all the miners came and broke up our laundry, chasing us out of town. They were going to hang us. We lost all our property and $365 in money, which members of the mob must have found.

Luckily most of our money was in the hands of Chinese bankers in San Francisco. I drew $500 and went east to Chicago, where I had a laundry for three years, during which I increased my capital to $2,500. After that I was four years in Detroit. I went home to China in 1897, but returned in 1898, and began a laundry business in Buffalo. But [the] Chinese laundry business now is not as good as it was ten years ago. American cheap labor in the steam laundries has hurt it. So I determined to become a general merchant, and with this idea I came to New York and opened a shop in the Chinese quarter, keeping silks, teas, porcelain, clothes, shoes, hats and Chinese provisions, which include shark's fins and nuts, lily bulbs and lily flowers, lychee nuts and other Chinese dainties, but do not include rats, because it would be too expensive to import them. The rat, which is eaten by the Chinese, is a field animal that lives on rice, grain and sugar cane. Its flesh is delicious. Many Americans who have tasted shark's fin and bird's nest soup and tiger lily flowers and bulbs are firm friends of Chinese cookery. If they could enjoy one of our fine rats they would go to China to live, so as to get some more.

American people eat ground hogs, which are very like these Chinese rats, and they also eat many sorts of food that our people would not touch. Those that have dined with us know that we understand how to live well.

The ordinary laundry shop is generally divided into three rooms. In front is the room where the customers are received, behind that a bedroom and in the back the workshop, which is also the dining room and kitchen. The stove and cooking utensils are the same as those of the Americans.

Work in a laundry begins early on Monday morning—about seven o'clock. There are generally two men, one of whom washes while the other does the ironing. The man who irons does not start in till Tuesday, as the clothes are not ready for him to begin till that time. So he has Sundays and Mondays as holidays. The man who does the washing finishes up on Friday night, and so he has Saturday and Sunday. Each works only five days a week, but those are long days—from seven o'clock in the morning till midnight.

During his holidays the Chinaman gets a good deal of fun out of life. There's a good deal of gambling and some opium smoking, but not so much as Americans imagine. Only a few of New York's Chinamen smoke opium. The habit is very general among rich men and officials in China, but not so much among poor men. I don't think it does as much harm as the liquor that the Americans drink. There's nothing so bad as a drunken man. Opium doesn't make people crazy.

Gambling is mostly fan tan, but there is a good deal of poker, which the Chinese have learned from Americans and can play very well.* They also gamble with dominoes and dice.

The fights among the Chinese and the operations of the hatchet men are all due to gambling. Newspapers often say that they are feuds between the six companies, but that is a mistake. The six companies are purely benevolent societies, which look after the Chinaman when he first lands here. They repre-

*fan tan: Traditional casino game in Chinese immigrant neighborhoods in the United States.

sent the six southern provinces of China, where most of our people are from, and they are like the German, Swedish, English, Irish and Italian societies which assist emigrants. When the Chinese keep clear of gambling and opium they are not blackmailed, and they have no trouble with hatchet men or any others.

About 500 of New York's Chinese are Christians, the others are Buddhists, Taoists, etc., all mixed up. These haven't any Sunday of their own, but keep New Year's Day and the first and fifteenth days of each month, when they go to the temple in Mott Street.

In all New York there are only thirty-four Chinese women, and it is impossible to get a Chinese woman out here unless one goes to China and marries her there, and then he must collect affidavits to prove that she really is his wife. That is in the case of a merchant. A laundryman can't bring his wife here under any circumstances, and even the women of the Chinese Ambassador's family had trouble getting in lately.

Is it any wonder, therefore, or any proof of the demoralization of our people if some of the white women in Chinatown are not of good character? What other set of men so isolated and so surrounded by alien and prejudiced people are more moral? Men, wherever they may be, need the society of women, and among the white women of Chinatown are many excellent and faithful wives and mothers.

Recently there has been organized among us the Oriental Club, composed of our most intelligent and influential men. We hope for a great improvement in social conditions by its means, as it will discuss matters that concern us, bring us in closer touch with Americans and speak for us in something like an official manner.

Some fault is found with us for sticking to our old customs here, especially in the matter of clothes, but the reason is that we find American clothes much inferior, so far as comfort and warmth go. The Chinaman's coat for the winter is very durable, very light and very warm. It is easy and not in the way. If he wants to work he slips out of it in a moment and can put it on again as quickly. Our shoes and hats also are better, we think, for our purposes, than the American clothes. Most of us have tried the American clothes, and they made us feel as if we were in the stocks.

I have found out, during my residence in this country, that much of the Chinese prejudice against Americans is unfounded, and I no longer put faith in the wild tales that were told about them in our village, though some of the Chinese, who have been here twenty years and who are learned men, still believe that there is no marriage in this country, that the land is infested with demons and that all the people are given over to general wickedness.

I know better. Americans are not all bad, nor are they wicked wizards. Still, they have their faults, and their treatment of us is outrageous.

The reason why so many Chinese go into the laundry business in this country is because it requires little capital and is one of the few opportunities that are open. Men of other nationalities who are jealous of the Chinese, because he is a more faithful worker than one of their people, have raised such a great outcry about Chinese cheap labor that they have shut him out of working on farms or in factories or building railroads or making streets or digging sewers. He cannot practice any trade, and his opportunities to do business are limited to his own countrymen. So he opens a laundry when he quits domestic service.

The treatment of the Chinese in this country is all wrong and mean. It is persisted in merely because China is not a fighting nation. The Americans would not dare to treat Germans, English, Italians or even Japanese as they treat the Chinese, because if they did there would be a war.

There is no reason for the prejudice against the Chinese. The cheap labor cry was always a falsehood. Their labor was never cheap, and is not cheap now. It has always commanded the highest market price. But the trouble is that the Chinese are such excellent and faithful workers that bosses will have no others when they can get them. If you look at men working on the street you will find an overseer for every four or five of them. That watching is not necessary for Chinese. They work as well when left to themselves as they do when someone is looking at them.

It was the jealousy of laboring men of other nationalities—especially the Irish—that raised all the outcry against the Chinese. No one would hire an Irishman, German, Englishman or Italian when he could get a Chinese, because our countrymen are so much more honest, industrious, steady, sober and painstaking. Chinese were persecuted, not for their vices, but for their virtues. There never was any honesty in the pretend fear of leprosy or in the cheap labor scare, and the persecution continues still, because Americans make a mere practice of loving justice. They are all for money making, and they want to be on the strongest side always. They treat you as a friend while you are prosperous, but if you have a misfortune they don't know you. There is nothing substantial in their friendship.

Wu-Ting-Fang talked very plainly to Americans about their ill treatment of our countrymen, but we don't see any good results. We hoped for good from Roosevelt. We thought him a brave and good man, but he has continued the exclusion of our countrymen, though all other nations are allowed to pour in here—Irish, Italians, Jews, Poles, Greeks, Hungarians, etc. It would not have been so if Mr. McKinley had lived.*

Irish fill the almshouses and prisons and orphan asylums, Italians are among the most dangerous of men, Jews are unclean and ignorant. Yet they are all let in, while Chinese, who are sober, or duly law-abiding, clean, educated and industrious, are shut out. There are few Chinamen in jails and none in the poor houses. There are no Chinese tramps or drunkards. Many Chinese here

*William McKinley, Jr. (1843–1901), twenty-fifth president of the United States, assassinated in 1901 in Buffalo by Leon Czolgosz.

have become sincere Christians, in spite of the persecution which they have to endure from their heathen countrymen. More than half the Chinese in this country would become citizens if allowed to do so, and would be patriotic Americans. But how can they make this country their home as matters now are! They are not allowed to bring wives here from China, and if they marry American women there is a great outcry.

All Congressmen acknowledge the injustice of the treatment of my people, yet they continue it. They have no backbone.

Under the circumstances, how can I call this my home, and how can anyone blame me if I take my money and go back to my village in China?

(1903)

Veronika and the Angelinos

Caspar Day

Veronika Mescavage was by nature and profession a Good Girl. Possibly a certain white glory of reputation was hers rather because the Mescavage boys were all Bad Boys, and Jonas in particular a Worst Boy, than on account of the virtues peculiar to the part. Her father concealed most of his good qualities from the Patch; her mother was an Awful Mean Lady to Drink. Great wonder was it, therefore, that the Christian virtues rather than the mortal sins should find in Veronika their tabernacle.

Vincas, the boarder, was Veronika's great partisan in well-doing. Veronika was nine, and Vincas twenty-six, with convictions on many matters.

"Here," Vincas would say, "is five cents, because you mended my shirt where the rat ate it. Also that you let the beer alone. A little beer is proper for men, but I do not believe in it for children. For, see, we shall grow like the Dagos in another ten years, our people, if the children learn drinking now. Where will the clean houses be found then? Where can a man board in decency? Who will be left to tell the truth except the greenhorns from the old country? Who will save money? Who will deserve good pay? Who will have respect? Nobody, see. We shall fall to being like the Dagos."

After these discussions, it was a relief to Veronika to contemplate the Angelino brood upon the opposite side of the street, and to observe that as yet the aristocratic fairness of her own race had not approached the russet browns of the Unwashed. The Angelinos kept a store and were decent enough for people of their blood; nevertheless, the Lithuanian neighborhood looked down upon them. To lower oneself to the Italian level was a horror not lightly to be contemplated.

Veronika had something on her mind, therefore, upon the August evening when she came and sat with Vincas on the bench under the mulberry tree.

"I did something today," she began.

"You did?" Vincas stopped cleaning his pipe and looked sidewise at the thin little figure in brown gingham. Vincas had come home from work at four o'clock; and from the way matters had gone since then he knew that all the Mescavage faults were on display. "It has been a bad day for good girls, has it?"

"Very," the child sighed. "But that is not it. I have found a baby, a new one. A baby that needs me!"

"Ah-h," said Vincas. If the rapture was not quite within his comprehension, he was at least able to receive a solemn confidence with sympathy. He was a comfortable friend.

"It has no hair at all, so I am rubbing lard into its head," Veronika continued blissfully. "And dirty, dir-ty! Tomorrow I go down there and wash it; those people don't know how. Anyway, the mother is going to work in the silk mill, so she will be busy. After it is cleaned, I shall love it!"

"Of course," he assented dutifully. "Is it a boy?"

"It is six weeks old. I don't know is it a boy or not a boy; I forgot to ask them. But its eyes are awful sore, my poor baby, and its neck. Could you give me a nickel, Vincas, to buy cold cream? And dare I steal one piece of your tar soap to clean it? I shall need soap. It rubs dirt in its little black eyes; that is the soreness."

"Certainly; steal one piece."

"But I can't bring it up here; that is one bad thing. I daresn't. My mother would holler at me," Veronika continued in English.

"I would hide it," Vincas advised in their own tongue. "Keep it to surprise her when it is all grown up to be a man."

The child sighed blissfully and nestled against his shoulder; her boarder always gave such soothing counsel.

"When I get grown up and am married with you I will have four twins a year," she promised, "so when one set are asleep you can always be riding the other set up and down the street in the two-baby carriage."

"Are they to sleep on the red velvet lounge?"

"Why, you said a cradle, Vincas! You said a little cradle with sheets! It will make more washing, of course; but then, I don't mind that!"

"So it was," the man agreed. "And what was I to have in my can when I worked dayshift? I forget what you said."

"Pie," Veronika beamed. "Pie and a garlic. A whole pie!"

"And when I work nightshift," he prompted.

"Herring. Or ham boiled. And sweet tea."

Vincas smacked his lips dutifully before he lit his pipe. It was a part of the regular program. But today had been such a very bad day that Veronika could not dwell long content in the imaginary possession of her household and four yearling twins. She moved restlessly upon the bench and looked about her in the dusk. Finally she wrought her vague trouble into words.

"You know it is really a lie, Vincas," said she. "All a lie. I don't want you to feel bad about it. But it is not so. I—I'm not *really* going to get married with you—nor put pie in your dinner pail."

"Not?" cried Vincas, gently wondering. "Why, it was all arranged. Dear, dear!"

"Not. I am really going to get married with Adam Walukas, down the street here. Or if he gets killed in the mines beforehand, then it will be an English boy named Gerrity. I promised them. This other, the story we tell, you and I, is just a lie."

"Let us go on telling it, though," he suggested. "We always do. We like it. We always tell it when we feel sad. There was the day I burned my hand. There was the time you fell—"

"No, no. You know you have to go back to the old country and pay some money and get the farm for your father, as soon as your bad brother finishes dying. That is one really true thing. And I have to get married with Adam and Aloysius in America. Another really true thing. We just say the other. It is—it is like Santy Claus, and Jesus-in-the-Barn that they put in Church. It is not true all the year, I mean; just once in a great while."

"Maybe," Vincas agreed. "All right; never mind about that. But how many dresses has your newfound baby got?"

"None. None at all. Just pieces of rag."

"All the easier to wash, then. Whose is it? Anybody near here?"

Veronika got to her knees and whispered in his ear.

"Its mother has come to stay at Angelino's. She is Dago."

Vincas whistled. "A *Dago* baby?"

"It's not! It's a nice baby, a dear baby! I'll wash it, I tell you, and it's too little and new to be Dago yet. It's just like any baby, only the sore eyes. It might grow yellow hair, if I keep it very clean. And I'll teach it our language every day when nobody is listening."

Vincas argued and dissuaded. Finally he yielded.

"Very good. But I am afraid it will turn out Dago in spite of you. Soap is not everything—But mind you, do not bring it home with you. And do not go over to the Dago's house nights, no matter if the baby cries; only daytimes, remember, when your ma isn't looking. She'd raise hell. I'd ought to tell her on you, but I won't."

For three weeks all went well. Day by day Veronika hurried through her housework before she fled to her new charge; there were no babies at home to need attention, and Mrs. Mescavage cared too little for her daughter's society to detain the child indoors unless there was work for her to do.

Many and many a doting confidence was given to Vincas during this happy period. Thus, the baby was a boy. He was not pink and white yet, like a normal Lithuish infant, but his tints improved. The Angelinos were horrified at so much washing of a baby. The Angelinos would not believe, at first, that Veronika had brought up six Lithuish babies to the walking-stage; only when they had made inquires and looked at samples did they grant her professional claims. Shortly the Angelinos made three garments for Nico, which had a definite architecture of their own and could by no means be transmuted into salt-bags or handkerchiefs or floor-mops or window-pane corks upon impulse; that Day of the First Shirt was a great day. Then the Angelinos themselves admitted that the sore eyes were growing healthier under the caustic régime of tar soap and clean clothing. Then the Angelinos themselves admitted that the baby loved Veronika better than its own mother.

A dreadful week befell when Mrs. Mescavage burned her foot and in consequence dedicated her leisure to pails of beer and balls of carpet-rags. Veronika could not slip away from the house for days; she was in attendance upon the invalid from dawn till nearly midnight. Vincas saw and understood the growing anguish in her eyes. On the evening of the sixth day he called her into the shed.

"It's been a-cryin' for you some," he said. "But that don't hurt a baby. The Dagos is takin' good care of it. I went over; I looked well at all they did. I never went in a Dago house before; they are dirty. Well, it was all right till today. Now it is a little sick. I frightened them on purpose, saying the boy would die; so they sent for the doctor. Tonight he comes. Tomorrow I guess I can make a plan with your mother to let you play all day up and down the streets."

A little diplomacy, accordingly, left Veronika free after the bread was baked and the morning's work done. She came into the Angelinos' kitchen in the nick of time. The story of her day was given to Vincas after dark.

"My baby was sick, so sick! That doctor you made them get, Vincas, was only a death-maker for Dagos. He says, 'Get a plaster.' They go to the drug-store and buy what he tells them. The plaster has English reading on it, but Mrs. Angelino can never read anything. It is a plaster with little holes in it and a cloth over the sticky side; you know, the kind that is good after you fall down cellar. Well! They pull off the cloth and soften the plaster with hot water and cut off little, little pieces. Then they make the baby eat them, those pieces, and half a banana. Oh, what a terrible time did I have choking those things out of my baby!"

"An' then I bet they was mad against you," commented the man.

"Naturally. They said I wasted their twenty-five cents that they paid for it. I said if they tried it again I would go for the policeman. Finally we all ran out the back gate and over to the drugstore; I carried the baby, and the Dago kids ran all around me, and the Angelino woman was yelling and holding out the plaster. My nose was bleeding, and her thumb that I had to bite. But the drug-store man said the baby would have died unless I got the plaster out. So I had satisfaction over her."

"Was the baby sick afterwards?"

"Oh, yes! Then we went back to the house again, she and I. And what do you think? I scolded them for being ignorant, and called them Dagos. They got angry and called me a Polander. Then I swore, and they swore, and we all talked at once and said we were not any such a thing—oh, a terrible time! But in the end we cried because we thought the baby would die, and became very good friends. I stayed there all day. She gave me a banana for my dinner, and tried to make all her children treat me with respect and get out from under my feet when I walked up and down with the baby."

The two days following the porous plaster incident went blissfully well. The third morning plunged the Mescavage family in a social abyss; and the vessel of wrath appointed for the defilement of the caste was Mrs. Angelino.

Veronika was sent at ten o'clock to buy a quart of molasses. At the gate she encountered Jonas, coming home early from the mine with a temper blacker than his face.

"Whatcher got, kid?" he demanded.

Veronika dodged, but Jonas caught her a smart blow on the side of the head. He enforced a profane inquiry with a shaking, and punctuated it with slaps.

"Ma sends me for molasses," the child admitted finally.

"Aw, cry, now! I'll molasses ye, ye big crybaby! Give us the pail. An' I want that there fifteen cents. Hand it over! Shut up yer squakin'. I didn't neither break yer wrist!"

The fifteen cents was unfortunately a quarter. Jonas took it and marched across the street. Veronika, weeping, crept back into the kitchen; experience had taught her that an accessory before the fact receives no mercy from either the capitalist or the embezzler.

"Well," demanded Mrs. Mescavage, "what have you done now, Rat-Eyes? Lost my money? Lost my pail? Lost my molasses?" Each domestic reverse, as she enumerated a list, was marked by the broomstick. "Tell it out, fool. A curse take my girls, anyway! My boys are worth ten of you. Well, liar, are you going to tell me what I ask?"

"Jonas took it. He took it off me, mother. He did, honest!"

"Shut that mouth! You should have been smart and told him I sent for five cents' worth of beer. He'd have taken five cents and stopped at that. It's your fault. I'll serve you. Down cellar you go, where the rats will eat you!"

With Veronika out of the way, Mrs. Mescavage waited ten minutes; then, anger outgrowing her inertia, she slammed the house-door and started down the street to look for Jonas.

Things were lively on Angelino's corner. All the children of the district were ranged about a noisy central groups of Italians. Upon the high porch, Luigi Angelino stood with two women, both screaming and talking at once. An Italian baker had stopped his wagon at the curb; by his signs and gestures the beholders knew that he was offering the vehicle as a police van. Rafael Angelino himself, a squat man in a wide felt hat, was dragging a youth down the high steps from his store.

Concetta, Rafael's wife, hung upon the stream-ship signboard in a horrid plight. Her face was bruised, her long hair unpinned and straggling. Her hands, freshly incarnadined each time she drew them from her nose, accused Rafael's prisoner. All the Angelinos were in a most unangelic temper. Only as Mrs. Mescavage reached the inner ring of spectators did the captive youth identify himself to her apprehension.

"Steala cigarettis, Missis," explained Rafael. His tone was businesslike. "Me, I don' tinka not'an; go down my cellair. My ol' 'oman t'inka ver' bada boy. She say, "Her-r-re, you to not steal dose t'ings outa store!' Boy, he not say back; he hitta ol' 'oman, brrreaka ta noses—knocks down floor. Now I getta heem 'rrested!"

As one man the Angelinos grinned their venomous glee. There was no doubt that their souls were set upon revenge. Luigi picked up the dinner can Jonas had dropped on the steps and removed its lid. Underneath were packages of cigarettes and tobacco.

"I let him get outside the store before I seized him. The law is stronger that way," cried Rafael to his family in Italian.

"Son, son, you put shame on us this day!" screamed Mrs. Mescavage, talking Lithuish. "To steal and get caught! To get caught by Dagos! Oi, Oi! Now what are we going to do?"

"Pay her money. Then her nose will stop bleeding," suggested the culprit.

"Talk Ingliss," Rafael ordered.

"I have none I can spare; only two months' rent, twelve dollars. And that must be saved for the house-boss."

"Pay that, then, for—"

"Ingliss! Ingliss!" vociferated the Angelic chorus in a breath.

"—for I am scared to go to jail. The police have another thing against me. Who knows what they will remember when they have a good look in my face?"

"You coma jail first. Talk Ingliss after. That talk no good for me!"

There was a short, sharp struggle on the sidewalk. When it ceased, the storekeeper sat astride the guilty Jonas.

"Now!" he announced. "You talka you Polandra way, me punch dese 'Merican my Dago way!" He illustrated.

Jonas Mescavage had not the temper for a losing fight. He wept. He begged for mercy. He promised money, friendship, patronage—all in English. His mother fell to her knees.

"Quit that, ma. Give 'er the money!"

Mrs. Mescavage heard; but so, alas, did the Angelinos. They held trumps and knew it; and like Pharaoh in a similar case, their hearts were hardened.

"Twenty dollars is nice to us, brother?" suggested Luigi in their private tongue.

"Forty," said the baker.

"Revenge is nicer to me," confessed the sanguinary Mrs. Angelino. The signboard upon which she leaned bore streaks of scarlet now. "Cut off one ear for me while you have him down. That is better than fifty dollars. I am your woman."

Freddie Tardello on the outskirts of the crowd began to scream with fright. English was his most familiar tongue, so that his terror translated itself: "Don't cut his ears off! Oh, oh!"

It was enough. Jonas' mother, with a wild cry, hurled herself beside Rafael on the sidewalk. She tore from inside her dress a knotted handkerchief and threw it to the Italian, reiterating monotonously, "Good Mister! Good Dago Mister!"

"Money!" cried Luigi. "How much?"

"Twelve dollars," replied the husband.

"Twelve dollars is too little. I want revenge."

The staccato words told nothing to the Lithuanian woman, but the tone said much. All the mother-passion of her heart rose in one mighty surge to save her best-loved boy. She sprang to her feet, facing the angry Italians on the high porch. Tears rained down her cheeks, her outstretched palms begged for mercy. As a suppliant she mounted the steps on her knees and crawled upon the dirty boards. Then, in a silence more awful than clamor, she drew herself forward and kissed her enemy's feet.

"Mine God! Oh, mine God!" cried somebody. The Lithuanians in the crowd turned and slipped to their houses, speechless; that degradation was too horrible for comment. But Mrs. Mescavage stayed, brazening out the shame, not ceasing her caresses. "Nice missis! Good missis! Please, good missis, you no kill my boy!"

The Italian woman took her triumph to full measure. Finally, she drew back coolly and shoved the petitioner with one thick, grimy foot.

"Vengeance is what I need. Twelve dollars is so little. Rafael, take the pup to jail."

A heartbroken cry came from the roadway. Veronika, in her brown gingham, flew up the steps and dashed herself into the central place. She snatched her mother's head from the dusty planks. She cradled it upon her knees, embracing it with meager, loyal arms; but her chin was high, and her eyes challenged them through tears. "Don't you do that, Concetta!" she cried. "She ain't none of your people for you to do them things to! Don't you shove her. Don't you darst!"

"Behold, the nursing child of our baby!" exclaimed Rafael from his couch on Jonas' ribs.

There followed a pause. Then Luigi laughed awkwardly; for the baby was his own.

"It is her mother, her own blood," spoke the neighbor woman, in Italian.

"She kept Maria's baby alive: yes. But her brother smashed my nose: yes."

"It pays," Rafael pronounced. "It just pays."

"Then take him to prison for stealing!" Concetta finished.

Luigi objected. "You forget the twelve dollars. The good girl has paid for the bad boy; we are her friends, and we call that a settled score. But why will not the twelve dollars pay for the cigarettes, sister, if the child has made peace already for your blood? Is it enough, eh?"

"It is enough," said the baker. "She is your friend."

"Enough," said Rafael and the neighbors.

"Enough," Concetta echoed. She threw out her hands in a sweeping gesture. "Let him go free. Only send them away out of my sight. I feel sick when I forgive anything. I wanted revenge."

Gloom deep and dreadful reigned in the house that night. Mrs. Mescavage had sat indoors, silent, brooding, waiting for callers who did not come. Father Mescavage had left the premises in a rage, stating that his absence might last a lifetime. Jonas had taken a week's vacation to go fishing. Joszef was spending his evening in a pleasanter place than home. Agati and Annie were at the silk mill working overtime. Veronika sat on a box by the coal-shed, weeping in the dark. There Vincas found her.

"I don't never darst go any place again," she sobbed in answer to his questions. "Folks is awful. I been fightin' two girls a'ready—an' now—I'm—tired—"

"You will be rested tomorrow," Vincas suggested. "And by the day after to-morrow they will forget and let you alone."

"I don't suppose I can never go near my baby again, neither; ma has found out about it now, an' the Dagos is all mad at us. An' I was jus' gettin' him so nice a'ready,—so fat,—an' awful lovely! He'd'a' been dead by this time, too, if I hadn't seed to him. Doctor said so."

"The Dagos ain't mad with you. That's why they let Johnny off, the most reason. 'Twasn't no money so much, nor—nor what your ma done. 'Twas on account o' youse tendin' the baby."

"I can't never—hold 'im no more again," sobbed Veronika. "They won't keep 'im clean—nor nothin'! An' I'd just learnt him talk some Lithuish yes-terday. Oh, oh!"

Vincas waited beside the shaken little figure with a hand on her hair.

"It's so awful," she groaned. "Jonas is gone off; he won't be workin'. Pa's gone off; he won't be workin'. Annie and Agati will be that mad when they find out, that they won't give ma no pay neither. There's just Joszef left; he don't make but a dollar-ten a day, even if he works steady. An' ma—she'll be drunk all the time."

"Oh, no; she can't," consoled the boarder. "She gave them Angelinos all her money. She won't drink. I'll tell Baroff's not to give her nothin' 'less she pays the money down. Will I?"

"An' then there's me! I'll be a-fightin' all times; an' I don't say I like much to fight. Some does, but I don't. Then I'll be a-swearin' all times; an' that's a sin, to swear. An' I don't like my ma no more. That ain't no good for me, is it? To be ashamed over my ma?"

As if to emphasize the cruelty of Veronika's position, a procession of chil-dren came up the street chanting:

Mis-sis Mescavage,
    There she goes,
I seen her crawlin'
    On her nose
To kiss the Dago's
    Dirty toes!

"Aloysius, he made up that song!" cried Veronika in a burst of woe. "He's an awful smart boy. But he says I can't marry him, not no more. The nasty ol' thing, I don't want to! But oh, Vincas, Vincas, the world is black, because I am ashamed of my mother! Why did she do that thing?"

The man stroked his hair as he replied in the old tongue:

"She had a good reason. Suppose—suppose your baby was to be put in jail by some cross old policeman; would you give him money to save the baby?"

"Yes, yes. Only I never have money, except a five cents."

"Would you kiss the policeman, if you had to? Think hard!"

"Yes, of course," cried the foster-mother. "Or fight him. Or tear him with scratches. Or maybe I could go to jail myself instead."

"See, then," spoke the counselor gently. "You would not be ashamed if it was for your baby. Now that is the way your mother felt. Consider: Jonas is her baby, the baby she likes best, even if he is a bad boy. So she did it for Jonas. Even to kiss a Dago was not too much, when it was to save Jonas out of prison. Look at the affair that way. There is not so much to be ashamed of, is there?"

A boy's treble rose shrilly in the street. "That's Adam," Veronika moaned. The faithless fiancé proceeded with the insulting solo:

> The Dago kicked her
>   In the snout;
> Says she, "Go on,
>   I'll chase ye out!"

"I can't marry Adam Walukas neither, can I? Nor I can't lick him, 'cause he's bigger than me. Oh, I shall stay always in this house, an' listen to what folks says about my mother! I'll get ashamed that I am called Mescavage, after a while!"

"Nonsense," spoke Vincas. He lifted her by the shoulders and took her bodily to their old seat under the mulberry tree. "Put two gray hairs in your braid every time you comb your hair, then you will grow up in a hurry, and you can get married to me, and your name will not be Mescavage any longer. You can go away to Oklahoma with me if you like. And the four twins will all be fat, beautiful babies, two of the kind that sleep all day, and two of the kind that sleep all night. Thus, they need only two clean dresses and two pairs of shoes, because—"

"Oh, Vincas, I want *four* pairs of shoes! You are rich. And you know you said—"

"Very good; four. And they shall have gray eyes and curly yellow hair as long as your finger, and no Dago will ever come near them to give them sores."

"Oh, I shall *love* them!" Veronika smiled in ecstasy through her tears. Then she faltered, her passionate little mother-soul shaken by an emotion more complex.

"Of course I shall always love them *best*," she promised. "But I would like to keep my Dago baby, too, if you can manage it. When a baby is sick, and has no hair and sore eyes, and such things, see—you—" she dropped into English desperately—"you can't give it up for nobody! You kinda love it more. Can't you verstand that?"

(1909)

What Is an American?
The Suicide of the Anglo-American

Honoré Willsie

Up in a stone quarry in Massachusetts, a few years ago, two men got jobs on the same day. The American of one man's name was Masso. He was a south European, short of body and long of arm. Masso had been in this country five years and spoke English fairly well.

The other man's name was Ezra. He was tall and lean and nervous. Ezra's forefathers once had held in grant from England the land on which the quarry lay, but Ezra's father had given it up. Farm labor was hard to get. The land thereabouts was being bought up by Poles and south Italian hucksters, who lived on what they could not sell and whose wives and children were their farm hands. Ezra's father could not compete with this condition. Ezra had drifted back from the city with the hope of buying, somehow, sometime, the old farm.

The two men were put at like work, at the same wage—two dollars a day. The quarry was one of a great string owned by a combination of companies. It was poorly equipped. Not a cent more of the profits was put back into the quarry than was absolutely essential for turning out stone. The result was crude methods, many accidents, and a constant inflow of raw hands

Masso found a house near the quarry. It was a shack, containing one room and a kitchen lean-to. Into this moved Masso with his wife and five children. The house looked good to them. In the old country their house had had one room and a dirt floor.

Ezra found a little four-room cottage, a good distance from the noise of the quarry. There was a porch and a bathroom. Into this moved Ezra with his wife and one child, a boy about twelve years old.

Masso's wife seemed to be at her housework all the time, but the house was always dirty, and so were the children. But they were healthy, and Mrs. Masso had a laugh that was good to hear.

Ezra's wife was nervous and energetic and wore the half-worried, half-wistful look of so many New England women. Her house and her one child were immaculate.

Masso managed to lay aside part of his wages each week toward the farm he was going to buy in the old country. But after the newspaper and little Ezra's magazine, by way of luxuries, had been paid for, not a cent of Ezra's wages was left.

Ezra and Masso, working shoulder to shoulder, day by day, developed a sort of liking for each other, in spite of the fact that Ezra held immigrants in utter contempt. At noon, when they sat in the shade of a stone block, eating their lunch, Ezra would try to get at Masso's ideas.

"What did you come to this country for, Masso?" he asked one hot July noon.

Masso gnawed his onion and bread thoughtfully. "Make money easy here," he answered, "then go back to old country rich."

"Well, what else?" urged Ezra.

Masso looked blank.

"I mean," said Ezra, did you like this Government better'n yours?" Did you like our ways better'n yours? Understand?"

Masso shrugged his shoulders. "Don't care 'bout gov'ment if I make the money. What did you come to this country for?"

Ezra flamed. "I was born here, you Wop you!* This very dirt here made the food that made me! Understand? I'm a part of this country same as the trees are! My folks left comfort and friends behind 'em and came to this country when it was full of Indians, to be free, *free;* can you get that? And what good did it do them? They larded the soil with their good sweat to make a place for fellows like you. And what do you care?"

"I work," said Masso stolidly. "I work all the time and I make the money. That's enough."

Ezra opened his mouth to reply, looked at the unresponsive face before him and subsided. Then he tried another tack.

"What started you over here? How'd you happen to think of coming?"

Masso understood this. "Over there you hear much about America and how ever' one get rich quick here. I hear, but it's like a story. I like to listen, but I'm pleased to stay where all my people lived. But in our part are agents of steamship companies, thousands of agents just in our little part of country. Those companies they have to have passengers, you see? So they talk all the time, fix it all smooth so you can come and tell 'bout places you can get work. Those agents they kept right after me and I come. That's all."

Ezra considered this for a few minutes. Then as he lighted his pipe he said: "I don't know anything about it except what I see and what I read in the papers. I ain't got anything personal against you. You're a human being like me, doing your best according to your light. But I'd like to bet that if they'd shut the doors after the Civil War and let those that was in the country have their chance, this country would be a whole lot farther along than it is now. I'll bet if they had fifty men in this quarry like me, instead of a hundred like you, it would turn out twice the work it does now."

Masso listened in a puzzled way and shook his head, as he did at most of Ezra's vagaries. But not only Masso is puzzled over the sort of speculation in which Ezra indulged. Men who have spent their lives in studying statistics and races are puzzled too.

Wop: Ethnic slur for Italians.

If America had closed her doors to immigration in 1830 and the birth rate of that period had continued for seventy years, instead of the 76,000,000 of people that we boasted in 1900 we would have had 100,000,000. This 100,000,000 would have been a homogeneous people, of strongly Anglo-Saxon type, and ideal. The chaos that has resulted from the constant introduction of new types would have been avoided.

Ever since 1830, when America first began to feel the tremendous influx from Europe, the native American birth rate has decreased progressively with the swell of immigration. It diminishes most markedly wherever the immigrant crowds most thickly. New England, once the most homogeneous portion of America, once having the highest birth rate, once the main source of what we call the American spirit, has now the greatest proportion of foreigners and the smallest native birth rate. It is not even holding its own. Massachusetts in her native birth rate and France can boast the greatest decline known in the Western world.

In 1900 the census for all the United States shows that the Anglo-American is by far the most unfruitful of all Americans. Where a Polish-American has a child once in two years, an Anglo-American will have a child once in five years. The south European—that is, the Slovak, the Russian Jew, the Magyar, the Greek, the Bohemian, and many other races—have for the past twenty years formed over eighty percent of our immigration. The first generation of these immigrants has shown itself to be extremely fertile. The south Italian, the Russian Jew, the Pole have the highest birth rate in the Western world. Eugenists say that this influx from south Europe must rapidly change the American type, must cause it to become darker and smaller, must make it more mercurial, fonder of music. That it will even change our type of crime. Murder, rape, and sex immorality will become more common than the Anglo-Saxon crimes of burglary, drunkenness, and vagrancy.

The change seems inevitable now. It is one of the world's hard facts of living that the Anglo-American must go. The only point of moment left in the matter is the way of his going and whether or not in his going he is any loss to America. Is there to be no trace of him left? Does he leave behind him an ideal sufficiently clean-cut, fundamental, and enduring to survive the floods of ignorance that are poured upon it?

The Anglo-American had an ideal. Even Ezra, sweating out his days in labor, had an ideal which it would take a second or third generation of Massos to get, if at all.

The blocks of stone were loaded onto flat cars by means of old-fashioned wooden-armed derricks that always were breaking and endangering the lives of the men. One day the guide rope of one of the biggest derricks broke and the great block of stone swept across the flat car, breaking the leg of a Polak and all but mashing the life out of a little Italian water boy.

Ezra was enraged. He went to the boss and demanded new equipment all around. The boss laughed.

"The equipment is good enough for a lot of Wops and Bohunks."*

"I'm not a Wop or a Bohunk!" retorted Ezra. "I won't work where you don't take any better care of your men than you do here."

The boss hesitated. The American workman was valuable in the intelligence he brought to his work.

"Well, I'll write to the company," he said, evasively.

Ezra's lips tightened. "You gotta get us some decent equipment," he growled.

He went back to his work, and that noon hour he struggled with Masso.

"Look here, Masso, they haven't any business to have such rotten derricks. I'll bet we can get them this way. That rush order for New York has got to be out tomorrow night or they lose money. Now we'll go out on strike this afternoon. Understand? Make 'em promise a good derrick and a crane before we'll go back. You tell the rest of the hands."

Ezra repeated this patiently until Masso understood. Then he finished his onion and shook his head.

"I don't want lose half a day pay while you talk."

"But you can get killed any minute the way things are now," persisted Ezra. Masso still shook his head. "I gotta work."

Angry and disgusted, Ezra went to the other men who could understand English. It was quite useless. "We gotta work," they said.

At first, Ezra declared he'd walk out by himself. He'd not stand it. But as he went on with his stone sawing and thought the matter out, he concluded that he was only wasting time and money to leave the job or to attempt to force better working conditions in the quarry.

"It's something bigger'n I am, I guess," he thought heavily. "It ain't only this quarry, it's every place I've worked. It's everywhere these foreigners willing to work with things such as us Americans can't stand, everywhere twenty of 'em waiting to undercut our pay. And the companies all banking on this very thing to make themselves rich."

A sense of suffocation, of blind hopelessness settled on Ezra.

"I don't see why I can't get down to macaroni and onions and a pigpen for a house," he muttered. "It's my only chance to compete with these fellows."

Early in November, when the work was getting slack but bitter hard in the raw weather, there came a ten percent cut in wages. Ezra, with the panicky feeling closing in on his heart, talked it over with his wife. It was of no use to quit and look for work that time of year, they decided.

Yet the twenty cents a day loss must be met. At first they thought of discontinuing the boy's magazine. But at last they decided that by Ezra giving up tobacco and by giving up cream for coffee and cereal, by getting no new clothes for themselves, they still could pay the rent for the pretty cottage with the bath-

---

Bohunk: Ethnic slur for almost any eastern European, Slavic group, though Bohemians (now called Czechs) were frequently specified.

room, still keep little Ezra well dressed and in school, and tide through the winter somehow—if there was no sickness.

The next morning Masso appeared on the job with a dirty-faced small boy.

Said Masso to Ezra: "I take him out school soon's I hear of the cut. Boss, he give him job as tool boy. He work cheaper than that American boy they got there."

"He's too small to work," said Ezra. "You'd ought to keep him in school. Give him a chance."

"Chance for what?" asked Masso.

"Chance to grow into a decent citizen," snarled Ezra with the old feeling of having his back to the wall while the pack worried him in front.

"Oh, he goes back to the old country with me in a few years!" said Masso. "He finds books no good over there."

The boy looked up quickly. "I ain't going back. Me, I'm an American!" he said. "I'll be rich some day."

The father gave him a push, and the boy went off to his work. John [*sic*] looked after him proudly. "That's right," he said. "He won't go back. He's good American now. My six children, they all Americans."

"Good Americans!" sneered Ezra. "What do you mean by good American?"

"Oh, he learn how to make much money quick!" answered Masso, nodding his head knowingly.

"That's not being an American!" shouted Ezra. "He'll never make an American, that kid!"

Masso scowled. "Why not?" he growled.

Ezra straightened his tired shoulders and looked out over the dreary waste of November fields beyond the quarry. It was the land that his fathers had held in grant from an English king. The fields that had made Ezra's flesh and blood were dotted with Italian huts. The lane where Ezra's mother had met his father when he returned crippled from Antietam was blocked by a Polak roadhouse.

Ezra looked from the fields back to the alien eyes of his hearer. He started to speak, then stopped.

Ezra thought: "My ancestors were immigrants too, but I know that they were Americans as soon as they landed here. This fellow isn't. He never can be." Then he said aloud:

"I don't know what makes an American of a person, unless it's the right kind of thing bringing him to this country."

Masso shrugged his shoulders. "I guess if you are an American, then to be an American you gotta be crazy."

But the question haunted Ezra. What was an American? And it may well puzzle any of us here in the United States. What *is* an American? Does taking out naturalization papers make an American? Does this produce from stolid ignorance the boasted American type? And what is the American type?

In the United States there are 33,000,000 people who are foreign born or of foreign parentage. They call themselves Americans. By what subtle alchemy did they change from Europeans to Americans? Or doesn't the word American mean anything more than an inhabitant of the United States? Can it mean anything more in this welter of types all claiming to be American?

If moved by a desire to worship God or to govern or to work, according to their own code, Ezra's forefathers came to a strange land, their contribution to that land is fundamentally different from Masso's who, pushed by money interests and bated by money interests, arrived in America with no desire save to make money and return to the old conditions.

Whether Masso's lack of high motive is the result of inherent brain poverty or of a brutal environment is a matter of greater importance to America than the tariff question. If due to the first, no amount of education of Masso or his children will bring this hereditary brain poverty to brain wealth. If due only to the second, little by little we may educate his succeeding generations of children to the American ideal—if there is one—and if we really use it! The Anglo-Saxon contributed the ideal that produced the Declaration of Independence and the Constitution and the Thirteenth Amendment to it. What is Masso contributing? Undoubtedly he will develop ideals. What will they be?

We have some foolish phrases. "The melting pot can fuse anything!" Yes, but fuse anything into what? "After all, the fittest will survive!" Yes, but fittest for what? Darwin didn't say that fittest meant best. He said that the man best *fitted* to his *environment* would survive, that practically survival of the fittest meant the survival of the most fertile.

Ezra had the one child. Every year of the three that Masso and Ezra worked together in the quarry Masso had a baby. As his wages went down and his birth rate went up, Masso merely moved into cheaper quarters, bought cheaper food, went dirtier and poorer clothed, and took another child out of school and put him or her to work.

Ezra heard of the birth of the eighth child with a grin of contempt for Masso without, and an overwhelming pang of envy and rebellion within. Ezra came of a fertile race. And yet he said:

"If I've got to live like a pig and bring my children up like pigs, I won't have them. To give my one the right chance is all I can possibly do. My Lord, Mary, all a man asks in the world is a chance to put the best of himself into his work and to bring up a family of children that will help the world along. And they won't let me!"

The thought of Masso's eight was dull misery to Ezra if he let himself think about it. Eight children! Eight bits of his own and Mary's flesh and blood to carry on the hopes in which he and she had failed. Eight tiny bulwarks against the race extinction, the imminence of which never left his soul. To father many children! To live up to the inalienable right of normal living beings to propagate each his own kind to the point of assuring race continuance.

The thing that differentiated Masso from Ezra was the thing that kept Ezra from having more children. Ezra had an ideal. The ideal of progress, of breeding better than he had been bred, the idea that demanded a certain standard of living. And rather than forego the ideal, Ezra committed race suicide.

Ezra never ceased to try in a quiet way to influence the immigrants with whom he worked to demand better working conditions. But his efforts were fruitless. When Ezra finally got the full connection between the importation of raw labor and the cheap running of plants, the heart within him failed. Not the least tragic aspect of the Anglo-American's disappearance is his consciousness of his own suffocation.

Nothing in the upbuilding of industry has been held so cheap as human life. This is one point where the upbuilders have seemed shortsighted. Ezra was worth two of Masso as an industrial unit. It would have been worthwhile to have doubled Ezra's wages and to have safeguarded Ezra's life, not only for what Ezra himself could contribute to industry, but so that he might have had enough children to insure some of them reaching maturity and in their turn contributing to industry. Little Ezra had small chance of maintaining Ezra's line. A man, by the law of averages, must have at least four children to stand a good chance of his line continuing.

But to industry the cheapest portion of its equipment has been its inexhaustible human labor supply. It was Ezra who had pleaded for the new derricks. It was Ezra who managed the decrepit machinery most deftly. And so it was Ezra who was sent to the danger spots, he having the keenest wits, the best knowledge of the danger spots. And so it was Ezra and Masso, his helper, who were caught under the giant block when the derrick broke from its moorings and dropped clean across the quarry.

It was too common a tragedy for even the local papers to give more than a passing column to it. And outside of the human pitifulness of the waste of it and the suffering to the mothers and the babies, one is not prepared to urge that the tragedy had special significance.

Had Masso known enough, before his broken chest choked him, he might have said: "It doesn't matter! After all, I have done a man's part. I have worked to the limit of my strength and I shall survive through my fertility. What I have done to America no one knows." But Masso was ignorant, and all that he said was some futile word to the priest who knelt in the sleet beside him. Masso never had gotten very far from the thought of his Maker.

Ezra, lifted to the edge of the quarry to lie on the border of the fields where his fathers had dreamed and hoped and sweated and fought, thought of the small Ezra and the losing fight ahead of the little fellow, and for the last time the sense of having his back to the wall, the pack suffocating him, closed in on him, blinded him and merged into the darkness into which none of us has seen. Ezra and his line were dead.

Had Ezra had an education and had he had a longer time for dying, he might have done the thing far more dramatically. He merely rasped out his life, a bloody, voiceless, broken thing on a brown November field, with all his dreams unspoken, all his ideals lost. He might, had things been otherwise, have seen the long sad glory of humanity's migrations, might have caught for an unspeakable second, as in a procession, that never-ceasing, never long-deflected onmoving of human life that must continue, regardless of race tragedy, as long as humans crave food either for the body or the soul. Ezra might have pictured himself as symbolizing one of those races which slip over the horizon into oblivion, unprotesting, silent. Only Ezra might have let himself break the silence, and, pausing to look into the face of the horde that was thrusting him over the brink, he might have said:

"We, who are about to die, salute thee!"

(1912)

Don't Bite the Hand That's Feeding You

Thomas Hoier and Jimmie Morgan

Last night, as I lay a-sleeping,
A wonderful dream came to me.
I saw Uncle Sammy weeping
For his children from over the sea;
They had come to him friendless and starving,
When from tyrant's oppression they fled.
But now they abuse and revile him,
Till at last in just anger he said:

"If you don't like your Uncle Sammy,
Then go back to your home o'er the sea,
To the land from where you came,
Whatever be its name,
But don't be ungrateful to me!
If you don't like the stars in Old Glory,
If you don't like the Red, White, and Blue,
Then don't act like the cur in the story,
Don't bite the hand that's feeding you!

"You recall the day you landed,
How I welcomed you to my shore?
When you came here empty handed,
And allegiance forever you swore?
I gathered you close to my bosom,
Of food and of clothes you got both,
So, when in trouble I need you,
You will have to remember your oath.

"If you don't like your Uncle Sammy,
Then go back to your home o'er the sea,
To the land from where you came,
Whatever be its name,

These song lyrics were first made popular by singer Billy Murray in 1915, during World War I. The song gained attention again during World War II. Gene Autry sings it in the film *Bells of Capistrano*, and though it was cut from the final edit, Judy Garland sang it for the film *For Me and My Gal*. Both films were released in 1942.

But don't be ungrateful to me!
If you don't like the stars in Old Glory,
If you don't like the Red, White, and Blue,
Then don't act like the cur in the story,
Don't bite the hand that's feeding you!"

(1915)

The Promised Land

Lewis E. MacBrayne

Having drawn his number in the pool formed to speculate on the daily run of the ship—a privilege that cost him one dollar, and gave him one chance in ten—the Hon. Frederick Baddington left the smoking-room and strolled down the deck to where his wife was sitting in her steamer-chair, snugly protected against the fresh breeze blowing from the sea by a heavy Scotch rug. He tossed his cigar over the rail and sat down beside her. She was a very attractive woman even at sea, where only a few women retain their good looks, and he was very fond of her.

"Fred, I have been thinking about the steerage," she said. "They are just what you want."

Baddington smiled. He knew his wife so well that he had been expecting the calling up of his immigration bill ever since the ship left Rotterdam. One reason for their trip abroad for the summer had been his desire to gather original material in support of the measure that he intended to introduce at the next session of Congress. He smiled to himself when he thought how few immigrants they had met during their travels. Surely there had been none at the Cecil in London, and none in the Embassy circles in Paris, and in the Netherlands they had not found them to any extent either in the museums or in the churches.

"There appears to be a heavy steerage list," he said. There had been nothing lower than second cabin on their trip over from New York.

"Five hundred and sixty," she answered; for she was of good Yankee descent, and took a just pride in figures.

"That is an omen or a coincidence," he said lightly. "It is just the size of my majority in the district last fall."

"I had forgotten that," she replied. The fact certainly was of interest.

The Hon. Frederick Baddington was a member of Congress. There are Congressmen who have been abroad several times. He had been one of that larger number who spend their summers at American resorts, not assuming that a knowledge of foreign conditions at firsthand is necessary in the business of making national laws.

In Washington Mrs. Baddington was not recognized as a political factor. That was due to the skillful management of her husband, who made it appear that in his home the consideration of political matters was ruled out; though there was a perfect domestic understanding as to the real part played by his wife in his political career.

She was a woman of superior education and wide social experience, and, like many other American women of similar qualifications, had that tireless energy that could not be satisfied with remaining a passive spectator to the progressive life about her. She was not of the class of women who desire the franchise for her sex. She was, however, of that more important class who hold their husbands to an intelligent account of the civic duties, and understand the value of a political career.

Baddington had been well aware of this before he entered the transitory stage of city and State politics that had paved the way for his seat in Congress. A man of university training and of cultured tastes, he would have devoted his energy to his private business, and buried his talents in his own library indefinitely, had not his wife directed them elsewhere. At the time of which we write he was, in many respects, a typical representative of the best element in his district; not a politician in the common acceptance of the word, but an honest, conscientious legislator; successful in business, and, consequently, well posted as to the trade conditions in his part of the country; a gentleman in society, and credited with having fair literary attainments.

The further discussion of the subject was interrupted at that point by the ringing of the dinner bell, and it was not until the following morning, as they started on their after-breakfast promenade, that it was resumed.

"I was down in the steerage before you came up," said Baddington as they reached the end of the promenade deck, and could look to the steerage deck below.

She at once lost interest in the gray lines of the sea, from which the fog was just lifting. "What did you find?" she asked.

"They are a sorry lot," he replied. "The Senator's bill, even if it was defeated, was not half strong enough."

The Senator's bill had aimed at a radical restriction of immigration, but had failed to pass the last Congress, partly for political reasons, and partly through the failure of the Western members to recognize its importance. But in Baddington's district the sentiment had been strongly in favor of it. His wife had pointed out the opportunity to win where the Senator had failed. He had been weak in the presentation of his bill. A more vigorous man, with all the facts at his command, would compel a favorable hearing; and success might mean as an ultimate reward an election as the Senator's successor. For these reasons it meant much to Mrs. Baddington that her husband was at last seriously interested in the subject, and she entered vigorously into the discussion as they stood where they could look down upon the mass of unwashed and unkempt humanity on the lower deck.

A number of Assyrian women were prostrate on one side of the steerage deck, unable to rally from the effects of a night of rough sea, while half a dozen unhappy-looking Cossacks, in high boots and astrakhan caps, dragged themselves back and forth in a hopeless promenade on the other; but a more striking picture was a group of half a hundred Roumanian Jews, huddled together in blankets, half drenched by the last wave that had broken over the bows.

Many of the men had soiled rags tied about their foreheads, the women were limp upon the deck in their misery; and the litter of children and kettles, and the evidence of woe unspeakable, completed a picture that might have been recalled from that past when the Jews encamped outside the walls of Jerusalem in helpless forlornness when driven out by their Babylonian conquerors.

"The doctor took me with him on his rounds this morning," said Baddington. "There are at least a dozen nationalities, and many families appear to be almost destitute."

"If that could be shown, would they be allowed to land in New York?" she asked suddenly.

"Certainly not," he replied. "Of what are you thinking?"

"Of your future!"

"Thank you. And your plan?" He knew that she had one in mind.

"When we reach New York you must turn back as many of these people as possible," she said. "The newspapers will send men to interview you, and you will talk. It will pave the way for your immigration bill."

"Mary, you are a born politician," he said with spirit.

"I am your obedient wife," she replied; and left him to think over what she had suggested.

Frederick Baddington, like many other members of Congress, was not a linguist. Waiters in Switzerland may speak three languages, and cabmen in Italy may know something of four; but this is a proof of the ascendancy of the Anglo-Saxon race. Even the fact that we are obliged to strain our knowledge of Latin to translate the State mottoes adopted by our forefathers is no argument that the times require any language other than English.

While Baddington was not a politician in the common sense, his power of political perception was entirely good, and the longer he considered his wife's suggestion, the clearer he recognized its feasibility. Now that he was prepared to make a systematic study of the steerage, he regretted his inability to speak any but his own language, and in his necessity he looked about him for an interpreter. He found one in the person of a Chicago man, Frank Louber by name, a genial fellow, somewhat past the prime of life. They became good friends under the advances made by the Congressman. His wife was observant, but held her peace for a couple of days. Then she asked her husband for a report of progress.

"We are progressing capitally," he told her. It was late in the afternoon, and their chairs were set forward, where they could watch the setting sun; for the ship was in the Gulf Stream, and the sea was a mass of undulating color. There were young people promenading the deck, and friendly groups were looking over the rail; while from the steerage below there came the sound of laughter, and of wild Assyrian singing.

The lower deck swarmed like an ant hill, for the somber dullness of the first storm had been cleared away by the sunshine, which was reflected in the bright headdress of the women, and the fantastic shirts and vests worn by the men. There was a deckhouse well forward, and this was now crowded with immigrants, seated with their backs to the wind, while in the midst of them, on a great coil of rope, a young couple sat simply, with arms about each other's waists, in the ecstasy of a happy courtship. Perfect health was stamped upon their faces. All else about them bespoke absolute poverty.

"If cleanliness is next to godliness, they are the most Godforsaken people that I have ever seen," the ship's doctor had said to Baddington. The Congressman repeated the statement to his wife, and added: "They don't know the first thing about sanitary laws, and fully half of them will be upon the State within a month after they land."

"If they land," suggested his wife.

"Yes, if they land," he corrected, laughingly.

Baddington was a systematic worker, and on the fifth day he had made such progress in his investigation that the first draft of his proposed immigration bill was written. It went even farther than the Senator's had ventured, but with the data that he would have at hand, he hoped to be able to carry it through to a triumphant passage.

Aided by Louber, he was now at work on the subject of wages paid to the immigrants in their own country. He already found that if they were willing to work for double, and, in many cases, for quadruple what they had received in their villages, the rate would still be so low as to prove a menace to American workmen. If he could learn something more definite of their antecedents, it would aid his object greatly. It was at this point that he made an important discovery.

It was on a Saturday morning, and going into steerage with Louber he found the Roumanians—two hundred or more Jews—gathered aft, as far away as possible from their fellow-passengers, for worship. For the time being the place had become a synagogue, and in the absence of a Rabbi one of the elders was reading from the Scriptures. His head, a type of the race, was covered in part by a little round hat, and a silky beard, streaked with gray, reached nearly to his waist. The attitude of the congregation was peculiarly devout, and the faces of the men were, for the moment, lifted above the sordid surroundings of the dingy, littered deck to a higher spiritual plane, in which there was both pride and a hope for the future.

"Clannish people," suggested Baddington, as they stood a little apart, watching the service.

"They came from the same village," replied the Chicago man.

"Indeed!" said the Congressman. "How did that happen?"

"They have suffered both from taxes and persecution, and the people of the village have been raising a fund for a year, to pay the passage of these, the most unfortunate, across the Atlantic."

"So they land as paupers!"

"Not exactly. They go to friends who left the village a year ago, and who have been saving from their earnings against the time of the coming of these people. But that is not the point. These Roumanians have tramped across Europe to Holland, three months by the way, footsore by day, and unsheltered in the open country at night, in order to reach Rotterdam and take passage upon this boat."

"You are certain that they tramped across Europe in order to immigrate?"

"Their chief men have told me in their own tongue, and they do not lie," replied Louber.

Baddington returned to the saloon deck for reflection. The picture of those believing people turned back at New York, after their weary weeks of tramping, came back sharply before his mind. He could not get the women and the children out of his mind, and he came very near stating the case to his wife for her judgment upon it.

But his wife had met a nobleman traveling incognito, and dragged him away for an introduction. In the evening he rejoined Louber, tramping the deck for his after-dinner cigar, and after a turn or two on the lee side of the ship he brought up the subject of the afternoon.

"I can't get those Roumanians out of my mind," he said. "It was only a few miles from Rotterdam, at Delfshaven, that the Pilgrims first set sail for America. What was it that influenced these people to go there?"

Louber stopped short in his walk and faced him. "Mr. Baddington," he said. "I wonder sometimes just how well you native Americans understand your own country. I am a German by birth, and while that country isn't a criterion for oppression, I have gained some knowledge of the conditions of the people in other lands. I want to tell you that where the United States is best known is not Berlin and Paris, but in the hills of Roumania, the villages of Armenia, and the deserts of Syria."

"I don't believe that I quite understand you."

"You have heard of the ancient cities of refuge?"

Baddington smiled. "I have some recollection of them," he replied. "I was a pupil at one time in a New England Sunday school."

Louber did not heed the answer.

"The United States is the refuge to which the oppressed of every land are looking," he said. "They don't come to you to overturn your institutions. They come asking only for the right to satisfy their hunger, to give their children something better than a life of poverty or dishonesty, to find a peaceful resting-place before old age forbids them to wander farther. Dirty? Of course they are dirty, sir. They've been in the dust so long that every sentiment but love of family and faint ambition has been stifled within them."

He spoke with such real eloquence that Baddington felt his blood stirring only as it did when he threw himself into the arena of debate in Congress. "You say that they have ambition," he said. "How can you prove it?"

"How can I prove it? I know it, even when I don't realize a tenth of the ambitions that exist among them. What are the ambitions of the first cabin deck? I am going back to my business; you to your politics. Mr. Sledger over there is a judge. Dr. Myer can afford to leave his patients whenever he wishes to go abroad. Jones, who throws away his money in the smoking-room, made it in the silver mines. They are all prosperous, and know to what they are returning. Now look over the rail at the scene down there in the twilight. Do you see that young couple on the coil of rope? They have been there together for the greater part of three days. It looks absurd enough on the face of it, but they are only anticipating a happy home in the land that they have never seen.

"Look at the old man still trying to read his book. I was talking with him this morning. He is a scholar, but an Armenian, and he saw his wife and daughter murdered in Turkey. Then look at that brown skinned lad staring at the sea. He told me that his sister was thrown into prison for repelling the insults of a tax collector in Russia."

He paused for a moment, and snapped the thumb and forefinger of his right hand vigorously, as though the action relieved him of the tension under which he was laboring. "They come to you in their ignorance, knowing far more of your land and your customs than you dream," he continued. "They are not cultured, and err because they still cling to their own customs. But I tell you that at heart, they are safe. They will work for you, fight for you, die for you; and their children will become the real Americans."

"But your proof?" asked Baddington, quietly.

"I came over in the steerage myself forty-five years ago, and both I and my sons have fought for your flag since then," replied Louber, and walked away abruptly.

Baddington paced the deck alone for half an hour. He was beginning to regret not having completed his education earlier in life with a study of European conditions. His data on the American side of the immigration question were sound. He knew the dangers of a lowered standard of wages, the relative increase in pauperism and crime due to the foreign element, and the undesirable quality of certain "machine made" citizenship. Yet there now stared him in the face this other side of the question—the pilgrimage from Roumania to nearly that same port in Holland from which his own honored ancestors had set sail for the same land of refuge nearly three centuries before. The first mate, who met him once on his solitary promenade, told him that the ship might sight land before another night, and this warned him of the necessity of a speedy decision as to the course that he should follow when New York was reached.

A ship bound from America to Europe sails at night into the cold East, but homeward bound again it seeks at sunset the golden West. The mate's prophecy came true, and by early evening there was land hard ahead in the yellow haze that hung over the sea. Everybody was upon the decks of the ship, and the Congressman and his wife stood with others looking over the rail into the changing West.

"Fred, there was a burial at sea this morning," Mrs. Baddington said suddenly.

"I had not heard that," he replied.

"It was a child in the steerage, ill since that day of the storm," she said. "A priest read the service, and they dropped the body into the sea in a sack. The mother fainted, though she has five poorly clad children left. It was an awful thing!"

The Baddingtons had lost their only son when a child. The Congressman understood why the incident had so deeply touched his wife.

"I have been thinking that it will be a great disappointment to many of these people to be sent back," she continued. "I inquired about the woman who lost her child. She is going to her husband, who settled in Syracuse six months ago. Isn't it possible—just possible, you know, that we may have been hasty in our conclusions? Are either of us, Fred, great enough to be the judge of all these people?"

It was a real effort for her to make this speech, but she was bound to do it, because it seemed right for her to do so. The death of the child had changed her whole view of the question, and if her husband still desired to carry out the plan that she had urged upon him, he must do it without her further aid.

"After all, if these people were really prosperous and happy, they would not wish to come to us, and there would be no need of immigration laws," he said, so kindly that she looked up into his face.

"See them now," she replied, directing his attention to the deck below. "You would hardly know them for the people who came aboard the ship."

The steerage passengers had cast away their remaining rags, and were dressed in clean and not unattractive garments. They had swarmed forward, and were hanging over the rails, their faces, too, toward the West. They crowded the bows, and the lovers stood, arm in arm, on the vantage ground of their coil of rope, chattering loudly, regardless of the rest of their world.

The outline of the land grew more distinct, until the islands of the outer harbor stood revealed. A wild shout rang out from the lower deck, and a Jew with a flowing beard and a round velvet cap threw his hand straight above his head and began to recite from the Scriptures. The young man whose arm was about the girl suddenly discovered that his coil of rope was a rostrum, and prepared to address the people below him. He clapped his hands, and the wild murmur of the throng gradually became hushed.

On the deck above, Mrs. Baddington had just asked her husband what steps he had decided to take against the immigrants, when she paused to listen to the curious sounds coming from below. A few voices were wavering in a song, gathering courage as others joined them, until, from the unintelligible chorus there finally came the clearly defined strains of a well-known air.

"Do you hear it? Do you hear it?" asked Mrs. Baddington, excitedly.

"I hear it."

"They are trying to sing 'America.'"

The Congressman had been tearing a sheet of closely written paper into small pieces. "Mary, there goes the first and last draft of my immigration bill," he said, as he threw it from his hand.

The pieces fell in a tiny shower upon the heads of the steerage.

(1902)

The Americanization of Roll-Down Joe

James B. Connolly

The latest development of American schooner came smartly to anchor in mid-stream.

From his perch in Crow's Nest, a cable-length abeam of the vessel, but mast-head high in the air, old Peter looked down on her with wonder and respect commingled. "The biggest mains'l ever swept past the Point! Look at the spread of it! Isn't that an ungodly armful to have to gather up on a jumping deck in a gale o' wind? Eighty-four-foot boom and fifty-two-foot gaff—you could sweep all the waters of the earth with all the searchlights of heaven and never a schooner of her tonnage would you find swingin' such a sail. And if you could find one, where but among American fishermen would you find a man would go outside a harbor in so much as a summer gale with that boom and that sail above it to be layin' out to looard of their rail?"

"But this man, Peter—he'll carry it?"

"Till all's blue. Eighty-four-foot boom! And I mind when they used to boast of their sixty-foot booms, and now the storm trys'ls of this one I expect'll lace to most that len'th."

"Portugee, ain't he, Peter ?"*

"Portugee-born," amended Peter, "but a good American citizen now."

"But isn't that surprising, Peter, his having the best out?"

"Surprisin'!" retorted Peter. "Meanin' because he's Portugee? Hmm. A sensible remark that, when so far's any of us can learn this man's ancestors were sailormen—navigators and world explorers—and a good many other things when your forefathers, or mine maybe, were tryin' to get up courage to visit the neighborin' mainland."

"But people new to this country."

"New people!" snorted Peter. "Man alive, where'd we be but for the new people? It's they puts the life into us. While the descendants of the old settlers are leanin' back in easy chairs, brains and bodies all used up, not an original notion left in 'em—from overwork, or overworry, or too much fat livin', or whatever 'tis that's ailin' them—it's the new people are coming along and gettin' things goin' again. Look right here in Gloucester now—is it the new blood, or the old, that's mannin' the fleet? And this same Roll-Down Joe—this

---

*The Portuguese were not typical among the "new immigrants," since they were not from southern and eastern Europe. In fact, John R. Commons points out that they came "not from Portugal, but from Cape Verde and Azores Islands, near equatorial Africa." The "nearly 9000 souls" who emigrated in 1906, he continues, went to either Hawaii or "New Bedford, Massachusetts, where they follow the fisheries in the summer" (*Race and Immigrants in America* [New York: Macmillan, 1907], 98–99).

Portugee immigrant, as they call him—industrious, upright, sober, intelligent—as are all but damn few of his kind that ever I see—he's standin' simply for one of the dozen big nations that's made us what we are or will make us what we're to be."

"But, how'd he get the name, Peter? Must be some story back of a name like that."

"It was while Joe was still but little known in Gloucester," began Peter, "but not so green that he hadn't managed to absorb a good many of the leadin' principles of the fishin' fleet, that him and Wesley Marrs were racin' home from the Western Banks one time, and after sixty hours of it Joe thought he needed a kink of sleep. So he started to go below, when the man to the wheel stopped him. It was blowin' hard then, the *Isabella* rollin' down pretty well under it. 'S'pose it gets worse while you're below, skipper, what'll I do?' asks the man to the wheel.

"'What you do? Why, keep her goin',' says Joe. 'Keep da *Isabell* goin', sure.'

"'But how long, skipper? There's a limit to everything—how long?'

"Joe studied a minute, then made a chalk line on the deck well up to wind'ard of the wheel-box. 'When she roll down to there, call me,' says Joe, and went below.

"'Cripes!' says the man to the wheel; 'when she rolls down to there, do you think you'll care whether you're called or not?'

"Well, I was the man to the wheel that time, and when I got to Gloucester I told the story, and ever since then they've called him Roll-Down Joe. He cert'nly promised even then to carry sail with the best of them.

"Well, 'twarn't long before people began to take notice of Joe. Most everybody, because there's always those who can never be brought to like those whose ways are different from their own. But the best people liked him. And you couldn't help it—he was so eager to win your goodwill and he set such store by what you said, you couldn't help but like him. I don't know but what most people of the South seem to be like that, don't they—want you to love 'em whatever else you do. There was nothing this man wouldn't do to please you. Nat'rally the killers began to take to him, and nat'rally, too, what they said was law to Joe. That was about the time when nothing'd do the killers but Oregon pine spars. Joe's were Georgia pine. 'What you want, Joe, is Oregon pine sticks,' says Wesley Marrs to him one day, and went on to demonstrate what beautiful implements his own were.

"Joe grew excited. 'I get dem,' he says. 'How mooch they costa—what? Fi' hundred dollar? No matt', I get dem,' says Joe. 'Fi' hundred, one t'ousand—no matt', I get dem. I wanta da ver' best.'

"'That's right, Joe—the best is none too good for you and me,' says Wesley; 'but don't go throwing away any five hundred dollars foolishly. Wait someday till you're out to sea and consult your almanac, Joe, and when them zodiac signs indicate a good breeze o' wind and a handy harbor, in conjunction, then do you slap everything you got to her, and—who knows?—it may be your

lucky day, and maybe them spars'll just nach'ally sag over the side o' themselves,' advised Wesley.

"Joe looked puzzled.

"'The insurance company'll have to pay for 'em then,' explains Wesley.

"'Ahh, da American way! Ver' good, ver' good,' shouted Joe, and a week later,
in a howlin' gale of wind, he sailed the *Isabella* back and forth of Halifax tryin'
to lift the masts out of her. But they were fine stout sticks and though they
buckled like umbrella ribs they just wouldn't come out, so Joe went on the
east'ard with the old sticks. But when next he met Wesley he apologized for not
doing better. 'May-bee ten ton more bal-last and a leet' more win' next time an'
I do eet,' he said to Wesley.

"Well, Joe, bringin' home the fish reg'larly as he did, was makin' a name for
himself among the fishermen. And doin' his best to live up to it, too. 'Twarn't
long before he got to where he shifted his drink from port wine to whiskey, and
could smoke fifteen-cent cigars on the curbstone like any American-born. Along
about there he came to me one day and said, 'Peter, I moost be one ceet-zen, one
American ceet-zen.' So I steered him up to City Hall, up to the proper grating in
the proper room where was a clerk, who, after he'd finished puttin' just the exact
point on his pencil and had manicured his nails once or twice again—and it
didn't take him any longer to do it than it would take a smart trawler to bait a
six-line string of gear, not more than twenty minutes maybe—he has time for
us. I explained what Joe was after and Joe told his name, a good old Portuguese
name, too; but it didn't seem to hit the fancy of this lad in the cage.

"'Do you expect me to spell or pronounce a name like that? Wonder you
wouldn't take some good local name.'

"Joe was a bit cast down—he had a bit of sentiment about his name. But he
was bound to be an American citizen, and thought if change of name was part
of it, why he'd change his name. So he tried to think of a good American name
and, recollectin' some of his skipper friends, 'Ahh, yess, yess—O'Don-nell,
Tom O'Don-nell,' he says.

"'Wrrh,' says the clerk. 'Look out the window at those signs across the street.'

"Joe looked, with an eye all the time for the fine big letters, and picked out
the biggest sign in sight. It read:

BURNHAM
COAL AND WOOD

The Burnham part of it was only of moderate size, while the 'Coal and Wood'
was in six-foot letters up and down so you couldn't go astray. The coal part,
happenin' to be to wind'ard, Joe picked that out for his, and, after carefully
copyin' it onto a piece of paper like a sign-painter, brought it to the clerk. 'One
good American name, hah?' he says.

"'That's better,' says the clerk, who, by the way, warn't throwin' any dazzlin'
reflections from any partic'larly bright side of his intelligence. 'But a wonder—

you wouldn't spell it right,' says he. 'C-o-l-e it should be,' and made out a paper for Joseph Cole, native of St. Michaels, Azores Islands, Portugal, and—"

Peter, happening to glance out to where the talkative, gesticulating, but active and efficient dark-bearded men were putting the great mainsail in stops, came to a pause. Presently, his eyes twinkling, he resumed: "And I s'pose that a couple of hundred years from now the genealogy sharks will be diggin' up a fine Anglo-Saxon pedigree for Joe's descendants, if it happens they want to get into one of those Who's Who societies we read about in the papers, as all the time guaranteein' which is the sure-enough thing. Joe's descendants—and they'll probably be numerous, for he's got seven children of his own already—they'll probably discover someday that they're descended from some fine old Northumberland family, so named because of the coalmining properties they owned, or maybe the pedigree experts will tell them they were so named because of their dark complexions.

"Well, Joe kept comin'. I saw him one night playin' duplicate whist in the Master Mariners' rooms, and he most burstin' with the things he wanted to say but couldn't, because some good friends told him 'twas against the rules to talk while you were playing whist, though everybody was talkin' around him. Says I, that's sure the finishin' touch. But it warn't. He didn't put on the last little rag polish to his Americanization till about the time he was expectin' his final naturalization papers, the papers that'd give him the right to vote. He was haddockin' in South Channel then, market-fishin' into Boston. And that's the devil's own fishin', let me tell you—night and day, rain or shine, till you fill her up—with those old-country fishermen, Dungarven, Claddagh and Kincaid men to set the pace. You need to be an iron man to stand it. And their everlastin' racin' to market! For whoever hits the Boston market right in haddockin' he's sure the boy that shares big, and blessed little if you don't hit it right, for those Boston dealers they cert'nly want it all.

"So the competition there is pretty keen, as you know, and nobody was any keener than Joe Cole to hold his own. We'd been hove-to under our fores'l for eight days waitin' for it to moderate so's we could get a chance to fish. A Tuesday morning that was, and not a vessel in the fleet, we felt sure, had a pound of fish in her hold. But such fishin' when we did shove the dories over! They must have been fair starved out down below, waitin' with their mouths open, and just over the right spot we must have been, for it was a fish to every hook. Next morning at five o'clock there was sixty thousand of fish iced below or ready to dress on deck. 'Sweeng her off,' says Joe, 'an' we mak' da market dees aft'noon.' 'Twas in Lent, and Joe could hardly hold himself when he thought of it. 'We ketcha da market dry,' says Joe, 'mak' plenta mon-ee dees trip, you see.'

"And the scheme did look good. It didn't seem possible that any vessel could have loaded up as fast as we did, and if we could get home that day, which seemed likely—a great sailin' breeze, with no more than a hundred and thirty-odd miles to the dock and twelve hours to do it in—it looked good. And of course if it *was* a fish famine after that long spell of bad weather, we cert'nly were in for a big trip.

"So off we went, across the channel and up by Cape Cod in good shape. And with the wind making all the time, we straightened out for a run across the Bay in fine spirits. Nothing, we thought then, could stop her from gettin' to T wharf, with hours to spare, nothing short of dismastin', and they bein' those same good old Georgia pine sticks that Joe had tried so hard to carry away off Halifax, we had no fear of that.

"We were belting along then, not ten miles from the lightship, the vessel hikin' everlastin'ly and the gang already spendin' their money—a couple up to the Boston Theatre; another looking over the bankbook with his wife—who just come back from depositin' forty dollars in the savings bank, and that made three hundred and twenty-nine dollars and fourteen cents, not countin' interest due but not yet entered; another chap was being measured for a nine-dollar pair o' pants, the only thing worryin' him was would he have a blue seam—when came a squall that struck us fair. Over she went, with most of her deck underwater. And stayed there for a while. But she was all right, she didn't quite capsize; only when she did come up we had to break out her topside plankin' with handspikes, so's the water could run off her deck before we could get her goin' again.

"And that would've been all right, only away up to wind'ard ten miles or more—we could just make her out—was a three-masted schooner hove-down. Only different from us, she showed no signs of coming up. Well, there was nothing to it but go up to her. And maybe Joe didn't look back longin'ly at the lightship when we wore' round.

"It must have taken us two hours to beat up—not much sea, but wind somethin' desp'rate—and when we got alongside we had to be everlastin'ly careful in takin' them off, and particularly careful with one gent, a passenger, who turned out to be her owner. He'd been takin' a cruise along the coast in this vessel of his. A big, fine-lookin', rosy chap, though not too rosy when we took him off; but a pretty decent kind, except that when he got his courage back he developed into one of those patronizin' kind that get on your nerves, the kind that look you over and think because you hustle for a livin' you must have lost any nat'ral intelligence you ever had, if ever you had any. You know— one of those 'my good man' kind of chaps.

"'I'll do something handsome for you, you'll see,' he says to Joe. This was after we'd got him dried out and the rosy color came into his face again. And pats Joe on the back, which Joe didn't quite like, comin' from a stranger; but you have to make allowances for a man whose life you've just saved, though just then Joe warn't payin' too much attention to this lad's speeches. Joe was mostly worryin' would he get to T wharf before five o'clock that afternoon or not.

"Well, we didn't get there; The market had been closed ten minutes when we dove into the slip. And you would 'a' had to sympathize with the skipper if you'd seen him sittin' on the cap-log fannin' himself with his sou'wester. He was downcast sure enough. 'Haddock seex centa an' da cod eight centa da poun'. Dees trip good for four t'ousan' dollar if we been in one leet' half hour ago.'

"Knowin' just how he felt, I tried hard to cheer him up. 'It may be even higher in the morning, skipper,' I said. 'If no other vessel comes in it's sure to,' I goes on, 'for with a Friday in Lent ahead of them they got to have the fish to fill the orders. And if it is, skipper, you'll have a market trip stock that'll go down to posterity.'

"Just to think of it made him smile—if nobody came in during the night!"

Peter stopped short and began to laugh softly. "I have to every time I think of it."

"What was it, Peter—nobody in?"

Peter roared. "Nobody in! Next mornin' there were thirty-five vessels into the dock. You couldn't see the harbor for masts and trys'ls hung up to dry. And fish! 1,764,589 pounds of fish to the dock that day. I remember the figures well, the record day of that year, and from eight and six cents a pound cod dropped to two and a quarter and haddock to a dollar and a quarter a hundred. Instead of stockin' four thousand we stocked less than nine hundred dollars. Instead of the crew sharing a hundred and fifty or sixty dollars apiece, we shared twenty-six dollars and twenty-three cents apiece for our two weeks of a winter trip.

"Well, you oughter seen Joe. 'Dam!' says he. 'Dam again all coasta-men that can-not han-del a ves-sel! Dam! T'ree t'ousan' dollar lost for one leet' squall! Dam! dam! dam!' in little explosions like a gasoline engine around deck.

"That same afternoon Joe's final papers came to him, and he went up to an Atlantic Avenue hotel with Wesley Marrs and Tom O'Donnell, his two great models, to look them over. They'd hardly gone when the owner he'd rescued from the three-master came down the dock lookin' for the skipper.

"He was rosy as any apple with good-humor and impatience, so I brought him up to the hotel. He pounced on Joe. 'Ha, I've found you! I've been up and down the dock looking for you, as this man'—meanin' me—'will tell you. You did me a good turn yesterday—good seamanship and a good spirit displayed. And I know that you must have lost sometime in doing it. Now, now. I kept track—three hours or more it must have been, and you shall be reimbursed—paid—and paid well for it.'

"Joe raised his hand, palm out, protestin'. 'No, no. For sav-ving life we can tak' no mon-ee.'

"'Now, now. I did not say this was for saving life.' And the smile of him! You'd think Joe was some three-year-old child he was talkin' to. 'No, not for saving life—allow me'—he goes on—'but for the time lost in saving life—for the time lost.'

"'For da time lost in sav-ving life I tak' no mon-ee,' repeats Joe.

"'But you must, captain. You really must let me have my way. And I will split no hairs over it. You and your men work hard, and your rewards, I know, are not great. Three hours for twenty-four men—how will that do?' and he held out some bills.

"'What ees it?' said Joe.

"'Why,' said the rescued chap, 'American money—a hundred dollars. See, five twenties. Now in the country where you come from—'

"'Yess,' interrupted Joe, 'in da countree where I come from a hund'ed dollar is mooch mon-ee, ver' mooch. But dere also we tak no mon-ee—not for sav-ving life.'

"'But you must,' said this chap, and forced the bills into Joe's hands.

"Joe looked at them as if he had never seen a twenty-dollar bill in his life before. 'My, such a heap!' he says after a little study, and held them up for Marrs and O'Donnell to look at, and after they'd had a look he crumpled them up in his fist, and then, straightening them out again and in the most absent-minded way in the world he reached over to the little alcohol lamp at the end of the bar, stuck one of them into the flame, and with it lit his cigar.

"The passenger jumped a yard into the air. 'My God!' he shrieked, 'what are you doing?'

"'What ees?' says Joe, surprised-like, at the same time stampin' what was left of the bill to ashes under his toe, and only then seemin' to take notice of what he had done. 'Ah, ah. I burn da mon-ee? What a mistak', sooch a mis-tak', ver' foolish. My brain it ees, what you say? bis-ee. But I will mak' a'right,' and diving into his jeans he pulled out a great wad of bills, from which he took a twenty and handed it with the other four bills to the passenger. The passenger drew back.

"'You do not weesh to tak'?' says Joe. 'It is for you, captain, and then the men, your crew—'

"'Ahh, for da crew?' and turned to where I was standing. 'Here, Peter, tak' dis mon-ee, dees fine gentla-man geev, an' buy see-gar, good see-gar, min' you. Seegar—er, no, see-gar-ette for da gang,' and tossed the hundred dollars over to me.

"By this time the passenger was making all kinds of queer faces. 'Have some drink?' asked Joe politely. And the man, kind of dazed still, said he guessed he'd take a little whiskey and soda.

"'Psst!' said Joe. His mustache curled and his earrings almost tinkled. 'Whis-key an' so-da! Dees no gang cheapa sport. Dees here Capta' Tom O'Don-nell, dees Capta' Wesley Marrs.' Then, rapping on the bar, Joe ordered the bartender to bring on a quart of the fizzy stuff, and after that another quart, and on top of that another, and was ordering another—all in a rush—and had spread out on the bar the papers that made him an American citizen, to call the man's attention to them, when he flew out the door. 'Ahh,' said Joe sadly, 'an' I wanta heem to see dese—what you call heem, dat long word, Tom?'

"'Naturali-zation papers, naturali-zation, and say it slow, Joe.'

"'Ahh, yess—what eet ees you say, Tom, what geev me vote—dat right?'

"'That's right, Joe, and 'twas treason to keep you waitin'. You ought to been votin' the day you hit the country, Joe.'

"Joe smiled. 'Anny-way, a good ceetzen now, hah, Tom—a good American ceet-zen Joe Cole now, hah, Wes-ley?'

"'That's what,' says Wesley. 'And the way you tossed that hundred to Peter, Joe, it was nothing less than—how is it they say, it in the theatre, Tom?'

"'Soo-per-r-b is the word, Wesley. With a gesture of sooperb contimpt, is the words they use.'

"'Ahh—,' said Joe, and reached for the fourth quart. 'We dreenk to one new American ceet-zen, Joe Cole! Mm—' he drew in his breath like a child—'and ahh, it tak' us to show dem da true American way. Hah, Tom? Ha, Wes-ley?'"

Peter had risen to mark on the blackboard the names of vessel and master, but with chalk in air he paused. "And I say with O'Donnell and Wesley 'tisn't the len'th of time a man's been in the country that makes a citizen of him. Joe was of more use to the country the first day he set foot on an American dock, of more use than many who'd vote to keep him out, of more use than many that's got ancestral halls and don't see anything right in the country nowadays, but who wouldn't themselves lose a night's sleep or the nail off a finger to make it right. Those others talk; but Joe's kind, whether he's Squarehead or Dutch, Polak or Dago, whatever he is—his is the kind that's always been throwin' a halo round the people and the institutions of the country he adopts. Joe's kind, that don't half the time know whether his country is right or wrong, and don't half the time care, is the kind that since nations were nations has gone out and died for the flag that's over them. And made but little fuss about it. And the horizon, you'll take notice, is blotted out with but few monuments to his mem-ory."

Carefully Peter was writing it down—"Schooner *Bonita*, master Joseph Cole," when—"But, Peter, did you really buy cigarettes for the money?"

The wrinkles spread from the corner of Peter's mouth till they reached to under his ears. "Hm—well, not for the whole hundred. But let me tell you, boy, what cigars we did smoke that day—they were cert'nly a damn swell brand."

(1907)

Mother America

Onorio Ruotolo

Great Mother, upon thee God has lavished
    all his favors,
And treasures and riches he concealed in thine
    earth, thy heaven, thy sea,
That other mothers might resort to thee,
That foundlings and the offspring of poor mothers
    and the forsterings of cruel stepmothers
    might resort to thee;
To eat of thy bread and drink of thy wine,
To unveil to the sun the treasures of thy breast,
To grow the laurel for thy brow and melt the gold
    for thy crown.
To hew the marble for thy throne and deck with stars
    of gold and silver, of green and crimson,
Thy mantle of Mother of Queen;
To sing thee the praises and the songs of all times
    and of all tongues, molten in the powerful throb
    of Faith renewed, of Love reborn.

We, orphans, sons of poor mothers, fosterlings of cruel
    stepmothers, came to thee, and thou didst welcome
    us with the immortal words:
"I am the mother of the Mothers and of the new family
    that is Humanity.
For all I have bread, work and happiness.
You are all my children, equal in joy and in sorrow,
    in war and in peace.
I would have all the love of the orphaned, for now I am
    their only mother, and I would have them forget
    their cruel stepmothers.

Yet would I not have them forget for love of me, their love
    for their poor Mothers far away, for I, too, am a Mother.
Share with me the love for those poor Mothers far away,
    for only thus can your love of me be true."

Dost thou remember, O Mother America,
Dost thou remember thine immortal words?

We adored thee on our knees,
And kissed thy feet, bedewing them with tender tears, as sons
    who have not lost a Mother, but in thee find her again.
We are thy children, born of thee, come to thee.

We have tilled thy soil,
Dug thy mines,
Tunneled thy mountains,
Raised thy spires, thy domes, thy temples, thine altars,
And we have laid the rails of thine iron ways;
With the sweat of our brow we have anointed thy machines
And with our blood we have watered thy fields;
That we might earn the right to thy bread,
That we might quench our thirst at thy fountains,
That with thine air we might breathe thy Freedom,
Defend the laws of thy Fathers
And honor thy flag;
That we might all be brothers through thy maternal love,
To rest at last within thy lap, in our eternal sleep;
That we might be called thy sons, born or fostered by thee,
America, our Queen-Mother.

(1925)

Alma Mater: The Immigrant at Columbia

Ajan Syrian

Gajor, richest of the Syrians, is my friend.
He sends me to the vast school,
Where the great square-winged houses circle
And call the young men in.
"Come! Come, beyond our pillars and our fountains!
Come from the restless, spending city,
Passionate and cold,
Her blistered mouth would drink you dry
Ere your eager hopes had found a soil and a sun
To draw them to a high bursting fragrance and a white,
    white bloom,
Roofing the world!
Come behind my gray-brown walls—
Even, strong, sober walls without towers.
Like a warm, still wine in the cup of youth,
Lift up your young blood here
To the lips of learning!"

O Alma Mater:
From the red, red dust, the long dead dust
Of ancient Syria, I come
To lie between thy feet of lasting bronze
And look up—and look up!
To see thy laureled head—
Massive, calm, with gloried brow—
Flame before the open portals of the House of Books;
Where the thoughts of noble men—
Dressed in all habits, speaking all tongues,
Gathered from all ages of time—
Meet like pilgrims at one shrine,
For the worship of service to thy sons.
O mother, thy brow shines loftily
Above the endless sullen roar of heavy whips
In the unmastered market of slaves!
What light is on thy face, brighter than the dawn?
It is the wind-flung beauty of her Torch—the Other Woman,
Who stands upon the sea as thou upon the land,

And lifts her light,
Beckoning the sons of weeping centuries
Out of their long dead dust, across the ten great seas,
Into this harbor!

    Ay, into this harbor have I come,
Where white sails of the world, like strings of a pearled lute,
Chant Liberty—and Liberty—and Liberty,
In the crashing wind of her lifted arm!
(Oh, chords from the smitten silver of light!)—
Mother, thy breast is bared and beating high to catch that
    song!

(1915)

PART II

The Assimilation Debate

The previous part discussed efforts in the period to restrict the numbers of immigrants from Asia, as well as from southern and eastern Europe and the Middle East. In this restrictionist climate, the United States also exerted great pressure on recently arrived immigrants to be absorbed by their new country at the expense of their old one. The selections in this part illustrate deep divisions over the idea of assimilation as a dominant mode of immigrant identity formation in the Progressive Era. As one of the most prevalent models of the period, the idea of assimilation suggested, with some starkness, that the task of new arrivals was to conform to the dominant Anglo-Saxon culture. Brander Matthews's 1922 essay "Are We Still Anglo-Saxons?" is representative of this strain of the assimilation debate. Matthews's fear was that immigrants were not sufficiently "subdued to what they lived in," and he illustrated how immigrants ought to act and feel by referring to immigration scholar Hjalmar H. Boyesen's experiences with Norwegian immigrants in Minnesota. The Norwegians, Boyesen noted, were "anxious to assert their solidarity with the older stock of Americans. They wanted to be like us; they accepted our traditions; they acquired our folkways; they shared our opinions and even our prejudices. They wished to become 'Anglo-Saxons' and to be recognized as 'Anglo-Saxons.'"[1] At its simplest core, assimilation was an effort to explain an immigrant's transition from family-based, self-sufficient village life to the centralized norms of the urban United States, even as these norms were never articulated fully. At the same time, assimilation reflected in large part the desire that immigrants renounce their past and submit to an Anglo-Saxon future in order to ensure a homogeneous (but ambiguously defined) national whole.

This part's opening essay by Theodore Roosevelt characterizes the subjugation model of assimilation represented by Matthews. Assimilation, for Roosevelt, was an urgent, nationalistic response to the alleged threats of mass immigration. In 1894, just two years after the Ellis Island facility was created to accommodate growing immigration from Europe—and twelve years after the Chinese Exclusion Act was passed to curtail Chinese immigration—Roosevelt extolled assimilation as a form of Americanization that would distinguish the country from what he saw as the "undersized" and "effeminate" yoke of European influence. The future of the United States, he argued, would depend "mainly on whether these newcomers do or do not throw themselves heartily into our national life, cease to be European, and become Americans like the rest of us." As is often the case in assimilation debates, much depends on how the writer defines the cultural responsibilities and rewards of U.S. citizenship. Roosevelt argued that immigrants would "harm both themselves and us" if they clung "to the speech, the customs, the ways of life, and the habits of thought of the Old World which they have left." Roosevelt so fervently believed in assimilation that he even suggested that St. Patrick's Day no longer be celebrated in the United States. Assimilation was less a prospect of mutual integration for Roosevelt and more a matter of "subduing" the immigrant's desire to "cling" to an Old World identity.

However, assimilation also could be portrayed in a more benign way, as a key component in the movement to "uplift" the masses so prevalent during the Progressive Era rather than as a form of exclusionary nationalism. In this vision, assimilation involved a process of mutual accommodation, where the dominant culture made room for its newest citizens, who in turn negotiated an equitable spot for themselves in their new country. Frances A. Kellor wrote in a 1919 issue of the *Yale Review* that this definition of assimilation was indeed the foremost "task of America," one in which the United States must "find the way by which these races, living on one soil, under one form of government, with no territorial lines, can be assimilated and become a part of [the country's] integral national life."[2] For someone such as Kellor, assimilation cast mutual integration as a noble, albeit difficult, duty that must be confronted by a culture whose government is unified but whose territorial boundaries nevertheless are always in flux.

In order to highlight these visions of assimilation based on models of subjugation and reform, Roosevelt's essay is followed in this part by poems written from the perspectives of nativists who envisioned assimilation as a process by which immigrant masses were rescued from Old World misery by an adoptive country eager to revivify its newly arrived future citizens. In this viewpoint, the relationship between immigrants and the culture to which they would assimilate is one of uplifting integration. Assimilation is a force that molds immigrants in the image of their new culture in poems such as C. A. Price's and Henry Blake Fuller's. Little is made of the power inequities that might arise in this process, and the nationalistic idealism of the assimilation debate is absorbed—implied rather than explicitly stated—by a position that suggests a beneficial relationship in which the adoptive country exerts equal parts pressure and compassion on its new immigrants.

This vision of assimilation as a mode of benevolence is explored further in other selections, which shift their primary setting to the U.S. public school classroom. One of the most powerful ideas in immigration debates in this era was the optimism among many that the primary location for a benign assimilation was the classroom, where the children of newly arrived immigrants would become Americanized. The U.S. public school system was a central means to promote Anglo-American cultural ideals among immigrants. To be sure, for many immigrants the promise of free public education was part of the allure of leaving their homelands in the first place. Yet, the value of such education is debated in ["Since I left South China"], by an anonymous Cantonese poet in San Francisco's Chinatown, and in Mary Antin's "The Lie." In ["Since I left South China"], the poet charts the vast difference between surface-level appearances and the less visible, but more enduring, effects of the U.S. educational system and what many saw as its attendant assimilationist mission. For the speaker of this poem, the consequences of assimilation sometimes can be simply new forms of ignorance. By contrast, in the classroom of Antin's story, the urge to assimilate instead leads to an optimistic dishonesty—what the teacher in her story describes bluntly as a "noble lie" that actually contributes to her pupil's assimilation. Either way, as a producer of an immigrant's alienation from his or her new culture, or as an optimistic impetus to accommodate oneself to a new culture, assimilation is portrayed increasingly in this part as a complicated process of loss and transformation for immigrants and natives alike.

In almost any setting, assimilation could be a source of turbulence for immigrants as well as for native-born. One of the major questions of the period, however, concerned the definition of exactly what immigrants should be assimilating into. If assimilation was the goal, then to what cultural norms should immigrants aspire? The difficulty of this question, as shown in the selections that follow, suggests that U.S. culture in itself was not as unified as assimilationists such as Matthews or Boyesen assumed. The selections by Sui Sin Far, Amy Lowell, and Claude McKay illustrate one of the primary problems of Progressive-Era assimilationist urgings: more often than not, as historian Russell A. Kazal points up, those demanding assimilation "did not clearly define the target society to which immigrants assimilated."[3] Even though in Sui Sin Far's story the family unit is the locus of assimilation, the consequences of assimilation are vexing because the family itself is split on how to define the most effective means of assimilation—through school, language, or customs, to name three possibilities—and split, too, on how to distinguish between adequate and overzealous assimilation. In a 1909 autobiographical essay, Sui Sin Far describes how the urgency to assimilate created a similar bifurcation in her own life; this disjunction is intensified by her mixed European and Chinese background. Assimilation threatened to wipe out her Chinese heritage at the same time that it promised, paradoxically, to unite her multiethnic identities. "I give my right hand to the Occidentals and my left hand to the Orientals," she writes, "hoping that between them they will not utterly destroy the insignificant connecting link."[4] The vitality, and eventually the threat, of this sardonically named "insignificant connecting link" is precisely what is at stake in her story of assimilation, "The Wisdom of the New," in this part.

At any moment that a new arrival might fear "the wisdom of the new," a nativist might at the same time implore "Are we still Anglo-Saxons?" the title question in the essay noted above.[5] In the anxious environment described by this essay, it would seem that the only choice available to the immigrant was to follow the example of the Norwegian immigrants in Minnesota and assimilate by surrendering to dominant Anglo-Saxon cultural practices. Yet, because the process of assimilation was defined ambiguously by the target society itself, the odds were stacked, politically so, against immigrants for whom the assimilation process often was shrouded in mystery. Describing the political realities of this ambiguity, The Independent wrote, "We are scathing in our criticism of the immigrant who fails to become a true American, but we pay little attention to the means by which his transformation must be accomplished."[6]

In the context of these debates over what the target society of assimilation was, and how much this undefined target society might be threatened by immigration, some suggested that the problem of immigration was the target society itself. The selections by poets Amy Lowell, a Boston native, and Claude McKay, a Jamaican immigrant, demonstrate the political realities for immigrants of assimilating to a hostile, ambiguously defined target society. Lowell was known as one of the early U.S. imagist poets, a group generally more interested in formal innovation than political engagement. Yet her poem "The Foreigner" dramatizes a decidedly political conflict: a duel between a nativist and an immigrant in which the new arrival resists assimilation precisely because it threatens to mutate him. Her archaic battle scene dramatizes a common nativist argument that assimilation would invigorate an overly civilized, even softened, United States; Lowell suggests that it is the immigrant, rather than the native, that U.S. culture should emulate. McKay's poem takes the political consequences of Lowell's argument even further, asserting that the decline of Anglo-Saxon culture is accelerated by its racial prejudices. With the parameters of assimilation ambiguous in the period, assimilation is made more difficult for the black immigrant who "darkly gazes" on the target culture; and, for McKay, the immigrant's function is not to assimilate to U.S. culture but to rebuild this culture from what he sees as the country's imminent ruin. Written as a traditional Shakespearean sonnet, the poem's form mirrors its content, prophesying the decline of the United States while speaking within a traditional Anglo-Saxon aesthetic mode. To borrow from Houston Baker's well-known arguments on Harlem Renaissance literature, McKay's mastery of traditional European poetic form is the vehicle for his deformation of the myth of European mastery (down to his ironic echoes of Percy Bysshe Shelley's "Ozymandius").[7] Much like the immigrant figure in Lowell's poem, McKay's speaker battles to deny the assimilation discourse its power to subjugate.

The combat metaphors found in Lowell's and McKay's poems offer the reminder that the divide between old country ideals and an ambiguously defined target society of assimilation exerted a terrible psychological stress on immigrants. This split between, on one hand, the pressures of loyalty to one's birthplace and, on the other hand, the pressures of Americanization, could create a difficult double-consciousness in immigrants. Kahlil Gibran's "Dead Are My People" explores this double-consciousness. Composed in the United States during the 1915 Syrian famine, the poem is grim in its portrayal of an immigrant torn between two cultures. Riven by both his allegiance to his homeland and the pressure to fold himself into a new land, Gibran questions the relevance of "the lamentation of an / Absent poet" during a time of national tragedy in the land of his birth. Gibran articulates the very sentiments for which *The Independent* reserved its "scathing critique"—the feelings of the immigrant torn between two cultures and resisting the call to assimilate. The psychological pressures of assimilation on immigrants are revisited later in this part, with what seems like the escapist fantasy of Ameen Rihani's poem, "I Dreamt I Was a Donkey-Boy Again." The poem seems at first glance a familiar account of immigrant homesickness. Yet the speaker's longings for Lebanon are shaped by the psychological pressures of assimilation. The dream that is central to the poem eventually signals a clearer story of the speaker's psychological struggles with assimilation than a straightforward narrative would—a more lucid portrayal of the disjunctive experience of assimilation than linear speech might provide.

The psychological stress of assimilation was also the product of a profound overlap between debates over assimilation and those over cultural pluralism. Immigrant Maurice Ravage emphasized a common theme in these debates in his 1917 essay, "Absorbing the Alien," suggesting that a pluralist consciousness is a necessary transitional state toward the ultimate end of assimilation. Cultural pluralism, he wrote, "is the period of transition and denationalization, when the alien has ceased to be his ancient self and has not yet become his new self."[8] This period, for Ravage, is one in which the assertion of the immigrant's "ancient self" is an articulation of "decay," serving the ultimate end of assimilation in which the immigrant's "whole spiritual constitution breaks up into its separate atoms, to be regrouped and rebuilt toward a new life." As Ravage saw it, the political potential of this eventual end-point of assimilation is a thoroughgoing revivification of the United States. The "spirit of the old Ghetto," he wrote, "has contributed to the revitalization of

America," where "college men are no longer eager to break strikes," and "thoughtful men and women of the more fortunate classes regard themselves no longer as a superior race of beings."[9]

This part ends with works that test the optimistic finality of assimilation typified by Ravage's image of unified groups—privileged natives and impoverished immigrants— reforming the country in the image of its liberal democratic ideals. The selections that follow demonstrate the pitfalls of assuming that immigrants themselves were a unified community either prepared to be absorbed into their new country or to resist assimilating. Achmed Abdullah's "A Simple Act of Piety" illustrates the internal hostilities produced among immigrant groups as they struggled to assimilate. Abdullah, an Afghan-Russian immigrant, represents one vector in assimilation debates of the period, in which immigrant groups delineated the target culture to which they would assimilate by defining themselves against this same culture's negative stereotypes of other immigrants. However, some literary figures of the time did not recognize that immigrants could reflect a heterogeneous mix of the dominant culture's tensions and conflicts. For instance, Abdullah's graceless portrayals of Chinese immigrants reflect nativists' racist stereotypes; yet, when "A Simple Act of Piety" was anthologized in *The Best Short Stories of 1918*, the volume's editor Edward J. O'Brien praised the story's "fine appreciation of the Oriental point of view" and its "fine crystallization of the poetry inherent in New York Chinatown life."[10] To be sure, we do not dispute that Abdullah's story was worthy of inclusion in the volume. O'Brien's vision of immigrant homogeneity, nevertheless, stands in stark contrast to the hostility within immigrant groups struggling to assimilate in Abdullah's portrayal of Chinatown, which he describes as a neighborhood that is "very sweet, very gentle—and very unhuman."

The difficulties of assimilation were even more vexing for Caribbean immigrants, whose double-consciousness as immigrants was heightened, as black Americans, by what W. E. B. Du Bois characterized in *The Souls of Black Folk* (1903) as the "double-consciousness" required for survival in a culture just a generation or two removed from its roots in a slave economy. Louis J. Parascandola explains that "the bipolar distinction of Black and White was alien to many Caribbean immigrants who had been brought up with many gradations between groups based upon racial complexion and class." Parascandola reports that Caribbean immigrants often "had their first encounters with racial prejudice in the United States."[11] Eric Walrond's "On Being Black" suggests that the racist exclusion of Caribbean immigrants such as himself from assimilation efforts offers, ironically, a better way of retaining ethnic identity than seen in the final story of this part—Edward Steiner's illustration of what is lost when a European immigrant assimilates "successfully." Walrond's protagonist opens the story looking to buy a new pair of eyeglasses. What he needs to see, of course, is more than just physical: the glasses are termed "goggles," as if protective rather than corrective eyewear. The salesman, an elderly Jewish immigrant, suggests much the same of the pair that the protagonist eventually purchases. "Here is a nice one, . . ." the salesman says. "Just the right kind of goggles to keep the dust from going into your eyes." With his new "goggles," the protagonist really does *see* the effects of assimilation, the extra price he pays for being a Caribbean immigrant, with the dust no longer in his eyes. "I did see," he tells the reader, explaining his moment of understanding the literal and figurative price of being denied assimilation: the tropics are closer, indeed, but only because "it pays"—literally—"to be black."

We hope that the works in this part demonstrate how the debate over assimilation could either be framed by the extremes of Matthews or Kellor, or nuanced by debates over exactly what the terms of assimilation were and which ethnic and racial groups were given preference over others. The works in this part revisit, and sometimes test, Ravage's assertion that the "tragedy" of assimilation is "lightened by a vast, rollicking farce and a broad beam of hope."[12] They demonstrate the rich, vexing conflicts of assimilation debates during the era. In doing so, these selections offer contrasting views on how new arrivals and natives defined themselves and participated in the liberal democratic institutions of the country even as they struggled to make sense of the unprecedented immigration changing the United States in this era.

Notes

1. Brander Matthews, quoted in "Are We Still Anglo-Saxons?" *The Literary Digest* (September 9, 1922): 31. Matthews admits that Boyesen's remarks are at least three decades old, which suggests that by 1922 it was difficult to find immigrants who would express such fervor to become Anglo-Saxons.

2. Frances A. Kellor, "What is Americanization?" *The Yale Review* 8 (January 1919): 282–299. Reprinted in *Immigration and Americanization: Selected Readings*, ed. Philip Davis (Boston: Ginn and Company, 1920), 623.

3. Russell A. Kazal, "Revisiting Assimilation: The Rise, Fall, and Reappraisal of a Concept in American Ethnic History," *The American Historical Review* 100, no. 2 (April 1995): 445.

4. Sui Sin Far, "Leaves from the Mental Portfolio of an Eurasian," *The Independent* 66 (January 21, 1909): 132.

5. "Are We Still Anglo-Saxons?" 31.

6. "The Honorable Hyphen," *The Independent* (June 12, 1916): 429.

7. For more on race and the politics of formal mastery, see Houston A. Baker, Jr., *Modernism and the Harlem Renaissance* (Chicago: University of Chicago Press, 1989).

8. M[aurice]. E. Ravage, "Absorbing the Alien," *Century* 95 (November 1917): 35.

9. Ibid., 36.

10. Edward J. O'Brien, "The Best Sixty American Short Stories, January to October, 1918: A Critical Summary," in *The Best Short Stories of 1918*, ed. Edward O'Brien (Boston: Small, Maynard, and Company, 1918), 374.

11. Louis Parascandola, introduction to *"Look for Me All Around You": Anglophone Caribbean Immigrants in the Harlem Renaissance*, ed. Louis Parascandola (Detroit: Wayne State University Press, 2005), 5. See also Nancy Foner, "West Indian Migration to New York: An Overview," in *Islands in the City: West Indian Migration to New York*, ed. Nancy Foner (Berkeley: University of California Press, 2001), 12–13; and Mary C. Waters, *Black Identities: West Indian Immigrant Dreams and American Realities* (New York: Russell Sage Foundation, 1999), 29–31.

12. Ravage, "Absorbing the Alien," 36.

True Americanism

Theodore Roosevelt

Patriotism was once defined as "the last refuge of a scoundrel"; and somebody has recently remarked that when Dr. Johnson gave this definition he was ignorant of the infinite possibilities contained in the word "reform."* Of course both gibes were quite justifiable, in so far as they were aimed at people who use noble names to cloak base purposes. Equally of course the man shows little wisdom and a low sense of duty who fails to see that love of country is one of the elemental virtues, even though scoundrels play upon it for their own selfish ends; and, inasmuch as abuses continually grow up in civic life as in all other kinds of life, the statesman is indeed a weakling who hesitates to reform these abuses because the word "reform" is often on the lips of men who are silly or dishonest.

What is true of patriotism and reform is true also of Americanism. There are plenty of scoundrels always ready to try to belittle reform movements or to bolster up existing iniquities in the name of Americanism; but this does not alter the fact that the man who can do most in this country is and must be the man whose Americanism is most sincere and intense. Outrageous though it is to use a noble idea as the cloak for evil, it is still worse to assail the noble idea itself because it can thus be used. The men who do iniquity in the name of patriotism, of reform, of Americanism, are merely one small division of the class that has always existed and will always exist,—the class of hypocrites and demagogues, the class that is always prompt to steal the watchwords of righteousness and use them in the interests of evil-doing.

The stoutest and truest Americans are the very men who have the least sympathy with the people who invoke the spirit of Americanism to aid what is vicious in our government or to throw obstacles in the way of those who strive to reform it. It is contemptible to oppose a movement for good because that movement has already succeeded somewhere else, or to champion an existing abuse because our people have always been wedded to it. To appeal to national prejudice against a given reform movement is in every way unworthy and silly. It is as childish to denounce free trade because England has adopted it as to advocate it for the same reason. It is eminently proper, in dealing with the tariff, to consider the effect of tariff legislation in time past upon other nations as well as the effect upon our own; but in drawing conclusions it is in the last degree

---

*Dr. Johnson: Samuel Johnson (1709–1784), poet and essayist, one of the most well known figures in English literature. Author of the *Dictionary of the English Language* (1755), the standard English dictionary until the early twentieth-century publication of the *Oxford English Dictionary*.

foolish to try to excite prejudice against one system because it is in vogue in some given country, or to try to excite prejudice in its favor because the economists of that country have found that it was suited to their own peculiar needs. In attempting to solve our difficult problem of municipal government it is mere folly to refuse to profit by whatever is good in the examples of Manchester and Berlin because these cities are foreign, exactly as it is mere folly blindly to copy their examples without reference to our own totally different conditions. As for the absurdity of declaiming against civil service reform, for instance, as "Chinese," because written examinations have been used in China, it would be quite as wise to declaim against gunpowder because it was first utilized by the same people. In short, the man who, whether from mere dull fatuity or from an active interest in misgovernment, tries to appeal to American prejudice against things foreign, so as to induce Americans to oppose any measure for good, should be looked on by his fellow countrymen with the heartiest contempt. So much for the men who appeal to the spirit of Americanism to sustain us in wrong-doing. But we must never let our contempt for these men blind us to the nobility of the idea which they strive to degrade.

We Americans have many grave problems to solve, many threatening evils to fight, and many deeds to do, if, as we hope and believe, we have the wisdom, the strength, the courage, and the virtue to do them. But we must face facts as they are. We must neither surrender ourselves to a foolish optimism, nor succumb to a timid and ignoble pessimism. Our nation is that one among all the nations of the earth which holds in its hands the fate of the coming years. We enjoy exceptional advantages, and are menaced by exceptional dangers; and all signs indicate that we shall either fail greatly or succeed greatly. I firmly believe that we shall succeed; but we must not foolishly blink the dangers by which we are threatened, for that is the way to fail. On the contrary, we must soberly set to work to find out all we can about the existence and extent of every evil, must acknowledge it to be such, and must then attack it with unyielding resolution. There are many such evils, and each must be fought after a fashion; yet there is one quality which we must bring to the solution of every problem,—that is, an intense and fervid Americanism. We shall never be successful over the dangers that confront us; we shall never achieve true greatness, nor reach the lofty ideal which the founders and preservers of our mighty Federal Republic have set before us, unless we are Americans in heart and soul, in spirit and purpose, keenly alive to the responsibility implied in the very name of American, and proud beyond measure of the glorious privilege of bearing it.

There are two or three sides to the question of Americanism, and two or three senses in which the word "Americanism" can be used to express the antithesis of what is unwholesome and undesirable. In the first place we wish to be broadly American and national, as opposed to being local or sectional. We do not wish, in politics, in literature, or in art, to develop that unwholesome parochial spirit, that over-exaltation of the little community at the expense of the great nation, which produces what has been described as the patriotism of the village, the patriotism of the belfry. Politically, the indulgence of this spirit was the chief cause of the calamities which befell the ancient republics of Greece, the medieval republics of Italy, and the petty States of Germany as it was in the last century. It is this spirit of provincial patriotism, this inability to take a view of broad adhesion to the whole nation that has been the chief among the causes that have produced such anarchy in the South American States, and which have resulted in presenting to us not one great Spanish-American federal nation stretching from the Rio Grande to Cape Horn, but a squabbling multitude of revolution-ridden States, not one of which stands even in the second rank as a power. However, politically this question of American nationality has been settled once for all. We are no longer in danger of repeating in our history the shameful and contemptible disasters that have befallen the Spanish possessions on this continent since they threw off the yoke of Spain. Indeed, there is, all through our life, very much less of this parochial spirit than there was formerly. Still there is an occasional outcropping here and there; and it is just as well that we should keep steadily in mind the futility of talking of a Northern literature or a Southern literature, an Eastern or a Western school of art or science. Joel Chandler Harris is emphatically a national writer; so is Mark Twain. They do not write merely for Georgia or Missouri or California any more than for Illinois or Connecticut; they write as Americans and for all people who can read English. St. Gaudens lives in New York; but his work is just as distinctive of Boston or Chicago. It is of very great consequence that we should have a full and ripe literary development in the United States, but it is not of the least consequence whether New York, or Boston, or Chicago, or San Francisco becomes the literary or artistic centre of the United States.

There is a second side to this question of a broad Americanism, however. The patriotism of the village or the belfry is bad, but the lack of all patriotism is even worse. There are philosophers who assure us that, in the future, patriotism will be regarded not as a virtue at all, but merely as a mental stage in the journey toward a state of feeling when our patriotism will include the whole human race and all the world. This may be so; but the age of which these philosophers speak is still several aeons distant. In fact, philosophers of this type are so very advanced that they are of no practical service to the present generation. It may be, that in ages so remote that we cannot now understand any of the feelings of those who will dwell in them, patriotism will no longer be regarded as a virtue, exactly as it may be that in those remote ages people will look down upon and disregard monogamic marriage; but as things now are and have been for two or three thousand years past, and are likely to be for two or three thousand years to come, the words "home" and "country" mean a great deal. Nor do they show any tendency to lose their significance. At present, treason, like adultery, ranks as one of the worst of all possible crimes.

One may fall very far short of treason and yet be an undesirable citizen in the community. The man who becomes Europeanized, who loses his power of doing good work on this side of the water, and who loses his love for his native land, is not a traitor; but he is a silly and undesirable citizen. He is as emphatically a noxious element in our body politic as is the man who comes here from abroad and remains a foreigner. Nothing will more quickly or more surely disqualify a man from doing good work in the world than the acquirement of that flaccid habit of mind which its possessors style cosmopolitanism.

It is not only necessary to Americanize the immigrants of foreign birth who settle among us, but it is even more necessary for those among us who are by birth and descent already Americans not to throw away our birthright, and, with incredible and contemptible folly, wander back to bow down before the alien gods whom our forefathers forsook. It is hard to believe that there is any necessity to warn Americans that, when they seek to model themselves on the lines of other civilizations, they make themselves the butts of all right-thinking men; and yet the necessity certainly exists to give this warning to many of our citizens who pride themselves on their standing in the world of art and letters, or, perchance, on what they would style their social leadership in the community. It is always better to be an original than an imitation, even when the imitation is of something better than the original; but what shall we say of the fool who is content to be an imitation of something worse? Even if the weaklings who seek to be other than Americans were right in deeming other nations to be better than their own, the fact yet remains that to be a first-class American is fifty-fold better than to be a second-class imitation of a Frenchman or Englishman. As a matter of fact, however, those of our countrymen who do believe in American inferiority are always individuals who, however cultivated, have some organic weakness in their moral or mental make-up; and the great mass of our people, who are robustly patriotic, and who have sound, healthy minds, are justified in regarding these feeble renegades with a half-impatient and half-amused scorn.

We believe in waging relentless war on rank-growing evils of all kinds, and it makes no difference to us if they happen to be of purely native growth. We grasp at any good, no matter whence it comes. We do not accept the evil attendant upon another system of government as an adequate excuse for that attendant upon our own; the fact that the courtier is a scamp does not render the demagogue any the less a scoundrel. But it remains true that, in spite of all our faults and shortcomings, no other land offers such glorious possibilities to the man able to take advantage of them, as does ours; it remains true that no one of our people can do any work really worth doing unless he does it primarily as an American. It is because certain classes of our people still retain their spirit of colonial dependence on, and exaggerated deference to, European opinion, that they fail to accomplish what they ought to. It is precisely along the lines where we have worked most independently that we have accomplished the greatest results; and it is in those professions where there has been no servility to, but merely a wise profiting by foreign experience, that we have produced our greatest men. Our soldiers and statesmen and orators; our explorers, our wilderness-winners, and commonwealth-builders; the men who have made our laws and seen that they were executed; and the other men whose energy and ingenuity have created our marvellous material prosperity— all these have been men who have drawn wisdom from the experience of every age and nation, but who have nevertheless thought, and worked, and conquered, and lived, and died, purely as Americans; and on the whole they have done better work than has been done in any other country during the short period of our national life.

On the other hand, it is in those professions where our people have striven hardest to mold themselves in conventional European forms that they have succeeded least; and this holds true to the present day, the failure being of course most conspicuous where the man takes up his abode in Europe; where he becomes a second-rate European, because he is over-civilized, over-sensitive, over-refined, and has lost the hardihood and manly courage by which alone he can conquer in the keen struggle of our national life. Be it remembered, too, that this same being does not really become a European; he only ceases being an American, and becomes nothing. He throws away a great prize for the sake of a lesser one, and does not even get the lesser one. The painter who goes to Paris, not merely to get two or three years' thorough training in his art, but with the deliberate purpose of taking up his abode there, and with the intention of following in the ruts worn deep by ten thousand earlier travelers, instead of striking off to rise or fall on a new line, thereby forfeits all chance of doing the best work. He must content himself with aiming at that kind of mediocrity which consists in doing fairly well what has already been done better; and he usually never even sees the grandeur and picturesqueness lying open before the eyes of every man who can read the book of America's past and the book of America's present. Thus it is with the undersized man of letters, who flees his country because he, with his delicate, effeminate sensitiveness, finds the conditions of life on this side of the water crude and raw; in other words, because he finds that he cannot play a man's part among men, and so goes where he will be sheltered from the winds that harden stouter souls. This emigre may write graceful and pretty verses, essays, novels; but he will never do work to compare with that of his brother, who is strong enough to stand on his own feet, and do his work as an American. Thus it is with the scientist who spends his youth in a German university, and can thenceforth work only in the fields already fifty times furrowed by the German ploughs. Thus it is with that most foolish of parents who sends his children to be educated abroad, not knowing—what every clear-sighted man from Washington and Jay down has known—that the American who is to make his way in America should be brought up among his fellow Americans.* It is among the people who like to consider themselves, and, indeed, to a large extent are, the

---

*John Jay: One of the principal founders of the United States, Jay (1745–1829) was the first chief justice of the Supreme Court, serving from 1789 to 1795. He coauthored the *Federalist Papers* (with James Madison and Alexander Hamilton).

leaders of the so-called social world, especially in some of the northeastern cities, that this colonial habit of thought, this thoroughly provincial spirit of admiration for things foreign, and inability to stand on one's own feet, becomes most evident and most despicable. We believe in every kind of honest and lawful pleasure, so long as the getting it is not made man's chief business; and we believe heartily in the good that can be done by men of leisure who work hard in their leisure, whether at politics or philanthropy, literature or art. But a leisure class whose leisure simply means idleness is a curse to the community, and in so far as its members distinguish themselves chiefly by aping the worst—not the best—traits of similar people across the water, they become both comic and noxious elements of the body politic.

The third sense in which the word "Americanism" may be employed is with reference to the Americanizing of the newcomers to our shores. We must Americanize them in every way, in speech, in political ideas and principles, and in their way of looking at the relations between Church and State. We welcome the German or the Irishman who becomes an American. We have no use for the German or Irishman who remains such. We do not wish German-Americans and Irish-Americans who figure as such in our social and political life; we want only Americans, and, provided they are such, we do not care whether they are of native or of Irish or of German ancestry. We have no room in any healthy American community for a German-American vote or an Irish-American vote, and it is contemptible demagogy to put planks into any party platform with the purpose of catching such a vote. We have no room for any people who do not act and vote simply as Americans, and as nothing else. Moreover, we have as little use for people who carry religious prejudices into our politics as for those who carry prejudices of caste or nationality. We stand unalterably in favor of the public school system in its entirety. We believe that English, and no other language, is that in which all the school exercises should be conducted. We are against any division of the school fund, and against any appropriation of public money for sectarian purposes. We are against any recognition whatever by the State in any shape or form of State-aided parochial schools. But we are equally opposed to any discrimination against or for a man because of his creed. We demand that all citizens, Protestant and Catholic, Jew and Gentile, shall have fair treatment in every way; that all alike shall have their rights guaranteed them. The very reasons that make us unqualified in our opposition to State-aided sectarian schools make us equally bent that, in the management of our public schools, the adherents of each creed shall be given exact and equal justice, wholly without regard to their religious affiliations; that trustees, superintendents, teachers, scholars, all alike shall be treated without any reference whatsoever to the creed they profess. We maintain that it is an outrage, in voting for a man for any position, whether State or national, to take into account his religious faith, provided only he is a good American. When a secret society does what in some places the American Protective Association seems to have done, and tries to proscribe Catholics both politically and socially, the members of such society show that they themselves are as utterly un-American, as alien to our school of political thought as the worst immigrants who land on our shores.* Their conduct is equally base and contemptible; they are the worst foes of our public school system, because they strengthen the hands of its ultramontane enemies; they should receive the hearty condemnation of all Americans who are truly patriotic.

The mighty tide of immigration to our shores has brought in its train much of good and much of evil; and whether the good or the evil shall predominate depends mainly on whether these newcomers do or do not throw themselves heartily into our national life, cease to be Europeans, and become Americans like the rest of us. More than a third of the people of the Northern States are of foreign birth or parentage. An immense number of them have become completely Americanized, and these stand on exactly the same plane as the descendants of any Puritan, Cavalier, or Knickerbocker among us, and do their full and honorable share of the nation's work. But where immigrants, or the sons of immigrants, do not heartily and in good faith throw in their lot with us, but cling to the speech, the customs, the ways of life, and the habits of thought of the Old World which they have left, they thereby harm both themselves and us. If they remain alien elements, unassimilated, and with interests separate from ours, they are mere obstructions to the current of our national life, and, moreover, can get no good from it themselves. In fact, though we ourselves also suffer from their perversity, it is they who really suffer most. It is an immense benefit to the European immigrant to change him into an American citizen. To bear the name of American is to bear the most honorable titles; and whoever does not so believe has no business to bear the name at all, and, if he comes from Europe, the sooner he goes back there the better. Besides, the man who does not become Americanized nevertheless fails to remain a European, and becomes nothing at all. The immigrant cannot possibly remain what he was, or continue to be a member of the Old-World society. If he tries to retain his old language, in a few generations it becomes a barbarous jargon; if he tries to retain his old customs and ways of life, in a few generations he becomes an uncouth boor. He has cut himself off from the Old World, and cannot retain his connection with it; and if he wishes ever to amount to anything he must throw himself heart and soul, and without reservation, into the new life to which he has come. It is urgently necessary to check and regulate our immigration, by much more drastic laws than now exist; and this should be done both to keep out laborers who tend to depress the labor market, and to keep out races which do not assimilate readily with our own, and unworthy individuals of all races—not only criminals, idiots, and paupers, but anarchists of the Most and O'Donovan Rossa type.†

American Protective Association: Anti-Catholic and anti-immigrant secret society active in the United States from 1887 to 1900.

†*Johann Most* (1846–1906), a German American anarchist; *O'Donovan Rossa* (1831–1915), a leader of the Irish Republican movement and prominent member of the Irish Republican Brotherhood.

From his own standpoint, it is beyond all question the wise thing for the immigrant to become thoroughly Americanized. Moreover, from our standpoint, we have a right to demand it. We freely extend the hand of welcome and of good fellowship to every man, no matter what his creed or birthplace, who comes here honestly intent on becoming a good United States citizen like the rest of us; but we have a right, and it is our duty, to demand that he shall indeed become so and shall not confuse the issues with which we are struggling by introducing among us Old-World quarrels and prejudices. There are certain ideas which he must give up. For instance, he must learn that American life is incompatible with the existence of any form of anarchy, or of any secret society having murder for its aim, whether at home or abroad; and he must learn that we exact full religious toleration and the complete separation of Church and State. Moreover, he must not bring in his Old-World religious race and national antipathies, but must merge them into love for our common country, and must take pride in the things which we can all take pride in. He must revere only our flag; not only must it come first, but no other flag should even come second. He must learn to celebrate Washington's birthday rather than that of the Queen or Kaiser, and the Fourth of July instead of St. Patrick's Day. Our political and social questions must be settled on their own merits, and not complicated by quarrels between England and Ireland, or France and Germany, with which we have nothing to do: it is an outrage to fight an American political campaign with reference to questions of European politics. Above all, the immigrant must learn to talk and think and *be* United States.

The immigrant of today can learn much from the experience of the immigrants of the past, who came to America prior to the Revolutionary War. We were then already, what we are now, a people of mixed blood. Many of our most illustrious Revolutionary names were borne by men of Huguenot blood—Jay, Sevier, Marion, Laurens. But the Huguenots were, on the whole, the best immigrants we have ever received; sooner than any other, and more completely, they became American in speech, conviction, and thought. The Hollanders took longer than the Huguenots to become completely assimilated; nevertheless they in the end became so, immensely to their own advantage. One of the leading Revolutionary generals, Schuyler, and one of the Presidents of the United States, Van Buren, were of Dutch blood; but they rose to their positions, the highest in the land, because they had become Americans and had ceased being Hollanders. If they had remained members of an alien body, cut off by their speech and customs and belief from the rest of the American community, Schuyler would have lived his life as a boorish, provincial squire, and Van Buren would have ended his days a small tavern keeper. So it is with the Germans of Pennsylvania. Those of them who became Americanized have furnished to our history a multitude of honorable names from the days of the Muhlenbergs onward; but those who did not become

Americanized form to the present day an unimportant body, of no significance in American existence.* So it is with the Irish, who gave to Revolutionary annals such names as Carroll and Sullivan, and to the Civil War men like Sheridan—men who were Americans and nothing else: while the Irish who remain such, and busy themselves solely with alien politics, can have only an unhealthy influence upon American life, and can never rise as do their compatriots who become straightout Americans.† Thus it has ever been with all people who have come hither, of whatever stock or blood. The same thing is true of the churches. A church which remains foreign, in language or spirit, is doomed. But I wish to be distinctly understood on one point. Americanism is a question of spirit, conviction, and purpose, not of creed or birthplace. The politician who bids for the Irish or German vote, or the Irishman or German who votes as an Irishman or German, is despicable, for all citizens of this commonwealth should vote solely as Americans; but he is not a whit less despicable than the voter who votes against a good American, merely because that American happens to have been born in Ireland or Germany. Knownothingism, in any form, is as utterly un-American as foreignism. It is a base outrage to oppose a man because of his religion or birthplace, and all good citizens will hold any such effort in abhorrence. A Scandinavian, a German, or an Irishman who has really become an American has the right to stand on exactly the same footing as any native-born citizen in the land, and is just as much entitled to the friendship and support, social and political, of his neighbors. Among the men with whom I have been thrown in close personal contact socially, and who have been among my staunchest friends and allies politically, are not a few Americans who happen to have been born on the other side of the water, in Germany, Ireland, Scandinavia; and there could be no better men in the ranks of our native-born citizens.

In closing, I cannot better express the ideal attitude that should be taken by our fellow citizens of foreign birth than by quoting the words of a representative American, born in Germany, the Honorable Richard Guenther, of Wisconsin. In a speech spoken at the time of the Samoan trouble he said: "We know as well as any other class of American citizens where our duties belong. We will work for our country in time of peace and fight for it in time of war,

---

Muhlenbergs: The Muhlenberg family, also the "Muhlenberg dynasty," a family of political, religious, and military leaders tracing back to the late eighteenth-century United States. The Muhlenbergs descend from Henry Muhlenberg (1711–1787), a German Lutheran minister who immigrated to the United States in 1742 and is considered the founder of the Lutheran Church in the United States.

†*Charles Carroll* (1737–1832), lawyer, member of the Continental Congress, and U.S. senator, whose grandfather was born in Ireland and immigrated to America from England. Carroll was the only Catholic signer of the Declaration of Independence. *John Sullivan* (1740–1795), American Revolutionary War general, member of the Continental Congress, and governor of New Hampshire, whose father immigrated to America from Ireland. *Philip Henry Sheridan* (1831–1888), Union general in the Civil War, whose parents immigrated to the United States from Ireland.

if a time of war should ever come. When I say our country, I mean, of course, our adopted country. I mean the United States of America. After passing through the crucible of naturalization, we are no longer Germans; we are Americans. Our attachment to America cannot be measured by the length of our residence here. We are Americans from the moment we touch the American shore until we are laid in American graves. We will fight for America whenever necessary. America, first, last, and all the time. America against Germany, America against the world; America, right or wrong; always America. We are Americans."

All honor to the man who spoke such words as those; and I believe they express the feelings of the great majority of those among our fellow American citizens who were born abroad. We Americans can only do our allotted task well if we face it steadily and bravely, seeing but not fearing the dangers. Above all we must stand shoulder to shoulder, not asking as to the ancestry or creed of our comrades, but only demanding that they be in very truth Americans, and that we all work together, heart, hand, and head, for the honor and the greatness of our common country.

(1900)

Ellis Island

C. A. Price

The Shapes press on,—mask after mask they wear,
　　Agape, we watch the never-ending line;
The crown of thought, the cap and bells are there,
　　And next the monk's hood see the morion shine.

Age on his staff and infancy's slow foot,
　　These we discern, if all else be disguise;
They fix on us an alien gaze and mute,
　　From the mysterious orbit of the eyes.

They come, they come, one treads the other's heel,
　　And some we laugh and some we weep to see,
And some we fear; but in the throng we feel
　　The might throb of our own destiny.

Outstretched their hands to take whate'er we give,
　　Honor, dishonor, daily bread or bane;
Not theirs to choose how we may bid them live—
　　But what we give we shall receive again.

America! charge not they fate to these;
　　The power is ours to mould them to mar,
But freedom's voice, far down the centuries,
　　Shall sound our choice from blazing star to star!

(1907)

The Alien

Henry Blake Fuller

As a child,
In her own native town,
She played amidst—
But you, complaisant reader,
Shall set the scene quite as you choose.
Make her loved region
Plainland or mountain, at your wish;
And her natal place
A close-built town of stuccoed fronts
With a baroque-façaded church for the dull priest,
Crushed down by a deep pediment;
Or let the church soar up in bulbous spires,
From many loose, disheveled shacks of wood.
(In either case, make nothing of the school.)
And let an unbridged river mope through wide marshes,
Or dash in headlong flight
Over a broad, sandy bottom to the sea.
Let there be many unwilling soldiers,
To cow their brothers of the streets and fields;
And tyrannous officials in abundant measure,
Who draw their sanction from some distant capital—
Or act without it;
And let there be a few stout hearts,
Impelled by hope, or misery, or courage,
Or all three,
To venture toward the other world.

She crossed at ten;
And after many days they showed her,
Thought a far-shimmering, watery haze,
A towering, iron-spiked head,
And told her she was free.

Free in the close-built streets of a tight-packed city;
Free in the swirling tide of the lately-come and the about-to-come;
Free to trip or trudge behind a push-cart
Through clattering ways; or, later,

To mouse beneath a counter
On which were heaped coarse gloves and shirts and shoes—
Or, an it please you better,
Stranger cheeses and odd fruits or vegetables
Plaited in strings or nettled in festoons.
And through it all—this newness—
One's own dear tongue, one's old home ways.

After a time, courted in the hurly-burly
By one from her own province;
Then another shop, better and bigger,
With their own infants playing on the floor,
Or chancing fate outside;
And one of these, a son,
Destined to be the family's morning-star—
Nay, its bright sun in the new heaven;
The brightest boy in school—
That school where this strange people
Offered—and compelled—instruction free.
Then, after some brief years,
Through which he sharpened up his wits
On theory and practice,
He took his father's petty shop and juggled it.
It grew within his hands, beneath their eyes,
To proportions quite unprecedented.
He walked the shining road of quick success,
Skipping from peak to peak.
At thirty-five
He labored in one palace, lived in another,
And hundreds from his mother's country,
And other hundreds of abject natives,
Slaved for his further good.

Soon her grandsons were sporting familiarly
Through picture-gallery or ballroom,
And harrying costly furniture,
Jacobean, Louis Seize or Empire—
It changed with passing seasons—
In childish games.
There were dinners, stately showy things,
From which she was discreetly absent.
There were receptions, with music, let us say,
At which she would appear briefly
In distant doorways,

Blinking dark, narrow eyes at the incredible scene,
And then retiring.
It was a strange, strange world—
A world apart from her,
And she apart from it.
She stumbled through its purlieus
(Gorgeous they seemed),
And stammered through its language
(One she had never rightly learned to speak).

In her retired bedroom
She gossiped with a few old cronies
Of origin like hers,
And slyly entertained her grandchildren,
When they would permit.
On certain designated days
Women, from somewhere,
Went by, to somewhere,
On public business—to "vote," she heard it said:
A thing repellent and incredible.
Other things, no less repellent and incredible
Were printed in the papers, she was told;
But these she never read.

In due course her grandsons
Turned lawyers, doctors, "business men,"
With weapons of offense and of defense
Unknown throughout her clan in earlier days.
More than ever was she safeguarded and entrenched
In this remote and alien world.

A great war came.
The quarrel had two sides, she heard.
How two?
Her heart, forgetful quite of old injustices,
Was with the land where stood the little town,
On mountain-stream or plain,
Which once had been her home,
The spot of her nativity.
And 'midst the family's recent splendors
The younger generations spoke up hotly
(With less discretion than they used outside)
About the exactions of "Americans"
As to the attitude of newer stocks;

And one young lad flung out,
In a moment of high exasperation,
That he would go and help his people's cause.
"Will they let you come back?" she quavered.
Laughter: and it was explained
That the means for letting people in
Were in good order,
But that the means for keeping people out
Were good as missing.

So, quietude.
The world was kind and fair;
Privileges were many; obligations, light.
A good old soul, all vague and isolate,
Rocked to and fro in her protected chamber;
A little in one world,
A little in another,
A good deal out of both;
But tending,
By all the strength of lengthening age
And early ties,
To drift backward toward that world—
For her at once both young and old—
Where she began.
Peace; let her fall asleep.
But let her sons keep open eyes—
And turn them the right way.

(1917)

Moses

Morris Abel Beer

Behold the hoary patriarch on Grand Street!* Not a whim
Nor idle pleasantry of mine—it's Moses—look at him!
From Sinai's mount he brought the Law in ages long ago,
And now he traffics candles here to keep the world aglow

(1917)

Grand Street: Major street on Manhattan's Lower East Side.

Old China

Morris Abel Beer

Hop Wah, the genial Chinaman, with steaming iron sings.
His heart is light because his little laundry shop takes wings,
And sailing o'er the silver skies, like birds in summer-time,
Through dreaming lanterned dells he strays as Bowery* belfries chime.

(1917)

Bowery: Neighborhood in southern Manhattan; a culturally vibrant area in the nineteenth century, the
Bowery was a struggling, impoverished neighborhood in the early twentieth century.

Songs of Gold Mountain

Anonymous

[Since I left South China]

Since I left South China,
I have changed my clothes to the Western style.
I seek praise for being neat and fashionable
Though I have yet to speak with an American tongue.
Smart in appearance—
Who dares to call me an ignorant fool?
A loose gown with wide sleeves brings only scurrilous remarks
And it gets you nowhere, even if you are modern in education.

Translated by Marlon K. Hom

The Lie

Mary Antin

I

The first thing about his American teachers that struck David Rudinsky was the fact that they were women, and the second was that they did not get angry if somebody asked questions. This phenomenon subverted his previous experience. When he went to *heder* (Hebrew school), in Russia, his teachers were always men, and they did not like to be interrupted with questions that were not in the lesson. Everything was different in America, and David liked the difference.

The American teachers, on their part, also made comparisons. They said David was not like other children. It was not merely that his mind worked like lightning; those neglected Russian waifs were almost always quick to learn, perhaps because they had to make up for lost time. The quality of his interest, more than the rapidity of his progress, excited comment. Miss Ralston, David's teacher in the sixth grade, which he reached in his second year at school, said of him that he never let go of a lesson till he had got the soul of the matter. "I don't think grammar is grammar to him," she said, "or fractions mere arithmetic. I'm not satisfied with the way I teach these things since I've had David. I feel that if he were on the platform instead of me, geography and grammar would be spliced to the core of the universe."

One difficulty David's teachers encountered, and that was his extreme reserve. In private conversation it was hard to get anything out of him except "yes, ma'am" and "no, ma'am," or, "I don't understand, please." In the classroom he did not seem to be aware of the existence of anybody besides Teacher and himself. He asked questions as fast as he could formulate them, and Teacher had to exercise much tact in order to satisfy him without slighting the rest of her pupils. To advances of a personal sort he did not respond, as if friendship were not among the things he hungered for.

It was Miss Ralston who found the way to David's heart. Perhaps she was interested in such things; they sometimes are, in the public schools. After the Christmas holidays, the children were given as a subject for composition, "How I spent the Vacation." David wrote in a froth of enthusiasm about whole days spent in the public library. He covered twelve pages with an account of the books he had read. The list included many juvenile classics in American history and biography; and from his comments it was plain that the little alien worshiped the heroes of war.

When Miss Ralston had read David's composition, she knew what to do. She was one of those persons who always know what to do, and do it. She asked

David to stay after school, and read to him, from a blue book with gilt letter-
ing, "Paul Revere's Ride" and "Independence Bell." That hour neither of them
ever forgot. To David it seemed as if all the heroes he had dreamed of crowded
around him, so real did his teacher's reading make them. He heard the clash
of swords and the flapping of banners in the wind. On the blackboard behind
Miss Ralston troops of faces appeared and vanished, like shadows that run
across a hillside when clouds are moving in the sky. As for Miss Ralston, she
said afterwards that she was the first person who had ever seen the real David
Rudinsky. That was a curious statement to make, considering that his mother
and father, and sundry other persons in the two hemispheres, had had some
acquaintance with David previous to the reading of "Paul Revere's Ride."
However, Miss Ralston had a way of saying curious things.

There were many readings out of school hours, after that memorable beginning. Miss Ralston did not seem to realize that the School Board did not
pay her for those extra hours that she spent on David. David did not know that
she was paid at all. He thought Teacher was born on purpose to read and tell
him things and answer his questions, just as his mother existed to cook his favorite soup and patch his trousers. So he brought his pet book from the library,
and when the last pupil was gone, he took it from his desk, and laid it on Miss
Ralston's, without a word; and Miss Ralston read, and they were both happy.
When a little Jewish boy from Russia goes to school in America, all sorts of
things are likely to happen that the School Board does not provide for. It might
be amusing to figure out the reasons.

David's reserve slowly melted in the glowing intimacy of these happy half-
hours; still he seldom made any comment on the reading at the time; he basked
mutely in the warmth of his teacher's sympathy. But what he did not say orally
he was very likely to say on paper. That also was one of Miss Ralston's discoveries. When she gave out the theme, "What I Mean to Do When I Grow Up,"
David wrote that he was going to be an American citizen, and always vote for
honest candidates, and belong to a society for arresting illegal voters. You see
David was only a greenhorn, and an excitable one. He thought it a very great
matter to be a citizen, perhaps because such a thing was not allowed in the
country he came from. Miss Ralston probably knew how it was with him, or
she guessed. She was great at guessing, as all her children knew. At any rate, she
did not smile as she read of David's patriotic ambitions. She put his paper
aside until their next quiet hour, and then she used it so as to get a great deal
out of him that he would not have had the courage to tell if he had not believed
that it was an exercise in composition.

This Miss Ralston was a crafty person. She learned from David about a
Jewish restaurant where his father sometimes took him, a place where a group
of ardent young Russians discussed politics over their inexpensive dinner. She
heard about a mass meeting of Russian Jews to celebrate the death of
Alexander III, "because he was a cruel tyrant, and was very bad to Jewish people." She even tracked some astonishing phrases in David's vocabulary to their

origin in the Sunday orations he had heard on the Common, in his father's company.

Impressed by these and other signs of paternal interest in her pupil's education, Miss Ralston was not unprepared for the visit which David's father paid her soon after these revelations. It was a very cold day, and Mr. Rudinsky shivered in his thin, shabby overcoat; but his face glowed with inner warmth as he discovered David's undersized figure in one of the front seats.

"I don't know how to say it what I feel to see my boy sitting and learning like this," he said, with a vibration in his voice that told more than his words. "Do you know, ma'am, if I didn't have to make a living, I'd like to stay here all day and see my David get educated. I'm forty years old, and I've had much in my life, but it's worth nothing so much as this. The day I brought my children to school, it was the best day in my life. Perhaps you won't believe me, ma'am, but when I hear that David is a good boy and learns good in school, I wouldn't change places with Vanderbilt the millionaire."

He looked at Miss Ralston with the eyes of David listening to "Paul Revere's Ride."

"What do you think, ma'am," he asked, as he got up to leave, "my David will be a good American, no?"

"He ought to be," said Miss Ralston, warmly, "with such a father."

Mr. Rudinsky did not try to hide his gratification.

"I am a citizen," he said, unconsciously straightening. "I took out citizen papers as soon as I came to America, four years ago."

So they came to the middle of February, when preparations for Washington's Birthday were well along. One day the class was singing "America," when Miss Ralston noticed that David stopped and stared absently at the blackboard in front of him. He did not wake out of his reverie till the singing was over, and then he raised his hand.

"Teacher," he asked, when he had permission to speak, "what does it mean, 'Land where my fathers died'?"

Miss Ralston explained, wondering how many of her pupils cared to analyze the familiar words as David did.

A few days later, the national hymn was sung again. Miss Ralston watched David. His lips formed the words "Land where my fathers died," and then they stopped, set in the pout of childish trouble. His eyes fixed themselves on the teacher's, but her smile of encouragement failed to dispel his evident perplexity.

Anxious to help him over his unaccountable difficulty, Miss Ralston detained him after school.

"David," she asked him, when they were alone, "do you understand 'America' now?"

"Yes, ma'am."

"Do you understand 'Land where my fathers died'?"

"Yes, ma'am."

"You didn't sing with the others."

"No, ma'am."

Miss Ralston thought of a question that would rouse him.

"Don't you like 'America,' David?" The boy almost jumped in his place.

"Oh, yes, ma'am, I do! I like 'America.' It's—fine."

He pressed his fist nervously to his mouth, a trick he had when excited.

"Then tell me, David, why you don't sing it."

David's eyes fixed themselves in a look of hopeless longing. He answered in a whisper, his pale face slowly reddening.

"*My* fathers didn't die here. How can I sing such a lie?"

Miss Ralston's impulse was to hug the child, but she was afraid to startle him. The attention she had lavished on the boy was rewarded at this moment, when her understanding of his nature inspired the answer to his troubled question. She saw how his mind worked. She realized, what a less sympathetic witness might have failed to realize, that behind the moral scruple expressed in his words, there was a sense of irreparable loss derived from the knowledge that he had no share in the national past. The other children could shout the American hymn in all the pride of proprietorship, but to him the words did not apply. It was a flaw in his citizenship, which he was so jealous to establish.

The teacher's words were the very essence of tact and sympathy. In her voice were mingled the yearning of a mother and the faith of a comrade.

"David Rudinsky, you have as much a right to those words as I or anybody else in America. Your ancestors did not die on our battlefields, but they would have if they'd had a chance. You used to spend all your time reading the Hebrew books, in Russia. Don't you know how your people—your ancestors, perhaps!—fought the Roman tyrants? Don't you remember the Maccabean brothers, and Bar Kochba, and—oh, you know about them more than I!* I'm ashamed to tell you that I haven't read much Jewish history, but I'm sure if we begin to look it up, we'll find that people of your race—people like your father, David—took a part in the fight for freedom, wherever they were allowed. And even in this country—David, I'm going to find out for you how many Jews there were in the armies of the Revolution. We don't think about it here, you see, because we don't ask what a man's religion is, as long as he is brave and good."

David's eyes slowly lost their look of distress as his teacher talked. His tense little face, upturned to hers, reminded her of a withered blossom that revives in the rain. She went on with increasing earnestness, herself interested in the discoveries she was making, in her need.

"I tell you the truth, David, I never thought of these things before, but I do believe that the Pilgrim Fathers didn't all come here before the Revolution. Isn't your father just like them? Think of it, dear, how he left his home, and

---

The Maccabean brothers: Judah Maccabee and his four brothers, who led a revolt against the Greeks in 167 BC, leading to Jewish independence in ancient Israel from 165 to 63 BC; *Bar Kochba:* Transliteration of Simon bar Kokhba, who led a revolt against the Romans in AD 132, leading to Jewish independence in Israel until AD 135.

came to a strange land, where he couldn't even speak the language. That was a great trouble, you know; something like the fear of the Indians in the old days. And didn't he come looking for the very same things? He wanted freedom for himself and his family, and a chance for his children to grow up wise and brave. You know your father cares more for such things than he does for money or anything. It's the same story over again. Every ship that brings your people from Russia and other countries where they are ill-treated is a *Mayflower*. If I were a Jewish child like you, I would sing 'America' louder than anybody else!"

David's adoring eyes gave her the thanks which his tongue would not venture to utter. Never since that moment, soon after his arrival from Russia, when his father showed him his citizenship papers, saying, "Look, my son, this makes you an American," had he felt so secure in his place in the world.

Miss Ralston studied his face in silence while she gathered up some papers on her desk, preparatory to leaving. In the back of her mind she asked herself to how many of the native children in her class the Fourth of July meant anything besides firecrackers.

"Get your things, David," she said presently, as she locked her desk. "It's time we were going. Think if we should get locked up in the building!"

David smiled absently. In his ears rang the familiar line, "Land where my fathers died—my fathers died—fathers died."

"It's something like the Psalms!" he said suddenly, himself surprised at the discovery.

"What is like the Psalms, dear?"

He hesitated. Now that he had to explain, he was not sure any more. Miss Ralston helped him out.

"You mean 'America,' sounds like the Psalms to you?"

David nodded. His teacher beamed her understanding. How did she guess wherein the similarity lay? David had in mind such moments as this when he said of Miss Ralston, "Teacher talks with her eyes."

Miss Ralston went to get her coat and hat from the closet.

"Get your things, David," she repeated. "The janitor will come to chase us out in a minute."

He was struggling with the torn lining of a coat sleeve in the children's dressing room, when he heard Miss Ralston exclaim,—

"Oh, David! I had almost forgotten. You must try this on. This is what you're going to wear when you speak the dialogue with Annie and Raymond. We used it in a play a few years ago. I thought it would do for you."

She held up a blue-and-buff jacket with tarnished epaulets. David hurried to put it on. He was to take the part of George Washington in the dialogue. At sight of the costume, his heart started off on a gallop.

Alas for his gallant aspirations! Nothing of David was visible outside the jacket except two big eyes above and two blunt boot toes below. The collar reached to his ears; the cuffs dangled below his knees. He resembled a scarecrow in the cornfield more than the Father of his Country.

Miss Ralston suppressed her desire to laugh.

"It's a little big, isn't it?" she said cheerily, holding up the shoulders of the heroic garment. "I wonder how we can make it fit. Don't you think your mother would know how to take up the sleeves and do something to the back?"

She turned the boy around, more hopeless than she would let him see. Miss Ralston understood more about little boys' hearts than about their coats.

"How old are you, David?" she asked, absently, wondering for the hundredth time at his diminutive stature. "I thought the boy for whom this was made was about your age."

David's face showed that he felt reproved. "I'm twelve," he said, apologetically.

Miss Ralston reproached herself for her tactlessness, and proceeded to make amends.

"Twelve?" she repeated, patting the blue shoulders. "You, speak the lines like a much older boy. I'm sure your mother can make the coat fit, and I'll bring the wig—a powdered wig—and the sword, David! You'll look just like George Washington!"

Her gay voice echoed in the empty room. Her friendly eyes challenged his. She expected to see him kindle, as he did so readily in these days of patriotic excitement. But David failed to respond. He remained motionless in his place, his eyes blank and staring. Miss Ralston had the feeling that behind his dead front his soul was running away from her.

This is just what was happening. David was running away from her, and from himself, and from the image of George Washington, conjured up by the scene with the military coat. Somewhere in the jungle of his consciousness a monster was stirring, and his soul fled in terror of its clutch. What was it— what was it that came tearing through the wilderness of his memories of two worlds? In vain he tried not to understand. The ghosts of forgotten impressions cackled in the wake of the pursuing monster, the breath of whose nostrils spread an odor of evil sophistries grafted on his boyish thoughts in a chimerical past.

His mind reeled in a whirlwind of recollection. Miss Ralston could not have understood some of the things David reviewed, even if he had tried to tell her. In that other life of his, in Russia, had been monstrous things, things that seemed unbelievable to David himself, after his short experience of America. He had suffered many wrongs,—yes, even as a little boy,—but he was not thinking of past grievances as he stood before Miss Ralston, seeing her as one sees a light through a fog. He was thinking of things harder to forget than injuries received from others. It was a sudden sense of his own sins that frightened David, and of one sin in particular, the origin of which was buried somewhere in the slime of the evil past. David was caught in the meshes of a complex inheritance; contradictory impulses tore at his heart. Fearfully he dived to the bottom of his consciousness, and brought up a bitter conviction: David Rudinsky, who called himself an American, who worshiped the names of the heroes, suddenly knew that he had sinned, sinned against his best friend, sinned even as he was planning to impersonate George Washington, the pattern of honor.

His white forehead glistened with the sweat of anguish. His eyes sickened, Miss Ralston caught him as he wavered and put him in the nearest seat.

"Why, David! What's the matter? Are you ill? Let me take this off—it's so heavy. There, that's better. Just rest your head on me, so."

This roused him. He wriggled away from her support, and put out a hand to keep her off.

"Why, David! What *is* the matter? Your hands are so cold—"

David's head felt heavy and wobbly, but he stood up and began to put on his coat again, which he had pulled off in order to try on the uniform. To Miss Ralston's anxious questions he answered not a syllable, neither did he look at her once. His teacher, thoroughly alarmed, hurriedly put on her street things, intending to take him home. They walked in silence through the empty corridors, down the stairs, and across the school yard. The teacher noticed with relief that the boy grew steadier with every step. She smiled at him encouragingly when he opened the gate for her, as she had taught him, but he did not meet her look.

At the corner where they usually parted David paused, steeling himself to take his teacher's hand; but to his surprise she kept right on, taking his crossing.

It was now that he spoke, and Miss Ralston was astonished at the alarm in his voice.

"Miss Ralston, where are you going? You don't go this way."

"I'm going to see you home, David," she replied firmly. "I can't let you go alone—like this."

"Oh, Teacher! Don't, please don't. I'm all right—I'm not sick,—it's not far—Don't, Miss Ralston, please."

In the February dusk, Miss Ralston saw the tears rise to his eyes. Whatever was wrong with him, it was plain her presence only made him suffer the more. Accordingly she yielded to his entreaty.

"I hope you'll be all right, David," she said, in a tone she might have used to a full-grown man. "Good bye." And she turned the corner.

II

All the way home Miss Ralston debated the wisdom of allowing him to go alone, but as she recalled his look and his entreating voice she felt anew the compulsion that had made her yield. She attributed his sudden breakdown entirely to overwrought nerves and remorsefully resolved not to subject him in the future to the strain of extra hours after school.

Her misgivings were revived the next morning, when David failed to appear with the ringing of the first gong, as was his habit. But before the children had taken their seats, David's younger brother, Bennie, brought her news of the missing boy.

"David's sick in bed," he announced in accents of extreme importance. "He didn't come home till awful late last night, and he was so frozen, his teeth knocked together. My mother says he burned like a fire all night, and she had to take little Harry in her bed, with her and papa, so's David could sleep all alone. We all went downstairs in our bare feet this morning, and dressed ourselves in the kitchen, so David could sleep."

"What is the matter with him? Did you have the doctor?"

"No, ma'am, not yet. The dispensary don't open till nine o'clock."

Miss Ralston begged him to report again in the afternoon, which he did, standing before her, cap in hand, his sense of importance still dominating over brotherly concern.

"He's sick, all right," Bennie reported. "He don't eat at all—just drinks and drinks. My mother says he cried the whole morning, when he woke up and found out he'd missed school. My mother says he tried to get up and dress himself, but he couldn't anyhow. Too sick."

"Did you have the doctor?" interrupted Miss Ralston, suppressing her impatience.

"No, ma'am, not yet. My father went to the dispensary, but the doctor said he can't come till noon, but he didn't. Then I went to the dispensary, dinner time, but the doctor didn't yet come when we went back to school. My mother says you can die ten times before the dispensary doctor comes."

"What does your mother think it is?"

"Oh, she says it's a bad cold, but David isn't strong, you know, so she's scared. I guess if he gets worse I'll have to stay home from school to run for the medicines."

"I hope not, Bennie. Now you'd better run along, or you'll be late."

"Yes, ma'am. Good bye."

"Will you come again in the morning and tell me about your brother?"

"Yes, ma'am. Good bye.—Teacher."

"Yes, Bennie?"

"Do you think you can do something—something—about his *record*? David feels dreadful because he's broke his record. He never missed school before, you know. It's—it's too bad to see him cry. He's always so quiet, you know, kind of like grown people. He don't fight or tease or anything. Do you think you can, Teacher?"

Miss Ralston was touched by this tribute to her pupil, but she could not promise to mend the broken record.

"Tell David not to worry. He has the best record in the school, for attendance and everything. Tell him I said he must hurry and get well, as we must rehearse our pieces for Washington's Birthday."

The next morning Bennie reeled off a longer story than ever. He described the doctor's visit in great detail, and Miss Ralston was relieved to gather that

David's ailment was nothing worse than grippe; unless, as the doctor warned, his run-down condition caused complications. He would be in bed a week or more, in any case, "and he ought to sleep most of the time, the doctor said."

"I guess the doctor don't know our David!" Bennie scoffed. "He never wants at all to go to sleep. He reads and reads when everybody goes to bed. One time he was reading all night, and the lamp went out, and he was afraid to go downstairs for oil, because he'd wake somebody, so he lighted matches and read little bits. There was a heap of burned matches in the morning."

"Dear me!" exclaimed Miss Ralston. "He ought not to do that. Your father ought not—Does your father allow him to stay up nights?"

"Sure. My father's proud because he's going to be a great man; a doctor, maybe." He shrugged his shoulders, as if to say, "What may not a David become?"

"David is funny, don't you think, Teacher?" the boy went on. "He asks such funny questions. What do you think he said to the doctor?"

"I can't imagine."

"Well, he pulled him by the sleeve when he took out the—the thing he puts in your mouth, and said kind of hoarse, 'Doctor, did you ever tell a lie?' Wasn't that funny?"

Miss Ralston did not answer. She was thinking that David must have been turning over some problem in his mind, to say so much to a stranger.

"Did you give him my message?" she asked finally.

"Yes 'm! I told him about rehearsing his piece for Washington's Birthday." Bennie paused.

"Well?"

"He acted so funny. He turned over to the wall, and cried and cried without any noise."

"The poor boy! He'll be dreadfully disappointed not to take his part in the exercises."

Bennie shook his head.

"That isn't for what he cries," he said oracularly.

Miss Ralston's attentive silence invited further revelations.

"He's *worrying* about something." Bennie brought out, rolling his head ominously.

"Why? How do you know?"

"The doctor said so. He told my father downstairs. He said, 'Make him tell, if you can, it may help to pull him off'—no, 'pull him up.' That's what the doctor said."

Miss Ralston's thoughts flew back to her last interview with David, two days before, when he had broken down so suddenly. Was there a mystery there? She was certain the boy was overwrought, and physically run down. Apparently, also, he had been exposed to the weather during the evening when he was taken ill; Bennie's chats indicated that David had wandered in the streets for hours. These things would account for the grippe, and for the abnormal fever of which Bennie boasted. But what was David worrying about? She resolved to go and see the boy in a day or two, when he was reported to be more comfortable.

On his next visit Bennie brought a message from the patient himself.

"He said to give you this, Teacher," handing Miss Ralston a journal. "It's yours. It has the pieces in it for Washington's Birthday. He said you might need it, and the doctor didn't say when he could go again to school."

Miss Ralston laid the journal carelessly on a pile of other papers. Bennie balanced himself on one foot, looking as if his mission were not yet ended.

"Well, Bennie?" Miss Ralston encouraged him. She was beginning to understand his mysterious airs.

"David was awful careful about that book," the messenger said impressively. "He said over and over not to lose it, and not to give it to nobody only you."

III

It was not till the end of the day that Miss Ralston took up the journal Bennie had brought. She turned the leaves absently, thinking of David. He would be so disappointed to miss the exercises! And to whom should she give the part of George Washington in the dialogue? She found the piece in the journal. A scrap of paper marked the place. A folded paper. Folded several times. Miss Ralston opened out the paper and found some writing.

> Dear Teacher Miss Ralston:
>   I can't be George Washington any more because I have lied to you. I must not tell you about what, because you would blame somebody who didn't do wrong.
>   Your friend,
>   DAVID RUDINSKY.

Again and again Miss Ralston read the note, unable to understand it. David, her David, whose soul was a mirror for every noble idea, had lied to her! What could he mean? What had impelled him? *Somebody who didn't do wrong.* So it was not David alone; there was some complication with another person. She studied the note word for word, and her eyes slowly filled with tears. If the boy had really lied—if the whole thing were not a chimera of his fevered nights—then what must he have suffered of remorse and shame! Her heart went out to him even while her brain was busy with the mystery.

She made a swift resolution. She would go to David at once. She was sure he would tell her more than he had written, and it would relieve his mind. She did not dread the possible disclosures. Her knowledge of the boy made her certain that she would find nothing ignoble at the bottom of his mystery. He was only a child, after all—an overwrought, sensitive child. No doubt he exaggerated his sin, if sin there were. It was her duty to go and put him at rest.

She knew that David's father kept a candy shop in the basement of his tenement, and she had no trouble in finding the place. Half the children in the neighborhood escorted her to the door, attracted by the phenomenon of a Teacher loose on their streets.

The tinkle of the shop bell brought Mr. Rudinsky from the little kitchen in the rear.

"Well, well!" he exclaimed, shaking hands heartily. "This is a great honor—a great honor." He sounded the initial *h*. "I wish I had a palace for you to come in, ma'am. I don't think there was such company in this house since it was built."

His tone was one of genuine gratification. Ushering her into the kitchen, he set a chair for her, and himself sat down at a respectful distance.

"I'm sorry," he began, with a wave of his hand around the room. "Such company ought not to sit in the kitchen, but you see—"

He was interrupted by Benny, who had clattered in at the visitor's heels, panting for recognition.

"Never mind, Teacher," the youngster spoke up, "we got a parlor upstairs, with a mantelpiece and everything, but David sleeps up there—the doctor said it's the most air—and you dassn't wake him up till he wakes himself."

Bennie's father frowned, but the visitor smiled a cordial smile.

"I like a friendly kitchen like this," she said quietly. "My mother did not keep any help when I was a little girl and I was a great deal in the kitchen."

Her host showed his appreciation of her tact by dropping the subject.

"I'm sure you came about David," he said.

"I did. How is he?"

"Pretty sick, ma'am. The doctor says it's not the sickness so much, but David is so weak and small. He says David studies too much altogether. Maybe he's right. What do you think, ma'am?"

Miss Ralston answered remorsefully.

"I agree with the doctor. I think we are all to blame. We push him too much when we ought to hold him back."

Here Bennie made another raid on the conversation.

"He's going to be a great man, a doctor maybe. My mother says—"

Mr. Rudinsky did not let him finish. He thought it time to insure the peace of so important an interview.

"Bennie," said he, "you will go mind the store, and keep the kitchen door shut."

Bennie's discomfiture was evident in his face. He obeyed, but not without a murmur.

"Let us make a covenant to take better care of David in the future."

Miss Ralston was speaking when Mrs. Rudinsky appeared in the doorway. She was flushed from the exertions of a hasty toilet, for which she had fled upstairs at the approach of "company." She came forward timidly, holding out a hand on which the scrubbing brush and the paring knife had left their respective marks.

"How do you do, ma'am?" she said, cordially, but shyly. "I'm glad to see you. I wish I can speak English better, I'd like to say how proud I am to see David's teacher in my haus."

"Why, you speak wonderfully!" Miss Ralston exclaimed, with genuine enthusiasm. "I don't understand how you pick up the language in such a short time. I couldn't learn Russian so fast, I'm sure."

"My husband makes us speak English all the time," Mrs. Rudinsky replied. "From the first day he said to speak English. He scolds the children if he hears they speak Jewish."

"Sure," put in her husband, "I don't want my family to be greenhorns." Miss Ralston turned a glowing face to him.

"Mr. Rudinsky, I think you've done wonders for your family. If all immigrants were like you, we wouldn't need any restriction laws." She threw all possible emphasis into her cordial voice. "Why, you're a better American than some natives I know!"

Mrs. Rudinsky sent her husband a look of loving pride.

"He wants to be a Yankee," she said.

Her husband took up the cue in earnest.

"Yes, ma'am," he said. "That's my ambition. When I was a young man, in the old country, I wanted to be scholar. But a Jew has no chance the old country; perhaps you know how it is. It wasn't the Hebrew books I wanted. I wanted to learn what the rest of the world learned, but a poor Jew had no chance in Russia. When I got to America, it was too late for me to go to school. It took me all my time and strength to make a living—I've never been much good in business, ma'am—and when I got my family over, I saw that it was the children would go to school for me. I'm glad to be a plain citizen, if my children will be educated Americans."

People with eyes and hands like Mr. Rudinsky's can say a great deal in a few words. Miss Ralston felt as if she had known him all his life, and followed his strivings in two worlds.

"I'm glad to know you, Mr. Rudinsky," she said in a low voice. "I wish more of my pupils had fathers like David's."

Her host changed the subject very neatly.

"And I wish the school children had more teachers like you. David likes you so much."

"Oh, he liked you!" the wife confirmed. "Please stay till he veks up. He'll be sorry to missed your visit."

While his wife moved quietly around the stove, making tea, Mr. Rudinsky entertained their guest with anecdotes of David's Hebrew-school days, and of his vain efforts to get at secular books.

"He was just like me," he said. "He wanted to learn everything. I couldn't afford a private teacher, and they wouldn't take him in the public school. He learned Russian all alone, and if he got a book from somewhere—a history or anything—he wouldn't eat or drink till he read it all."

Mrs. Rudinsky often glanced at David's teacher, to see how her husband's stories were impressing her. She was too shy with her English to say more than was required of her as hostess, but her face, aglow with motherly pride, showed how she participated in her husband's enthusiasm.

"You see yourself, ma'am, what he is," said David's father, "but what could I make of him in Russia? I was happy when he got here, only it was a little late. I wished he started in school younger."

"He has time enough," said Miss Ralston. "He'll get through grammar school before he's fourteen. He's twelve now, isn't he?"

"Yes, ma'am—no, ma'am! He's really fourteen now, but I made him out younger on purpose."

Miss Ralston looked puzzled. Mr. Rudinsky explained.

"You see, ma'am, he was twelve years when he came, and I wanted he should go to school as long as possible, so when I made his school certificate, I said he was only ten. I have seven children, and David is the oldest one, and I was afraid he'd have to go to work, if business was bad, or if I was sick. The state is a good father to the children in America, if the real fathers don't mix in. Why should my David lose his chance to get educated and be somebody, because I am a poor business man, and have too many children? So I made out that he had to go to school two years more."

He narrated this anecdote in the same simple manner in which he had told a dozen others. He seemed pleased to rehearse the little plot whereby he had insured his boy's education. As Miss Ralston did not make any comment immediately, he went on, as if sure of her sympathy.

"I told you I got my citizen papers right away when I came to America. I worked hard before I could bring my family—it took me four years to save the money—and they found a very poor home when they got here, but they were citizens right away. But it wouldn't do them much good, if they didn't get educated. I found out all about the compulsory education, and I said to myself that's the policeman that will keep me from robbing my David if I fail in business."

He did not overestimate his visitor's sympathy. Miss Ralston followed his story with quick appreciation of his ideals and motives, but in her ingenuous American mind one fact separated itself from the others: namely, that Mr. Rudinsky had falsified his boy's age, and had recorded the falsehood in a public document. Her recognition of the fact carried with it no criticism. She realized that Mr. Rudinsky's conscience was the product of an environment vastly different from hers. It was merely that to her mind the element of deceit was something to be accounted for, be it ever so charitably, whereas in Mr. Rudinsky's mind it evidently had no existence at all.

"So David is really fourteen years old?" she repeated incredulously. "Why, he seems too little even for twelve! Does he know?—Of course he would know! I wonder that he consented—"

She broke off, struck by a sudden thought. "Consented to tell a lie" she had meant to say, but the unspoken words diverted her mind from the conversation. It came upon her in a flash that she had found the key to David's mystery. His note was in her pocketbook, but she knew every word of it, and now everything was plain to her. The lie was this lie about his age, and the person he wanted to shield was his father. And for that he was suffering so!

She began to ask questions eagerly.

"Has David said anything about—about a little trouble he had in school the day he became ill?"

Both parents showed concern. "Trouble? What trouble?"

"Oh, it was hardly trouble—at least, I couldn't tell myself."

"David is so hard to understand sometimes," his father said.

"Oh, I don't think so!" the teacher cried. "Not when you make friends with him. He doesn't say much, it's true, but his heart is like a crystal."

"He's too still," the mother insisted, shaking her head. "All the time he's sick, he don't say anything, only when we ask him something. The doctor thinks he's worrying about something, but he don't tell."

The mother sighed, but Miss Ralston cut short her reflections.

"Mrs. Rudinsky—Mr. Rudinsky," she began eagerly, "*I* can tell you what David's troubled about."

And she told them the story of her last talk with David, and finally read them his note.

'And this lie," she ended, "you know what it is, don't you? You've just told me yourself, Mr. Rudinsky."

She looked pleadingly at him, longing to have him understand David's mind as she understood it. But Mr. Rudinsky was very slow to grasp the point.

"You mean—about the certificate? Because I made out that he was younger?"

Miss Ralston nodded.

"You know David has such a sense of honor," she explained, speaking slowly, embarrassed by the effort of following Mr. Rudinsky's train of thought and her own at the same time. "You know how he questions everything—sooner or later he makes everything clear to himself—and something must have started him thinking of this matter lately—Why, of course! I remember I asked him his age that day, when he tried on the costume, and he answered as usual, and then, I suppose, he suddenly *realized* what he was saying. I don't believe he ever *thought* about it since—since you arranged it so, and now, all of a sudden—"

She did not finish, because she saw that her listeners did not follow her. Both their faces expressed pain and perplexity. After a long silence, David's father spoke.

"And what do *you* think, ma'am?"

Miss Ralston was touched by the undertone of submission in his voice. Her swift sympathy had taken her far into his thoughts. She recognized in his story one of those ethical paradoxes which the helpless Jews of the Pale, in their search for a weapon that their oppressors could not confiscate, have evolved for their self-defense. She knew that to many honest Jewish minds a lie was not a lie when told to an official; and she divined that no ghost of a scruple had disturbed Mr. Rudinsky in his sense of triumph over circumstances, when he invented the lie that was to insure the education of his gifted child. With David, of course, the same philosophy had been valid. His father's plan for the protection of his future, hinging on a too familiar sophistry, had dropped innocuous into his consciousness; until, in a moment of spiritual sensitiveness, it took on the visage of a sin.

"And what do *you* think, ma'am?"

David's father did not have to wait a moment for her answer, so readily did her insight come to his defense. In a few eager sentences she made him feel that she understood him perfectly and understood David perfectly.

"I respect you the more for that lie, Mr. Rudinsky. It was—a *noble* lie!" There was the least tremor in her voice. "And I love David for the way *he* sees it."

Mr. Rudinsky got up and paced slowly across the room. Then he stopped before Miss Ralston.

"You are very kind to talk like that, Miss Ralston," he said, with peculiar dignity. "You see the whole thing. In the old country we had to do such things so many times that we—got used to them. Here—here we don't have to." His voice took on a musing quality. "But we don't see it right away when we get here. I meant nothing, only just to keep my boy in school. It was not to cheat anybody. The state is willing to educate the children. I said to myself I will tie my own hands, so that I can't pull my child after me if I drown. I did want my David should have the best chance in America."

Miss Ralston was thrilled by the suppressed passion in his voice. She held out her hand to him, saying again, in the low tones that come from the heart, "I am glad I know you, Mr. Rudinsky."

There was unconscious chivalry in Mr. Rudinsky's next words. Stepping to his wife's side, he laid a gentle hand on her shoulder, and said quietly, "My wife has been my helper in everything."

Miss Ralston, as we know, was given to seeing things. She saw now, not a poor immigrant couple in the first stage of American respectability, which was all there was in the room to see, but a phantom procession of men with the faces of prophets, muffled in striped praying shawls, and women radiant in the light of many candles, and youths and maidens with smoldering depths in their eyes, and silent children who pushed away joyous things for—for—

Dreams don't use up much time. Mr. Rudinsky was not aware that there had been a pause before he spoke again.

"You understand so well, Miss Ralston. But David"—he hesitated a moment, then finished quickly. "How can he respect me if he feels like that?"

His wife spoke tremulously from her corner.

"That's what I think."

"Oh, don't think that!" Miss Ralston cried. "He does respect you—he understands. Don't you see what he says: *I can't tell you—because you would blame somebody who didn't do wrong.* He doesn't blame you. He only blames himself. He's afraid to tell me because he thinks I can't understand."

The teacher laughed a happy little laugh. In her eagerness to comfort David's parents, she said just the right things, and every word summed up an instantaneous discovery. One of her useful gifts was the ability to find out truths just when she desperately needed them. There are people like that, and some of them are school teachers hired by the year. When David's father cried, "How can he respect me?" Miss Ralston's heart was frightened while it beat one beat. Only one. Then she knew all David's thoughts between the terrible, "I have lied," and the generous, "But my father did no wrong." She guessed what the struggle had cost to reconcile the contradictions; she imagined his bewilderment as he tried to rule himself by his newfound standards, while seeking excuses for his father in the one he cast away from him as unworthy of an American. Problems like David's are not very common, but then Miss Ralston was good at guessing.

"Don't worry, Mr. Rudinsky," she said, looking out of her glad eyes. "And you, Mrs. Rudinsky, don't think for a moment that David doesn't understand. He's had a bad time, the poor boy, but I know—Oh, I must speak to him! Will he wake soon, do you think?"

Mr. Rudinsky left the room without a word.

"It's all right," said David's mother, in reply to an anxious look from Miss Ralston. "He sleeps already the whole afternoon."

It had grown almost dark while they talked. Mrs. Rudinsky now lighted the lamps, apologizing to her guest for not having done so sooner, and then she released Bennie from his prolonged attendance in the store.

Bennie came into the kitchen chewing his reward, some very gummy confection. He was obliged to look the pent-up things he wanted to say, until such time as he could clear his clogged talking-gear.

"Teacher," he began, before he had finished swallowing, "What for did you say—"

"Bennie!" his mother reproved him, "You must shame yourself to listen by the door."

"Well, there wasn't any trade, ma," he defended himself, "only Bessie Katz, and she brought back the peppermints she bought this morning, to change them for taffy, but I didn't because they were all dirty, and one was broken—"

Bennie never had a chance to bring his speeches to a voluntary stop. Somebody always interrupted. This time it was his father, who came down the stairs, looking so grave that even Bennie was impressed.

"He's awake," said Mr. Rudinsky. "I lighted the lamp. Will you please come up, ma'am?"

He showed her to the room where David lay, and closed the door on them both. It was not he, but Miss Ralston, the American teacher, that his boy needed. He went softly down to the kitchen, where his wife smiled at him through unnecessary tears.

Miss Ralston never forgot the next hour, and David never forgot. The woman always remembered how the boy's eyes burned through the dusk of the shadowed corner where he lay. The boy remembered how his teacher's voice palpitated in his heart, how her cool hands rested on his, how the lamplight made a halo out of her hair. To each of them the dim room with its scant furnishings became a spiritual rendezvous.

What did the woman say, that drew the sting of remorse from the child's heart, without robbing him of the bloom of his idealism? What did she tell him that transmuted the offense of ages into the marrow and blood of persecuted virtue? How did she weld in the boy's consciousness the scraps of his mixed inheritance, so that he saw his whole experience as an unbroken thing at last? There was nobody to report how it was done. The woman did not know, nor the child. It was a secret born of the boy's need and the woman's longing to serve him; just as in nature every want creates its satisfaction.

When she was ready to leave him, Miss Ralston knelt for a moment at David's bedside, and once more took his small, hot hands in hers.

"And I have made a discovery, David," she said, smiling in a way of her own. "Talking with your parents downstairs I saw why it was that the Russian Jews are so soon at home here in our dear country. In the hearts of men like your father, dear, is the true America."

(1913)

A Great Man

Adriana Spadoni

The boy sat on the leathern bench beside old Ettore, the cobbler. He sat hunched forward, his head down between his shoulders, his near-sighted brown eyes staring straight before him.

"So, so." The old man nodded his rough gray head. "The machine went— *zip!* And the finger of Luigi lay on the floor."

The boy shuddered. His pale face contracted. The cobbler smiled grimly.

"*Bene.* It makes nothing. It is not the finger of *Signor*, the owner. The finger of one small guinea! What is it? And for such you faint. It is not wonderful that the boss says, 'We want no such boys.'"

"But—I—saw it—wriggled, master, and—it—made—me sick."

"Surely. It moved—the finger—of Luigi—calling men—to witness— deaf—men." The words trailed off. Old Ettore bent over his work. When he looked up again, the boy was watching him. The cobbler laid aside his work and put both gnarled hands on Michele's shoulders.

"Eh, little one," he whispered softly, "thou art learning. The things the old man tells here in the shop, they are true, all true, is it not?"

The boy nodded. "They are true, master."

"*Ecco!* They are true." The old man's hands dropped from Michele's shoulders. "Here mending shoes of the poor I have learned. I, who fought with the great Garibaldi to make our Italy one, know now there is no Italy, no America.* There is only the rich man and the poor man. And, like the machine in thy factory, the rich man cuts in pieces the soul of the poor. Here, working, I think and learn, learn always, Michele, and I teach thee." The cobbler's eyes burned. His voice came thick through his gray beard.

"Master," Michele Soracco's soft brown eyes pleaded, "will you not ask the father that I stay here and make shoes with thee. It is twice now in one year that they say to me 'Go' from those big noisy places."

The old man's hands went out eagerly. Then they dropped back into his lap. He shook his head slowly. "No, no, Michele; such work is for the old—those who have lived, and have—only to cut the leather—and to think. Thou art young, sixteen. At that age I was a soldier. Thou, too, must fight."

The boy's eyes filled. He bit his lip. Then his head went down upon the counter. "But, not out there, master—I can't—I can't." For a moment the cobbler sat watching the narrow, heaving shoulders. Then he bent and raised the boy.

Garibaldi: Giuseppe Garibaldi (1807–1882), Italian soldier famous for military actions that contributed to the unification of Italy.

"But, Michele, *mio*, my more than son, what else is possible?"

The boy wrenched himself free. His breath came in choking gasps. His thin hands beat the air, as if to tear a passage for the words. "I would tell to the world the things you tell me. I would not let them cut the fingers and say 'Go' because I cannot laugh—when—the finger—moves. I would learn—everything in—the world. I would write—in the papers of this—wickedness. I would teach—all men—as you teach—me." His straining hands tore the words from the depths of his soul and threw the secret in the cobbler's eyes.

The old man bent forward. His lips twitched. For a moment they moved noiselessly. Then the words came slowly, dropping like tiny stones into space. "Thou—would teach others—to all men—the thoughts—born here—*my* thoughts?"

The door banged open. A small, dirty boy poked in his head.

"Dinner, Michele. There's good spaghetti tonight." He vanished.

The boy did not move. He sat gazing dully into the leather scraps on the floor. The old man, motionless, leaned forward as if he had died in that position. At last the boy got up wearily, without a word, and went. When he had been gone some time, old Ettore stirred, rubbed his hand across his eyes, and began to work. As he pared the new sole he nodded, whispering to himself:

"Why not? Why *not*? He has the brain clear like glass. A few years— to study—in books—and then—together—we teach the world. The way— there—is only—to find the—way."

The boy climbed slowly through the blackness to the top floor of the tenement above. As he opened the door his mother turned from the stove with an iron pot in her hands. She stopped, holding the pot close, and looked quickly back and forth between Michele and the table. For a moment they went on eating, sucking the spaghetti noisily, their faces close to their plates. When they had swallowed the mouthful he had interrupted, they looked up. There was faint curiosity in the eyes of the two boarders, eating a little apart. Carmela moved over to make room for him. Teresa giggled, Beppo laughed outright. The three younger children wriggled. The dark, hairy man at the head of the table sat half turned, breathing heavily, his eyes hard with contempt.

"*Ecco,*" he said at last, "Michelena has come home to eat."

The two boarders roared with laughter. At the feminizing of his name anger broke Michele's nervous fear.

"Am I a stone," he screamed, "to see a finger—go—dripping—" His voice broke. He trembled from head to foot.

"Bah! Thou art a fool, a woman! A finger? Is it thy finger? A fine thing for a father to hear!" He rose. His strong hands, palms up, appealed to the men at the end of the table. "Thy son faints like a girl to see a finger cut. I have seen hands, twice an arm, and once a man was caught in a belt—"

The boy put his hands before his face. The gesture angered the man. He strode across and gripped Michele by the shoulder.

"Husband!" The woman put down the pot.

"Silence! Tomorrow I will take this baby to Paolo, who makes the fine business to carry dirt in a shovel. Perhaps he is not afraid of a shovel."

Without warning the boy suddenly wrenched himself free. Beside himself with anger, he screamed, beating the air with his thin hands, a ridiculous duplicate of the man before him. "I will not! I will not!"

For a moment the man listened. Then he shook the boy. "Silence!" he roared. "I do not understand? I cannot read? I cannot write? At sixteen thou speakest to the father like a dog." His rage choked him. He pushed the boy away. "Go. Eat the food thy old father earns. Tomorrow we talk again." He took his hat and went out to his night's work.

The boy ate his supper alone. The three children ran down to play in the hot dust of the street. The two boarders went out. When the dishes were done, Maria Soracco brought a great bundle of coats from the corner. They sewed in swift silence, broken only by the screaming of children in the street below, the loud, hoarse voices of men in endless argument, the whir of machines from near tenements. When it was late, the three children crawled up sleepily and went to bed. Teresa and Beppo nodded over the black coats.

"Go. We can finish." Maria Soracco smiled approvingly at the finished pile.

She and Michele and Carmela sewed on until the coats were done. As she smoothed the last coat she touched Michele's hand lightly.

"Forget the angry words of thy father, little one. He loves thee, and would be proud of thee, and always that pig of a Santucci tells, 'My Guiseppe is not yet fifteen, and he makes five dollars a week!' And the father thought to see thee growing to be a great man also. In the old country, when thou wert yet a baby, he said always, 'He is smarter than other boys, my Michele.' And now before others he must have shame for thee."

"I will not make that stupidness with a shovel. Such is work for a dog."

"*Bene.* Then thou must go out before he returns in the morning, for he has the heart sore because of thee and will do as he says."

Michele went into the kitchen and threw his mattress down beside the two men already asleep. In a few moments he heard the heavy breathing of his mother from the next room. One of the men began to snore, making choking noises and turning heavily from side to side. Michele felt a wall closing in upon him, sealing him forever in the hot, breathless kitchen. It was a long time before he slept, tossing restlessly on the warm mattress.

He was up early and out before old Ettore had taken the shutters from his shop. He walked along aimlessly through the dirty streets littered with scraps of garbage and half-dressed babies with old pale faces sitting solemnly in dark hallways. Soon the streets began to fill, heavy wagons rumbled by. More people poured out from the houses. Whistles blew. The hurrying stream gathered him in and bore him along. The whole world was working up to its tremendous daily speed. He walked more slowly. From time to time he stopped before a factory and went in. Sometimes he went in response to scrawled placards hanging in doorways. He turned from each refusal with a little sigh of relief, which was lost in anxiety before he reached the next place.

Late in the afternoon he came back. He had found nothing. As he passed the shop old Ettore rose quickly from his bench and made violent motions for him to enter. His eyes twinkling, his whole face radiant, the old man led the boy mysteriously into the little room behind the shop.

"Whist!" With his horny finger along the bridge of his nose, he winked solemnly.

"Singor Dottore, at your service." He bowed clumsily, chuckling with happiness. The boy laughed in response. Suddenly the old man's eyes grew serious. He put both hands on Michele's shoulders. "*Caro,* dost remember the Protestant House on Houston Street where the children make classes for many things? And Miss Mildred, who always said, 'I want Michele Soracco to do this, to do that'?"

"Surely, I remember. I went sometimes to the class for little soldiers."

"*Ecco!* They are good people. They think to make the world better with song and little gifts to children, but the hearts are good. Often they come here to have the shoes fixed, but most often comes Miss Mildred. And always she stays a little to talk. I tell her of the old Italy and of Garibaldi. She listens with both ears. And she never goes without to ask, 'Michele Soracco, is he well? A fine boy, Michele. He has a good head. It is a misfortune he cannot go to school. He would be a great man.' And I say always, 'There are many children and the father is a poor man. Michele must work.' Patience, what use to make too many words?"

Michele looked up, smiling. "She says I have a good head." The tone was complacent.

"Little peacock! So. Be not too proud. Others also have heads, and the worst is not this one." The old man tapped his gray mop. "Listen. Last night I sat alone, sad in the heart because of thee. And I said, there is much money in the world and it takes only a little for my Michele to go to school. In an hour many rich men spend enough; and then, sudden, like thunder—the idea came. At the Protestant House they do much for the poor—often foolish things. Here is something not foolish. I will go and talk with Miss Mildred."

The boy began to tremble. "Master—a"

The old man bent and gathered the boy close. "Michele," he whispered, "it is true, true. This morning she came. She talked to the father. He listened like one to a crazy woman, but he said yes. Each week they will pay to him five dollars for a year that he will let thee go to school. After that—there are other ways. She came afterwards to the shop and the eyes were bright like stars. Why, baby, crying! Psh! A man—to—cry—because—"

The old man and the boy cried together.

At last the cobbler dried his eyes. "Come, come!" He bustled about importantly. "All day I wait for thee to return to make a feast." He brought a small bottle of wine, sausage, crisp Roman bread, and little cakes of nuts from a shelf. When he had spread the table, he went chuckling into the shop. "For two hours the shop is closed. The cobbler celebrates the birth of his son."

While they ate old Ettore talked, planning the future, prophesying many things. Michele listened. He felt that he had died and was in a strange world. He scarcely heard what old Ettore was saying. Like frightened rabbits, his thoughts scurried about in the future. His brain whirled. He was too good to be wasted. Men saw his value. When the last crumb was eaten, the cobbler pushed back his chair.

"And now I must return to my shoes. But there will be many nights so, for thou wilt study down here, where it is quiet, and read the books to me, the English books, telling me the meaning."

He kissed the boy on both cheeks, and for a moment Michele clung to him.

As the boy opened the door Carmela and her mother looked up from the coats. Michele sat down. He felt awkward and self-conscious, as if he didn't "belong." He watched and waited for them to speak. When his mother reached the end of the seam, she took the pins from her mouth and passed the coat to the boy.

"There are three dozens, and they must be finished." Michele threaded his needle and began to sew.

Michele sat staring—he sat in the old way, hunched forward, his head between his shoulders—over the city roofs, towards the setting sun. Slowly, as if moving against his will, Michele's hand went to his pocket. He drew out a square white envelope, opened it in the same mechanical way, and laid six narrow pieces of cardboard on the arm of the chair.

He saw them so clearly: the dark, hairy man with a ragged black mustache and broken nails; the fat, shapeless woman with tired eyes and patient, beast-like shoulders; shy, awkward Carmela; Amadeo, with the green plaid suit, oily hair, and creaking patent leather shoes. Teresa, with her mountain of puffs, her tight skirt, and low-cut lace waist. And Ettore—old mumbling Ettore, with his piercing eyes. Michele took the cards in his trembling hands and tore them to bits. The white scraps dropped to the floor.

Cold sweat broke out on Michele's face. His slim brown hands clenched.

"There's no credit to them. They've lost nothing in my years here. I've tutored enough to support myself and turned my scholarship money over to them. What more can they ask?"

The scraps of paper on the floor stared at him with accusing eyes. He turned to the window again. All about him lights from huge apartment houses glowed through the dusk. The deserted streets were clean and still. He could fell the smooth, well-ordered mechanism of comfortable homes; could feel it sharply, the reality of the new life into which he had grown so easily. It seemed to close about him, touching his flesh like his own clothes. Between this and the tenement where once a month he spent an agonizing Sunday afternoon there lay a million miles of thought and space. And he had climbed the million miles alone.

"Maybe they've forgotten the day," he said. "If not, it will only be a *festa* more or less. What can graduation exercises mean to them? When I do not come, they will wait a while, but not for long. Some day I will explain."

Michele felt his face flush. The room was dark now; he could barely see the scattered papers on the floor. Slowly he undressed and groped his way to bed. It was morning before he slept.

In his shop old Ettore sat stitching in the flickering gaslight. From time to time he stopped, bent his gray head, and listened. Twice he went to the door. At eleven he put away his work, swept the floor, and put up the shutters. But he did not lock the door. He came back to his bench and sat with his eyes on the clock, his hands idle in his leather apron.

At twelve he turned the big key in the lock, then he went slowly, as if very, very tired, into the little room behind the shop. In the center of the table lay two plates, cakes, and a bottle of wine. He opened the window and threw the cakes out in the darkness of the alleyway.

Early the next morning he was at his bench. He worked steadily without looking at the clock, nor did he go once to the door. From time to time through the long hot forenoon little Pietro came down from the top floor to report the progress of his mother's baking.

"Most surely it will be a fine feast, a very fine feast." The old man nodded without stopping his work.

Late in the afternoon Maria Soracco came. Her eyes were troubled. "It is almost five o'clock," she said. "Soon the husband will be home, and Michele has not come. Last night I had a bed ready for him with clean sheets, a bed for him alone. Perhaps he was busy, but today we know not how to go to the school. I am afraid. Too much study is bad for the head. By the hope of Paradise, if my Michele is sick—"

"Holy Mary, have pity on an old fool! I have a head like a broken sieve." The cobbler dropped his work and began searching his pockets, shrugging his shoulders, mumbling angrily at his own stupidity. "*Macce!*" he growled. "No matter. I remember the words. This morning I had from our own Michele a little letter. Last night he was busy. He told me the way to the school. I am to show the way."

"Thanks be to the Holy Mother!" Maria Soracco breathed a deep sigh of relief. "The husband said I was foolish, but—the heart of a mother. It makes me afraid, this working with the head. What if my Michele were sick among those strangers—Americans with hearts of ice?"

The old man's hands made a soothing gesture, but he did not look at Maria. "Michele is well," he said, gruffly. "At seven I come. Yes?"

Maria Soracco bustled happily from the shop. The cobbler looked at the leather he held. "*Ecco*," he smiled crookedly, "the danger is not always to the hear from those books; no—it—is not—always to the head."

Tomoasso Soracco went first, elbowing his way slowly through the crowd that packed the vestibule of the auditorium. His women followed. Old Ettore brought up the rear. Maria, a little frightened, held fast to Tomasso's coat. Carmela and Teresa, their eyes bright with wonder, stared happily about. Through the wide doors ahead they caught glimpses of a great hall, with gay pennants hanging from the high ceiling and hundreds of lights. Above the low hum about them they could hear the steady shuffle of many people moving to their seats.

At last Tomasso reached the door. They were almost the last of the line.

"Tickets!" a young man dressed like the bridegroom in the window of Giuseppe, the tailor, held out his hand. "Tickets, please!"

"Tickets!" Tomasso shook his head, spread both empty hands to witness, and nodded violently.

"No one admitted without tickets. Step aside, please."

Tomasso Soracco's good humor vanished. He turned angrily to Teresa. "Come here. Tell this donkey in his barbarous tongue that we come to see Michele. We are the family of Michele, and have nothing to pay."

Those who were waiting to be seated turned quickly. Someone laughed. "Tell as I say," roared Tomasso. Then the throng at the door parted. Through an opening Maria suddenly saw Michele. The red roses on her hat danced madly as she waved to him.

"*Figlio, figlio*," she cried, "come quick! Explain to this crazy one." Tomasso shrugged his contempt of the young man and waited with folded arms for Michele.

For a moment Michele stood just as he was when the crowd opened and the shrill voice of his mother came to his ears. Then he moved slowly forward. His face was white and set. He turned to the boy at the door. "These are my people," he said, distinctly; "I think—they must—have forgotten their tickets."

In the still of dawn as before the birth of a new world he moved down the hall toward the front seats reserved for relatives. He saw the suppressed smiles in the women's eyes at the bobbing red roses on his mother's hat. He heard people sniff as they passed, scenting the strong, cheap perfume Teresa used. As they clattered noisily into their seats his mother whispered: "He is getting old, that Ettore. Through his stupidness with the tickets the trouble came."

Michele moved off toward the platform. His place was with the honor men of his class. Somehow he found his seat. He sat down, staring blankly before him. He applauded mechanically when the others did. Vaguely he knew that one number of the program after another was gone through, checked off as done forever. He heard nothing. From time to time he glanced toward the seats where his people sat. They were all sitting forward, interested, curious, a little awed. Once he caught old Ettore's eyes full on him. But the cobbler might have been dead, so rigid was the mask of his face. Michele trembled as if from cold. Then the blood rushed in a boiling stream to his head. He heard his name called. Michele stood up and stepped forward to take his degree. He saw the President's lips moving. He saw the paper in the President's outstretched hand. In the stillness, like two quick cracks of a pistol, he heard his mother's tense whisper, *"Che fa? Che fa?"* and his father's quivering, "Silence! They make him—a gift." He looked about like a criminal trying to escape. In the smooth flat level of faces before him something caught and held his eye. Old Ettore sat forward, his great gray head erect, his twisted brown hands clasped tightly against his gray beard. Carmela's shy eyes glowed with excitement. Teresa's pretty, assertive face claimed him defiantly. But Tomasso Soracco and Maria, his wife, sat quietly hand in hand and the big tears ran unheeded down their cheeks.

It was over. He had slipped away with his people and they had brought him in triumph to the "feast." There was Pepe, the fat "boss"; and Luigi, whose finger had gone "zip" in the machine; and the Santuccis, who had once brought the news of his fainting to Tomasso. Every one was red-faced from eating, and very happy. They laughed and talked, shouting one above the other. Tomasso Soracco kept bringing fresh bottles of wine. Maria filled and refilled the plates with little cakes. It seemed to Michele that he had been sitting for years at the table and had eaten mountains of small cakes. Every now and then Maria Soracco stopped to pat him on the shoulder.

"He loves yet the little cakes of his mother, my fine son!" And every time Michele answered, "They are the best cakes in the world."

But at last it was impossible to drink another glass of wine or eat another cake. Silence fell in the stifling room. Then, with the air of having waited for just this moment, Pepe stood up. Those about the table leaned forward expectantly, grasping their glasses in answer to Pepe's, held high in his right hand. Pepe cleared his throat.

"Friends, it gives me great pleasure to be here tonight with this happy family and with you all, my very good friends." Pepe's round bullet head rolled on his shoulders as if he would include even the furnishing of the room in his good will. "I am proud to be here. I rejoice with our good compatriot Tomasso Soracco, with his good wife, and with his fine son, Michele." Pepe bowed. "We are proud of you, Michele Soracco—we, your family, your friends, all the Italians of New York." Pepe's fat left hand extended New York to include the universe. "You are not yet twenty-two, and already you are first in your class, above the sons of rich Americans. You have brains, Michele Soracco, brains." Pepe paused dramatically. A murmur of approval ran about the table. Michele felt a hot wave of pity and love and self-consciousness sweep over him. Tears stung the back of his eyes.

"*Ecco!* For that reason, here and now, I offer you, for your own sake and in sign of appreciation for the faithful service of your good father" (Pepe's full black eyes touched softly the oval chin of Teresa), "*one—hundred—dol—lars* a month as padrone of the men I send next week to Wisconsin for one year to make the roads of the State. *Ecco!* One—hundred—dollars."

Tomasso Soracco half rose from his chair. He sank back. He looked helplessly about. No one stirred. They sat, looking toward him, as if the words of Pepe had been a thunder bolt that had killed them where they sat.

Michele's eyes went about the table from face to face. He was smiling faintly. He saw the long, flat roads of gray dust and dark, heavy men tearing the earth. The smile crept down from his eyes to his lips. Instinctively his eyes sought Ettore's. He felt strangely like a little boy again, running down to the old cobbler. He saw again Luigi's finger wriggling on the floor. The smile deepened. But Ettore did not glance from the plate before him. The smile died slowly in Michele's face. He sat staring at the old man. Suddenly he began to tremble. Maria Soracco buried her face in her hands. She sobbed:

"He—said it—always, 'Our—Michele will be a great man.'"

Michele's laugh broke the stillness. He stood up. His glass clicked with Pepe's. "A million thanks, Signor Manelli; for one year I will make the roads of the State."

"To Michele!" cried old Ettore, and his shaking hand spilled the wine as he drank.

(1913)

The Wisdom of the New

Sui Sin Far

I

Old Li Wang, the peddler, who had lived in the land beyond the sea, was wont to declare: "For every cent that man makes here, he can make one hundred there."

"Then, why," would ask Sankwei, "do you now have to move from door to door to fill your bowl with rice?"

And the old man would sigh and answer:

"Because where one learns how to make gold, one also learns how to lose it."

"How to lose it!" echoed Wou Sankwei. "Tell me all about it."

So the old man would tell stories about the winning and the losing, and the stories of the losing were even more fascinating than the stories of the winning.

"Yes, that was life," he would conclude. "Life, life."

At such times the boy would gaze across the water with wistful eyes. The land beyond the sea was calling to him.

The place was a sleepy little south coast town where the years slipped by monotonously. The boy was the only son of the man who had been the town magistrate.

Had his father lived, Wou Sankwei would have been sent to complete his schooling in another province. As it was he did nothing but sleep, dream, and occasionally get into mischief. What else was there to do? His mother and sister waited upon him hand and foot. Was he not the son of the house? The family income was small, scarcely sufficient for their needs; but there was no way by which he could add to it, unless, indeed, he disgraced the name of Wou by becoming a common fisherman. The great green waves lifted white arms of foam to him, and the fishes gleaming and lurking in the waters seemed to beseech him to draw them from the deep; but his mother shook her head.

"Should you become a fisherman," said she, "your family would lose face. Remember that your father was a magistrate."

When he was about nineteen there returned to the town one who had been absent for many years. Ching Kee, like old Li Wang, had also lived in the land beyond the sea; but unlike old Li Wang he had accumulated a small fortune.

"'Tis a hard life over there," said he. "But 'tis worth while. At least one can be a man and can work at what work comes his way without losing face." Then he laughed at Wou Sankwei's flabby muscles, at his soft, dark eyes, and plump, white hands.

"If you lived in America," said he, "you would learn to be ashamed of such beauty."

Whereupon Wou Sankwei made up his mind that he would go to America, the land beyond the sea. Better any life than that of a woman man.

He talked long and earnestly with his mother. "Give me your blessing," said he. "I will work and save money. What I send home will bring you many a comfort, and when I come back to China, it may be that I shall be able to complete my studies and obtain a degree. If not, my knowledge of the foreign language which I shall acquire will enable me to take a position which will not disgrace the name of Wou."

His mother listened and thought. She was ambitious for her son whom she loved beyond all things on earth. Moreover, had not Sik Ping, a Canton merchant, who had visited the little town two moons ago, declared to Hum Wah, who traded in palm leaves, that the signs of the times were that the son of a cobbler, returned from America with the foreign language, could easier command a position of consequence than the son of a school teacher unacquainted with any tongue but that of his motherland?

"Very well," she acquiesced; "but before you go I must find you a wife. Only your son, my son, can comfort me for your loss."

II

Wou Sankwei stood behind his desk, busily entering figures in a long yellow book. Now and then he would thrust the hair pencil with which he worked behind his ears and manipulate with deft fingers a Chinese counting machine. Wou Sankwei was the junior partner and bookkeeper of the firm of Leung Tang Wou & Co. of San Francisco. He had been in America seven years and had made good use of his time. Self-improvement had been his object and ambition, even more than the acquirement of a fortune, and who, looking at his fine, intelligent face and listening to his careful English, could say that he had failed?

One of his partners called his name. Some ladies wished to speak to him. Wou Sankwei hastened to the front of the store. One of his callers, a motherly looking woman, was the friend who had taken him under wing shortly after his arrival in America. She had come to invite him to spend the evening with her and her niece, the young girl who accompanied her.

After his callers had left, Sankwei returned to his desk and worked steadily until the hour for his evening meal, which he took in the Chinese restaurant across the street from the bazaar. He hurried through with this, as before going to his friend's house, he had a somewhat important letter to write and mail. His mother had died a year before, and the uncle, to whom he was writing, had taken his wife and son into his home until such time as his nephew could send for them. Now the time had come.

Wou Sankwei's memory of the woman who was his wife was very faint. How could it be otherwise? She had come to him but three weeks before the sailing of the vessel which had brought him to America, and until then he had not seen her face. But she was his wife and the mother of his son. Ever since he had worked in America he had sent money for her support, and she had proved a good daughter to his mother.

As he sat down to write he decided that he would welcome her with a big dinner to his countrymen.

"Yes," he replied to Mrs. Dean, later on in the evening, "I have sent for my wife."

"I am so glad," said the lady. "Mr. Wou"—turning to her niece—"has not seen his wife for seven years."

"Deary me!" exclaimed the young girl. "What a lot of letters you must have written!"

"I have not written her one," returned the young man somewhat stiffly.

Adah Charlton looked up in surprise. "Why—" she began.

"Mr. Wou used to be such a studious boy when I first knew him," interrupted Mrs. Dean, laying her hand affectionately upon the young man's shoulder. "Now, it is all business. But you won't forget the concert on Saturday evening."

"No, I will not forget," answered Wou Sankwei.

"He has never written to his wife," explained Mrs. Dean when she and her niece were alone, "because his wife can neither read nor write."

"Oh, isn't that sad!" murmured Adah Charlton, her own winsome face becoming pensive.

"They don't seem to think so. It is the Chinese custom to educate only the boys. At least it has been so in the past. Sankwei himself is unusually bright. Poor boy! He began life here as a laundryman, and you may be sure that I must have been hard on him, for, as the son of a petty Chinese Government official, he had not been accustomed to manual labor. But Chinese character is wonderful; and now after seven years in this country, he enjoys a reputation as a business man amongst his countrymen, and is as up to date as any young American."

"But, Auntie, isn't it dreadful to think that a man should live away from his wife for so many years without any communication between them whatsoever except through others."

"It is dreadful to our minds, but not to theirs. Everything with them is a matter of duty. Sankwei married his wife as a matter of duty. He sends for her as a matter of duty."

"I wonder if it is all duty on her side," mused the girl.

Mrs. Dean smiled. "You are too romantic, Adah," said she. "I hope, however, that when she does come, they will be happy together. I think almost as much of Sankwei as I do of my own boy."

III

Pau Lin, the wife of Wau Sankwei, sat in a corner of the deck of the big steamer, awaiting the coming of her husband. Beside her, leaning his little queued head against her shoulder, stood her six-year-old son. He had been ailing throughout the voyage, and his small face was pinched with pain. His mother, who had been nursing him every night since the ship had left port, appeared very worn and tired. This, despite the fact that with a feminine desire to make herself fair to see in the eyes of her husband, she had arrayed herself in a heavily embroidered purple costume, whitened her forehead and cheeks with powder, and tinted her lips with carmine.

He came at last, looking over and beyond her. There were two others of her county-women awaiting the men who had sent for them, and each had a child, so that for a moment he seemed somewhat bewildered. Only when the ship's officer pointed out and named her, did he know her as his. Then he came forward, spoke a few words of formal welcome, and lifting the child into his arms, began questioning her as to its health.

She answered in low monosyllables. At his greeting she had raised her patient eyes to his face—the face of the husband whom she had not seen for seven long years—then the eager look of expectancy which had crossed her own faded away, her eyelids drooped, and her countenance assumed an almost sullen expression.

"Ah, poor Sankwei!" exclaimed Mrs. Dean, who with Adah Charlton stood some little distance apart from the family groups.

"Poor wife!" murmured the young girl. She moved forward and would have taken in her own white hands the ringed ones of the Chinese woman, but the young man gently restrained her. "She cannot understand you," said he. As the young girl fell back, he explained to his wife the presence of the stranger woman. They were there to bid her welcome; they were kind and good and wished to be her friends as well as his.

Pau Lin looked away. Adah Charlton's bright face, and the tone in her husband's voice when he spoke to the young girl, aroused a suspicion in her mind—a suspicion natural to one who had come from a land where friendship between a man and woman is almost unknown.

"Poor little thing! How shy she is!" exclaimed Mrs. Dean.

Sankwei was glad that neither she nor the young girl understood the meaning of the averted face.

Thus began Wou Sankwei's life in America as a family man. He soon became accustomed to the change, which was not such a great one after all. Pau Lin was more of an accessory than a part of his life. She interfered not at all with his studies, his business, or his friends, and when not engaged in housework or sewing, spent most her time in the society of one or the other of the merchants' wives who lived in the flats and apartments around her own. She kept up the Chinese custom of taking her meals after her husband or at a separate table, and observed faithfully the rule laid down for her by her late mother-in-law: to keep a quiet tongue in the presence of her man. Sankwei, on his part, was always kind and indulgent. He bought her silk dresses, hair ornaments, fans, and sweetmeats. He ordered her favorite dishes from the Chinese restaurant. When she wished to go out with her women friends, he hired a carriage, and shortly after her advent erected behind her sleeping room a chapel for the ancestral tablet and gorgeous goddess which she had brought over seas with her.

Upon the child both parents lavished affection. He was a quaint, serious little fellow, small for his age and requiring much care. Although naturally much attracted to his mother, he became also very fond of his father who, more like an elder brother than a parent, delighted in playing all kinds of games with him, and whom he followed about like a little dog. Adah Charlton took a great fancy to him and sketched him in many different poses for a book on Chinese children which she was illustrating.

"He will be strong enough to go to school next year," said Sankwei to her one day. "Later on I intend to put him through an American college."

"What does your wife think of a Western training for him?" inquired the young girl.

"I have not consulted her about the matter," he answered. "A woman does not understand such things."

"A woman, Mr Wou," declared Adah, "understands such things as well as and sometimes better than a man."

"An American woman, maybe," amended Sankwei; "but not a Chinese."

From the first Pau Lin had shown no disposition to become Americanized, and Sankwei himself had not urged it.

"I do appreciate the advantages of becoming westernized," said he to Mrs. Dean whose influence and interest in his studies in America had helped him to become what he was, "but it is not as if she had come here as I came, in her learning days. The time for learning with her is over."

One evening, upon returning from his store, he found the little Yen sobbing pitifully.

"What!" he teased, "A man—and weeping."

The boy tried to hide his face, and as he did so, the father noticed that his little hand was red and swollen. He strode into the kitchen where Pau Lin was preparing the evening meal.

"The little child who is not strong—is there anything he could do to merit the infliction of pain?" he questioned.

Pau Lin faced her husband. "Yes, I think so," said she.

"What?"

"I forbade him to speak the language of the white women, and he disobeyed me. He had words in that tongue with the white boy from the next street."

Sankwei was astounded.

"We are living in the white man's country," said he. "The child will have to learn the white man's language."

"Not my child," answered Pau Lin.

Sankwei turned away from her. "Come, little one," said he to his son, "we will take supper tonight at the restaurant, and afterward Yen shall see a show."

Pau Lin laid down the dish of vegetables which she was straining and took from a hook a small wrap which she adjusted around the boy.

"Now go with thy father," said she sternly.

But the boy clung to her—to the hand which had punished him. "I will sup with you," he cried, "I will sup with you."

"Go," repeated his mother, pushing him from her. And as the two passed over the threshold, she called to the father: "Keep the wrap around the child. The night air is chill."

Late that night, while father and son were peacefully sleeping, the wife and mother arose, and lifting gently the unconscious boy, bore him into the next room where she sat down with him in a rocker. Waking, he clasped his arms around her neck. Backwards and forwards she rocked him, passionately caressing the wounded hand and crooning and crying until he fell asleep again.

The first chastisement that the son of Wou Sankwei had received from the mother was because he had striven to follow in the footsteps of his father and use the language of the stranger.

"You did perfectly right," said old Sien Tau the following morning, as she leaned over her balcony to speak to the wife of Wou Sankwei. "Had I again a son to rear, I should see to it that he followed not after the white people."

Sien Tau's son had married a white woman, and his children passed their granddame on the street without recognition.

"In this country, she is most happy who has no child," said Lae Choo, resting her elbow upon the shoulder of Sien Tau. "A Toy, the young daughter of Lew Wing, is as bold and free in her ways as are the white women, and her name is on all the men's tongues. What prudent man of our race would take her as wife?"

"One needs not to be born here to be made a fool of," joined in Pau Lin, appearing at another balcony door. "Ting of Hum Wah. From sunrise till midnight he worked for fourteen years, then a white man came along and persuaded from him every dollar, promising to return doublefold within the moon. Many moons have risen and waned, and Hum Wah still waits on this side of the sea for the white man and his money. Meanwhile, his father and mother, who looked long for his coming, have passed beyond returning."

"The new religion—what trouble it brings!" exclaimed Lae Choo. "My man received word yestereve that the good old mother of Chee Ping—he who was baptized a Christian at the last baptizing in the Mission around the corner—had her head secretly severed from her body by the steadfast people of the village, as soon as the news reached there. 'Twas the first violent death in the records of the place. This happened to the mother of one of the boys attending the Mission corner of my street."

"No doubt, the poor old mother, having lost face, minded not so much the losing of her head," sighed Pau Lin. She gazed below her curiously. The American Chinatown held a strange fascination for the girl from the seacoast village. Streaming along the street was a motley throng made up of all nationalities. The sing-song voices of girls whom respectable merchants' wives shudder to name, were calling to one another from high balconies up shadowy alleys. A fat barber was laughing hilariously at a drunken white man who had fallen into a gutter; a withered old fellow, carrying a bird in a cage, stood at the corner entreating passersby to have a good fortune told; some children were burning punk on the curbstone. There went by a stalwart Chief of the Six Companies engaged in earnest confab with a yellow-robed priest from the joss house.* A Chinese dressed in the latest American style and a very blonde woman, laughing immoderately, were entering a Chinese restaurant together. Above all the hubbub of voices was heard the clang of electric cars and the jarring of heavy wheels over cobblestones.

Pau Lin raised her head and looked her thoughts at the old woman, Sien Tau.

"Yes," nodded the dame, "'tis a mad place in which to bring up a child."

Pau Lin went back into the house, gave little Yen his noonday meal, and dressed him with care. His father was to take him out that afternoon. She questioned the boy, as she braided his queue, concerning the white women whom he visited with his father.

It was evening when they returned—Wou Sankwei and his boy. The little fellow ran up to her in high glee. "See, mother," said he, pulling off his cap, "I am like father now. I wear no queue."

The mother looked down upon him—at the little round head from which the queue, which had been her pride, no longer dangled.

"Ah!" she cried. "I am ashamed of you; I am ashamed!"

The boy stared at her, hurt and disappointed.

"Never mind, son," comforted his father. "It is all right."

Pau Lin placed the bowls of seaweed and chickens' livers before them and went back to the kitchen where her own meal was waiting. But she did not eat. She was saying within herself: "It is for the white woman he has done this; it is for the white woman!"

Later, as she laid the queue of her son within the trunk wherein lay that of his father, long since cast aside, she discovered a picture of Mrs. Dean, taken when the American woman had first become the teacher and benefactress of the youthful laundryman. She ran over with it to her husband. "Here," said she; "it is a picture of one of your white friends." Sankwei took it from her almost reverently. "That woman," he explained, "has been to me as a mother."

---

*_joss house:_ Temple for worship of Chinese deities from Buddhism, Confucianism, and Taoism; also used for prayers and offerings to ancestors.

"And the young woman—the one with the eyes the color of blue china—is she also as a mother?" inquired Pau Lin gently.

But for all her gentleness, Wou Sankei flushed angrily.

"Never speak of her," he cried. "Never speak of her!"

"Ha, ha, ha! Ha, ha, ha!" laughed Pau Lin. It was a soft and not unmelodious laugh; but to Wou Sankwei it sounded almost sacrilegious.

Nevertheless, he soon calmed down. Pau Lin was his wife, and to be kind to her was not only his duty but his nature. So when his little boy climbed into his lap and besought his father to pipe him a tune, he reached for his flute and called to Pau Lin to put aside work for that night. He would play her some Chinese music. And Pau Lin, whose heart and mind, undiverted by change, had been concentrated upon Wou Sankwei ever since the day she had become his wife, smothered, for the time being, the bitterness in her heart, and succumbed to the magic of her husband's playing—a magic which transported her in thought to the old Chinese days, the old Chinese days whose impression and influence ever remain with the exiled sons and daughters of China.

IV

That a man should take to himself two wives, or even three, if he thought proper, seemed natural and right in the eyes of Wou Pau Lin. She herself had come from a home where there were two broods of children and where her mother and her father's other wife had eaten their meals together as sisters. In that home there had not always been peace; but each woman, at least, had the satisfaction of knowing that her man did not regard or treat the other woman as superior. To each had fallen the common lot—to bear children to the man, and the man was master of all.

But, oh! the humiliation and shame of bearing children to a man who looked up to another woman—and a woman of another race—as being above the common uses of women. There is a jealousy of the mind more poignant than any mere animal jealousy.

When Wou Sankwei's second child was two weeks old, Adah Charlton and her aunt called to see the little one, and the young girl chatted brightly with the father and played merrily with Yen, who was growing strong and merry. The American women could not, of course, converse with the Chinese; but Adah placed beside her a bunch of beautiful flowers, pressed her hand, and looked down upon her with radiant eyes. Secure in the difference of race, in the love of many friends, and in the happiness of her chosen work, no suspicion whatever crossed her mind that the woman whose husband was her aunt's protégé tasted everything bitter because of her.

After the visitors had gone, Pau Lin, who had been watching her husband's face while the young artist was in the room, said to him:

"She can be happy who takes all and gives nothing."

"Takes all and gives nothing," echoed her husband. "What do you mean?"

"She has taken all your heart," answered Pau Lin, "but she has not given you a son. It is I who have had that task."

"You are my wife," answered Wou Sankwei. "And she—oh! how can you speak of her so? She, who is as a pure water flower—a lily!"

He went out of the room, carrying with him a little painting of their boy, which Adah Charlton had given to him as she bade him goodbye and which he had intended showing with pride to the mother.

It was on the day that the baby died that Pau Lin first saw the little picture. It had fallen out of her husband's coat pocket when he lifted the tiny form in his arms and declared it lifeless. Even in that first moment of loss Pau Lin, stopping to pick up the portrait, had shrunk back in horror, crying: "She would cast a spell! She would cast a spell!"

She set her heel upon the face of the picture and destroyed it beyond restoration.

"You know not what you say and do," sternly rebuked Sankwei. He would have added more, but the mystery of the dead child's look forbade him.

"The loss of a son is as the loss of a limb," said he to his childless partner, as under the red glare of the lanterns they sat discussing the sad event.

"But you are not without consolation," returned Leung Tsao. "Your first-born grows in strength and beauty."

"True," assented Wou Sankwei, his heavy thoughts becoming lighter.

And Pau Lin, in her curtained balcony overhead, drew closer her child and passionately cried:

"Sooner would I, O heart of my heart, that the light of thine eyes were also quenched, than that thou shouldst be contaminated with the wisdom of the new."

V

The Chinese women friends of Wou Pau Lin gossiped among themselves, and their gossip reached the ears of the American woman friend of Pau Lin's husband. Since the days of her widowhood Mrs. Dean had devoted herself earnestly and wholeheartedly to the betterment of the condition and the up-lifting of the young workingmen of Chinese race who came to America. Their appeal and need, as she had told her niece, was for closer acquaintance with the knowledge of the Western people, and *that* she had undertaken to give them, as far as she was able. The rewards and satisfactions of her work had been rich in some cases. Witness Wou Sankwei.

But the gossip had reached and much perturbed her. What was it that they said Wou Sankwei's wife had declared—that her little son should not go to an American school nor learn the American learning. Such bigotry and narrow-mindedness! How sad to think of! Here was a man who had benefited and profited by living in America, anxious to have his son receive the benefits of a Western education—and here was this man's wife opposing him with her ignorance and hampering him with her unreasonable jealousy.

Yes, she had heard that too. That Wou Sankwei's wife was jealous—jealous—and her husband the most moral of men, the kindest and the most generous.

"Of what is she jealous?" she questioned Adah Charlton. "Other Chinese men's wives, I have known, have had cause to be jealous, for it is true some of them are dreadfully immoral and openly support two or more wives. But not Wou Sankwei. And this little Pau Lin. She has everything that a Chinese woman could wish for."

A sudden flash of intuition came to the girl, rendering her for a moment speechless. When she did find words, she said:

"Everything that a Chinese woman could wish for, you say. Auntie, I do not believe there is any real difference between the feelings of a Chinese wife and an American wife. Sankwei is treating Pau Lin as he would treat her were he living in China. Yet it cannot be the same to her as if she were in their own country, where he would not come in contact with American women. A woman is a woman with intuitions and perceptions, whether Chinese or American, whether educated or uneducated, and Sankwei's wife must have noticed, even on the day of her arrival, her husband's manner toward us, and contrasted it with his manner toward her. I did not realize this before you told me that she was jealous. I only wish I had. Now, for all her ignorance, I can see that the poor little thing became more of an American in that one half hour on the steamer than Won Sankwei, for all your pride in him, has become in seven years."

Mrs. Dean rested her head on her hand. She was evidently much perplexed.

"What you say may be, Adah," she replied after a while; "but even so, it is Sankwei whom I have known so long, who has my sympathies. He has much to put up with. They have drifted seven years of life apart. There is no bond of interest or sympathy between them, save the boy. Yet never the slightest hint of trouble has come to me from his own lips. Before the coming of Pau Lin, he would confide in me every little thing that worried him, as if he were my own son. Now he maintains absolute silence as to his private affairs."

"Chinese principles," observed Adah, resuming her work. "Yes, I admit Sankwei has some puzzles to solve. Naturally, when he tries to live two lives—that of a Chinese and that of an American."

"He is compelled to that," retorted Mrs. Dean. "Is it not what we teach these Chinese boys—to become American? And yet, they are Chinese, and must, in a sense, remain so."

Adah did not answer.

Mrs. Dean sighed. "Poor, dear children, both of them," mused she. "I feel very low-spirited over the matter. I suppose you wouldn't care to come downtown with me. I should like to have another chat with Mrs. Wing Sing."

"I shall be glad of the change," replied Adah, laying down her brushes.

Rows of lanterns suspended from many balconies shed a mellow, moon-shiny radiance. On the walls and doors were splashes of red paper inscribed with hieroglyphics. In the narrow streets, booths decorated with flowers, and banners and screens painted with immense figures of josses diverted the eye; while bands of musicians in gaudy silks, shrilled and banged, piped and fluted.

Everybody seemed to be out of doors—men, women, and children—and nearly all were in holiday attire. A couple of priests, in vivid scarlet and yellow robes, were kowtowing before an altar covered with a rich cloth, embroidered in white and silver. Some Chinese students from the University of California stood looking on with comprehending, half-scornful interest; three girls lavishly dressed in colored silks, with their black hair plastered back from their faces and heavily bejeweled behind, chirped and chattered in a gilded balcony above them like birds in a cage. Little children, their hands full of half-moon-shaped cakes, were pattering about, with eyes, for all the hour, as bright as stars.

Chinatown was celebrating the Harvest Moon Festival, and Adah Charlton was glad that she had an opportunity to see something of the celebration before she returned East. Mrs. Dean, familiar with the Chinese people and the mazes of Chinatown, led her around fearlessly, pointing out this and that object of interest and explaining to her its meaning. Seeing that it was a gala night, she had abandoned her idea of calling upon the Chinese friend.

Just as they turned a corner leading up to the street where Wou Sankwei's place of business and residence was situated, a pair of little hands grasped Mrs. Dean's skirt and a delighted little voice piped: "See me! See me!" It was little Yen, resplendent in mauve-colored pantaloons and embroidered vest and cap. Behind him was a tall man who both women recognized.

"How do you happen to have Yen with you?" Adah asked.

"His father handed him over to me as a sort of guide, counselor, and friend. The little fellow is very amusing."

"See over here," interrupted Yen. He hopped over the alley to where the priests stood by the altar. The grown people followed him.

"What is that man chanting?" asked Adah. One of the priests had mounted a table, and with arms outstretched toward the moon sailing high in the heavens, seemed to be making some sort of an invocation.

Her friend listened for some moments before replying:

"It is a sort of apotheosis of the moon. I have heard it on a like occasion in Hankow, and the Chinese *bonze* who officiated gave me a translation. I almost know it by heart. May I repeat it to you?"

Mrs. Dean and Yen were examining the screen with the big josses.

"Yes, I should like to hear it," said Adah.

"Then fix your eyes upon Diana."

"Dear and lovely moon, as I watch thee pursuing thy solitary course o'er the silent heavens, heart-easing thoughts steal o'er me and calm my passionate soul. Thou art so sweet, so serious, so serene, that thou causest me to forget the stormy emotions which crash like jarring discords across the harmony of life, and bringest to my memory a voice scarce ever heard amidst the warring of the world—love's low voice.

"Thou art so peaceful and so pure that it seemeth as if naught false or ignoble could dwell beneath thy gentle radiance, and that earnestness—even the earnestness of genius—must glow within the bosom of him on whose head thy beams fall like blessings.

"The magic of thy sympathy disburtheneth me of many sorrows and thoughts, which like the songs of the sweetest sylvan singer, are two dear and sacred for the careless ears of day, gush forth with unconscious eloquence when thou art the only listener.

"Dear and lovely moon, there are some who say that those who dwell in the sunlit fields of reason should fear to wander through the moonlit valleys of imagination; but I, who have ever been a pilgrim and a stranger in the realm of the wise, offer to thee the homage of a heart which appreciates that thou graciously shinest—even on the fool."

"Is that really Chinese?" queried Adah.

"No doubt about it—in the main. Of course, I cannot swear to it word for word."

"I should think that there would be some reference to the fruits of the earth—the harvest. I always understood that the Chinese religion was so practical."

"Confucianism is. But the Chinese mind requires two religions. Even the most commonplace Chinese has yearnings for something above everyday life. Therefore, he combines with his Confucianism, Buddism—or, in this country, Christianity."

"Thank you for the information. It has given me a key to the mind of a certain Chinese in whom Auntie and I are interested."

"And who is this particular Chinese in whom you are interested?"

"The father of the little boy who is with us tonight."

"Wou Sankwei! Why, here he comes with Lee Tong Hay. Are you acquainted with Lee Tong Hay?"

"No, but I believe Aunt is. Plays and sings in vaudeville, doesn't he?"

"Yes; he can turn himself into a German, a Scotchman, an Irishman, or an American, with the greatest of ease, and is as natural in each character as he is as a Chinaman. Hello, Lee Tong Hay."

"Hello, Mr. Stimson."

When her friend was talking to the lively young Chinese who had answered his greeting, Adah went over to where Wou Sankwei stood speaking to Mrs. Dean.

"Yen begins school next week," said her aunt, drawing her arm within her own. It was time to go home.

Adah made no reply. She was settling her mind to do something quite out of the ordinary. Her aunt often called her romantic and impractical. Perhaps she was.

VI

"Auntie went out of town this morning," said Adah Charlton. "I phoned for you to come up, Sankwei, because I wished to have a personal and private talk with you."

"Any trouble, Miss Adah?" inquired the young merchant. "Anything I can do for you?"

Mrs. Dean often called upon him to transact little business matters for her or to consult with him on various phases of her social and family life.

"I don't know what I would do without Sankwei's head to manage for me," she often said to her niece.

"No," replied the girl, "you do too much for us. You always have ever since I've known you. It's a shame for us to have allowed you."

"What are you talking about, Miss Adah? Since I came to America your aunt has made this house like a home to me, and of course, I take an interest in it and like to do anything for it that a man can. I am always happy when I come here."

"Yes, I know you are, poor old boy," said Adah to herself.

Aloud she said: "I have something to say to you which I would like you to hear. Will you listen, Sankwei?"

"Of course I will," he answered.

"Well then," went on Adah, "I asked you to come here today because I have heard that there is trouble at your house and that your wife is jealous of you."

"Would you please not talk about that, Miss Adah. It is a matter which you cannot understand."

"You promised to listen and heed. I do understand, even though I cannot speak to your wife nor find out what she feels and thinks. I know you, Sankwei, and I can see just how the trouble has arisen. As soon as I heard that your wife was jealous I knew why she was jealous."

"Why?" he queried.

"Because," she answered unflinchingly, "you are thinking far too much of other women."

"Too much of other women?" echoed Sankwei dazedly. "I did not know that."

"No, you didn't. That is why I am telling you. But you are, Sankwei. And you are becoming too Americanized. My aunt encourages you to become so, and she is a good woman with the best and highest motives; but we are all liable to make mistakes, and it is a mistake to try and make a Chinese man into an American—

if he has a wife who is to remain as she always has been. It would be different if you were not married and were a man free to advance. But you are not."

"What am I to do then, Miss Adah? You say that I think too much of other women besides her, and that I am too much Americanized. What can I do about it now that it is so?"

"First of all you must think of your wife. She has done for you what no American woman would do—came to you to be your wife, love you and serve you without even knowing you—took you on trust altogether. You must remember that for many years she was chained in a little cottage to care for your ailing and aged mother—a hard task indeed for a young girl. You must remember that you are the only man in the world to her, and that you have always been the only one that she has ever cared for. Think of her during all the years you are here, living a lonely, hard-working life—a baby and an old woman her only companions. For this, she had left all her own relations. No American woman would have sacrificed herself so.

"And, now, what has she? Only you and her housework. The white woman reads, plays, paints, attends concerts, entertainments, lectures, absorbs herself in the work she likes, and in the course of her life thinks of and cares for a great many people. She has much to make her happy besides her husband. The Chinese woman has him only."

"And her boy."

"Yes, her boy," repeated Adah Charlton, smiling in spite of herself, but lapsing into seriousness the moment after. "There's another reason for you to drop the American for a time and go back to being a Chinese. For the sake of your darling little boy, you and your wife should live together kindly and cheerfully. That is much more important for his welfare than that he should go to the American school and become Americanized."

"It is my ambition to put him through both American and Chinese schools."

"But what he needs most of all is a loving mother."

"She loves him all right."

"Then why do you not love her as you should? If I were married I would not think my husband loved me very much if he preferred spending his evenings in the society of other women than in mine, and was so much more polite and deferential to other women than he was to me. Can't you understand now why your wife is jealous?"

Wou Sankwei stood up.

"Goodbye," said Adah Charlton, giving him her hand.

"Goodbye," said Wou Sankwei.

Had he been a white man, there is no doubt that Adah Charlton's little lecture would have had a contrary effect from what she meant it to have. At least, the lectured would have been somewhat cynical as to her sincerity. But Wou Sankwei was not a white man. He was a Chinese and did not see any reason for insincerity in a matter as important as that which Adah Charleton had brought before him. He felt himself exiled from Paradise, yet it did not occur to him to question, as a white man would have done, whether the angel with the flaming sword had authority for her action. Neither did he lay the blame for things gone wrong upon any woman. He simply made up his mind to make the best of what was.

VIII

It has been a peaceful week in the Wou household —the week before little Yen was to enter the American school. So peaceful indeed that Wou Sankwei had begun to think that his wife was reconciled to his wishes with regard to the boy. He whistled softly as he whittled away at the little ship he was making for him. Adah Charlton's suggestions had set coursing a train of thought which had curved around Pau Lin so closely that he had decided that, should she offer any further opposition to the boy's attending the American school, he would not insist upon it. After all, though the American language might be useful during this century, the wheel of the world would turn again, and then it might not be necessary at all. Who could tell? He came very near to expressing himself thus to Pau Lin.

And now it was the evening before the morning that little Yen was to march away to the American school. He had been excited all day over the prospect, and to calm him, his father finally told him to read aloud a little story from the Chinese book which he had given him on his first birthday in America and which he had taught him to read. Obediently the little fellow drew his stool to his mother's side and read in his childish sing-song the story of an irreverent lad who came to great grief because he followed after the funeral of his grand-father and regaled himself on the crisply roasted chickens and loose-skinned oranges which were left on the grave for the feasting of the spirit.

Wou Sankwei laughed heartily over the story. It reminded him of some of his own boyish escapades. But Pau Lin stroked silently the head of the little reader, and seemed lost in reverie.

A whiff of fresh salt air blew in from the Bay. The mother shivered, and Wou Sankwei, looking up from the fastening of the boat's rigging, bade Yen close the door. As the little fellow came back to his mother's side, he stumbled over her knee.

"Oh, poor mother!" he exclaimed with quaint apology. "'Twas the stupid feet, not Yen."

"So," she replied, curling her arm around his neck, "'tis always the feet. They are to the spirit as the cocoon to the butterfly. Listen, and I will sing you the song of the Happy Butterfly."

She began singing the old Chinese ditty in a fresh birdlike voice. Wou Sankwei, listening, was glad to hear her. He liked having everyone around him cheerful and happy. That had been the charm of the Dean household.

The ship was finished before the little family retired. Yen examined it, critically at first, then exultingly. Finally, he carried it away and placed it carefully in the closet where he kept his kites, balls, tops, and other treasures. "We will set sail with it tomorrow after school," said he to his father, hugging gratefully that father's arm.

Sankwei rubbed the little round head. The boy and he were great chums.

What was that sound which caused Sankwei to start from his sleep? It was just on the border land of night and day, and unusual time for Pau Lin to be up. Yet, he could hear her voice in Yen's room. He raised himself on his elbow and listened. She was softly singing a nursery song about some little squirrels and a huntsman. Sankwei wondered at her singing in that way at such an hour. From where he lay he could just perceive the child's cot and the silent child figure lying motionless in the dim light. How very motionless! In a moment Sankwei was beside it.

The empty cup with its dark dregs told the tale.

The thing he loved the best in all the world—the darling son who had crept into his heart with his joyousness and beauty—had been taken from him—by her who had given.

Sankwei reeled against the wall. The kneeling figure by the cot arose. The face of her was solemn and tender.

"He is saved," smiled she, "from the Wisdom of the New."

In grief too bitter for words the father bowed his head upon his hands.

"Why! Why!" queried Pau Lin, gazing upon him bewilderedly. "The child is happy. The butterfly mourns not o'er the shed cocoon."

Sankwei put up his shutters and wrote this note to Adah Charlton:

I have lost my boy through an accident. I am returning to China with my wife whose health requires a change.

(1912)

The Foreigner

Amy Lowell

Have at you, you Devils!
 My back's to this tree,
For you're nothing so nice
 That the hind-side of me
Would escape your assault.
 Come on now, all three!

Here's a dandified gentleman,
 Rapier at point,
And a wrist which whirls round
 Like a circular joint.
A spatter of blood, man!
 That's just to anoint

And make supple your limbs.
 'Tis a pity the silk
Of your waistcoat is stained.
 Why! Your heart's full of milk,
And so full, it spills over!
 I'm not of your ilk.

You said so, and laughed
 At my old-fashioned hose,
At the cut of my hair,
 At the length of my nose.
To carve it to pattern
 I think you propose.

Your pardon, young Sir,
 But my nose and my sword
Are proving themselves
 In quite perfect accord.
I grieve to have spotted
 Your shirt. On my word!

And hullo! You Bully!
 That blade's not a stick

To slash right and left,
  And my skull is too thick
To be cleft with such cuffs
  Of a sword. Now a lick

Down the side of your face,
  What a pretty, red line!
Tell the taverns that scar
  Was an honor. Don't whine
That a stranger has marked you.
  The tree's there, You Swine!

Did you think to get in
  At the back, while your friends
Made a little diversion
  In front? So it ends,
With your sword clattering down
  On the ground. 'Tis amends

I make for your courteous
  Reception of me,
A foreigner, landed
  From over the sea
Your welcome was fervent,
  I think you'll agree.

My shoes are not buckled
  With gold, nor my hair
Oiled and scented; my jacket's
  Not satin, I wear
Corded breeches, wide hats,
  And I make people stare!

So I do, but my heart
  Is the heart of a man,
And my thoughts cannot twirl
  In the limited span
'Twixt my head and my heels,
  As some other men's can.

I have business more strange
  Than the shape of my boots,
And my interests range
  From the sky, to the roots

Of this dung-hill you live in,
　　You half-rotted shoots

Of a mouldering tree!
　　Here's at you, once more.
You Apes! You Jack-fools!
　　You can show me the door,
And jeer at my ways,
　　But you're pinked to the core.

And before I have done,
　　I will prick my name in
With the front of my steel,
　　And your lily-white skin
Shall be printed with me.
　　For I've come here to win!

(1914)

America

Claude McKay

Although she feeds me bread of bitterness,
And sinks into my throat her tiger's tooth,
Stealing my breath of life, I will confess
I love this cultured hell that tests my youth!
Her vigor flows like tides into my blood,
Giving me strength erect against her hate.
Her bigness sweeps my being like a flood.
Yet as a rebel fronts a king in state,
I stand within her walls with not a shred
Of terror, malice, not a word of jeer.
Darkly I gaze into the days ahead,
And see her might and granite wonders there,
Beneath the touch of Time's unerring hand,
Like priceless treasures sinking in the sand.

(1921)

Dead Are My People

Kahlil Gibran
(Written in exile during the famine in Syria)

World War I

Gone are my people, but I exist yet,
Lamenting them in my solitude . . .
Dead are my friends, and in their
Death my life is naught but great
Disaster.

The knolls of my country are submerged
By tears and blood, for my people and
My beloved are gone, and I am here
Living as I did when my people and my
Beloved were enjoying life and the
Bounty of life, and when the hills of
My country were blessed and engulfed
By the light of the sun.

My people died from hunger, and he who
Did not perish from starvation was
Butchered with the sword; and I am
Here in this distant land, roaming
Amongst a joyful people who sleep
Upon soft beds, and smile at the days
While the days smile upon them.

What can an exiled son do for his
Starving people, and of what value
Unto them is the lamentation of an
Absent poet?

Were I an ear of corn grown in the earth
Of my country, the hungry child would
Pluck me and remove with my kernels
The hand of Death from his soul. Were
I a ripe fruit in the gardens of my
Country, the starving woman would

Gather me and sustain life. Were I
A bird flying in the sky of my country,
My hungry brother would hunt me and
Remove with the flesh of my body the
Shadow of the grave from his body.
But alas! I am not an ear of corn
Grown in the plains of Syria, nor a
Ripe fruit in the valley of Lebanon;
This is my disaster, and this is my
Mute calamity which brings humiliation
Before my soul and before the phantoms
Of the night . . . This is the painful
Tragedy which tightens my tongue and
Pinions my arms and arrests me usurped
Of power and of will and of action.
This is the curse burned upon my
Forehead before God and man.

And often they say to me,
"The disaster of your country is
Nothing to the calamity of the
World, and the tears and blood shed
By your people are as nothing to
The rivers of blood and tears
Pouring each day and night in the
Valleys and plains of the earth . . ."

Yes, but the death of my people is
A silent accusation; it is a crime
Conceived by the head of the unseen
Serpents . . . It is a songless and
Sceneless tragedy . . . And if my
People had attacked the despots
And oppressors and died as rebels,
I would have said, "Dying for
Freedom is nobler than living in
The shadow of weak submission, for
He who embraces death with the sword
Of Truth in his hand will eternalize
With the Eternity of Truth, for Life
Is weaker than Death and Death is
Weaker than Truth."

If my nation had partaken in the war
Of all nations and had died in the
Field of battle, I would say that
The raging tempest had broken with
Its might the green branches; and
Strong death under the canopy of
The tempest is nobler than slow
Perishment in the arms of senility.
But there was no rescue from the
Closing jaws . . . My people dropped
And wept with the crying angels.

If an earthquake had torn my
Country asunder and the earth had
Engulfed my people into its bosom,
I would have said, "A great and
Mysterious law has been moved by
The will of divine force, and it
Would be pure madness if we frail
Mortals endeavored to probe its
Deep secrets . . ."
By my people did not die as rebels;
They were not killed in the field
Of battle; nor did the earthquake
Shatter my country and subdue them.
Death was their only rescuer, and
Starvation their only spoils.

My people and your people, my Syrian
Brother, are dead . . . What can be
Done for those who are dying? Our
Lamentations will not satisfy their
Hunger, and our tears will not quench
Their thirst; what can we do to save
Them from between the iron paws of
Hunger? My brother, the kindness
Which compels you to give a part of
Your life to any human who is in the
Shadow of losing his life is the only
Virtue which makes you worthy of the
Light of day and the peace of the
Night . . . Remember, my brother,

That the coin which you drop into
The withered hand stretching toward
You is the only golden chain that
Binds your rich heart to the
Loving heart of God . . .

(1916)

Translated by Anthony Rizcallah Ferris

A Simple Act of Piety

Achmed Abdullah

His affair that night was prosy. He was intending the murder of an old Spanish woman around the corner, on the Bowery, whom he had known for years, with whom he had always exchanged courteous greetings, and whom he neither liked nor disliked.*

He did kill her; and she knew that he was going to the minute he came into her stuffy, smelly shop, looming tall and bland, and yellow, and unearthly Chinese from behind the shapeless bundles of secondhand goods that cluttered the doorway. He wished her good evening in tones that were silvery, but seemed tainted by something unnatural. She was uncertain what it was, and this very uncertainty increased her horror. She felt her hair rise as if drawn by a shivery wind.

At the very last she caught a glimmer of the truth in his narrow-lidded, purple-black eyes. But it was too late.

The lean, curved knife was in his hand and across her scraggy throat—there was a choked gurgle, a crimson line broadening to a crimson smear, a thudding fall—and that was the end of the affair as far as she was concerned.

A minute later Nag Hong Fah walked over to the other end of Pell Street and entered a liquor store which belonged to the Chin Sor Company, and was known as the "Place of Sweet Desire and Heavenly Entertainment." It was the gathering place for the Chinese-born members of the Nag family, and there he occupied a seat of honor because of his wealth and charity and stout rectitude.

He talked for about half an hour with the other members of his clan, sipping fragrant, sun-dried Formosa tea mixed with jessamine flowers, until he had made for himself a bulletproof alibi.

The alibi held.

For he is still at liberty. He is often heard to speak with regret—nor is it hypocritical regret—about the murder of Señora Garcia, the old Spanish woman who kept the shop around the corner. He is a good customer of her nephew, Carlos, who succeeded to her business. Nor does he trade there to atone, in a manner, for the red deed of his hands, but because the goods are cheap.

He regrets nothing. To regret, you must find sin in your heart, while the murder of Señora Garcia meant no sin to him. It was to him a simple action, respectable, even worthy.

Bowery: Neighborhood in southern Manhattan; a culturally vibrant area in the nineteenth century, the Bowery was a struggling, impoverished neighborhood in the early twentieth century.

For he was a Chinaman, and although it all happened between the choco-late-brown of the Hudson and the murky, cloudy gray of the North River, the tale is of the Orient. There is about it an atmosphere of age-green bronze; of first-chop chandoo and spicy aloewood; of gilt, carved statues brought out of India when Confucius was young; of faded embroideries, musty with the scent of the dead centuries. An atmosphere which is very sweet, very gentle—and very unhuman.

The Elevated roars above. The bluecoat shuffles his flat feet on the greasy as-phalt below. But still the tale is of China—and the dramatic climax, in a Chinaman's story, from a Chinaman's slightly twisted angle, differs from that of an American.

To Nag Hong Fah this climax came not with the murder of Señora Garcia, but with Fanny Mei Hi's laugh as she saw him with the shimmering bauble in his hands and heard his appraisal thereof.

She was his wife, married to him honorably and truly with a narrow gold band and a clergyman and a bouquet of wired roses bought cheaply from an itinerant Greek vendor, and handfuls of rice thrown by facetious and drunken members of both the yellow race and the white.

Of course, at the time of his marriage, a good many people around Pell Street whispered and gossiped. They spoke of the curling black smoke and slavery and other gorgeously, romantically wicked things. Miss Edith Rutter, the social settlement investigator, spoke of—and to—the police.

Whereas Nag Hong Fah, who had both dignity and a sense of humor, in-vited them all to his house: gossipers, whisperers, Miss Edith Rutter, and Detective Bill Devoy of the Second Branch, and bade them look to their hearts' content; and whereas they found no opium, no sliding panels, and hidden cupboards, no dread Mongol mysteries, but a neat little steam heated flat, fur-nished by Grand Rapids via Fourteenth Street, German porcelain, a case of blond Milwaukee beer, a five-pound humidor of shredded Kentucky burlap tobacco, a victrola, and a fine, big Bible with brass clamp and edges and M. Doré's illustrations.

"Call again," he said as they were trooping down the narrow stairs. "Call again any time you please. Glad to have you—aren't we, kid?" chucking his wife under the chin.

"You bet yer life, you fat old yellow sweetness!" agreed Fanny; and then—as a special barbed shaft leveled at Miss Rutter's retreating back: "Say! Any time yer wanta lamp my wedding certificate—it's hangin' between the fottygraphs of the President and the Big Boss—all framed up swell!"

He had met her first one evening in a Bowery saloon, where she was in-troduced to him by Mr. Brian Neill, the owner of the saloon, a gentleman from out the County Armagh, who had spattered and muddied his proverbial Irish chastity in the slime of the Bowery gutters, and who called himself her uncle.

This latter statement had to be taken with a grain of salt. For Fanny Mei Hi was not Irish. Her hair was golden, her eyes blue. But otherwise she was Chinese. Easily nine-tenths of her. Of course she denied it. But that is neither here nor there.

She was not a lady. Couldn't be—don't you see—with that mixed blood in her veins, Mr. Brian Neill acting as her uncle, and the standing pools of East Side vice about her.

But Nag Hong Fah, who was a poet and a philosopher, besides being the proprietor of the Great Shanghai Chop Suey Palace, said that she looked like a golden-haired goddess of evil, familiar with all the seven sins. And he added—this to the soothsayer of his clan, Nag Hop Fat—that he did not mind her having seven, nor seventeen nor seven times seventeen bundles of sin, as long as she kept them in the sacred bosom of the Nag family.

"Yes," said the soothsayer, throwing up a handful of painted ivory sticks and watching how they fell to see if the omens were favorable. "Purity is a jewel to the silly young. And you are old, honorable cousin—"

"Indeed," chimed in Nag Hong Fah, "I am old and fat and sluggish and extremely wise. What price is there in purity higher than there is contained in the happiness and contentment of a respectable citizen when he sees menchildren playing gently about his knees?"

He smiled when his younger brother, Nag Sen Yat, the opium merchant, spoke to him of a certain Yung Quai.

"Yung Quai is beautiful," said the opium merchant "and young—and of an honorable clan—and—"

"And childless! And in San Francisco! And divorced from me!"

"But there is her older brother, Yung Long, the head of the Yung clan. He is powerful and rich—the richest man in Pell Street! He would consider this new marriage of yours a disgrace to his face. Chiefly since the woman is a foreigner!"

"She is not. Only her hair and her eyes are foreign."

"Where hair and eyes lead, the call of the blood follows," rejoined Nag Sen Yat, and he reiterated his warning about Yung Long.

But the other shook his head.

"Do not give wings to trouble. It flies swiftly without them," he quoted. "Too, the soothsayer read in the painted sticks that Fanny Mei Hi will bear me sons. One—perhaps two. Afterward, if indeed it be so that the drop of barbarian blood has clouded the clear mirror of her Chinese soul, I can always take back into my household the beautiful and honorable Yung Quai, whom I divorced and sent to California because she is childless. She will then adopt the sons which the other woman will bear me—and everything will be extremely satisfactory."

And so he put on his best American suit, called on Fanny, and proposed to her with a great deal of dignity and elaborate phrases.

"Sure I'll marry you," said Fanny. "Sure! I'd rather be the wife of the fattest, yellowest Chink in New York than live the sorta life I'm livin'—see, Chinkie-Toodles?"

"Chinkie-Toodles" smiled. He looked her over approvingly. He said to himself that doubtless the painted sticks had spoken the truth, that she would bear him men-children. His own mother had been a river-girl, purchased during a drought for a handful of parched grain; and had died in the odor of sanctity, with nineteen Buddhist priests following her gaily lacquered coffin, wagging their shaven polls ceremoniously, and mumbling flattering and appropriate verses from "Chin-Kong-Ching."

Fanny, on the other hand, though wickedly and lyingly insisting on her pure white blood, knew that a Chinaman is broadminded and free handed, that he makes a good husband, and beats his wife rather less often than a white man of the corresponding scale of society.

Of course, gutter bred, she was aggressively insistent upon her rights.

"Chinkie-Toodles," she said the day before the wedding, and the gleam in her eyes gave point to the words, "I'm square—see? An' I'm goin' to travel square. Maybe I haven't always been a poifec' lady, but I ain't goin' to bilk yer, get me? But—" She looked up, and suddenly, had Nag Hong Fah known it, the arrogance, the clamorings, and the tragedy of her mixed blood were in the words that followed: "I gotta have a dose of freedom. I'm an American—I'm white—say!"— seeing the smile which he hid rapidly behind his fat hand—"yer needn't laugh. I *am* white, an' not a painted Chinese doll. No sittin' up an' mopin' for the retoin of my fat, yellow lord an' master in a stuffy, stinky, punky five-by-four cage for me! In other woids, I resoive for my little golden-haired self the freedom of asphalt an' electric lights, see? An' I'll play square—as long as you'll play square," she added under her breath.

"Sure," he said. "You are free. Why not? I am an American. Have a drink?" And they sealed the bargain in a tumbler of Chinese rice whisky, cut with Bourbon, and flavored with aniseed and powdered ginger.

The evening following the wedding, husband and wife, instead of a honeymoon trip, went on an alcoholic spree amid the newly varnished splendors of their Pell Street flat. Side by side, in spite of the biting December cold, they leaned from the open window and brayed an intoxicated paean at the Elevated structure which pointed at the stars like a gigantic icicle stood on end, frozen, austere—desolate, for all its clank and rattle, amid the fragrant warm reek of China which drifted from shutters and cellar gratings.

Nag Hong Fah, seeing Yung Long crossing the street, thought with drunken sentimentality of Yung Long's sister whom he had divorced because she had borne him no children, and extended a boisterous invitation to come up.

"Come! Have a drink!" he hiccupped.

Yung Long stopped, looked, and refused courteously, but not before he had leveled a slow, appraising glance at the golden-haired Mei Hi, who was shouting by the side of her obese lord. Yung Long was not a bad looking man, standing there in the flickering light of the streetlamp, the black shadows cutting the pale yellow, silky sheen of his narrow, powerful face as clean as with a knife.

"Swell looker, that Chink!" commented Fanny Mei Hi as Yung Long walked away; and her husband, the liquor warming his heart into generosity, agreed:

"Sure! Swell looker! Lots of money! Let's have another drink!"

Arrived at the sixth tumbler, Nag Hong Fah, the poet in his soul released by alcohol, took his blushing bride upon his knee and improvised a neat Cantonese love ditty; but when Fanny awakened the next morning with the sobering suspicion that she had tied herself for life to a drunkard, she found out that her suspicion was unfounded.

The whisky spree had only been an appropriate celebration in honor of the man-child on whom Nag Hong Fah had set his heart; and it was because of this unborn son and the unborn son's future that her husband rose from his tumbled couch, bland, fat, without headache or heartache, left the flat, and bargained for an hour with Yung Long, who was a wholesale grocer, with warehouses in Canton, Manila, New York, San Francisco, Seattle, and Vancouver, British Columbia.

Not a word was said about either Yung Quai or Fanny. The talk dealt entirely with canned bamboo sprouts and preserved leeches, and pickled star-fruit, and brittle almond cakes. It was only after the price had been decided upon and duly sealed with the right phrases and palm touching palm—afterwards, though nothing in writing had passed, neither party could recede from the bargain without losing face—that Yung Long remarked,

"By the way, the terms are cash—spot cash," and he smiled.

For he knew that the restaurant proprietor was an audacious merchant who relied on long credits and future profits, and to whom in the past he had always granted ninety days' leeway without question or special agreement.

Nag Hong Fah smiled in his turn; a slow, thin, enigmatic smile.

"I brought the cash with me," he replied, pulling a wad of greenbacks from his pocket, and both gentlemen looked at each other with a great deal of mutual respect.

"Forty-seven dollars and thirty-three cents saved on the first business of my married life," Nag Hong Fah said to his assembled clan that night at the Place of Sweet Desire and Heavenly Entertainment. "Ah, I shall have a fine, large business to leave to the man-child which my wife shall bear me!"

And the man-child came—golden-haired, blue-eyed, yellow-skinned, and named Brian in honor of Fanny's apocryphal uncle who owned the Bowery saloon. For the christening Nag Hong Fah sent out special invitations—pink cards lettered with virulent magenta, and bordered with green forget-me-nots and purple roses, with an advertisement of the Great Shanghai Chop Suey

Palace on the reverse side. He also bestowed upon his wife a precious bracelet of cloudy white jade, earrings of green jade cunningly inlaid with blue feathers, a chest of carved Tibetan soapstone, a bottle of French perfume, a pound of Mandarin blossom tea for which he paid seventeen dollars wholesale, a set of red Chinese sables, and a new Caruso record for the victrola.

Fanny liked the last two best; chiefly the furs, which she wore through the whirling heat of an August day, as soon as she was strong enough to leave her couch, on an expedition to her native pavements. For she held fast to her proclaimed right that hers was the freedom of asphalt and electric light—not to mention the back parlor of her uncle's saloon, with its dingy, musty walls covered with advertisements of eminent Kentucky distilleries and the indelible traces of many generations of flies, with its gangrened tables, its battered cuspidors, its commingling atmosphere of poverty and sloth, of dust and stale beer, of cheese sandwiches, wet weeds, and cold cigars.

"Getta hell outa here!" she admonished a red-powdered bricklayer who came staggering across the threshold of the back parlor and was trying to encircle her waist with amatory intent. "I'm a respectable married woman—see?" And then to Miss Ryan, the sidekick of her former riotous spinster days, who was sitting at a corner table dipping her pretty little upturned nose into a foaming schooner: "Take my tip, Mamie, an' marry a Chink! That's the life, believe me!"

Mamie shrugged her shoulders.

"All right for you, Fan, I guess," she replied. "But not for me. Y' see—ye're mostly Chink yerself—"

"I ain't! I ain't! I'm white—wottya mean callin' me a Chink?" And then, seeing signs of contrition on her friend's face: "Never mind. Chinkie-Toodles is good enough for me. He treats me white, all right, all right!"

Nor was this an overstatement of the actual facts.

Nag Hong Fah was good to her. He was happy in the realization of his fatherhood, advertised every night by lusty cries which reverberated through the narrow, rickety Pell Street house to find an echo across the street in the liquor store of the Chin Sor Company, where the members of his clan predicted a shining future for father and son.

The former was prospering. The responsibilities of fatherhood had brought an added zest and tang to his keen, bartering Mongol brain. Where before he had squeezed the dollar, he was now squeezing the cent. He had many a hard tussle with the rich Yung Long over the price of tea and rice and other staples, and never did either one of them mention the name of Yung Quai, nor that of the woman who had supplanted Yung Quai in the restaurant keeper's affections.

Fanny was honest. She traveled the straight and narrow, as she put it to herself. "Nor ain't it any strain on my feet," she confided to Miss Ryan. For she was happy and contented. Life, after all, had been good to her, had brought her prosperity and satisfaction at the hands of a fat Chinaman, at the end of her fantastic, twisted, unclean youth, and there were moments when, in spite of herself, she felt herself drawn into the surge of that Mongol race which had given her nine-tenths of her blood—a fact which formerly she had been in the habit of denying vigorously.

She laughed her happiness through the spiced, warm mazes of Chinatown, her firstborn cuddled to her breast, ready to be friends with everybody.

It was thus that Yung Long would see her walking down Pell Street as he sat in the carved window seat of his store, smoking his crimson-tassled pipe, a wandering ray of sun dancing through the window, breaking into prismatic colors, and wreathing his pale, serene face with opal vapors.

He never failed to wave his hand in courtly greeting.

She never failed to return the civility.

Some swell looker, that Chink. But—Gawd!—she was square, all right, all right!

A year later, after Nag Hong Fah, in expectation of the happy event, had acquired an option on a restaurant farther uptown, so that the second son might not be slighted in favor of Brian, who was to inherit the Great Shanghai Chop Suey Palace, Fanny sent another little crossbreed into the reek and riot of the Pell Street world. But when Nag Hong Fah came home that night, the nurse told him that the second-born was a girl—something to be entered on the debit, not the credit, side of the family ledger.

It was then that a change came into the marital relations of Mr. and Mrs. Nag Hong Fah.

Not that the former disliked the baby daughter, called Fanny, after the mother. Far from it. He loved her with a sort of slow, passive love, and he could be seen on an afternoon rocking the wee bundle in his stout arms and whispering to her, crooning Cantonese fairy-lilts: all about the god of small children whose face is a candied plum, so that the babes like to hug and kiss him and, of course, lick his face with their little pink tongues.

But this time there was no christening, no gorgeous magenta-lettered invitations sent to the chosen, no happy prophecies about the future.

This time there were no precious presents of green jade and white jade heaped on the couch of the young mother.

She noticed it. But she did not complain. She said to herself that her husband's new enterprise was swallowing all his cash; and one night she asked him how the new restaurant was progressing.

"What new restaurant?" he asked blandly.

"The one uptown, Toodles—for the baby—"

Nag Hong Fah laughed carelessly.

"Oh—I gave up that option. Didn't lose much."

Fanny sat up straight, clutching little Fanny to her.

"You—you gave it up?" she asked. "Wottya mean—gave it up?"

Then suddenly inspired by some whisper of suspicion, her voice leaping up extraordinarily strong: "You mean you gave it up—because—because little Fanny is—a *goil?*"

He agreed with a smiling nod.

"To be sure! A girl is fit only to bear children and clean the household pots."

He said it without any brutality, without any conscious male superiority; simply as a statement of fact. A melancholy fact, doubtless. But a fact, unchangeable, stony.

"But—but—" Fanny's gutter flow of words floundered in the eddy of her amazement, her hurt pride and vanity. "I'm a woman myself—an' I—"

"Assuredly you are a woman and you have done your duty. You have borne me a son. Perhaps, if the omens be favorable you will bear me yet another. But this—this girl—" He dismissed little Fanny with a wave of his pudgy, dimpled hand as a regrettable accident, and continued, soothingly: "She will be taken care of. Already I have written to friends of our clan in San Francisco to arrange for a suitable disposal when the baby has reached the right age." He said it in his mellow, precise English. He had learned it at a night school, where he had been the pride and honor of his class.

Fanny had risen. She left her couch. With a swish-swish of knitted bed slippers she loomed up on the ring of faint light shed by the swinging petroleum lamp in the center of the room. She approached her husband, the baby held close to her heart with her left hand, her right hand aimed at Nag Hong Fah's solid chest like a pistol. Her deep set, violet-blue eyes seemed to pierce through him.

But the Chinese blood in her veins—shrewd, patient—scotched the violence of her American passion, her American sense of loudly clamoring for right and justice and fairness. She controlled herself. The accusing hand relaxed and fell gently on the man's shoulder. She was fighting for her daughter, fighting for the drop of white blood in her veins, and it would not do to lose her temper.

"Looka here, Chinkie-Toodles," she said. "You call yerself a Christian, don't yer? A Christian an' an American. Well, have a heart. An' some sense! This ain't China, Toodles. Lil Fanny ain't goin' to be weighed an' sold to some rich brother Chink at so many seeds per pound. Not much! She's gonna be eddycated. She's gonna have her chance, see? She's gonna be independent of the male beast an' the sorta life wot the male beast likes to hand to a skoit. Believe me, Toodles, I know what I'm talkin' about!"

But he shook his stubborn head. "All has been settled," he replied. "Most satisfactorily settled!"

He turned to go. But she rushed up to him. She clutched his sleeve.

"Yer—yer don't mean it? Yer can't mean it!" she stammered.

"I do, fool!" He made a slight, weary gesture as if brushing away the incomprehensible. "You are a woman—you do not understand—"

"Don't I, though!"

She spoke through her teeth. Her words clicked and broke like dropping icicles. Swiftly her passion turned into stone, and as swiftly back again, leaping out in a great, spattering stream of abuse.

"Yer damned, yellow, stinkin' Chink! Yer—yer— Wottya mean—makin' me bear children—yer own children— an' then—" Little Fanny was beginning to howl lustily, and she covered her face with kisses. "Say kiddie, it's a helluva dad you've drawn! A helluva dad! Look at him—standin' there! Greasy an' yellow an'— Say—he's willin' to sell yer into slavery to some other beast of a Chink! Say—"

"You are a—ah—a Chink yourself, fool!"

"I ain't! I'm white—an' square—an' decent—an'—"

He lit a cigarette and smiled placidly, and suddenly she knew that it would be impossible to argue, to plead with him. Might as well plead with some sardonic, deaf immensity, without nerves, without heart. And then, womanlike, the greater wrong disappeared in the lesser.

"Ye're right. I'm part Chink myself—an' damned sorry for myself because of it! An' that's why I know why yer gave me no presents when lil Fanny was born. Because she's a girl! As if that was my fault, yer fat, sneerin' slob, yer! Yah! That's why yer gave me no presents—I know! I know what it means when a Chink don't give no presents to his wife when she gives boith to a child! Make me lose face—that's wottya call it, ain't it? An' I thought fer a while yer was savin' up the ducats to give lil Fanny a start in life!

"Well, yer got another guess comin'! Yer gonna do wot I tell yer, see? Yer gonna open up that there new restaurant uptown, an' yer gonna give me presents! A bracelet, that's what I want! None o' yer measly Chink jade, either; but the real thing, get me? Gold an' diamonds, see?" and she was still talking as he, unmoved, silent, smiling, left the room and went down the creaking stairs to find solace in the spiced cups of the Palace of Sweet Desire and Heavenly Entertainment.

She rushed up to the window and threw it wide. She leaned far out, her hair framing her face like a glorious, disordered aureole, her loose robe slipping from her gleaming shoulders, her violet eyes blazing fire and hatred.

She shouted at his fat, receding back:

"A bracelet, that's what I want! That's what I'm gonna get, see? Gold an' diamonds! Gold an' diamonds, yer yellow pig, yer!"

It was at that moment that Yung Long passed her house. He heard, looked up, and greeted her courteously, as was his wont. But this time he did not go straight on his way. He looked at her for several seconds, taking in the soft lines of her neck and shoulders, the small, pale oval of her face with the crimson of her broad, generous mouth, the white flash of her small, even teeth, and the blue, sombre orbit of her eyes. With the light of the lamp shining in back, a breeze rushing in front past the open window, the wide sleeves of her dressing gown fluttered like immense, rosy butterfly wings.

Instinctively she returned his gaze. Instinctively, straight through her rage and heartache, the old thought came to her mind:

Swell looker—that Chink!

And then, without realizing what she was doing, her lips had formed the thought into words:

"Swell looker!"

She said it in a headlong and vehement whisper that drifted down, through the whirling reek of Pell Street—sharp, sibilant, like a message.

Yung Long smiled, raised his neat bowler hat, and went on his way.

Night after night Fanny returned to the attack, cajoling, caressing, threatening, cursing.

"Listen here, Chinkie-Toodles—"

But she might as well have tried to argue with the sphinx for all the impression she made on her eternally smiling lord. He would drop his amorphous body into a comfortable rocker, moving it up and down with the tips of his felt-slippered feet, a cigarette hanging loosely from the right corner of his coarse, sagging lips, a cup of lukewarm rice whisky convenient to his elbow, and watch her as he might the gyrations of an exotic beetle whose wings had been burned off. She amused him. But after a while continuous repetition palled the amusement into monotony, and, correctly Chinese, he decided to make a formal complaint to Brian O'Neill, the Bowery saloonkeeper, who called himself her uncle.

Life, to that prodigal of Erin, was a rather sunny arrangement of small conveniences and small, pleasant vices. He laughed in his throat and called his "nephew" a damned, sentimental fool.

"Beat her up!" was his calm, matter-of-fact advice. "Give her a good old hiding, an' she'll feed outa yer hand, me lad!"

"I have—ah—your official permission, as head of her family?"

"Sure. Wait. I'll lend ye me blackthorn. She knows the taste of it."

Nag Hong Fah took both advice and blackthorn. That night he gave Fanny a severe beating and repeated the performance every night for a week until she subsided.

Once more she became the model wife, and happiness returned to the stout bosom of her husband. Even Miss Rutter, the social settlement investigator, commented upon it. "Real love is a shelter of inexpugnable peace," she said when she saw the Nag Hong Fah family walking down Pell Street, little Brian toddling on ahead, the baby cuddled in her mother's arms.

Generously Nag Hong Fah overlooked his wife's petty womanish vanities; and when she came home one afternoon, flushed, excited, exhibiting a shimmering bracelet that was encircling her wrist, "just imitation gold an' diamonds, Chinkie-Toodles!" she explained. "Bought it outa my savings—thought yer wouldn't mind, see? Thought it wouldn't hurt yer none if them Chinks here-abouts think it was the real dope an' yer gave it to me"—he smiled and took her upon his knee as of old.

"Yes, yes," he said, his pudgy hand fondling the intense golden gleam of her tresses. "It is all right. Perhaps—if you bear me another son—I shall give you a real bracelet, real gold, real diamonds. Meanwhile you may wear this bauble."

As before she hugged jealously her proclaimed freedom of asphalt and electric lights. Nor did he raise the slightest objections. He had agreed to it at the time of their marriage and, being a righteous man, he kept to his part of the bargain with serene punctiliousness.

Brian Neill, whom he chanced to meet one afternoon in Señora Garcia's secondhand emporium, told him it was all right.

"That beatin' ye gave her didn't do her any harm, me beloved nephew," he said. "She's square. God help the lad who tries to pass a bit o' blarney to her." He chuckled in remembrance of a Finnish sailor who had beaten a sudden and undignified retreat from the back parlor into the saloon, with a ragged scratch crimsoning his face and bitter words about the female of the species crowding his lips. "Faith, she's square! Sits there with her little glass o' gin an' her auld chum, Mamie Ryan—an' them two chews the rag by the hour—talkin' about frocks an' frills, I doubt not—"

Of course, once in a while she would return home a little the worse for liquor. But Nag Hong Fah, being a Chinaman, would mantle such small short-comings with the wide charity of his personal laxity.

"Better a drunken wife who cooks well and washes the children and keeps her tongue between her teeth than a sober wife who reeks with virtue and breaks the household pots," he said to Nag Hop Fat, the soothsayer. "Better an honorable pig than a cracked rose bottle."

"Indeed! Better a fleet mule than a hamstrung horse," the other wound up the pleasant round of Oriental metaphors, and he reinforced his opinion with a chosen and appropriate quotation from the "Fo-Sho-Hing-Tsan-King."

When late one night that winter, a high wind booming from the north and washing the snow-dusted Pell Street houses with its cutting blast, Fanny came home with a jag, a chill, and a hacking cough, and went down with pneumonia seven hours later, Nag Hong Fah was genuinely sorry. He turned the management of his restaurant over to his brother, Nag Sen Yat, and sat by his wife's bed, whispering words of encouragement, bathing her feverish forehead, changing her sheets, administering medicine, doing everything with fingers as soft and deft as a woman's.

Even after the doctor had told him three nights later that the case was hopeless and that Fanny would die—even after, as a man of constructive and practical brain, he had excused himself for a few minutes and had sat down in the back room to write a line to Yung Quai, his divorced wife in San

Francisco, bidding her hold herself in readiness and including a hundred dollars for transportation—he continued to treat Fanny Mei Hi with the utmost gentleness and patience.

Tossing on her hot pillows, she could hear him in the long watches of the night breathing faintly, clearing his throat cautiously so as not to disturb her; and on Monday morning—he had lifted her up and was holding her close to help her resist the frightful, hacking cough that was shaking her wasted frame—he told her that he had reconsidered about little Fanny.

"You are going to die," he said placidly, in a way, apologetically, "and it is fitting that your daughter should make proper obeisance to your departed spirit. A child's devotion is best stimulated by gratitude. And little Fanny shall be grateful to you. For she will go to a good American school and, to pay for it, I shall sell your possessions after you are dead. The white jade bracelet, the earrings of green jade, the red sables—they will bring over four thousand dollars. Even this little bauble"—he slipped the glittering bracelet from her thin wrist—"this, too, will bring a few dollars. Ten, perhaps twelve; I know a dealer of such trifles in Mott Street who—"

"Say!"

Her voice cut in, raucous, challenging. She had wriggled out of his arms. An opaque glaze had come over her violet-blue eyes. Her whole body trembled. But she pulled herself on her elbows with a terrible, straining effort, refusing the support of his ready hands.

"Say! How much did yer say this here bracelet's worth?"

He smiled gently. He did not want to hurt her woman's vanity. So he increased his first appraisal.

"Twenty dollars," he suggested. "Perhaps twenty-one. Do not worry. It shall be sold to the best advantage—for your little daughter—"

And then, quite suddenly, Fanny burst into laughter—gurgling laughter that shook her body, choked her throat, and leaped out in a stream of blood from her tortured lungs.

"Twenty dollars!" she cried. "Twenty-one! Say, you poor cheese, that bracelet alone'll pay for lil Fanny's eddycation. It's worth three thousand! It's real, real—gold an' diamonds! Gold an' diamonds! Yung Long gave it to me, yer poor fool!" And she fell back and died, a smile upon her face, which made her look like a sleeping child, wistful and perverse.

A day after his wife's funeral Nag Hong Fah, having sent a ceremonious letter, called on Yung Long in the latter's store. In the motley, twisted annals of Pell Street the meeting, in the course of time, has assumed the character of something epic, something Homeric, something almost religious. It is mentioned with pride by both the Nag and the Yung clans; the tale of it has drifted to the Pacific Coast; and even in far China wise men speak of it with a hush of reverence as they drift down the river on their painted houseboats in peach-blossom time.

ACHMED ABDULLAH • 155

Yung Long received his caller at the open door of his shop.

"Deign to enter first," he said, bowing.

Nag Hong Fah bowed still lower.

"How could I dare to?" he retorted, quoting a line from the "Book of Ceremonies and Exterior Demonstrations," which proved that the manner is the heart's inner feeling.

"*Please* deign to enter first," Yung Long emphasized and again the other gave the correct reply: "How should I dare?"

Then, after a final request, still protesting, he entered as he was bidden. The grocer followed, walked to the east side of the store and indicated the west side to his visitor as Chinese courtesy demands.

"Deign to choose your mat," he went on and, after several coy refusals, Nag Hong Fah obeyed again, sat down, and smiled gently at his host.

"A pipe?" suggested the latter.

"Thanks! A simple pipe of bamboo, please, with a plain bamboo mouthpiece and no ornaments!"

"No, no!" protested Yung Long. "You will smoke a precious pipe of jade with a carved amber mouthpiece and crimson tassels!"

He clapped his hands, whereupon one of his young cousins entered with a tray of nacre, supporting an opium lamp, pipes and needles and bowls, and horn and ivory boxes neatly arranged. A minute later the brown opium cube was sizzling over the open flame, the jade pipe was filled and passed to Nag Hong Fah, who inhaled the gray, acrid smoke with all the strength of his lungs, then returned the pipe to the boy, who refilled it and passed it to Yung Long.

For a while the two men smoked in silence—men of Pell Street, men of lowly trade, yet men at whose back three thousand years of unbroken racial history, racial pride, racial achievements, and racial calm, were sitting in a solemn, graven row—thus dignified men.

Yung Long was caressing his cheek with his right hand. The dying, crimson sunlight danced and glittered on his well-polished fingernails.

Finally he broke the silence.

"Your wife is dead," he said with a little mournful cadence at the end of the sentence.

"Yes." Nag Hong Fah inclined his head sadly; and after a short pause: "My friend, it is indeed reasonable to think that young men are fools, their brains hot and crimson with the blinding mists of passion, while wisdom and calm are the splendid attributes of older men—"

"Such as—you and I?"

"Indeed!" decisively.

Yung Long raised himself on his elbows. His oblique eyes flashed a scrutinizing look and the other winked a slow wink and remarked casually that a wise and old man must first peer into the nature of things, then widen his knowledge, then harden his will, then control the impulses of his heart, then entirely correct himself—then establish good order in his family.

"Truly spoken," agreed Yung Long. "Truly spoken, O wise and older brother! A family! A family needs the strength of a man and the soft obedience of a woman."

"Mine is dead," sighed Nag Hong Fah. "My household is upset. My children cry."

Yung Long slipped a little fan from his wide silken sleeves and opened it slowly.

"I have a sister," he said gently, "Yung Quai, a childless woman who once was your wife, O wise and older brother."

"A most honorable woman!" Nag Hong Fah shut his eyes and went on: "I wrote to her five days ago, sending her money for her railway fare to New York."

"Ah!" softly breathed the grocer; and there followed another silence.

Yung Long's young cousin was kneading, against the pipe, the dark opium cubes which the flame gradually changed into gold and amber.

"Please smoke," advised the grocer.

Nag Hong Fah had shut his eyes completely, and his fat face, yellow as old parchment, seemed to have grown indifferent, dull, almost sleepy.

Presently he spoke:

"Your honorable sister, Yung Quai, will make a most excellent mother for the children of my late wife."

"Indeed."

There was another silence, again broken by Nag Hong Fah. His voice held a great calmness, a gentle singsong, a bronze quality which was like the soft rubbing of an ancient temple gong; green with the patina of the swinging centuries.

"My friend," he said, "there is the matter of a shimmering bracelet given by you to my late wife—"

Yung Long looked up quickly; then down again as he saw the peaceful expression on the other's bland features and heard him continue:

"For a while I misunderstood. My heart was blinded. My soul was seared with rage. I—I am ashamed to own up to it—I harbored harsh feelings against you. Then I considered that you were the older brother of Yung Quai and a most honorable man. I considered that in giving the bracelet to my wife you doubtless meant to show your appreciation for me, your friend, her husband. Am I not right?"

Yung Long had filled his lungs with another bowlful of opium smoke. He was leaning back, both shoulders on the mat so as the better to dilate his chest and to keep his lungs filled all the longer with the fumes of the kindly philosophic drug.

"Yes," he replied after a minute or two. "Your indulgent lips have pronounced words full of harmony and reason. Only—there is yet another trifling matter."

"Name it. It shall be honorably solved."

Yung Long sat up and fanned himself slowly.

"At the time when I arranged a meeting with the mother of your children," he said, "so as to speak to her of my respectful friendship for you and to bestow upon her a shimmering bracelet in proof of it, I was afraid of the wagging, leaky tongues of Pell Street. I was afraid of scandal and gossip. I therefore met your wife in the back room of Señora Garcia's store, on the Bowery. Since then I have come to the conclusion that perhaps I acted foolishly. For the foreign woman may have misinterpreted my motives. She may talk, thus causing you as well as me to lose face, and besmirching the departed spirit of your wife. What sayeth the 'Li-Ki'? 'What is whispered in the private apartments must not be shouted outside.' Do you not think that this foreign woman should—ah—"

Nag Hong Fah smiled affectionately upon the other.

"You have spoken true words, O wise and older brother," he said rising. "It is necessary for your and my honor, as well as for the honor of my wife's departed spirit, that the foreign woman should not wag her tongue. I shall see to it tonight." He waved a fat, deprecating hand. "Yes—yes. I shall see to it. It is a simple act of family piety—but otherwise without much importance."

And he bowed, left the store, and returned to his house to get his lean knife.

(1918)

I Dreamt I Was a Donkey-Boy Again

Ameen Rihani

I dreamt I was a donkey-boy again.

Out on the sun-swept roads of Baalbek, I tramp behind my burro, trailing my
mulayiah.

At noon, I pass by a garden redolent of mystic scents and tarry awhile.

Under an orange tree, on the soft green grass, I stretch my limbs. The daisies,
the anemones, and the cyclamens are round me pressing:

The anemone buds hold out to me their precious rubies; the daisies kiss me in
the eyes and lips; and the cyclamens shake their powder in my hair.

On the wall, the roses are nodding, smiling; above me the orange blossoms surrender themselves to the wooing breeze; and on yonder rock the salamander sits, complacent and serene.

I take a daisy, and, boy as boys go, question its petals:

Married man or monk, I ask, plucking them off one by one,

And the last petal says, Monk.

I perfume my fingers with crumpled cyclamens, cover my face with the dark-
eyed anemones, and fall asleep.

And my burro sleeps beneath the wall, in the shadow of nodding roses.

And the black-birds too are dozing, and the bulbuls flitting by whisper with
their wings, "salaam."

Peace and salaam!

The bulbul, the black-bird, the salamander, the burro, and the burro-boy, are
to each other shades of noon-day sun:

Happy, loving, generous, and free;—

As happy as each other, and as free.

We do what we please in Nature's realm, go where we please;

No one's offended, no one ever wronged.

No sentinels hath Nature, no police.

But lo, a goblin taller than the tallest poplar, who carries me upon his neck to
the Park in far New York.

Here women, light-heeled, heavy-haunched, pace up and down the flags in
graceful gait.

My roses these, I cry, and my orange blossoms.

But the goblin placed his hand upon my mouth, and I was dumb.

The cyclamens, the anemones, the daisies, I saw them, but I could not speak to
them.

The goblin placed his hand upon my mouth, and I was dumb.

O take me back to my own groves, I cried, or let me speak.

But he threw me off his shoulders in a huff, among the daisies and the cycla-
     mens.
Alone among them, but I could not speak.
He had tied my tongue, the goblin, and left me there alone.
And in front of me, and towards me, and beside me,
Walked Allah's fairest cyclamens and anemones.
I smell them, and the tears flow down my cheeks;
I can not even like the noon-day bubul
Whisper with my wings, salaam!
I sit me on a bench and weep.
And in my heart I sing
O, let me be a burro-boy again;
O, let me sleep among the cyclamens
Of my own land.

(1911)

On Being Black

Eric Walrond

I

I go to an optician for a pair of goggles. My eyes are getting bad and my wife insists upon my getting them. For a long time I have hesitated to do so. I hated to be literary—that is, to look literary. It is a fad, I believe. On an afterthought I am convinced she is right; I need them. My eyes are paining me. Moreover, the lights in the subway are blindingly dark, and head swirling. Again, the glitter of spring sends needles through my skull. I need the things badly. I decide to go to the optician's. I go. It is a Jewish place. Elderly is the salesman. I put my cards on the table. . . . "Fine day, isn't it?" He rubs and twists his pigmy fingers and ambles back to the rear. A moment later he returns. With him is a tray of jewelry—lenses and gold rings, diamonds and silver frames. Fine, dainty, effeminate things.

"Here is a nice one," chirps the old gentleman in a sing-song tone, as he tries to fit it on to my nose. "Just the right kind of goggles to keep the dust from going into your eyes. Only the other day I sold—"

At first I feel as if it is one of these confounded new fangled things. Overnight they come, these new styles. Ideas! Here, I whisper to myself, is a new one on me. But I look again. It has a perforated bit of tin on either side of it like the black star-eyed guard on a horse's blinker.

"Oh, I can show you others, if you don't like that one. Want one with a bigger dust piece? I have others back here. Don't be afraid, I'll fix you up. All the colored chauffeurs on Cumberland Street buy their glasses here."

"But I am not a chauffeur," I reply softly. Were it a Negro store, I might have said it with a great deal of emphasis, of vehemence. But being what it is, and knowing that the moment I raise my voice I am accused of "uppishness," I take pains—oh such pains, to be discreet. I wanted to bellow into his ears, "Don't think every Negro you see is a chauffeur." But the man is overwhelmingly amused. His snow-white head is bent—bent over the tray of precious gold, and I can see his face wrinkle in an atrociously cynical smile. But I cannot stand it—that smile. I walk out.

II

I am a stenographer. I am in need of a job. I try the employment agencies. I battle with anemic youngsters and giggling flappers. I am at the tail end of a long line—only to be told the job is already filled. I am ignorantly optimistic. America is a big place; I feel it is only a question of time and perseverance. Encouraged, I go into the tall office buildings on Lower Broadway. I try everyone of them. Not a firm is missed. I walk in and offer my services. I am black, foreign-looking and a curio. My name is taken. I shall be sent for, certainly, in case of need. "Oh, don't mention it sir. . . . Glad you came in. . . . Good morning." I am smiled out. I never hear from them again.

Eventually I am told that that is not the way it is done here. What typewriter do I use? Oh,—. Well, go to the firm that makes them. It maintains an employment bureau, for the benefit of users of its machine. There is no discrimination there; go and see them. Before I go I write stating my experience and so forth. Are there any vacancies? In reply I get a flattering letter asking me to call. I do so.

The place is crowded. A sea of feminine faces disarms me. But I am no longer sensitive. I've got over that—long since. I grind my teeth and confidently take my seat with the mob. At the desk the clerks are busy telephoning and making out cards. I am just one of the crowd. One by one the girls, and men, too, are sent out after jobs. It has been raining and the air is frowsy. The Jewish girls are sweating in their war paint. At last they get around to me. It is my turn.

I am sitting away down at the front. In order to get to me the lady is obliged to do a lot of detouring. At first I thought she was about to go out, to go past me. But I am mistaken. She takes a seat right in front of me, a smile on her wrinkled old-maidish face. I am sure she is the head of the department. It is a situation that requires a strong diplomatic hand. She does not send one of the girls. She comes herself. She is from Ohio, I can see that. She tries to make me feel at home by smiling broadly in my face.

"Are you Mr.—?"

"Yes."

"That's nice. Now how much experience you say you've had?" She is about to write.

"I stated all that in the letter, I think. I've had five years. I worked for—"

"Oh yes, I have it right here. Used to be secretary to Dr.—. Then you worked for an export house, and a soap manufacturer. Also as a shorthand reporter on a South American paper. That is interesting; quite an experience for a young man, isn't it?"

I murmur unintelligibly.

"Well," continues the lady, "we haven't anything at present—"

"But I thought you said in your letter that there is a job vacant. I've got it here in my pocket. I hope I haven't left it at home—"

"That won't suit you. You see it—it—is a post that requires: banking experience. One of the biggest banks in the city. Secretary to the vice president. Ah, by the way; come to think of it, you're just the man for it. You know Mr.— of Lenox Avenue? You do! I think the number is—. Yes, here it is. Also one of his cards. Well, if I were you I would go and see him. Good day."

Dusk is on the horizon. I am once more on Broadway. I am not going to see the man on Lenox Avenue. It won't do any good. The man she is sending me to is a pupil of mine!

III

My wife's health is not very good and I think of sending her to the tropics. I write to the steamship company and in reply I receive a sheaf of booklets telling me all about the blueness of the Caribbean, the beauty of Montega Bay [sic], and the fine a la carte service at the Myrtle Bank Hotel. I am intrigued— I think that is the word—by a three months' cruise at a special rate of $150.00. I telephone the company in an effort to get some information as to sailing dates, reservations, and so forth.

"I understand," I say to the young man who answers the telephone. "I understand that you have a ship sailing on the tenth. I would like to reserve a berth at the $150.00 you are at present offering."

"White or colored?"

"Colored."

Evidently the clerk is consulting someone. But his hand is over the mouthpiece and I can not hear what he is saying. Presently—

"Better come in the office and make reservations."

"What time do you close?"

"Five o'clock."

"What time is it now, please?"

"Ten to."

"Good," I hurry, "I am at Park Place now. Do you think if I hop on a Broadway trolley I can make it before five?"

"I don't know," unconcernedly.

I am at the booking desk. It is three minutes to five. The clerks, tall, lean, light-haired youths, are ready to go home. As I enter a dozen pairs of eyes are fastened upon me. Murmuring. Only a nigger. Again the wheels of life grind on. Lots are cast—I am not speaking metaphorically. The joke is on the Latin. Down in Panama he is a government clerk. Over in Caracas, a tinterillo,* and in Mexico, a scientifico. I know the type. Coming to New York, he shuns the society of Spanish-Americans. On the subway at night he reads the *New York Journal* instead of *La Prensa*.† And on wintery evenings, you can always find him around Seventy-second Street and Broadway. The lad before me is dark, has crystal brown eyes, and straight black hair.

---

tinterillo: a lower-level clerk; also, a disreputable lawyer.

†*La Prensa*: established in New York City in 1913, one of the oldest and most respected Spanish-language newspapers in the United States.

"I would like," I begin, "to reserve a passage for my wife on one of your steamers to Kingston. I want to get it at the $150.00 rate."

"Well, it is this way." I am positive he is from Guayaquil. "It will cost you $178.00."

"Why $178.00?"

"You see, the passage alone is $170.00."

"A hundred and seventy dollars! Why, this booklet here says $150.00 round trip. You must have made a mistake."

"You see, this $150.00 rate is for three in a room, and all the rooms on the ship sailing on the tenth are already taken up."

"All right," I decide. "the date is inconsequential. What I want is the $150.00 rate. Reserve a berth for me on any ship that is not already filled up I don't care how late in the summer it is. I have brought a deposit along with me—"

I am not truculent. Everything I say I strive to say softly, unoffensively—especially when in the midst of a color-ordeal!

"Well, you'd have to get two persons to go with her." The Peruvian is independent. "There are only three berths in a stateroom, and if your wife wants to take advantage of the $150.00 rate, she will have to get two other colored persons to go with her."

"I s-e-e!" I mutter dreamily. And I did see!

"Come in tomorrow and pay a deposit on it, if you want to. It is five o'clock and—"

I am out on the street again. From across the Hudson a gurgling wind brings dust to my nostrils. I am limp, static, emotionless. There is only one line to Jamaica, and I am going to send her by it. It is the only thing to do. Tomorrow I am going back, with the $178.00. It pays to be black.

(1922)

A Slavic Oklahoman

Edward A. Steiner

He talked to me until dawn, and when he left me I could not sleep, for he had told me his own story; how he had lost the name by which he was baptized, had forgotten his native tongue, had forsaken his mother's faith and but dimly remembered the name of his old home. For twenty years his mind and soul had been absorbed in Oklahoma; her size, her wealth, her prospects.

My coming and speaking had recalled to him the fact that he was a Slav by birth, that his childhood had been in a foreign land, and that he once had a soul which reached beyond the desire to own fertile soil in his adopted state. He remembered that he had loved, and that his real name was not the one by which he was now known.

"I don't recall the name of our village," he said; "but we had four days' journey to Trieste and my name was Demetrius Gondory."

"Gondory," I said; "then you are a Southern Slav; because if you were from the North you would pronounce it softly with an H.

"Don't you remember anything of your language?"

"Yes," he said; "I remember a song in my mother tongue." And he sang for me as we walked from the church to my hotel:

> "Oh! Thou poor river Save
> Fret no against thy shores."

From the song and the way he sang, I traced him to the shores of that mountain stream, where it is young and turbulent. He had never seen it where it broadens and carries ships to the ocean; nor did he know the cities below it and above it, only the names of two mountains which overshadow his village. To him then, I recalled its name which has five consonants and only one vowel, but it was music to his ears and he repeated it a dozen times.

"That's it!" he cried; "I could always see it with my eyes but I could not speak it with my tongue.

"America," he said, "gives a man more than any other country, but it takes away more. It took from me my name, my native speech, my mother's faith; it almost blotted out for me my cradle home, and what has it given me?

"They call me John, although the priest baptized me Demetrius. They have filled my soul with the love of gold until it is like a cash register which responds only to the touch on the dollar key. My brain is full of the red dust of Oklahoma and they have put into my blood the love for a fight until I am like a bulldog. Say, I can't talk without snarling.

"I run a newspaper which is just a series of barks. They say it is picturesque for I use no dashes—I just give them God Almighty's Hell, and they seem to like it. Of course I have fought for some things worthwhile, and before I am through I am going to see a few of the gang in the penitentiary; you may stake your bottom dollar on that.

"Now my story. The dominant feeling in my childhood was fear. Witches, devils, evil spirits of all sorts haunted me, and religion was the great bugaboo to drive away the other bugaboos. Say, I feel it creeping over me now, that old fear. Talk about devils! I can see their red, licking tongues of fire when I am alone in the dark—hundreds, thousands of them, and I am afraid that when the end comes, my fighting blood will turn to buttermilk, and I shall crawl back into the shelter of the Church.

"My mother was a sweet, timid creature; my father was brutal, and when I was not afraid of the devils I was afraid of him. I remember a phrase he used; it was something like this: '*Za decu je u zapecku mesto.*' Do you know what it means?"

"Yes," I replied. "The place for the children is behind the bake-oven."

"Yes, that must be it, for he used to drive me behind an old brick oven which took up a third of the living room. It was dark as a pocket and hot as Hell, and I could see nothing but devils. When you hear me saying devil every other minute, remember that I have personal acquaintance with his Satanic Majesty, and that when I swear I mean no harm. I have heard all sorts of cuss words from the day I was born, and you know out here in Oklahoma they belong to the native dialect.

"My mother dedicated me to the Church to appease the devils that tormented her, and I became an acolyte at ten years of age. I fought the bunch of holy kinds for the privilege of carrying the sacred water or the censor; for only then did I feel safe.

"I don't know how old I was when a wonderful thing happened to me—my uncle came back from America. He looked to me like a lord and he acted like one. He got the whole town drunk, he had the band playing for him all night, he swore at the gendarmes and he brought my mother a gold ring.

"He talked about nothing but America—his farm and mills. He said he had a flour mill, a sawmill, carriage and horses and cows, and so many pigs that he couldn't count them. He persuaded my father to let me go with him. An aunt of mine was going along to be his housekeeper, his wife having died, and I was to go as his adopted son and heir.

"I must have strutted around that blessed town like a peacock. I put on woolen clothes and a black hat, and I wore real leather shoes for the first time in my life. My job as an acolyte went to a cousin of mine, who, before I left, sprinkled me all over with holy water to guard me against the evil spirits I might encounter. My mother wept and prayed, and made me kneel before the crucifix and promise two things, which she most feared might happen: never to forsake the Roman Catholic faith and not to marry an American wife.

"My uncle lived in Illinois, in a most desolate and forsaken place. His farm was a poor, rundown affair and his mills consisted of a feed grinder under the roof of his barn, while the sawmill was a handsaw and the usual buck.

"I had to work hard; plow the corn and do the chores while my uncle frequented saloons in the neighboring town. He took me there occasionally and regaled me with a glass or two of beer. There I learned my first English, and I collected such a fine lot of swear words that I have not had to learn much in that direction since.

"I grew physically like a weed; I had plenty to eat, good air and lots of exercise, but mentally and spiritually I didn't grow an inch. I lived in the world of evil spirits, witches and devils which I brought with me and I did not have even the consolation of the incense and the holy water. My aunt and I went to church. The priest was German and I added a few words of his language to my own, but of the consolation of religion I received very little.

"One day my uncle, in a drunken fit, drove me from the farm. Most likely I was impudent for I am that now, to a superlative degree. I went to town and got a job in a saloon in which my uncle was a good customer. My work consisted in keeping the filthy barroom reasonably clean, and in waiting on customers when the boss had imbibed too much of his own wet goods.

"I slept in the billiard room on a pool table, another one being a bed for the saloonkeeper's brother who kept a butcher shop next door. He was a consumptive, and in the darkness of the night his hacking cough nearly drove me crazy. One night he bled to death right on that pool table and I was along with him till morning. You can't imagine with what horrors my whole being was filled.

"The night after the funeral as I lay there at midnight I would have given anything to have heard even the hacking cough of the consumptive. I saw nothing but corpses and spirits. I shook as if I had the ague. I grew desperate. I went behind the bar, took a box of sulphur matches and poured whiskey over them; it was the only poison of which I knew and I was about to drink it when I heard music, a waltz tune. I heard just as if it was a dream—it went to my brain and drove the witches and devils and the fear all out of me.

"I left the saloon and went after it. It came from the Masonic Hall up in the third story of the temple. I climbed up those stairs as if I were climbing to Heaven. Say, they may talk about us immigrants being illiterate but we know music, and that's culture.

"Music saved me from death, if from nothing else. I looked into that hall and to me it was like a king's chamber. The men and women who danced were as far removed from me as the saloon in which I worked was from the cloud under which cherubim and seraphim kneel before the ark.

"Do you know what the one thought was that held me and lifted me, and nearly saved me? To live! So to live that some day I should be worthy to min-gle with those people. I stood entranced by the melody, the swaying bodies, the cleanliness and the beauty. I felt like a great poet must feel when he is lifted into his seventh heaven.

"There was one young girl upon whom my love-hungry eyes especially rested, and I said to myself—I don't know just why I said it—I shall dance with her some day in this very room; and who knows what she will say to me, and I will say to her? While I was held by the vision I was suddenly brought to earth by some one shouting: 'Look at the funny little Dutchman!' Then I bolted downstairs, resolved not to be a Dutchman, and more strongly resolved to be a man.

"I could keep you here ten days telling you what happened in the next ten years. Jiminy crickets! I got the Dutchman or the Slav or whatever it is out of my nature. I climbed high enough to dance with that young woman in that blooming town. I never entered that saloon nor any saloon. I was offered bar-keeper's wages; the beer brewer wanted me to work in his office. I think I might have managed to own the whole blasted brewery, but that music and that young woman led me on to better things.

"Of course it wasn't anything big that I got to be; just a bookkeeper in a clothing store, but it's heaps better than bottle washer in a saloon, and I was climbing, you bet! In six months I could talk English. I read like a fiend: Dickens, Longfellow, Old Homer, the Bible. I sat under an old oak tree one Sunday reading Longfellow's 'Muratori Salutamus,' and I cried like a baby, be-cause its music ravished my ears and its pathos wrung my heart.

"*She* passed by and I joined her, and went to church with her, the first time I was in a Protestant church. They had a revival meeting on and they sang hymn tunes which first moved my feet as if I were going to dance, and then they began to grip my heart as if I should die unless I obeyed their pleading.

"Say, you may talk about that stuff not being good music; it does the job just the same. That plaintive, 'Why not?' 'Why not?' sung by five hundred people, usually women and children, with their shrill voices which rack your nerves and make you feel like a sinner who is pursued by the devil—it's great music; it was for me.

"I don't remember much of what the preacher said. It was about the devil and Hell, about sin and perdition, and when he pled with men to repent I jumped up, and was the first one at the altar.

"I writhed like an epileptic on that floor. I tell you I know how all those great souls felt: St. Augustine, St. Francis and Luther, those who lived in the middle ages, for I had not outgrown them; I was there. To me that was the first call to repentance, the first way of escape opened.

"I fought for hours with the devil who wanted me back; I saw his licking tongue and when he couldn't prevail against me he called other devils to his aid. Then he called my mother and I saw her with her rosary in the hand, kneeling with me and begging me not to forsake the Mother Church. I bolted for the door, but there *she* stood, the woman for whom my heart yearned, and she led me back and I found peace.

"I have read a whole lot of psychology since. I know William James almost by heart. I have outgrown all that emotional Methodism; but as I think back I know that I stood on a pure mountain height, one which I have never reached again, for I became like Lucifer; but that's another story."

He chewed the end of his cigar nervously.

"Say, honestly, am I not boring you? I am talking to you as if you were my father confessor."

When I assured him that I was willing to stay awake all night to listen to him, he continued:

"That girl whom I loved as I have never loved since, wouldn't, couldn't marry me. She was much older; she was rich, cultured, and I was still a rough human, no more a Slav and scarcely yet an American. I knew she did just the right thing, but she threw me over a precipice, and I never stopped falling till— well, I am ahead of my story.

"I began to drink and the old alcohol-soaked germs in me—my ancestors' drunken ghosts—cried for more and more, till I was again in the gutter. I drifted West further and further and got fairly on my feet in Kansas. I say on my feet. I was a boozer still, but I was among boozers.

"Say, those were wild days and great days. I helped to make cities out of lonely prairies; I moved county seats, and helped to elect Congressmen and United States Senators. The state was in a delirium and I helped to make that. People were real estate crazy and I acted like the craziest of them all.

"We are a slow, sluggish race; you said that tonight. I know how slow my own blood runs, but I out-Yankeed the Yankees in my pace; not in the drinking line alone, nor in playing cards, though I could bluff them at their own game, but in that bigger game which they call business. Say, honest," he said, "you ought to go to bed!"

But he was so eager to tell and I was so eager to listen that he continued, although the porters were mopping the floor and moving the chairs, and were quite anxious to have us gone.

"I began, as you know, as a farmer; I became a bartender; I then went into the clothing business. I have worked in a grocery store, slung hash in a restaurant, driven cabs, carried hods. I owned a pantatorium, then I became a reporter. Honestly, I believe I was at every kind of business except selling subscription books and life insurance.

"Talk about the immobility of the Slav! They have made mercury out of the iron in me. I am sure my pulse goes a good many beats faster than the Creator ordained it should. I have traveled through every state in the Union, and I have not bought a burial lot yet, for I'll be slugged if I know where I want to wait for Gabriel's trumpet.

"Once I made a big pile of money, and I went back to Illinois, for I had not forgotten *her*, never for a minute. Talk about your great emotions! Is there anything bigger, do you think, than that going back to where you were born, I mean consciously born, born again? Where at sixteen years of age you crawled out of the womb of ignorance and superstition, and began to live, intellectually and spiritually?

"I have a sneaking notion, now that I have heard you speak of us Slavs, that I want to go back to where my body was born, and where she who bore me lies buried, but I am sure it couldn't mean as much to me as that other going back meant. No one recognized me. I had grown from a youth into a man, into an old man almost, for I had gone the pace which crowds years into a calendar page.

"I went out to the farm first. I hired a carriage to take me, the kind they use at funerals and weddings. The old man still lived; he looked exactly like his farm, seedy and broken down, run down at the heel. I thanked God for the deliverance from that place and that kind of life.

"I then went to the saloon; it had prospered to the degree that my uncle's farm had deteriorated. There were fine pictures, plate glass, and a barkeeper in a white jacket. I then went to the clothing store. It also had changed and changed for the better. And then I went to see *her*.

"I rang the doorbell and waited for her in the parlor. She came. There was a cherub of a baby in her arms, and a three-year-old kid was pulling at her skirts as if determined to pull them off. She didn't recognize me, and I made for the door, stammering apologies. She must have thought me crazy.

"I went up to the dance hall in the Masonic Temple and I cried right there by the closed doors. I guess it's easier for a Slav to cry than for a Yankee. Then I made for the tree under which I used to read poetry, and I had a good look at the Methodist church, and there too I blubbered like a baby. I left town as soon as I could, and going through Chicago the old devils got hold of me again and I blew in every cent I had—I needn't tell you how.

"Then I came to this blooming town and slept on this very hill where this hotel stands, but there was nothing above me but the stars, and under me the red soil of Oklahoma. There was red soil over me too, for the wind blew great guns, and I swallowed dirt enough to feel that I was the owner of some real estate at least, even if I didn't have a red copper in my pocket.

"It's different now. I am a stockholder in this hotel; I own a printing shop and newspaper. They call me a scrapper and I am. I have fought and am still fighting. I have made enemies enough so that I have to keep in fighting trim all the time. You will hear lots of lies about me, but no one will tell you that I haven't fought fair. I could have sold myself and my interests a dozen times; I have refused to touch their dirty money. I have fought for the farmers; say, I am a farmer still at heart. My ancestors, you said, were an agricultural people."

"Yes," I replied, "they were people of the plow and not of the sword."

"That's right," he said. "I am a child of the soil; I feel it in my blood. I have started more fights than a bulldog, but from what you said tonight I fight like a Slav, clumsily and ill-sustained. I lack confidence in myself and in others. The only thing I have confidence in is the blooming state.

"It's bound to be the greatest state in the Union, the center of population. It has the soil and the climate. It can raise better cotton than Louisiana; it beats Nebraska for corn and California for fruit. It has them all beaten, for we have two crops on top of the soil and three crops beneath it: coal, gas and oil, and then our natural resources are not yet developed."

He talked fifteen minutes more about Oklahoma; her constitution, her schools and churches, and then I laid my hand upon his shoulder and looking into his face, aglow from the enthusiasm of his deliverance, I said:

"Verily, Demetrius Gondory, thou art an American."

(1911)

PART III

The Melting Pot Debate

At the turn of the twentieth century, many citizens attributed America's greatness to characteristics inherited from a single stock of people, whether that stock was called Anglo-Saxon, Nordic, or even "old immigrant." As discussed in Part II, this explanation of the nation's greatness bolstered the movement to require immigrants to assimilate fully to the dominant culture. One way to oppose such assimilation, then, was to point out weak spots in mainstream U.S. culture, and this strategy was used by those who championed another view of the United States, namely, the melting pot vision. For instance, in a 1907 essay titled "The American of the Future," Brander Matthews said that "it is only stubborn pride, singularly out of place in an American of the twentieth century, which makes us dread evil consequences" brought about by mixing with immigrants from southern and eastern Europe. "The suave manner of the Italian," he continued, "may modify in time the careless discourtesy which discredits us now in the eyes of foreign visitors. The ardor of the Slav may quicken our appreciation of the fine arts." Though he admitted that some of the strengths of the current American character might be lessened, he added that "there is no reason to suppose that in the future we shall not make our profit out of the best that every contributing blood can bring to us."[1] In other words, on the whole, a brighter tomorrow meant not eradicating immigrant characteristics but incorporating them.

Another reason the melting pot was favored over assimilation is simply that not all immigrants were convinced that their cultures were worth abandoning. In the speech that opens this part, Joseph Štýbr told his audience that "it is impossible to Americanize a man in the sense lately so often expressed and demanded: that he should forget his native land, that he should forget his mother tongue, that he should forget everything he was before he came to this country and should become 100 percent American." As a Czech immigrant, Štýbr knew all too well about efforts to indoctrinate one country with another's culture. Prior to World War I, under the thumb of the Habsburg Empire, Czechs were pressured to abandon their own culture in favor of Austria's, including supplanting the Czech language with German. The outcome, Štýbr explained, was that their hostility toward the government and their refusal to conform could be expressed in German. In other words, while assimilation certainly does occur to a degree, it is a rare immigrant who completely erases his or her former identity in the process of becoming an American. As such, Štýbr recommended seeing this process as a slow one, and he used images of the melting pot to articulate his alternative.

In the early twentieth century, many shared Štýbr's preference for the melting pot vision of the United States over the one that attributed the nation's greatness solely to its Anglo-Saxon traditions. No doubt, the popularity of this preference was at least partly sparked by Israel Zangwill's play *The Melting Pot*, which premiered in 1908 and is credited with having popularized the title phrase. Its lead character, David Quixano, sees in America a chance to raise humanity above religious and racial bigotry. In the finale, he points to New York harbor during a blazing sunset and proclaims it to be "the great Melting

Pot." He continues, "Ah, what a stirring and seething! Celt and Latin, Slav and Teuton, Greek and Syrian,—black and yellow . . . How the great Alchemist melts and fuses them with his purging flame! Here shall they all unite to build the Republic of Man and the Kingdom of God." America's glory, he prophesies, will outshine that of Rome and Jerusalem.[2] Though the exact phrase "the melting pot" seems not to have been used, the essential idea that Zangwill dramatizes was not new. It is typically traced back to Hector St. John de Crèvecoeur's *Letters from an American Farmer* (1782), where Crèvecoeur first asked the famous question, "What, then, is the American, this new man?" He said, "I could point out to you a family whose grandfather was an Englishman, whose wife was Dutch, whose son married a French woman, and whose present four sons have now four wives of different nations. *He* is an American . . . Here individuals of all nations are melted into a new race of men, whose labours and posterity will one day cause great changes in the world."[3] Though American Indians and Africans were conspicuously absent, Crèvecoeur's melting pot, like Zangwill's, envisioned a nation in which immigrants contributed traits to an evolving, homogeneous national people. *Melting* together is key here. Rather than the assimilationists' notion that remaining unified (in the sense of erasing diversity) keeps the nation strong, advocates of the melting pot argued that melting would keep the nation unified and make it stronger.

This is important in that it differentiates the melting pot vision of the nation from other visions, the assimilationist as well as the cultural pluralist. Zangwill's play was so popular that the script was marketed as book. In its afterword, the playwright summed up the message he had hoped to convey: "The process of American amalgamation is not assimilation or simple surrender to the dominant type, as is popularly supposed, but an all-round give-and-take by which the final type may be enriched or impoverished."[4] Here, Zangwill defined the melting pot in contrast to the "simple surrender to the dominant type" advocated by proponents of complete assimilation. Indeed, as Werner Sollors explains, the melting pot metaphor itself was appropriated to signify assimilation to Anglo-American culture, as exemplified by the graduation ceremony of the Ford Motor Company's English classes for foreign-born employees. Donned in foreign clothing, graduates disembarked from a mock-up of a ship and entered a huge melting pot. They then emerged wearing "American" suits and waving flags, symbolically cleansed of their ethnic origins by "the baptismal blessings of the melting pot." Sollors also points out that Horace Kallen's essay "Democracy Versus the Melting-Pot" (1915), which is reprinted in our part exploring cultural pluralism, ends with "an image of harmonious musical fusion which was presented as a radical alternative to the melting pot, while it resembles the struggles of Zangwill's protagonist David Quixano to compose an American symphony."[5] The flexibility the image had in the early twentieth century possibly accounts for the looseness with which the phrase is sometimes used today, as when one says "America is a melting pot" to mean simply that it is a place where people of diverse ethnicities live together.

Nonetheless, in 1923, Charlotte Perkins Gilman had Zangwill's definition in mind when she wrote an essay titled "Is America Too Hospitable?" Gilman's stance was, yes, America was too hospitable in regard to immigration. "With glowing enthusiasm we have seized upon one misplaced metaphor, and call our country now a 'melting pot'. . . ," she said, adding that this metaphor was "stupidly" chosen. A melting pot must be "carefully filled with weighed and measured proportions of such ores as will combine to produce known results. If you put into a melting pot promiscuous shovelfuls of anything that comes handy you do not get out of it anything of value, and you may break the pot." Miscegenation is what worried Gilman, who pointed out that the United States was familiar with "the various blends of black and white, and the wisest of both races prefer the pure stock." Similarly, the "Eurasian mixture" was "generally considered unfortunate by most observers," and even combining "European races" was dangerous. Many Americans shared this view expressed by Gilman: "The American people, as a racial stock, are mainly of English descent, mingled with the closely allied Teutonic and Scandinavian strains . . . together with some admixture of the Celt and Gael."[6] With Americans defined as those descended from northern and western Europe, the "new immigrants" from southern and eastern Europe stood beside African Americans, Asian Americans, Asian immigrants, and others as perceived threats to the nation's racial strength. The arrival of the "new immigrants" in unprecedented numbers exacerbated a growing disillusionment with the melting pot as a national metaphor felt by more Americans than just Gilman.

An image that Gilman used to close her essay forms the basis of her poem, "The Melting Pot," the next selection in this part. The disgust with indiscriminate mixing that she expresses there is reflected less metaphorically in a song called "The Argentines, the Portuguese, and the Greeks." Though the lyrics point out that the immigrants' give-and-take with mainstream American culture has had a largely negative impact, they also note that these newcomers have also learned the national anthem while the native-born have not. In the end, the song reveals a curious fear that immigrants threaten the native-born population by having the drive to become economically superior. As counter-statements to Štýbr's endorsement of the melting pot and Zangwill's comparatively rhapsodic treatment of it, Gilman's poem and the song establish how this vision stirred just as much controversy as did the prospects of restriction and complete assimilation.

The next set of works offer at least slightly more balanced views of the melting pot vision. Jeanette Dailey and Ernest Poole look at the children of mixed parentage, both authors suggesting that such individuals face daunting and even tragic challenges. Charles Chesnutt, Abraham Cahan, and Florence Converse then take different stances on the prospect of mixed marriages. Concern about marriages and sexual unions between the races—the biological side of the melting pot as opposed to its cultural side—has deep roots in U.S. history. Before the nineteenth century, racial differences were sometimes attributed to environmental factors. One theory, for instance, attributed them to climate: races went from light to dark as they approached the equator. However, by the time James Fenimore Cooper wrote *The Last of the Mohicans* (1826), race was generally designated as being a matter of reproduction and, in the rhetoric of the time, a matter of blood. In *"Miscegenation": Making Race in America*, Elise Lemire points out that Cooper's main character Hawk-eye is insistent about having only the blood of a white man. "Because he is a simple woodsman who lives with Indians," Lemire explains, "readers are meant to understand that, in constantly referring to blood, Hawk-eye is using the most basic and even perhaps pre-cultural terms to describe the essence of being a 'white man.'" Hawk-eye figures prominently in the novel's two marriage plots: one involving Heyward and Alice, two white characters; and the other comprised of a triangle with Cora, who is of mixed black and white parentage, and Indian characters Uncas and Magua. Insofar as the former succeeds and the latter ends in tragedy, Lemire concludes that Hawk-eye's "role in the narrative is to register disapproval of inter-racial sexual unions and to otherwise disallow them while instead enabling the intra-racial ones."[7]

It is wrong, though, to assume that all prominent nineteenth-century writers portrayed racially mixed unions as objectionable, as Lemire notes in her discussion of Louisa May Alcott's short story "M.L." Published in 1863, the story valorized "an inter-racial marriage for the way in which it began to open the racist eyes of the couple's community" and was part of an abolistionist effort to combat hostilities toward intermarriage between blacks and whites.[8] Such views persisted until long after the Civil War, though in 1896, for instance, Willis Boughton advocated racial fusion and, specifically, an end to laws forbidding the marriage of blacks and whites as a way to fully realize racial equality in the United States. Boughton summed up the melting pot ethos by declaring, "Old races have often been supplanted by those of inferior culture but of superior energy. More often, however, by fusion of different racial types and by the mingling of various tribes and peoples, have been evolved new races superior to any of the original types." In fact, according to Boughton, the greatness of Greece and Rome was achieved only after racial conflicts were resolved through fusion.[9]

A similar position was espoused a few years later by Charles Chesnutt in a series of essays that originally appeared in the *Boston Evening Transcript*. His thesis was that "the future American race—the future American ethnic type—will be formed of a mingling . . . of the various racial varieties which make up the present population of the United States." Chesnutt addressed only American Indians, African Americans, and whites. The fusion of American Indians and whites, he said, would occur swiftly because "there is no prejudice against the Indian blood, in solution. A half or quarter-breed, removed from the tribal environment, is freely received among white people." However, for African Americans and whites, there would be no "sudden and wholesale amalgamation," and like Boughton, he cited "the laws which prevail in all the Southern States, without exception, forbidding the intermarriage of white persons and persons of color" among the major obstacles.[10] Curiously, Chesnutt's short story "Uncle Wellington's Wives" reveals seemingly irresolvable conflicts facing those attempting to achieve racial equality between black and white through marriage in the North. It is telling that Chesnutt's African American character seeks a white wife among only immigrants, whose status as "white" was presumably somewhat less rigid than with native-born white women.

Since the biological ramifications of the melting pot had a long legacy in literature, writers could draw upon this tradition and adapt it to new groups. Earlier in this part, we see Dailey adapting the "tragic mulatto" character to issues involving Chinese immigrants. Later, Converse dramatizes that even a marriage between Irish American Maggie and Italian-immigrant Umberto could be complicated by what were then described as "the dissimilarities of race." However, the melting pot could also be understood in terms of immigrants' cultural contributions to their new country. In "The Alien in the Melting Pot," for instance, Frederick J. Haskin catalogues the many roles that immigrants play in the country's industry and manufacturing. In stark contrast, H. T. Tsiang addresses the restrictions that Chinese immigrants faced while simply trying to earn a living, and in doing so, he comments on how Asian immigrants were prevented from contributing to the melting pot in the diverse ways that Haskin lists. In "A Yellow Man and a White," Eleanor Gates combats anti-Chinese prejudice by introducing readers to Fong Wu, a sort of Chinese "superman" who is, in a sense, a one-man melting pot of the world's medical cures. Implied in this story is a comment upon how bigotry and, specifically, restriction laws deprive the United States of the world's wisdom that, otherwise, immigrants might contribute to the nation.

Catalina Páez then shifts the focus to the ways that cultural contributions might take the form of folkways. This tale is clearly influenced by something historian John Higham refers to as "the doctrine of 'immigrant gifts.'" He explains that immigrant parents frequently experienced disturbing ruptures between themselves and their rapidly assimilated children. To remedy these problems, Jane Addams and other settlement leaders "began in the nineties to develop programs for conserving and celebrating the holidays, customs, folksongs, and languages of the nationalities in the neighborhood." In doing so, they "argued that each immigrant group had a tangible contribution to make to the building of American culture." Higham deems this approach to be "a modification of the melting-pot tradition," in that it puts a cultural twist on the biological fusion of the races idea that previously had dominated melting pot discourse.[11] Carl Sandburg similarly suggests that the folksy leisure activities of Hungarian immigrants—specifically, accordion playing, beer drinking, and family picnicking—offer Americans an insight into happiness that they have lost to advanced learning and industrial progress.

Sandburg's poem draws a curious sketch of the era, one in which middle-class Americans are successful in work and education but are out of touch with happiness. He was not alone in this view. "We know little of the joy of living," wrote Ernest Crosby about his fellow Americans in an essay published in 1904. With the period's habit of generalizing, he added, "We take our holidays sadly, and laugh with mental reservations. The European comes to us with a new capacity for mirth, a genius for joviality and sociability."[12] Perhaps, underneath it all, this points to a basic difference between those who advocated assimilation to the dominant culture and those who favored the melting pot. With all the pitfalls of nostalgia, the former located happiness in the past, in the "old immigrant" culture they believed had made the United States better than virtually any other country in the world. Clinging to that culture was vital to them. The latter sought happiness in the future and saw immigrants as the guides to—indeed, the very material of—that brighter day.

Notes

1. Brander Matthews, "The American of the Future," *Century* (July 1907): 479.
2. Israel Zangwill, *The Melting Pot* (New York: Macmillan, 1924), 184–185.
3. J. Hector St. John de Crèvecoeur, *Letters from an American Farmer* (New York: Penguin, 1986), 69–70.
4. Israel Zangwill, afterword, *The Melting Pot* (New York: Macmillan, 1924), 203.
5. Werner Sollors, *Beyond Ethnicity: Consent and Descent in American Culture* (New York: Oxford University Press, 1986), 89, 97.
6. Charlotte Perkins Gilman, "Is America Too Hospitable?" *Forum* (October 1923): 1985, 1988.

7. Elise Lemire, *"Miscengenation": Making Race in America* (Philadelphia: University of Pennsylvania, 2002), 35, 45.

8. Ibid., 115.

9. Willis Boughton, "The Negro's Place in History," *The Arena* 16 (1896): 616–617.

10. Charles Chesnutt, "The Future American," *MELUS* 15 (1988): 97–98, 104.

11. John Higham, *Strangers in the Land: Patterns of American Nativism, 1860–1925*, (New York: Atheneum, 1963), 121–122.

12. Ernest Crosby, "The Immigration Bugbear," *Arena* (December 1904): 601.

Americanization

Joseph Štýbr

There is an old saying among the Czechs, "Sing the praises of him whose bread you eat." This axiom expresses fittingly the basic principle of Americanization. It is both right and proper that a man who has adopted this land for his country and is eating its bread should sing its praises, in other words, that he should become American. The question only is, how it should be done so that the country might find in him a loyal and useful citizen, and he in turn might find in the country the right kind of domicile, a satisfactory substitute for his native land, so that he might live contented and happy; for only then will he become a good citizen.

It has been often said that Americanization means an amalgamation of the foreigner. What is amalgamation? Originally in chemistry, it is a process by which mercury and some other metal, usually of the precious sort, are alloyed into a new substance, rather unstable, from which by heat or other means the original metals may easily be recovered. I do not know whether the use of the term was really premeditated, but my impression is that it has been well chosen. For in truth take any amalgamated citizen and heat him up, and you will soon be able to tell where he hails from—just like in the chemical process. Therefore it appears to me that it is impossible to Americanize a man in the sense lately so often expressed and demanded: that he should forget his native land, that he should forget his mother tongue, that he should forget everything he was before he came to this country and should become 100 percent American. All we can justly ask and expect from him is that he become a loyal citizen of this country and obey its laws and respect its institutions, and with that he will pass for a good citizen.

When I came to this country 28 years ago, I landed clad in the apparel of the latest cut of Europe at that time. I wore a pair of rather severely pointed shoes. One day, as I walked along the street, a group of school boys passed me, and an urchin from their midst gave me a slight glance and remarked to his chums, "Gee. I wouldn't like this fellow to give me a kick from behind!" They laughed, but I took the hint. I really thanked the little fellow in my mind; I went directly to a shoe store and bought myself a new pair of shoes. The rest of my apparel soon followed; I improved my English; in due time I acquired the citizenship and ultimately became so thoroughly Americanized that now, after 28 years, I am called upon to speak for the Czechs of our community.

The editors of *The Czechoslovak Review* note that "Americanization" is the text of a speech Štýbr gave to the Pittsburgh Chamber of Commerce on May 3, 1919.

You will notice that Americanization in my case began with the feet, and it may seem a rather strange procedure; nevertheless, if you are intent upon Americanizing a foreigner, I would suggest to begin with the feet. Teach him to walk in the American life; teach him how to grasp things in the American light; do it all in a kind and benevolent manner, and you are bound to gain his heart and convince his head. Never begin with his head as it has been lately advocated; the head is too round and too hard an object to break over the knee. To begin denationalization with the head is a German method, and we Czechs know all about it from our experience. We have been taught the German language at home so efficiently that in time we were able to tell the Germans plainly in their own tongue what we thought of them, and then we left our oppressed native land to seek the land of liberty. If you will attempt to compel the foreigner to do something similar, he may learn how to tell you in plain English what he thinks of you, but then your purpose may be spoiled. And remember, gentlemen, that if the foreigner will be docile and willing and will see his best interest in becoming speedily Americanized, that he can hardly do it in any other way except by imitating you and your ways in order to produce the golden American amalgam, and ultimately you will be able to see yourself in him like in a mirror. If you wish to like and admire your own reflection, put into him that which is the best and most admirable in you. Show yourselves to him in the right way; protect him from evil influences and above all protect him from exploitation of the "also citizen" whose only design is the foreigner's scalp. And do not forget, gentlemen, that while the foreigner is undergoing Americanization he also is constantly living in memories and in comparisons, and bear with him patiently when, on account of recalling to his mind things he believes were better in his old home, he cannot promptly see things that may be better here in their proper light.

The process of Americanization along these lines is naturally slow and requires a good bit of patience from both sides. It would be unnatural, unreasonable and even immoral to expect the foreigner to forget all that he was before he fell into the amalgamating pot. It would be unnatural and unreasonable because it is physically impossible; and it would be immoral because it is contrary to the law of God. How can anyone ask me to forget my father who is sleeping his eternal sleep in my native land; and how can I think of him and forget the beautiful land where he is resting?

So you see, gentlemen, that Americanization, as I say, is much slower process than many of us may imagine, and I do not believe that the hyphen can be expunged within one generation. That, however, does not necessarily mean that the Americanized foreign-born citizen should or does love his adopted country less than his American-born fellow citizen. In the end, whether fully conscious or partly conscious of the fact, we are all working toward one end in preparing this beautiful and great, but still young and somewhat raw, country for the happiness of our future generations. And while each of us is doing his bit to his best ability, the great melting pot is boiling hot and working overtime. It does not matter much where we originally hail from, as old Omar put it,

> "Whether at Naishapúr or at Babylon;
> Whether the Cup with sweet or bitter run;
> The Wine of Life keeps oozing drop by drop;
> The Leaves of Life keep falling one by one."*

And when our labors are done and we shall have laid our weary heads to our eternal rest, then our children will sing together with your children,

> "Land where our fathers died,
> Land of the pilgrims' pride—"

and then the process of Americanization will be completed.

(1919)

---

*From "Rubaiyat of Omar Khayyam," translated by Edward Fitzgerald.

The Melting Pot

Charlotte Perkins Gilman

A melting pot has to be made
    With particular care,
And carefully sampled and weighed
As to nature, proportion and grade
    Are the ores mingled there.

Let the metaphor change in your mind
    To an effort to bake,
Of eggs, butter, and flour you will find,
With milk, sugar and raisins combined,
    You compose a good cake.

Or taking salt, pepper and meat,
    With an onion or two,
Tomatoes, and maybe a beet,
Fine herbs and some celery sweet,
    A good soup you may brew.

But if all these ingredients here
    Should commingle at will,
Neither cake nor yet soup will appear,
There's one name for a mixture so queer—
    That is swill.

(c. 1923)

The Argentines, the Portuguese, and the Greeks

Arthur M. Swanstrom and Carey Morgan

Columbus discovered America in Fourteen Ninety-two
Then came the English and the Dutch, the Frenchman and the Jew
Then came the Swede and the Irishman, who helped the country grow
Still they keep a-coming, and now ev'rywhere you go

There's the Argentines and the Portuguese, the Armenians and the Greeks
One sells you papers, one shines your shoes, another shaves the whiskers off
 your cheeks
When you ride again in a subway train, notice who has all the seats
You'll find they're held by the Argentines, and the Portuguese, and the Greeks

I am in love with the sweetest girl, and the sweetest girl loves me
But though she's sweet and hard to beat, our ideas don't agree
I like to eat in the swell cafes, terrapin and wine
My girl has a diff'rent craze, and she just loves to dine

With the Argentines and the Portuguese, the Armenians and the Greeks
She loves to frolic down among the garlic, and her breath will knock you over
 when she speaks
But the thing I dread is the year we're wed and our child is aged three weeks
It will look just like all the Argentines, and the Portuguese, and the Greeks

There's the Oldsmobile, and the Hupmobile, and the Cadillac, and the Ford
They are the motors you and I can own, the kind most anyone can afford
But the Cunninghams and the Mercedes and the Rolls Royce racing freaks
Ah! they all belong to the Argentines, and the Portuguese, and the Greeks

There's the Argentines and the Portuguese, the Armenians and the Greeks
They don't know the language, they don't know the law, but they vote in the
 country of the free
And a funny thing, when we start to sing "My Country 'Tis of Thee"
None of us know the words but the Argentines, and the Portuguese, and the
 Greeks

There's the Argentines and the Portuguese, the Armenians and the Greeks
They all love their "licker," they don't give a nickel for the stuff that runs in
 rivers, brooks, and creeks

So there'll come a day when they sail away from this land where laws are freaks
And we'll all be aboard with the Argentines, and the Portuguese, and the
    Greeks

There's the little flat, where you hang your hat—has a mystery I'll explain
The janitor is Irish, the hall boy is a coon, and the elevator fellow is a Dane
But who is the gent that collects the rent at the end of each four weeks
Ah! that is all done by the Argentines, and the Portuguese, and the Greeks

(1920)

Sweet Burning Incense

Jeanette Dailey

Maurice Moore and his bride, Lilian, flushed with love and excitement, followed the guide and his party down through Chinatown. The streets were brilliantly decorated with lanterns, bright-colored flags; lilies potted in odd vases bloomed along their path; fire-works illumined the whole district, for it was the celebration of the Chinese New Year.

Lilian's dreamy blue eyes peeped, from under her brown sailor, up at the tall, wide-awake husband at her side; she clung tightly to his arm, but half heeding his remarks, herself charmed into silence by the scene.

They visited the shops crowded with jade, peacock-feathered fans, Oriental parasols, quaint pottery, dragon-embroidered cloths of silver and gold. Then, on they went to a Joss house, smoky with sweet-burning incense, smoldering upon altars where, perhaps, prince and princess had the Buddha.*

The guide led them through long dark alleys, down into basements, where several large families dwelt together in one room, divided into apartments by bright draperies and ornamented screens.

From dark alleys, he guided the party up long winding stairways, into one of the finest Tong houses of the city.† As they admired the old paintings, the hand-carved teakwood furniture, Lilian, standing apart, saw her reflection in a mirror, framed in blue and gold, enameled with curious Chinese emblems. Closing her eyes, the fumes of the sweet-burning incense cast on the spell of the Orient, vivid with mystery. In place of a brown tailored suit, she saw a silk jacket and pantalets embroidered with blue birds. The blue eyes, the mass of yellow, fluffy hair, that she knew as her own. Why, what strange thing was this? Black hair arranged in Oriental style framed her face, and black, almond-shaped eyes peered at her. Lilian brushed her hand across her eyes and opened them quickly.

"I—I'm mesmerized by this sweet-burning incense. I must go out," she murmured to herself; and immediately pushed her husband out of the room, ahead of the guide.

They stopped next at the Chinese concert. The music sounded to Maurice like a whole symphony of discords. To Lilian there was harmony in the weird

---

The editor who introduced this work in the *Overland Monthly* notes that it "received second prize in a competition of the California Writemany Club, in which many prominent literary people competed." Below its title is this description: "The Race Question, Garnished by Pathos and Romance."

*Joss house: Temple for worship of Chinese deities from Buddhism, Confucianism, and Taoism; also used for prayers and offerings to ancestors.

†Tong house: Meeting house for a Tong society, part secret society and part mutual aid organization for Chinese immigrants.

sounds—and something more. A new bewildering emotion possessed her. It was as if the thing she heard was familiar—yet, not familiar. The music pulled at her heart-strings, and seemed to say, "Don't you remember?" "Remember what?" she said, aloud; then blushing for her own silliness, looked around to see if anyone had heard her.

"I've had enough of this!" exclaimed Maurice, and, leaving the party, they went into one of the Chinese tearooms.

A peculiar odor of burning incense greeted them; and Lilian at once bought a package, with instructions that she must never inhale too much of it in a closed room, for they burned this incense only a few seconds at a time, just to get the sweet Oriental odor, without the sleepy effect. The old Poppy man, as Lilian named him, informed her that he never sold that incense to customers, but she was different, for she had told him of her mania for sweet-burning incense. The tearoom decorated with lanterns, many-colored, shed a soft light upon the cozy corners behind the screens. Lilies potted with tiny pebbles sprung forth from clumps of melted bottles. A big round table stood in the center of the room, where tea, cakes, preserved ginger and candied Chinese fruit were served.

"Come out of it, Lilian! Shake the trance and drink your tea," Maurice exclaimed, as he teasingly pinched her arm.

"Do you notice, Maurice, this burning incense mesmerizes one? It fascinates me, yet I'm afraid."

"Oh, shucks, honey!" Maurice said, patting her hand. "Why, there's nothing to fear, with a big husky like me to protect you."

"But, Maurice," she urged, "down in the Tong house I had a strange vision. I saw myself change into a Chinese maiden—black hair, almond-shaped eyes, and all."

"Lilian dear, believe me it's nothing but the weird atmosphere, and perhaps the excitement of our runaway marriage."

"Look, Maurice!" she insisted; "I was like that little Chinese girl over there, the one who served us tea. Do you think she's pretty?"

"Oh, she's rather attractive. But, no China for me! I'd just as soon have colored blood as a yellow streak. But come! It's time for me to take you home, honey."

Later, Lilian placed the burning joss sticks on her dresser, slowing inhaling their perfumed incense.* She stood before the mirror brushing her fluffy yellow hair, thankful that her vision of Oriental black hair and almond-shaped eyes was only a dream, brought on by the mysterious influence of sweet-burning incense.

"Oh, Aunt Mary!" she cried as her foster aunt came into the room, "I'm the happiest girl in the world! You can't find any fault with Maurice, Aunty, for he's the best, the dearest, and—"

---

joss stick: Type of incense burned at a Chinese altar.

"Lilian, my darling child!" interrupted Aunt Mary, "I want you to be happy; and I feel Maurice is all that you say." Lilian saw Aunt Mary's soft white hair and troubled face in the mirror over her shoulder.

"But Aunty, why look so serious, then? Maurice is working up a big law practice now; and we are going to have the dearest little bungalow, with yellow and baby crimson roses playing hide and seek all over it."

"It is all on the good qualities of Maurice that I forgive you for getting married without my consent, and against your father's wishes. You were not to marry until you were eighteen; and you were first to read a letter—"

"Yes, but if daddy were alive I know he would forgive when he met Maurice."

Aunt Mary kissed Lilian, and hastily left the room without speaking further upon the subject. Lilian bent low over the joss sticks, inhaling their sweet perfume.

"I wonder why Aunt Mary opposed our marriage before I was eighteen?" she mused. "Well, I'm eighteen today, and we haven't been married so many moons." Lilian shook out her mass of yellow hair around her shoulders, and tucked a flower over her ear. "I wonder, how would I have looked in a bridal veil and orange blossoms; and Maurice, serious-looking, with a white flower on his lapel, standing under a bower of roses, promising to honor and obey, while the solemn minister read the ceremony? I can hear the congregation whisper, 'He is so tall, and dark, and handsome; what could he have seen in that baby-faced blonde?'" Dreaming, she glanced into the mirror again. Instead of orange blossoms, she saw lilies, Chinese lilies, in her hair! Hurriedly she smothered the joss candles, though something seemed to say, "Look! Don't you remember?"

She told herself, "This sweet-burning incense fascinates me; yet, it is getting on my nerves—I'm seeing things."

"Lilian dear," said her aunt, as she came back into the room, "where is Maurice?"

"Oh, he's downstairs smoking, and looking over some papers before he goes to bed. Why, Auntie?"

"You are eighteen, dearie, and I feel it is my duty to tell you all I know about your family history, even if you did disobey, and get married."

"But Auntie, you always told me you didn't know anything; that my daddy gave me away when I was born; that I never had a real mother. And that I must not marry before I was eighteen. So we just ran away and got married, anyway."

"Lilian, your father loved you dearly. He never gave you away; he only left you in my care, until his return from abroad; but he died over there. Your mother died when you were born, and your father was so grieved over it that he could not speak of her. He even named you for your mother."

Aunt Mary stroked the girl's soft yellow hair. "You resemble your father some; the same blue-gray eyes, only his were melancholy eyes, while yours are happy ones. He was a large man, and you are such a wee thing!"

"But why did my father put all of these things in the way of my marriage?"

Aunt Mary hastily took a letter from the desk and handed it to Lilian. "This letter is from your father, dear, and you were to read it upon your eighteenth birthday. It has been all this time in the safety deposit box. I took it out yesterday."

The sweet odor of burning incense filled the room. Lilian tore open the envelope. At that moment did a spirit hand lay a finger of warning on Aunt Mary's arm? She reached out and took the letter. Her hand trembled.

"I—I—I think I've given you the wrong letter, dear." Aunt Mary glanced at the letter, read it again carefully, without looking up.

Lilian spoke a trifle impatiently. "Aunt Mary, is it the right letter?"

Aunt Mary hurriedly tucked the missive into her belt; in a choked voice she whispered, "I—I was mistaken, Lilian dear; this is not for your eyes." She hastily left the room, without any further explanation, just as Maurice entered, smiling.

"Don't run away, Aunt Mary," he said, "just because I came."

"Maurice," said Lilian, closing the door, "Aunt Mary acted queerly tonight. She brought me a letter, saying it was from father, and after looking it over she said it was a mistake; it wasn't meant for me."

"Well, honey, perhaps she did bring the wrong letter."

"Oh, but my name was on it!"

"That's nothing, honey," argued Maurice, "she may have put the name on the wrong letter."

He walked over and snuffed out the light of the joss sticks.

"Why the burning incense tonight, Lilian? That's what upsets you, honey; it always does; yet you insist upon lighting the darn things. I'm like Aunt Mary—I believe your sweet-burning incense is bad luck."

He took her in his arms and talked to her of other things; of their future, of their bungalow, wreathed in crimson and yellow roses hanging over the front door, sending out the fragrance of welcome. He talked of love and happiness, rather than of sorrow and mystery, until Lilian forgot all else, and her dreamy blue eyes smiled again.

And the days went by in golden procession. Lilian happy in looking toward the future, delighted now with the love of her husband.

The sun came out after the morning shower and shone upon the raindrops, glistening like so many stars in the almond trees. The moisture gladdened the blue bird's throat as he sipped the honeydew. Lilian knelt by her hope chest and gently fingered the dainty nainsooks, trimmed with baby laces and blue ribbons; she laid them one by one on Maurice's lap. Aunt Mary came into the room just as Lilian held up a wee shirt embroidered with buttonhole stitch of white silk floss. "Look Aunt Mary! Aren't they darlings?" She hugged them closely to her. Maurice caressed lightly the tiny garments that lay across his knee, fearful that his big hands might crush them. The love light lingered in his frank eyes and his gaze rested upon her golden, sun-kissed hair.

Aunt Mary's kindly face brightened, and tears shone in her eyes as she spoke softly, "I wish every blessing upon you, my children." She took the baby shirt from Lilian and held it out, smiling through her tears. "How tiny and precious! Perhaps this one is as small as was the swaddling cloth of our Savior."

"Auntie, I wonder if father would be pleased if he were here? And, Aunt Mary, what became of father's letter? Haven't you found it yet? You never speak of it anymore."

"It is too late now, Lilian dear. You must never read it."

"Never read daddy's letter? And why not, Auntie?" Lilian opened wide her dreamy blue eyes. The odor of sweet-burning incense stifled the room.

"Lilian, my child, why do you insist upon burning those joss sticks? I—I hate the odor. The fumes choke me." Evasively Aunt Mary had turned the subject, as she had done whenever Lilian had questioned her upon the matter. Maurice quickly extinguished the smoldering fire of the joss sticks and remarked, "Lilian is cultivating a perfect mania for incense, Aunt Mary."

"But why, Auntie," insisted Lilian, not to be turned aside, "why can't I read father's letter? Why is it too late?"

"Because, Lilian dear, you were not to read it if you were married before you were eighteen. And, besides, it wouldn't bring you happiness to read it now."

"But Auntie, where is the letter?" Maurice gently tried to draw Lilian away, begging her to forget the past and its mystery, and just be happy in today.

"Oh, Auntie! Where is the letter?" she sobbed. "I want it. I must know my father better, and my people."

"Lilian dear, forgive me! I love you as my own." She patted her fluffy yellow hair. "I did it for you. I burned the letter—for you are a happy bride. It is all for the best."

The hour of Lilian's trial came, passed. The sun's rays slyly crept through the drawn shutters, playing hide and seek upon the little white crib, with the big blue bow upon the foot, that stood in the corner of the room. The doctor and the nurse bent down low over the baby basket. A faint cry, then a louder one, greeted their ears. "Yes, he'll live," answered the doctor.

"But it's a shame!" the young nurse whispered, "for the child is plainly marked."

"Yes, yes," spoke the doctor worriedly. "I don't understand; there's a mystery somewhere."

Aunt Mary tiptoed softly into the room over toward the little white crib; she pulled the blankets down and peeped in. "May I see the baby now? Is he all right?" As she gazed her face became horror-stricken; she gave a low moan. "Oh, merciful heavens! It's true; it is true! Lilian's father was right after all." Without glancing toward Lilian, Aunt Mary fled from the room.

The doctor called to the young father, who was bending low over Lilian; "Your son will live." A baby's cry filled the room. Maurice came quickly to the little crib and took the child in his arms. He held him up in the light. "Why, Doc!" he cried, "he looks exactly like a Chinese baby—color, hair, almond-shaped eyes, and all."

He scrutinized the baby carefully. "Do you suppose, Doc, that Lilian could have marked the child?" He related their trip through Chinatown, the effect upon Lilian, and her mania for sweet-burning incense.

"Perhaps, Maurice. It is possible." The doctor caught at the suggestion. He slapped Maurice on the back. "The baby will doubtless change color as he grows older."

Maurice held the baby up close to his heart. "I love you, little fellow, for you are mine and Lilian's baby," he said with emotion. Tucking the baby in his little white basket trimmed with the blue satin bow, he went back to Lilian again.

"Is baby all right, Maurice?" Lilian enquired eagerly; "does he look like you—or me?"

He bent over and kissed her forehead, her soft yellow hair. "Baby's all right. You must be quiet now, honey, and rest. I have another call for that case out of town that I put off yesterday, and I just can't delay longer. Goodbye, dear; I'll write every night and wire every morning."

"Auntie," Lilian called, later on, as Aunt Mary slipped quietly into the room, "bring baby to me. I want to see him."

"He's—he's asleep," Aunt Mary answered hesitatingly.

"Please Auntie, I won't wake him. I must see him."

Aunt Mary picked up baby and blanket, and carried them to Lilian, placing the child in her arms. She gave a tender, searching look—then cried:

"Raise the shades! I—I can't see him well. He—he—looks so yellow. Take him away!" I want my baby!" She burst into tears. "Is—is—he—all right? Tell me, Auntie."

"Yes, Lilian, my child; everything will be all right. You must not worry. There, now go to sleep." And Aunt Mary spoke soothingly.

In her weakened state Lilian was easily persuaded. But there came a day, when the baby was two weeks old, that Lilian, after gazing silently at him for a time, turned determinedly to Aunt Mary.

"His father will be home tomorrow. Tell me what you have been keeping from me. I must know. Why does this baby look—Chinese?"

"He has Chinese blood flowing in his veins."

"Oh, Auntie, it isn't true! Tell me it isn't true," sobbed Lilian.

"Yes, my dear child, it is true." Sorrow and love were written upon the Aunt's face. "The biggest mistake of my life was that I didn't read the letter the day your father gave it to me to put in the safety deposit box. For in that he told the love story about your mother. She was a Chinese girl."

"Don't, Auntie!" cried Lilian; "I—can't endure it. I hate Chinese people! I hate my mother! I hate my father. I hate myself! I—I—almost hate my—baby."

"But, Lilian dear, your father loved you. If you could only remember how much he made of you, and how he talked to you when you were small." Aunt Mary stroked the girl's hair. "Your father did love you. He gave you his name, Ware, and your mother's name, Lilian."

"Oh, Auntie! Maurice will hate me! He will! He will! I wanted to make him happy."

"No, Lilian; Maurice loves you too well to ever hate you."

Aunt Mary reasoned and soothed Lilian into a more quiet state. She had to go into town on an errand, and must leave her with only a little nurse girl.

"Bring baby to me, Auntie." She kissed him and cuddled him in her arms. "I love you, for you are mine and his, my Maurice."

When the Aunt had gone, Lilian at once called the nurse girl to her. "Get me the incense out of the bottom dresser drawer. It is in that package, wrapped in brown paper. There, that's it. Now, light it, and set it close, here at my side. Close the shutters and leave us alone, for the incense will soothe us to sleep, to rest."

Lilian hugged the tiny baby within her arms, and her golden head on the pillow, lay with a smile in her dreamy blue eyes.

"Oh, sweet-burning incense! I never knew that I would need you. Baby, we will sleep, you and I, alone, all alone."

The burning incense filled the room with a sweet, soothing odor. Lilian and her baby drifted into dreamland, while the poison fumes grew more powerful. Lilian, with her baby cuddled in her arms, floated on and on, like a sacred lily in full bloom, with a tiny bud blossoming at her side; tossed upon muddy stream, first troubled, then peaceful. At last she rested in that country where there are no lines drawn, of color, or of race, and where every child is loved of God.

The candles flickered, flickered, then died away, leaving only the sweet perfume of the burning incense.

(1921)

Salvatore Schneider—A Story of New York

Ernest Poole

"T'ank Gott, he's a Schneider!" old Otto would mutter in deep relief. And so he was—a Schneider huge beyond all bounds. As he sat at the cashier's desk in the snug little butcher shop of his sire, the prodigious body of Salvatore hour by hour overflowed like a wagonload of hay, until only the bending, creaking legs of the chair remained in view. Customers glanced at him in surprise; startled babies took one look and ducked their heads in speechless fright. But even babies learned to trust and gaze in solemn wonder. For through the whole vast labyrinth of his veins the Schneider blood flowed quietly, as it had flowed for long generations; while from morning to night the eyes were serious, steadily fixed, as Salvatore made out the bills.

But blood is a mysterious thing. Already it had produced this exuberance out of Otto and Margarita his wife, who were both rotund little people. What other surprise lurked deep in this fortress of flesh? Otto had never ceased watching. He was taking no chances.

Nineteen years before, in that mighty welding of peoples which is to bring forth someday a strange new race of men in the hybrid city of Greater New York, Otto had become a daring pioneer. Reckless for once in his life, romantic and blind with emotion, he had married the lovely young daughter of an Italian greengrocer nearby. But when he had roused to what he had done and its possible bearing upon his career, then Otto had opened his steady blue eyes and had never quite closed them since. On the christening day, when Margarita, in all the appealing weakness and charm of brand new motherhood, begged that the bambino be named Salvatore, Otto gave in. But this was the last of Italy's triumphs. Day by day and year by year, every trace of that fiery land of the South was toned away. Margarita grew plump and submissive and beaming; Otto grew stout and cheery and brisk. And working in happy domestic accord, they had bred in the pliable soul of their son all the virtues of order, frugality, thrift, and hard, patient application to work.

So here the budding monster sat, flowering slowly but surely into a sober businessman. And the danger sprung from the reckless past seemed buried forever behind.

Salvatore suddenly heaved a monstrous quivering sigh.

A lovely April day was nearing its end. The air was delicious with fresh earthy odors. Even the ragged old tree across the street was donning a delicate garb of green. Children were scampering, shouting like mad; old people were blissfully dozing on doorsteps; important young lovers came slowly by. The genial sun's last beams poured over the tenement roofs and bathed it all in a rich, warm light. And from the North River beyond, deep and muffled and strangely disturbing, sounded the voice of an ocean liner outward bound for the world of the winds and the rolling waves eternally free.

Restlessness, the insidious longings of nights and days, tugging at the heart-strings—all burst softly forth in Salvatore's sigh. Then he began making out a new bill:

Two pounds Sirloin Steak. . . @ .20 .40
Three pounds Wiener Schnitzel. . . @ .25 .75
One pound—

All at once, with a crash of drum and cymbal, a hurdy-gurdy wheeled into action close by the open door.* The noise was deafening. With a frown of indignation Salvatore looked around—and stared.

Through the open window at his elbow a girl was gazing at him in amazement and delight. When Salvatore scowled with all the annoyance of pompous eighteen, her eyes only sparkled the brighter, her head nodded twice in vigorous approval, and in Italian she whispered:

"Madre de Dio, come splendido quel nomo, *come magnifico!*"

Salvatore understood, his rosy cheeks turned suddenly a darker hue, and at this time she threw back her airy young head and laughed so joyously that even he relented. On his face there appeared a quiet, indulgent smile; as a huge Newfoundland dog might stare at a kitten, so Salvatore looked down upon the girl. And seeing this, she gave an odd, graceful hitch to her skirts, shifted her tambourine with a tinkle, and stood there wholly oblivious under his eyes. Over her head was a kerchief of gray with little gold spangles; from under the edges the soft black hair strayed in negligent, lazy fashion, and under the black arched eyebrows were two assertive gray eyes that now looked up again—challenging, mocking, elusive, curious, prying with eager scrutiny right into Salvatore's soul.

With a nervous laugh he tossed her a nickel. She caught the coin in her tambourine, looked at it, flushed like a child, and then flashed upon him a smile so intimate and warm that Salvatore grunted and fell back aghast. And at this the girl sprang nimbly away. With her old father she seized the crazy piano and trundled it swiftly down the street. And Salvatore, left alone, gazed dumbfounded into the deepening twilight, his two great black eyes in scandalous disaccord with the rest of him; twinkling, eager, restless, dazed, almost ready to flash.

But in the morning, running one ponderous finger slowly and carefully down the columns of figures, his heavy brows had lowered again, the eyes were buried, the whole mammoth face was sluggish as before.

---

hurdy-gurdy: Commonly, a stringed instrument resembling a fiddle (also known as a *wheel fiddle*). But beginning in the eighteenth century, *hurdy-gurdy* also referred to a small portable barrel organ, often played by impoverished street musicians. The hurdy-gurdy in "Salvatore Schneider—A Story of New York" refers to this latter version of the instrument.

When again the drum and cymbal crashed and those disturbing gray eyes gazed in at him he slowly turned and surveyed the creature in grave disapproval. She dropped her eyes and stood abashed, and with a low grunt of satisfaction Salvatore resumed his work. After a time he glanced up again. She was standing motionless, both hands hanging limp at her sides. She did not even raise her eyes to his, but stood with grave interest watching his work.

So she came day after day in the balmy weeks that followed, derisive no longer, sneering and prying no longer, respectfully curious, humble, strangely intent, waiting until he should toss her the coin. The coin was his sign of dismissal, and the girl always obeyed. And now with the first sharp trill of uneasiness gone, he felt safe, this colossal man of eighteen. The whole silent drama was hidden from Otto and Margarita by the high counter behind. And Salvatore, who until now had barely looked on the face of a woman, would look at the stranger with all the serene assurance of a sagacious old man of the world, and her big eyes would open wide and look frankly back into his.

"My name is Gemma," she said abruptly in the midst of one of these mutual stares. Salvatore good-humoredly nodded and bent again over his work, feeling a curious, brand new tingling up and down his spine.

"I knew you could," she said softly, still in Italian.

"Could what?" growled Salvatore.

"You are doing it now—speaking like me! You are Italian! I knew it! You are Italian—like me!"

Salvatore looked hastily round, saw that he was alone in the shop, gave a grunt of relief, turned back and surveyed her in silence.

"How old are you?" he asked gruffly. Gemma glanced over her shoulder, gave that peculiarly graceful hitch to her skirt, dropped her head on one side and looked at him gravely.

"Seventeen," she said. Salvatore stared. He had thought her at least twenty-five, and something romantic inside of him dropped. But she saw the change in his face, and in an instant her eyes had half closed, she drew into herself, grew strange, mysterious, wise, like a gypsy witch.

"I am older than you," she said slowly, with a provoking smile. He gave a short laugh of amusement.

"I am," she said calmly, "because I know more." And all at once she threw back her head and laughed till the tears shone bright in her eyes. She stopped. Her voice grew mysterious, thrilling and low: "What do you see," she asked, "on the streets—in the night?" Salvatore watched her uneasily.

"I mind my own business," he growled. She eyed him with scorn.

"That is stupid," she said severely. "You should *never* mind your own business! You should watch!" He scowled.

"Watch what?" he asked, but the enchantress was already back with the white old man at the curb; and together they trundled the battered old instrument noisily down the street.

In the evening, seated in front of the shop, he loomed unassailable, placidly puffing great circles of smoke. When he saw the pair coming he made no sign, except to throw one backward glance at Otto busily talking far in the rear of the shop. When they stopped at the curbstone before him and the music burst gaily forth, and the enchantress came forward, her tambourine in her hand— the unflinching monster only took out a match from his box and carefully held it over the bowl of his already glowing pipe. When she raised the tambourine slowly over her head and softly beat time to the music, and began bending and turning, her eyes dilating and filling with strange, uncanny delight; when as the throb of music came faster her lithe young body responded, twisting, tossing and whirling into mad rollicking life—still Salvatore the Schneider sat motionless, strictly attending to business, puffing in dignified silence like an old Indian warrior chief. But he took out his pipe with a breath of relief as the crowd closed in between them.

She came many nights. She sang. And her crude, deep voice, like her dancing, was of swiftly changing moods; now rough, impatient, fiercely stirring; now low and appealing and hungry; and again radiant, laughing, mocking and gay. Some evenings Margarita would slowly steal out of the shop and stand with arms akimbo—beaming. Once with a sudden suspicion she cast a look of uneasiness down at her precious son, but the giant gave such a stony grunt that Margarita breathed easy and listened and watched to her heart's content.

One night in early May the old hurdy-gurdy stopped a block down the street. The moon shone bright and clear; he could see Gemma, dim, fantastic and airy, dancing like a sprite. Then the crowd closed round her, and Salvatore lounged far back on the stoop, confidently waiting until she should come. But a few moments later he sat up and scowled. The crowd was dispersing; the pair had turned and were going back by the way they had come!

This happened five nights.

And then one evening slowly the huge bulk of Salvatore reared from the stoop, and with his black felt hat tipped carelessly back on his flaxen head, the stem of his long Dutch pipe in his teeth, and the bowl in his great right hand, he lumbered off from the safe Schneider shop, off into the sparkling night!

Once loosed from his moorings, through the long, balmy evenings of May, Salvatore roamed hither and thither; now aimlessly, dazed, seeing nothing at all; and now watching life with genial eyes.

Every night in the course of his rambles Salvatore would cautiously loiter into the dark outskirts of a crowd that had gathered round an old hurdy-gurdy. But never once did Gemma notice his presence. Often this colossal moth would approach the flame many times in one night; between his approaches he would make studious detours around tenement blocks, or far down by the docks, strolling out on the end of an empty pier, gazing off into the gleaming old river, and smoking silently, except for now and then a muffled grunt of longing.

Evening by evening, the tinkle and bang of the battered piano floated steadily down the west side of Manhattan, each night farther away from the snug and respectable Schneider abode, each night farther down toward the teeming, scandalous, joyous quarter where live the children of the South.

One night in the middle of June, after a slow and sagacious detour, he found the piano waiting just at the head of a long, dark street which he had never entered before. So narrow it was that the tenement roofs seemed meeting above in the distance; below in the canyon for blocks and blocks the pavement was black with a surging mass; and in arches and long festoon, tiny lights by thousands were twinkling festive and fairy-like; and out of it all came the hum of voices so thrilling with gladness that Salvatore pushed back his hat and stood rooted fast to the spot.

In a moment, caught by the tide, he was quickly jostled along. Towering high over all the heads, he looked delightedly this way and that at the swarthy faces, the flashing laughs, and the excited black eyes. All around him the soft flowing speech rose voluble, eager, and gay. Songs floated lightly about, and shouts and long ringing peals of mirth. At the third corner, on a rough platform over the street, a big brass band was booming; below were old women and children and men and girls—a whirling, shrieking throng; and from a fire-escape close above, two merry scamps were hurling confetti in snowy showers down over the heads.

Suddenly, from behind him, Gemma came spinning on the feet light as air, tossing and bending and stamping and banging the old tambourine, circling round him and laughing unsteadily out of her half-closed eyes. In an instant, before he had time to escape, he found himself in a circle of hundreds of faces; glad shouts of "Gemma! Gemma!" rang from the crowd; and with one fiery upward glance Gemma came spinning straight into his arms, jerked him round with a merry shriek—and Salvatore was dancing!

Tumultuous cheers resounded. From the street all around, from row upon row of windows above, the eyes of his countrymen flashed into his. And with his whole great soul a fiery furnace, he gamboled and pranced and swung his arms; while high above all the shouting and dominating it all, there suddenly thundered a laugh so prodigious it tore the air! With one hand clutching Gemma's young arm, his bulging cheeks palpitating with glee, the demeanor of Schneider forever lost and the soul of Italy bursting out in his eyes, Salvatore shook with the sheer joy of life and fairly bellowed his mirth.

And truly that was a festival night. Before all the crowd did he kiss Gemma square on her blushing cheek. When in a rage she sprang off in the crowd, he chased her and caught her; seizing the handle of the piano, he turned it furiously round and round; and in sonorous Italian he shouted, "Dance—dance—dance!" Off she whirled; and as the crowd began roaring a ballad in time to her dancing, Salvatore joined in, catching words here and there and laughing between. And when at last the band music was over, Gemma sent home her weary old father; the giant gripped the piano shafts; and together, chuckling, laughing, jabbering fast and low, those two went wandering off in the night.

After that, every evening for weeks, Salvatore would sluggishly rise from the Schneider home doorstep and lazily drift down the street, turn the corner, hasten his pace, and jog contentedly off to the appointed corner. Gemma was always waiting alone; for her stooping, old father, worn by the work of the long, hot day, was only too glad to rest at night. And in the powerful hands of its jovial master the crazy old instrument crashed forth its music as though to proclaim that the weary old world had had a fresh birth and that life was suddenly dazzling new.

Salvatore the vagabond beamed upon life. Gemma the witch began teaching him how to pry into its secrets; with a slowly increasing intensity, she forced his eyes open and held his gaze as though she would burn the love of it all forever deep into its soul.

Sometimes as she danced and Salvatore watched her, all unconsciously his hand on the grinder would revolve faster and faster, until, gasping for breath, the girl would stop and seize his arm. And then, quite forgetting the faces around, they would look at each other and laugh till the tears rolled down their glistening cheeks.

Through the midsummer nights the bellowing laugh of Salvatore rose above all the street's bedlam of sounds, like a huge advertisement announcing the fun. It thickened the crowd, it doubled the pennies; and when the wise Gemma saw this, she taught him to bring it in at just the right moments in perfect accord with her dances and songs. So startling was the effect and so captivating to the simple Italians, that little by little he added rough jokes of his own, loud indignant remarks, pathetic roars of appeal to bystanders. And the great voice of the jovial monster ringing free and glad in his mother tongue seemed heralding forth to all the world the mirth and the loves and the throbbing life of the happy-go-lucky South.

But when at last the streets grew hushed, when the fire escapes were filled with the sleepers, the moon sank over the tenement roofs, and the stars grew dim in the misty skies, then Salvatore would go slowly back as though drawn by some irresistible power, back to his neat and snowy couch and sleep and the orderly business life in the shop of his Teuton sire.

And here by day, as week followed week, over the cheery home there crept an ominous shadow. The anxious parents suspected; but, knowing their son, they resolutely refrained from the questions that might only bring on the storm. Margarita was silent and giddy, feeling that she was the source of it all. Otto barely uttered a word, indignantly hacking and sawing his steaks. Only each morning when, in increasing numbers, the bills came back for correction, he carefully looked them over, went to the desk, and silently pointed out the mistakes.

And little by little, from the innermost depths of Salvatore's soul, there rose insistent and sharp and clear the still, small voice of Schneider.

In the ominous silence he scowled. He scowled at the glances that he could feel, at the whispered words that came to his ears. He scowled at every mistake in the bills, as it loomed a mute accusing witness under Otto's finger. He melted and burned with the midsummer's heat. He cursed his head that was aching and dull from the sleep he had missed in his rovings. He ground his teeth and strove to be careful, clear, and exact. But in his work the mistakes swelled day by day, and the gloom of the butcher shop deepened. So through the dragging, sweltering weeks a Schneider by day and a Salvatore by night struggled to win that mammoth soul.

At last, one stifling morning in August, when the short, rosy finger of Otto pointed to five mistakes in one bill, then up leaped Salvatore! Speechless, he stood all aquiver with mortification and rage. Undaunted, vigilant, careful, stout little Otto looked steadily up; his breath came hard, but when he spoke his voice was low and solemn:

"So! . . . So—my poy—now you see! No man can attend to his beesnees when he is a vagapond effery night! . . . So! . . . And now you must choose." Here Otto suddenly swallowed hard, but his voice was quiet as ever: "You must choose for yourself, my poy," he said. "I will do noddings to boss you."

For one moment longer the giant glared down. Then without warning his head jerked back, the great neck shook, and for the first and only time the house of Schneider rang with that scandalous bellow of mirth. It ended. And Salvatore lurched from his desk and out through the door, and then unsteadily, blindly, swiftly up the street.

Back in the shop, Margarita stood like one in a dream. Slowly the tears welled in her eyes and trickled down her cheeks. She turned to her husband and laid one hand on his trembling arm.

"Otto," she whispered imploringly, "Otto! Don't—don't be so angry!"—her voice broke in a frightened sob. "Otto," she wailed, "I did my best! How could I *help* being born?" Again did Otto swallow hard.

"*You* couldn't help," he said tenderly. "*You* vas *already* born—*you* couldn't help." He squeezed her hand reassuringly. "Wait," he said, "he will come back, Margarita; he is a goot poy! He will come back!"

And little Margarita's sobs gradually subsided. She dried her eyes and sat quietly down to her sewing. And after an hour of silent work, she looked up with a guilty light in her eyes.

"*Madre Dio*," she thought, "what a magnificent laugh!" And Margarita sighed.

Far and wide did Salvatore roam over Manhattan that day, dark and lowering, like a bull who has broken his pasture bounds.

But at night, haggard and pale, the prodigal came home. He said not a word, but went up to bed, and fell into heavy sleep.

The next day he was up bright and early. Without one break or even a grunt he worked at his desk through the long, sultry hours. And that evening, and for three nights thereafter, Salvatore sat on the doorstep, quietly smoking the pipe of peace, of honest repose from a day well spent.

But on the fourth evening, moment by moment the mountainous bulk of him seemed to tighten. Suddenly, with breath that was like an explosion, he rose, jammed his broad black hat firmly down over his eyes, and with a look of heroic decision strode off to the old place of meeting.

Swinging sharply around the corner, he met Gemma face to face. At first she did not see him. She stood by the old hurdy-gurdy, alone and staring across the street in a way that made Salvatore stop short. When she saw him, Gemma gave a quick gasp and both hands leaped to her throat. Then her face cleared and relaxed; and looking up into his scowling visage the girl laughed triumphantly, long and low.

But Salvatore was in no joking mood. With a solemn, businesslike frown he advanced, took her hand, squeezed it until she winced with the pain, and growled:

"Now I know what I want to do! We will go to a priest, we will be married, and then we will go to my father and mother! Let him try! What can he say? *My mother herself was Italian!*"

As Gemma looked up, her face slowly changed, grew utterly dazed. For a moment she seemed to grasp nothing. But all at once her eyes fairly crackled with wrath.

"Me?" she gasped. *"Like your mother?"*

"Yes," said Salvatore, suddenly beaming. "Don't be afraid. You can be just the same."

"Me? . . . *Me the same?*" She started to laugh, stopped, looked at him again, pursed her red lips and spoke in a tone of withering scorn:

"Salvatore! I have seen your mother in the shop! And rather than be a Signora Schneider like her I would wrap my throat tight, tight in my hair, and pull and pull until I was dead! Ugh!" She threw up both expressive young hands.

Salvatore was dumb with amazement. Thrice he tried and could not utter a word. But as he glared down at Gemma, slowly his cheeks puffed out and out in swelling indignation.

"Goodbye!" he burst out at last. He flounced around heavily and started away.

"No! Salvatore! No—no—no!" Her strong, supple fingers clung tight to one of his arms; the girl was panting between her teeth. And instant she seemed hesitating. "No!" she whispered. "I will not tell!"

"Tell what?" he asked roughly. She shook her head, and her face broke into a flashing smile.

"Salvatore. Come." Her voice was coaxing and tremulous now. "Come. One evening more—only one. It is not so much. When I dance I can think; when I sing I can see! And then I will tell you what we can do! We will find a good way, a beautiful way! Come! Salvatore! Come!"

And Salvatore gave in.

That night they hardly knew where they wandered; they barely saw the swarthy faces pressing close around. The eyes of Gemma kept hungrily turning up to the face of her lover, striving to grip again the vagabond spirit that she had wakened to life. Salvatore himself could feel this part of him rise to respond. But his old self, the old Schneider self of sobriety, order, and thrift, this too rose to the struggle. And while the witch danced till the tenement street was a mass of delighted faces, while she sang with the fiery heat of the old mountain songs that had once made him thrill with strange new dreams and longings, Salvatore stood at his post firm as the ancient Colossus of Rhodes.* His face was fixed in a gloomy scowl, through which the new soul of him broke only in faint occasional gleams. And the bellowing laugh was silent now, buried deep in the fortress. Stoutly did the house of Schneider stand the storm that night.

At last when the struggle had gone on for hours, after a desperate tingling effort which brought tremendous applause, when Gemma turned and met as before only that stony expression of gloom, her dusky face grew suddenly white. She came to him swiftly, stamped her foot, threw her lithe young body into a posture of terrible scorn, and with one hand outstretched and shaking, the girl poured forth her pent up wrath:

"Now go! Go back to your Schneiders, your sausages, cows—and pigs! Go back! Go to sleep. Grow fatter than all the pigs in the world—and eat! You are good for nothing—nothing—*nothing!* Go!"

Salvatore looked down at his feet, gave a short angry laugh, and turned and went quickly away.

And Gemma, facing the crowd with cheeks that now were flaming, went into peal upon peal of wild hysterical laughter.

"Who," she shouted at last, "who will play while I dance?"

Three gallant countrymen sprang to the grinder. And laughing and shrieking in gay little bursts, the airy witch whirled round and round, till the whole street echoed with long and resounding "Bravos!" of applause.

Since then, in the snug little butcher shop, nine long, happy years have glided smoothly by.

And now each morning, his books held firmly under his arm, a neat and decorous youngster trots dutifully to school. His face is plump, his stiff little flaxen curls peep demurely from under his cap; as he goes, his serious, steady blue eyes, attending strictly to business, are fixed determinedly straight ahead. And to give not the slightest chance for a doubt, his name is Otto Gottfried Schneider.

(1908)

Colossus of Rhodes: One of the Seven Wonders of the Ancient World, the Colossus of Rhodes (statue of the Greek god Helios) was the tallest statue of the ancient world. Finished in 280 BC, the statue was destroyed by an earthquake in 224 BC. See also Emma Lazarus's paean to the Statue of Liberty, "The New Colossus," in Part I of this book.

Uncle Wellington's Wives

Charles W. Chesnutt

I

Uncle Wellington Braboy was so deeply absorbed in thought as he walked
slowly homeward from the weekly meeting of the Union League, that he let his
pipe go out, a fact of which he remained oblivious until he had reached the little frame house in the suburbs of Patesville, where he lived with aunt Milly, his
wife.* On this particular occasion the club had been addressed by a visiting
brother from the North, Professor Patterson, a tall, well-formed mulatto, who
wore a perfectly fitting suit of broadcloth, a shiny silk hat, and linen of dazzling
whiteness,—in short, a gentleman of such distinguished appearance that the
doors and windows of the offices and stores on Front Street were filled with
curious observers as he passed through that thoroughfare in the early part of
the day. This polished stranger was a traveling organizer of Masonic lodges,
but he also claimed to be a high officer in the Union League, and had been in-
vited to lecture before the local chapter of that organization at Patesville.

The lecture had been largely attended, and uncle Wellington Braboy had occupied a seat just in front of the platform. The subject of the lecture was "The
Mental, Moral, Physical, Political, Social, and Financial Improvement of the
Negro Race in America," a theme much dwelt upon, with slight variations, by
colored orators. For to this struggling people, then as now, the problem of
their uncertain present and their doubtful future was the chief concern of life.
The period was the hopeful one. The Federal Government retained some ves-
tige of authority in the South, and the newly emancipated race cherished the
delusion that under the Constitution, that enduring rock on which our liber-
ties are founded, and under the equal laws it purported to guarantee, they
would enter upon the era of freedom and opportunity which their Northern
friends had inaugurated with such solemn sanctions. The speaker pictured in
eloquent language the state of ideal equality and happiness enjoyed by colored people at the North: how they sent their children to school with the white
children; how they sat by white people in the churches and theatres, ate with
them in the public restaurants, and buried their dead in the same cemeteries.
The professor waxed eloquent with the development of his theme, and, as a

---

Union League: Union Leagues established in the South after 1867 were social, civic, and political organizations for newly freed African Americans during the Reconstruction. A number of Union Leagues were
formed in the North during the Civil War as support organizations for the Union, and continue as contemporary charitable organizations.

finishing touch to an alluring picture, assured the excited audience that the intermarriage of the races was common, and that he himself had espoused a white woman.

Uncle Wellington Braboy was a deeply interested listener. He had heard something of these facts before, but his information had always come in such vague and questionable shape that he had paid little attention to it. He knew that the Yankees had freed the slaves, and that runaway negroes had always gone to the North to seek liberty; any such equality, however, as the visiting brother had depicted, was more than uncle Wellington had ever conceived as actually existing anywhere in the world. At first he felt inclined to doubt the truth of the speaker's statements; but the cut of his clothes, the eloquence of his language, and the flowing length of his whiskers, were so far superior to anything uncle Wellington had ever met among the colored people of his native State, that he felt irresistibly impelled to the conviction that nothing less than the advantages claimed for the North by the visiting brother could have produced such an exquisite flower of civilization. Any lingering doubts uncle Wellington may have felt were entirely dispelled by the courtly bow and cordial grasp of the hand with which the visiting brother acknowledged the congratulations showered upon him by the audience at the close of his address.

The more uncle Wellington's mind dwelt upon the professor's speech, the more attractive seemed the picture of Northern life presented. Uncle Wellington possessed in large measure the imaginative faculty so freely bestowed by nature upon the race from which the darker half of his blood was drawn. He had indulged in occasional daydreams of an ideal state of social equality, but his wildest flights of fancy had never located it nearer than heaven, and he had felt some misgivings about its practical working even there. Its desirability he had never doubted, and the speech of the evening before had given a local habitation and a name to the forms his imagination had bodied forth. Giving full rein to his fancy, he saw in the North a land flowing with milk and honey,—a land peopled by noble men and beautiful women, among whom colored men and women moved with the ease and grace of acknowledged right. Then he placed himself in the foreground of the picture. What a fine figure he would have made in the world if he had been born at the free North! He imagined himself dressed like the professor, and passing the contribution box in a white church; and most pleasant of his dreams, and the hardest to realize as possible, was that of the gracious white lady he might have called wife. Uncle Wellington was a mulatto, and his features were those of his white father, though tinged with the hue of his mother's race; and as he lifted the kerosene lamp at evening, and took a long look at his image in the little mirror over the mantelpiece, he said to himself that he was a very good-looking man, and could have adorned a much higher sphere in life than that in which the accident of birth had placed him. He fell asleep and dreamed that he lived in a two-story brick house, with a spacious flower garden in front, the whole enclosed by a high iron fence; that he kept a carriage and servants, and never did a stroke of work. This was the highest style of living in Patesville, and he could conceive of nothing finer.

Uncle Wellington slept later than usual the next morning, and the sunlight was pouring in at the open window of the bedroom, when his dreams were interrupted by the voice of his wife, in tones meant to be harsh, but which no ordinary degree of passion could rob of their native unctuousness.

"Git up f'm dere, you lazy, good-fuh-nuffin' nigger! Is you gwine ter sleep all de mawnin'? I's ti'ed er dis yer runnin' 'roun' all night an' den sleepin' all day. You won't git dat tater patch hoed ovuh terday 'less'n you git up f'm dere an' git at it."

Uncle Wellington rolled over, yawned cavernously, stretched himself, and with a muttered protest got out of bed and put on his clothes. Aunt Milly had prepared a smoking breakfast of hominy and fried bacon, the odor of which was very grateful to his nostrils.

"Is breakfus' done ready?" he inquired, tentatively, as he came into the kitchen and glanced at the table.

"No, it ain't ready, an' 't ain't gwine ter be ready 'tel you tote dat wood an' water in," replied aunt Milly severely, as she poured two teacups of boiling water on two tablespoonfuls of ground coffee.

Uncle Wellington went down to the spring and got a pail of water, after which he brought in some oak logs for the fireplace and some lightwood for kindling. Then he drew a chair toward the table and started to sit down.

"Wonduh what's de matter wid you dis mawnin' anyhow," remarked aunt Milly. "You must 'a' be'n up ter some devilment las' night, fer yo' recommemb'ance is so po' dat you fus' fergit ter git up, an' den fergit ter wash yo' face an' hands fo' you set down ter de table. I don' 'low nobody ter eat at my table dat a-way."

"I don' see no use 'n washin' 'em so much," replied Wellington wearily. "Dey gits dirty ag'in right off, an' den you got ter wash 'em ovuh ag'in; it's jes' pilin' up wuk what don' fetch in nuffin'. De dirt don' show nohow, 'n' I don' see no advantage in bein' black, ef you got to keep on washin' yo' face 'n' han's jes' lack w'ite folks." He nevertheless performed his ablutions in a perfunctory way, and resumed his seat at the breakfast table.

"Ole 'oman," he asked, after the edge of his appetite had been taken off, "how would you lack ter live at de Norf?"

"I dunno nuffin' 'bout de Norf," replied aunt Milly. "It's hard 'nuff ter git erlong heah, whar we knows all erbout it."

"De brother what 'dressed de meetin' las' night say dat de wages at de Norf is twicet ez big ez dey is heah."

"You could make a sight mo' wages heah ef you'd 'ten' ter yo' wuk better," replied aunt Milly.

Uncle Wellington ignored this personality, and continued, "An' he say de cullud folks got all de privileges er de w'ite folks,—dat dey chillen goes ter school tergedder, dat dey sets on same seats in chu'ch, an' sarves on jury, 'n' rides on de kyars an' steamboats wid de w'ite folks, an' eats at de fus' table."

"Dat 'u'd suit you," chuckled aunt Milly, "an' you'd stay dere fer de secon' table, too. How dis man know 'bout all dis yer foolis'ness?" she asked incredulously.

"He come f'm de Norf," said uncle Wellington, "an' he 'speunced it all hisse'f."

"Well, he can't make me b'lieve it," she rejoined, with a shake of her head.

"An' you wouldn' lack ter go up dere an' 'joy all dese privileges?" asked uncle Wellington, with some degree of earnestness.

The old woman laughed until her sides shook. "Who gwine ter take me up dere?" she inquired.

"You got de money yo'se'f."

"I ain' got no money fer ter was'e," she replied shortly, becoming serious at once; and with that the subject was dropped.

Uncle Wellington pulled a hoe from under the house, and took his way wearily to the potato patch. He did not feel like working, but aunt Milly was the undisputed head of the establishment, and he did not dare to openly neglect his work. In fact, he regarded work at any time as a disagreeable necessity to be avoided as much as possible.

His wife was cast in a different mould. Externally she would have impressed the casual observer as a neat, well-preserved, and good-looking black woman, of middle age, every curve of whose ample figure—and her figure was all curves—was suggestive of repose. So far from being indolent, or even deliberate in her movements, she was the most active and energetic woman in the town. She went through the physical exercises of a prayer meeting with astonishing vigor. It was exhilarating to see her wash a shirt, and a study to watch her do it up. A quick jerk shook out the dampened garment; one pass of her ample palm spread it over the ironing board, and a few well-directed strokes with the iron accomplished what would have occupied the ordinary laundress for half an hour.

To this uncommon, and in uncle Wellington's opinion unnecessary and unnatural activity, his own habits were a steady protest. If aunt Milly had been willing to support him in idleness, he would have acquiesced without a murmur in her habits of industry. This she would not do, and, moreover, insisted on his working at least half the time. If she had invested the proceeds of her labor in rich food and fine clothing, he might have endured it better; but to her passion for work was added a most detestable thrift. She absolutely refused to pay for Wellington's clothes, and required him to furnish a certain proportion of the family supplies. Her savings were carefully put by, and with them she had bought and paid for the modest cottage which she and her husband occupied. Under her careful hand it was always neat and clean; in summer the little yard was gay with bright-colored flowers, and woe to the heedless pickaninny who should stray into her yard and pluck a rose or a verbena! In a stout oaken chest under her bed she kept a capacious stocking, into which flowed a steady stream of fractional currency. She carried the key to this chest in her pocket, a proceeding regarded by uncle Wellington with no little disfavor. He was of the opinion—an opinion he would not have dared to assert in her presence—that his wife's earnings were his own property; and he looked upon this stocking as a drunkard's wife might regard the saloon which absorbed her husband's wages.

Uncle Wellington hurried over the potato patch on the morning of the conversation above recorded, and as soon as he saw aunt Milly go away with a basket of clothes on her head, returned to the house, put on his coat, and went uptown.

He directed his steps to a small frame building fronting on the main street of the village, at a point where the street was intersected by one of the several creeks meandering through the town, cooling the air, providing numerous swimming holes for the amphibious small boy, and furnishing waterpower for gristmills and sawmills. The rear of the building rested on long brick pillars, built up from the bottom of the steep bank of the creek, while the front was level with the street. This was the office of Mr. Matthew Wright, the sole representative of the colored race at the bar of Chinquapin County. Mr. Wright came of an "old issue" free colored family, in which, though the negro blood was present in an attenuated strain, a line of free ancestry could be traced beyond the Revolutionary War. He had enjoyed exceptional opportunities, and enjoyed the distinction of being the first, and for a long time the only colored lawyer in North Carolina. His services were frequently called into requisition by impecunious people of his own race; when they had money they went to white lawyers, who, they shrewdly conjectured, would have more influence with judge or jury than a colored lawyer, however able.

Uncle Wellington found Mr. Wright in his office. Having inquired after the health of the lawyer's family and all his relations in detail, uncle Wellington asked for a professional opinion.

"Mistah Wright, ef a man's wife got money, whose money is dat befo' de law—his'n er her'n?"

The lawyer put on his professional air, and replied: "Under the common law, which in default of special legislative enactment is the law of North Carolina, the personal property of the wife belongs to her husband."

"But dat don' jes' tech de p'int, suh. I wuz axin' 'bout money."

"You see, uncle Wellington, your education has not rendered you familiar with legal phraseology. The term 'personal property' or 'estate' embraces, according to Blackstone, all property other than land, and therefore includes money. Any money a man's wife has is his, constructively, and will be recognized as his actually, as soon as he can secure possession of it."

"Dat is ter say, suh—my eddication don' quite 'low me ter understan' dat—dat is ter say"—

"That is to say, it's yours when you get it. It isn't yours so that the law will help you get it; but on the other hand, when you once lay your hands on it, it is yours so that the law won't take it away from you."

Uncle Wellington nodded to express his full comprehension of the law as expounded by Mr. Wright, but scratched his head in a way that expressed some disappointment. The law seemed to wobble. Instead of enabling him to stand up fearlessly and demand his own, it threw him back upon his own efforts; and the prospect of his being able to overpower or outwit aunt Milly by any ordinary means was very poor.

He did not leave the office, but hung around awhile as though there were something further he wished to speak about. Finally, after some discursive remarks about the crops and politics, he asked, in an offhand, disinterested manner, as though the thought had just occurred to him:—

"Mistah Wright, w'ile's we're talkin' 'bout law matters, what do it cos' ter git a defoce?"

"That depends upon circumstances. It isn't altogether a matter of expense. Have you and aunt Milly been having trouble?"

"Oh no, suh; I was jes' a-wond'rin'."

"You see," continued the lawyer, who was fond of talking, and had nothing else to do for the moment, "a divorce is not an easy thing to get in this State under any circumstances. It used to be the law that divorce could be granted only by special act of the legislature; and it is but recently that the subject has been relegated to the jurisdiction of the courts."

Uncle Wellington understood a part of this, but the answer had not been exactly to the point in his mind.

"S'pos'n', den, jes' fer de argyment, me an' my ole 'oman sh'd fall out en wanter separate, how could I git a defoce?"

"That would depend on what you quarreled about. It's pretty hard work to answer general questions in a particular way. If you merely wished to separate, it wouldn't be necessary to get a divorce; but if you should want to marry again, you would have to be divorced, or else you would be guilty of bigamy, and could be sent to the penitentiary. But, by the way, uncle Wellington, when were you married?"

"I got married 'fo' de wah, when I was livin' down on Rockfish Creek."

"When you were in slavery?"

"Yas, suh."

"Did you have your marriage registered after the surrender?"

"No, suh; never knowed nuffin' 'bout dat."

After the war, in North Carolina and other States, the freed people who had sustained to each other the relation of husband and wife as it existed among slaves, were required by law to register their consent to continue in the marriage relation. By this simple expedient their former marriages of convenience received the sanction of law, and their children the seal of legitimacy. In many cases, however, where the parties lived in districts remote from the larger towns, the ceremony was neglected, or never heard of by the freedmen.

"Well," said the lawyer, "if that is the case, and you and aunt Milly should disagree, it wouldn't be necessary for you to get a divorce, even if you should want to marry again. You were never legally married."

"So Milly ain't my lawful wife, den?"

"She may be your wife in one sense of the word, but not in such a sense as to render you liable to punishment for bigamy if you should marry another woman. But I hope you will never want to do anything of the kind, for you have a very good wife now."

Uncle Wellington went away thoughtfully, but with a feeling of unaccustomed lightness and freedom. He had not felt so free since the memorable day when he had first heard of the Emancipation Proclamation. On leaving the lawyer's office, he called at the workshop of one of his friends, Peter Williams, a shoemaker by trade, who had a brother living in Ohio.

"Is you hearn f'm Sam lately?" uncle Wellington inquired, after the conversation had drifted through the usual generalities.

"His mammy got er letter f'm 'im las' week; he's livin' in de town er Groveland now."

"How's he gittin' on?"

"He says he gittin' on monst'us well. He 'low ez how he make five dollars a day w'itewashin', an' have all he kin do."

The shoemaker related various details of his brother's prosperity, and uncle Wellington returned home in a very thoughtful mood, revolving in his mind a plan of future action. This plan had been vaguely assuming form ever since the professor's lecture, and the events of the morning had brought out the detail in bold relief.

Two days after the conversation with the shoemaker, aunt Milly went, in the afternoon, to visit a sister of hers who lived several miles out in the country. During her absence, which lasted until nightfall, uncle Wellington went uptown and purchased a cheap oilcloth valise from a shrewd son of Israel, who had penetrated to this locality with a stock of notions and cheap clothing. Uncle Wellington had his purchase done up in brown paper, and took the parcel under his arm. Arrived at home he unwrapped the valise, and thrust into its capacious jaws his best suit of clothes, some underwear, and a few other small articles for personal use and adornment. Then he carried the valise out into the yard, and, first looking cautiously around to see if there was any one in sight, concealed it in a clump of bushes in a corner of the yard.

It may be inferred from this proceeding that uncle Wellington was preparing for a step of some consequence. In fact, he had fully made up his mind to go to the North; but he still lacked the most important requisite for traveling with comfort, namely, the money to pay his expenses. The idea of tramping the distance which separated him from the promised land of liberty and equality

had never occurred to him. When a slave, he had several times been impor-
tuned by fellow servants to join them in the attempt to escape from bondage,
but he had never wanted his freedom badly enough to walk a thousand miles
for it; if he could have gone to Canada by stagecoach, or by rail, or on horse-
back, with stops for regular meals, he would probably have undertaken the
trip. The funds he now needed for his journey were in aunt Milly's chest. He
had thought a great deal about his right to this money. It was his wife's savings,
and he had never dared to dispute, openly, her right to exercise exclusive control over what she earned; but the lawyer had assured him of his right to the
money, of which he was already constructively in possession, and he had therefore determined to possess himself actually of the coveted stocking. It was im-
practicable for him to get the key of the chest. Aunt Milly kept it in her pocket
by day and under her pillow at night. She was a light sleeper, and, if not awakened by the abstraction of the key, would certainly have been disturbed by the
unlocking of the chest. But one alternative remained, and that was to break
open the chest in her absence.

There was a revival in progress at the colored Methodist church. Aunt Milly
was as energetic in her religion as in other respects, and had not missed a single one of the meetings. She returned at nightfall from her visit to the country
and prepared a frugal supper. Uncle Wellington did not eat as heartily as usual.
Aunt Milly perceived his want of appetite, and spoke of it. He explained it by
saying that he did not feel very well.

"Is you gwine ter chu'ch ternight?" inquired his wife.

"I reckon I'll stay home an' go ter bed," he replied. "I ain't be'n feelin' well
dis evenin', an' I 'spec' I better git a good night's res'."

"Well, you kin stay ef you mine ter. Good preachin' 'u'd make you feel better, but ef you ain't gwine, don' fergit ter tote in some wood an' lighterd 'fo' you
go ter bed. De moon is shinin' bright, an' you can't have no 'scuse 'bout not
bein' able ter see."

Uncle Wellington followed her out to the gate, and watched her receding form
until it disappeared in the distance. Then he reentered the house with a quick
step, and taking a hatchet from a corner of the room, drew the chest from under
the bed. As he applied the hatchet to the fastenings, a thought struck him, and
by the flickering light of the pine-knot blazing on the hearth, a look of hesitation might have been seen to take the place of the determined expression his face
had worn up to that time. He had argued himself into the belief that his present
action was lawful and justifiable. Though this conviction had not prevented him
from trembling in every limb, as though he were committing a mere vulgar theft,
it had still nerved him to the deed. Now even his moral courage began to weaken.
The lawyer had told him that his wife's property was his own; in taking it he was
therefore only exercising his lawful right. But at the point of breaking open the
chest, it occurred to him that he was taking this money in order to get away from
aunt Milly, and that he justified his desertion of her by the lawyer's opinion that
she was not his lawful wife. If she was not his wife, then he had no right to take

the money; if she was his wife, he had no right to desert her, and would certainly have no right to marry another woman. His scheme was about to go to ship-wreck on this rock, when another idea occurred to him.

"De lawyer say dat in one sense er de word de ole 'oman is my wife, an' in anudder sense er de word she ain't my wife. Ef I goes ter de Norf an' marry a w'ite 'oman, I ain't commit no brigamy, 'caze in dat sense er de word she ain't my wife; but ef I takes dis money, I ain't stealin' it, 'caze in dat sense er de word she is my wife. Dat 'splains all de trouble away."

Having reached this ingenious conclusion, uncle Wellington applied the hatchet vigorously, soon loosened the fastenings of the chest, and with trem-bling hands extracted from its depths a capacious blue cotton stocking. He emptied the stocking on the table. His first impulse was to take the whole, but again there arose in his mind a doubt—a very obtrusive, unreasonable doubt, but a doubt, nevertheless—of the absolute rectitude of his conduct; and after a moment's hesitation he hurriedly counted the money—it was in bills of small denominations—and found it to be about two hundred and fifty dollars. He then divided it into two piles of one hundred and twenty-five dollars each. He put one pile into his pocket, returned the remainder to the stocking, and replaced it where he had found it. He then closed the chest and shoved it under the bed. After having arranged the fire so that it could safely be left burning, he took a last look around the room, and went out into the moonlight, lock-ing the door behind him, and hanging the key on a nail in the wall, where his wife would be likely to look for it. He then secured his valise from behind the bushes, and left the yard. As he passed by the woodpile, he said to himself—

"Well, I declar' ef I ain't done fergot ter tote in dat lighterd; I reckon de ole 'oman'll ha' ter fetch it in herse'f dis time."

He hastened through the quiet streets, avoiding the few people who were abroad at that hour, and soon reached the railroad station, from which a northbound train left at nine o'clock. He went around to the dark side of the train, and climbed into a second-class car, where he shrank into the darkest corner and turned his face away from the dim light of the single dirty lamp. There were no passengers in the car except one or two sleepy negroes, who had got on at some other station, and a white man who had gone into the car to smoke, accompanied by a gigantic bloodhound.

Finally the train crept out of the station. From the window uncle Wellington looked out upon the familiar cabins and turpentine stills, the new barrel fac-tory, the brickyard where he had once worked for some time; and as the train rattled through the outskirts of the town, he saw gleaming in the moonlight the white headstones of the colored cemetery where his only daughter had been buried several years before.

Presently the conductor came around. Uncle Wellington had not bought a ticket, and the conductor collected a cash fare. He was not acquainted with uncle Wellington, but had just had a drink at the saloon near the depot, and felt at peace with all mankind.

"Where are you going, uncle?" he inquired carelessly.

Uncle Wellington's face assumed the ashen hue which does duty for pallor in dusky countenances, and his knees began to tremble. Controlling his voice as well as he could, he replied that he was going up to Jonesboro, the terminus of the railroad, to work for a gentleman at that place. He felt immensely relieved when the conductor pocketed the fare, picked up his lantern, and moved away. It was very unphilosophical and very absurd that a man who was only doing right should feel like a thief, shrink from the sight of other people, and lie instinctively. Fine distinctions were not in uncle Wellington's line, but he was struck by the unreasonableness of his feelings, and still more by the discomfort they caused him. By and by, however, the motion of the train made him drowsy; his thoughts all ran together in confusion; and he fell asleep with his head on his valise, and one hand in his pocket, clasped tightly around the roll of money.

II

The train from Pittsburg drew into the Union Depot at Groveland, Ohio, one morning in the spring of 187—, with bell ringing and engine puffing; and from a smoking car emerged the form of uncle Wellington Braboy, a little dusty and travel-stained, and with a sleepy look about his eyes. He mingled in the crowd, and, valise in hand, moved toward the main exit from the depot. There were several tracks to be crossed, and more than once a watchman snatched him out of the way of a baggage truck, or a train backing into the depot. He at length reached the door, beyond which, and as near as the regulations would permit, stood a number of hackmen, vociferously soliciting patronage. One of them, a colored man, soon secured several passengers. As he closed the door after the last one he turned to uncle Wellington, who stood near him on the sidewalk, looking about irresolutely.

"Is you goin' uptown?" asked the hackman, as he prepared to mount the box.

"Yas, suh."

"I'll take you up fo' a quahtah, ef you want ter git up here an' ride on de box wid me."

Uncle Wellington accepted the offer and mounted the box. The hackman whipped up his horses, the carriage climbed the steep hill leading up to the town, and the passengers inside were soon deposited at their hotels.

"Whereabouts do you want to go?" asked the hackman of uncle Wellington, when the carriage was emptied of its last passengers.

"I want ter go ter Brer Sam Williams's," said Wellington.

"What's his street an' number?"

Uncle Wellington did not know the street and number, and the hackman had to explain to him the mystery of numbered houses, to which he was a total stranger.

"Where is he from?" asked the hackman, "and what is his business?"

"He is f'm Norf Ca'lina," replied uncle Wellington, "an' makes his livin' w'itewashin'."

"I reckon I knows de man," said the hackman. "I 'spec' he's changed his name. De man I knows is name' Johnson. He b'longs ter my chu'ch. I'm gwine out dat way ter git a passenger fer de ten o'clock train, an' I'll take you by dere."

They followed one of the least handsome streets of the city for more than a mile, turned into a cross street, and drew up before a small frame house, from the front of which a sign, painted in white upon a black background, announced to the reading public, in letters inclined to each other at various angles, that whitewashing and kalsomining were "dun" there. A knock at the door brought out a slatternly looking colored woman. She had evidently been disturbed at her toilet, for she held a comb in one hand, and the hair on one side of her head stood out loosely, while on the other side it was braided close to her head. She called her husband, who proved to be the Patesville shoemaker's brother. The hackman introduced the traveler, whose name he had learned on the way out, collected his quarter, and drove away.

Mr. Johnson, the shoemaker's brother, welcomed uncle Wellington to Groveland, and listened with eager delight to the news of the old town, from which he himself had run away many years before, and followed the North Star to Groveland. He had changed his name from "Williams" to "Johnson," on account of the Fugitive Slave Law, which, at the time of his escape from bondage, had rendered it advisable for runaway slaves to court obscurity. After the war he had retained the adopted name. Mrs. Johnson prepared breakfast for her guest, who ate it with an appetite sharpened by his journey. After breakfast he went to bed, and slept until late in the afternoon.

After supper Mr. Johnson took uncle Wellington to visit some of the neighbors who had come from North Carolina before the war. They all expressed much pleasure at meeting "Mr. Braboy," a title which at first sounded a little odd to uncle Wellington. At home he had been "Wellin'ton," "Brer Wellin'ton," or "uncle Wellin'ton;" it was a novel experience to be called "Mister," and he set it down, with secret satisfaction, as one of the first fruits of Northern liberty.

"Would you lack ter look 'roun' de town a little?" asked Mr. Johnson at breakfast next morning. "I ain' got no job dis mawnin', an' I kin show you some er de sights."

Uncle Wellington acquiesced in this arrangement, and they walked up to the corner to the streetcar line. In a few moments a car passed. Mr. Johnson jumped on the moving car, and uncle Wellington followed his example, at the risk of life or limb, as it was his first experience of streetcars.

There was only one vacant seat in the car and that was between two white women in the forward end. Mr. Johnson motioned to the seat, but Wellington shrank from walking between those two rows of white people, to say nothing of sitting between the two women, so he remained standing in the rear part of the car. A moment later, as the car rounded a short curve, he was pitched sidewise into the lap of a stout woman magnificently attired in a ruffled blue calico gown. The lady colored up, and uncle Wellington, as he struggled to his feet amid the laughter of the passengers, was absolutely helpless with embarrassment, until the conductor came up behind him and pushed him toward the vacant place.

"Sit down, will you," he said; and before uncle Wellington could collect himself, he was seated between the two white women. Everybody in the car seemed to be looking at him. But he came to the conclusion, after he had pulled himself together and reflected a few moments, that he would find this method of locomotion pleasanter when he got used to it, and then he could score one more glorious privilege gained by his change of residence.

They got off at the public square, in the heart of the city, where there were flowers and statues, and fountains playing. Mr. Johnson pointed out the courthouse, the post office, the jail, and other public buildings fronting on the square. They visited the market nearby, and from an elevated point, looked down upon the extensive lumberyards and factories that were the chief sources of the city's prosperity. Beyond these they could see the fleet of ships that lined the coal and iron ore docks of the harbor. Mr. Johnson, who was quite a fluent talker, enlarged upon the wealth and prosperity of the city; and Wellington, who had never before been in a town of more than three thousand inhabitants, manifested sufficient interest and wonder to satisfy the most exacting *cicerone*. They called at the office of a colored lawyer and member of the legislature, formerly from North Carolina, who, scenting a new constituent and a possible client, greeted the stranger warmly, and in flowing speech pointed out the superior advantages of life at the North, citing himself as an illustration of the possibilities of life in a country really free. As they wended their way homeward to dinner uncle Wellington, with quickened pulse and rising hopes, felt that this was indeed the promised land, and that it must be flowing with milk and honey.

Uncle Wellington remained at the residence of Mr. Johnson for several weeks before making any effort to find employment. He spent this period in looking about the city. The most commonplace things possessed for him the charm of novelty, and he had come prepared to admire. Shortly after his arrival, he had offered to pay for his board, intimating at the same time that he had plenty of money. Mr. Johnson declined to accept anything from him for board, and expressed himself as being only too proud to have Mr. Braboy remain in the house on the footing of an honored guest, until he had settled himself. He lightened in some degree, however, the burden of obligation under which a prolonged stay on these terms would have placed his guest, by soliciting from the latter occasional small loans, until uncle Wellington's roll of money began to lose its plumpness, and with an empty pocket staring him in the face, he felt the necessity of finding something to do.

During his residence in the city he had met several times his first acquaintance, Mr. Peterson, the hackman, who from time to time inquired how he was getting along. On one of these occasions Wellington mentioned his willingness to accept employment. As good luck would have it, Mr. Peterson knew of a vacant situation. He had formerly been coachman for a wealthy gentleman residing on Oakwood Avenue, but had resigned the situation to go into business for himself. His place had been filled by an Irishman, who had just been discharged for drunkenness, and the gentleman that very day had sent word to Mr. Peterson, asking him if he could recommend a competent and trustworthy coachman.

"Does you know anything erbout hosses?" asked Mr. Peterson.

"Yas, indeed, I does," said Wellington. "I wuz raise' 'mongs' hosses."

"I tol' my ole boss I'd look out fer a man, an' ef you reckon you kin fill de 'quirements er de situation, I'll take yo' roun' dere termorrer mornin'. You wants ter put on yo' bes' clothes an' slick up, fer dey're partic'lar people. Ef you git de place I'll expec' you ter pay me fer de time I lose in 'tendin' ter yo' business, fer time is money in dis country, an' folks don't do much fer nuthin'."

Next morning Wellington blacked his shoes carefully, put on a clean collar, and with the aid of Mrs. Johnson tied his cravat in a jaunty bow which gave him quite a sprightly air and a much younger look than his years warranted. Mr. Peterson called for him at eight o'clock. After traversing several cross streets they turned into Oakwood Avenue and walked along the finest part of it for about half a mile. The handsome houses of this famous avenue, the stately trees, the wide-spreading lawns, dotted with flower beds, fountains and statuary, made up a picture so far surpassing anything in Wellington's experience as to fill him with an almost oppressive sense of its beauty.

"Hit looks lack hebben," he said softly.

"It's a pootty fine street," rejoined his companion, with a judicial air, "but I don't like dem big lawns. It's too much trouble ter keep de grass down. One er dem lawns is big enough to pasture a couple er cows."

They went down a street running at right angles to the avenue, and turned into the rear of the corner lot. A large building of pressed brick, trimmed with stone, loomed up before them.

"Do de gemman lib in dis house?" asked Wellington, gazing with awe at the front of the building.

"No, dat's de barn," said Mr. Peterson with good-natured contempt; and leading the way past a clump of shrubbery to the dwelling house, he went up the back steps and rang the doorbell.

The ring was answered by a buxom Irishwoman, of a natural freshness of complexion deepened to a fiery red by the heat of a kitchen range. Wellington thought he had seen her before, but his mind had received so many new impressions lately that it was a minute or two before he recognized in her the lady whose lap he had involuntarily occupied for a moment on his first day in Groveland.

"Faith," she exclaimed as she admitted them, "an' it's mighty glad I am to see ye ag'in, Misther Payterson! An' how hev ye be'n, Misther Payterson, since I see ye lahst?"

"Middlin' well, Mis' Flannigan, middlin' well, 'ceptin' a tech er de rheumatiz. S'pose you be'n doin' well as usual?"

"Oh yis, as well as a dacent woman could do wid a drunken baste about the place like the lahst coachman. O Misther Payterson, it would make yer heart bleed to see the way the spalpeen cut up a-Saturday! But Misther Todd discharged 'im the same avenin', widout a characther, bad 'cess to 'im, an' we've had no coachman sence at all, at all. An' it's sorry I am"—

The lady's flow of eloquence was interrupted at this point by the appearance of Mr. Todd himself, who had been informed of the men's arrival. He asked some questions in regard to Wellington's qualifications and former experience, and in view of his recent arrival in the city was willing to accept Mr. Peterson's recommendation instead of a reference. He said a few words about the nature of the work, and stated his willingness to pay Wellington the wages formerly allowed Mr. Peterson, thirty dollars a month and board and lodging.

This handsome offer was eagerly accepted, and it was agreed that Wellington's term of service should begin immediately. Mr. Peterson, being familiar with the work, and financially interested, conducted the new coachman through the stables and showed him what he would have to do. The silver-mounted harness, the variety of carriages, the names of which he learned for the first time, the arrangements for feeding and watering the horses,—these appointments of a rich man's stable impressed Wellington very much, and he wondered that so much luxury should be wasted on mere horses. The room assigned to him, in the second story of the barn, was a finer apartment than he had ever slept in; and the salary attached to the situation was greater than the combined monthly earnings of himself and aunt Milly in their Southern home. Surely, he thought, his lines had fallen in pleasant places.

Under the stimulus of new surroundings Wellington applied himself diligently to work, and, with the occasional advice of Mr. Peterson, soon mastered the details of his employment. He found the female servants, with whom he took his meals, very amiable ladies. The cook, Mrs. Katie Flannigan, was a widow. Her husband, a sailor, had been lost at sea. She was a woman of many words, and when she was not lamenting the late Flannigan's loss,—according to her story he had been a model of all the virtues,—she would turn the batteries of her tongue against the former coachman. This gentleman, as Wellington gathered from frequent remarks dropped by Mrs. Flannigan, had paid her attentions clearly susceptible of a serious construction. These attentions had not borne their legitimate fruit, and she was still a widow unconsoled,—hence Mrs. Flannigan's tears. The housemaid was a plump, good-natured German girl, with a pronounced German accent. The presence on washdays of a Bohemian laundress, of recent importation, added another to the variety of ways in which the English tongue was mutilated in Mr. Todd's kitchen. Association with the white women drew out all the native gallantry of the mulatto, and Wellington developed quite a helpful turn. His politeness, his willingness to lend a hand in kitchen or laundry, and the fact that he was the only male servant on the place, combined to make him a prime favorite in the servants' quarters.

It was the general opinion among Wellington's acquaintances that he was a single man. He had come to the city alone, had never been heard to speak of a wife, and to personal questions bearing upon the subject of matrimony had always returned evasive answers. Though he had never questioned the correctness of the lawyer's opinion in regard to his slave marriage, his conscience had never been entirely at ease since his departure from the South, and any positive denial of his married condition would have stuck in his throat. The inference naturally drawn from his reticence in regard to the past, coupled with his expressed intention of settling permanently in Groveland, was that he belonged in the ranks of the unmarried, and was therefore legitimate game for any widow or old maid who could bring him down. As such game is bagged easiest at short range, he received numerous invitations to tea parties, where he feasted on unlimited chicken and pound cake. He used to compare these viands with the plain fare often served by aunt Milly, and the result of the comparison was another item to the credit of the North upon his mental ledger. Several of the colored ladies who smiled upon him were blessed with good looks, and uncle Wellington, naturally of a susceptible temperament, as people of lively imagination are apt to be, would probably have fallen a victim to the charms of some woman of his own race, had it not been for a strong counter-attraction in the person of Mrs. Flannigan. The attentions of the lately discharged coachman had lighted anew the smouldering fires of her widowed heart, and awakened longings which still remained unsatisfied. She was thirty-five years old, and felt the need of someone else to love. She was not a woman of lofty ideals; with her a man was a man—

"For a' that an' a' that;"

and, aside from the accident of color, uncle Wellington was as personable a man as any of her acquaintance. Some people might have objected to his complexion; but then, Mrs. Flannigan argued, he was at least half white; and, this being the case, there was no good reason why he should be regarded as black.

Uncle Wellington was not slow to perceive Mrs. Flannigan's charms of person, and appreciated to the full the skill that prepared the choice tidbits reserved for his plate at dinner. The prospect of securing a white wife had been one of the principal inducements offered by a life at the North; but the awe of white people in which he had been reared was still too strong to permit his taking any active steps toward the object of his secret desire, had not the lady herself come to his assistance with a little of the native coquetry of her race.

"Ah, Misther Braboy," she said one evening when they sat at the supper table alone,—it was the second girl's afternoon off, and she had not come home to supper,—"it must be an awful lonesome life ye've been afther l'adin', as a single man, wid no one to cook fer ye, or look afther ye."

"It are a kind er lonesome life, Mis' Flannigan, an' dat's a fac'. But sence I had de privilege er eatin' yo' cookin' an' 'joyin' yo' society, I ain' felt a bit lonesome."

"Yer flatthrin' me, Misther Braboy. An' even if ye mane it"—

"I means eve'y word of it, Mis' Flannigan."

"An' even if ye mane it, Misther Braboy, the time is liable to come when things'll be different; for service is uncertain, Misther Braboy. An' then you'll wish you had some nice, clean woman, 'at knowed how to cook an' wash an' iron, ter look afther ye, an' make yer life comfortable."

Uncle Wellington sighed, and looked at her languishingly.

"It 'u'd all be well ernuff, Mis' Flannigan, ef I had n' met you; but I don' know whar I's ter fin' a colored lady w'at'll begin ter suit me after habbin' libbed in de same house wid you."

"Colored lady, indade! Why, Misther Braboy, ye don't nade ter demane yer-self by marryin' a colored lady—not but they're as good as anybody else, so long as they behave themselves. There's many a white woman 'u'd be glad ter git as fine a lookin' man as ye are."

"Now *you're* flattrin' *me*, Mis' Flannigan," said Wellington. But he felt a sudden and substantial increase in courage when she had spoken, and it was with astonishing ease that he found himself saying:—

"Dey ain' but one lady, Mis' Flannigan, dat could injuce me ter want ter change de lonesomeness er my singleness fer de 'sponsibilities er matermony, an' I'm feared she'd say no ef I'd ax her."

"Ye'd better ax her, Misther Braboy, an' not be wastin' time a-wond'rin'. Do I know the lady?"

"You knows 'er better 'n anybody else, Mis' Flannigan. *You* is de only lady I'd be satisfied ter marry after knowin' you. Ef you casts me off I'll spen' de rest er my days in lonesomeness an' mis'ry."

Mrs. Flannigan affected much surprise and embarrassment at this bold declaration.

"Oh, Misther Braboy," she said, covering him with a coy glance, "an' it's rale 'shamed I am to hev b'en talkin' ter ye ez I hev. It looks as though I'd b'en doin' the coortin'. I didn't drame that I'd b'en able ter draw yer affections to mesilf."

"I's loved you ever sence I fell in yo' lap on de streetcar de fus' day I wuz in Groveland," he said, as he moved his chair up closer to hers.

One evening in the following week they went out after supper to the residence of Rev. Caesar Williams, pastor of the colored Baptist church, and, after the usual preliminaries, were pronounced man and wife.

III

According to all his preconceived notions, this marriage ought to have been the acme of uncle Wellington's felicity. But he soon found that it was not without its drawbacks. On the following morning Mr. Todd was informed of the marriage. He had no special objection to it, or interest in it, except that he was opposed on principle to having husband and wife in his employment at the same time. As a consequence, Mrs. Braboy, whose place could be more easily filled than that of her husband, received notice that her services would not be required after the end of the month. Her husband was retained in his place as coachman.

Upon the loss of her situation Mrs. Braboy decided to exercise the married woman's prerogative of letting her husband support her. She rented the upper floor of a small house in an Irish neighborhood. The newly wedded pair furnished their rooms on the installment plan and began housekeeping.

There was one little circumstance, however, that interfered slightly with their enjoyment of that perfect freedom from care which ought to characterize a honeymoon. The people who owned the house and occupied the lower floor had rented the upper part to Mrs. Braboy in person, it never occurring to them that her husband could be other than a white man. When it became known that he was colored, the landlord, Mr. Dennis O'Flaherty, felt that he had been imposed upon, and, at the end of the first month, served notice upon his tenants to leave the premises. When Mrs. Braboy, with characteristic impetuosity, inquired the meaning of this proceeding, she was informed by Mr. O'Flaherty that he did not care to live in the same house "wid naygurs." Mrs. Braboy resented the epithet with more warmth than dignity, and for a brief space of time the air was green with choice specimens of brogue, the altercation barely ceasing before it had reached the point of blows.

It was quite clear that the Braboys could not longer live comfortably in Mr. O'Flaherty's house, and they soon vacated the premises, first letting the rent get a couple of weeks in arrears as a punishment to the too fastidious landlord. They moved to a small house on Hackman Street, a favorite locality with colored people.

For a while, affairs ran smoothly in the new home. The colored people seemed, at first, well enough disposed toward Mrs. Braboy, and she made quite a large acquaintance among them. It was difficult, however, for Mrs. Braboy to divest herself of the consciousness that she was white, and therefore superior to her neighbors. Occasional words and acts by which she manifested this feeling were noticed and resented by her keen-eyed and sensitive colored neighbors. The result was a slight coolness between them. That her few white neighbors did not visit her, she naturally and no doubt correctly imputed to disapproval of her matrimonial relations.

Under these circumstances, Mrs. Braboy was left a good deal to her own company. Owing to lack of opportunity in early life, she was not a woman of many resources, either mental or moral. It is therefore not strange that, in order to relieve her loneliness, she should occasionally have recourse to a glass of beer, and, as the habit grew upon her, to still stronger stimulants. Uncle Wellington himself was no teetotaler, and did not interpose any objection so long as she kept her potations within reasonable limits, and was apparently none the worse for them; indeed, he sometimes joined her in a glass. On one of these occasions he drank a little too much, and, while driving the ladies of Mr. Todd's family to the opera, ran against a lamppost and overturned the carriage, to the serious discomposure of the ladies' nerves, and at the cost of his situation.

A coachman discharged under such circumstances is not in the best position for procuring employment at his calling, and uncle Wellington, under the pressure of need, was obliged to seek some other means of livelihood. At the suggestion of his friend Mr. Johnson, he bought a whitewash brush, a peck of lime, a couple of pails, and a handcart, and began work as a whitewasher. His first efforts were very crude, and for a while he lost a customer in every person he worked for. He nevertheless managed to pick up a living during the spring and summer months, and to support his wife and himself in comparative comfort.

The approach of winter put an end to the whitewashing season, and left uncle Wellington dependent for support upon occasional jobs of unskilled labor. The income derived from these was very uncertain, and Mrs. Braboy was at length driven, by stress of circumstances, to the washtub, that last refuge of honest, able-bodied poverty, in all countries where the use of clothing is conventional.

The last state of uncle Wellington was now worse than the first. Under the soft firmness of aunt Milly's rule, he had not been required to do a great deal of work, prompt and cheerful obedience being chiefly what was expected of him. But matters were very different here. He had not only to bring in the coal and water, but to rub the clothes and turn the wringer, and to humiliate himself before the public by emptying the tubs and hanging out the wash in full view of the neighbors; and he had to deliver the clothes when laundered.

At times Wellington found himself wondering if his second marriage had been a wise one. Other circumstances combined to change in some degree his once rose-colored conception of life at the North. He had believed that all men were equal in this favored locality, but he discovered more degrees of inequality than he had ever perceived at the South. A colored man might be as good as a white man in theory, but neither of them was of any special consequence without money, or talent, or position. Uncle Wellington found a great many privileges open to him at the North, but he had not been educated to the point where he could appreciate them or take advantage of them; and the enjoyment of many of them was expensive, and, for that reason alone, as far beyond his reach as they had ever been. When he once began to admit even the possibility of a mistake on his part, these considerations presented themselves to his mind with increasing force. On occasions when Mrs. Braboy would require of him some unusual physical exertion, or when too frequent applications to the bottle had loosened her tongue, uncle Wellington's mind would revert, with a remorseful twinge of conscience, to the *dolce far niente* of his Southern home; a film would come over his eyes and brain, and, instead of the red-faced

Irishwoman opposite him, he could see the black but comely disk of aunt Milly's countenance bending over the washtub; the elegant brogue of Mrs. Braboy would deliquesce into the soft dialect of North Carolina; and he would only be aroused from this blissful reverie by a wet shirt or a handful of suds thrown into his face, with which gentle reminder his wife would recall his attention to the duties of the moment.

There came a time, one day in spring, when there was no longer any question about it: uncle Wellington was desperately homesick.

Liberty, equality, privileges, —all were but as dust in the balance when weighed against his longing for old scenes and faces. It was the natural reaction in the mind of a middle-aged man who had tried to force the current of a sluggish existence into a new and radically different channel. An active, industrious man, making the change in early life, while there was time to spare for the waste of adaptation, might have found in the new place more favorable conditions than in the old. In Wellington age and temperament combined to prevent the success of the experiment; the spirit of enterprise and ambition into which he had been temporarily galvanized could no longer prevail against the inertia of old habits of life and thought.

One day when he had been sent to deliver clothes he performed his errand quickly, and boarding a passing street car, paid one of his very few five-cent pieces to ride down to the office of the Hon. Mr. Brown, the colored lawyer whom he had visited when he first came to the city, and who was well known to him by sight and reputation.

"Mr Brown," he said, "I ain' gitt'n' 'long very well wid my ole 'oman."

"What's the trouble?" asked the lawyer, with business-like curtness, for he did not scent much of a fee.

"Well, de main trouble is she doan treat me right. An' den she gits drunk, an' wuss'n dat, she lays vi'lent han's on me. I kyars de marks er dat 'oman on my face now."

He showed the lawyer a long scratch on the neck.

"Why don't you defend yourself?"

"You don' know Mis' Braboy, suh; you don' know dat 'oman," he replied, with a shake of the head. "Some er dese yer w'ite women is monst'us strong in de wris'."

"Well, Mr. Braboy, it's what you might have expected when you turned your back on your own people and married a white woman. You weren't content with being a slave to the white folks once, but you must try it again. Some people never know when they've got enough. I don't see that there's any help for you; unless," he added suggestively, "you had a good deal of money."

"'Pears ter me I heared somebody say sence I be'n up heah, dat it wuz 'gin de law fer w'ite folks an' colored folks ter marry."

"That was once the law, though it has always been a dead letter in Groveland. In fact, it was the law when you got married, and until I introduced a bill in the legislature last fall to repeal it. But even that law didn't hit cases like yours. It was unlawful to make such a marriage, but it was a good marriage when once made."

"I don' jes' git dat th'oo my head," said Wellington, scratching that member as though to make a hole for the idea to enter.

"It's quite plain, Mr. Braboy. It's unlawful to kill a man, but when he's killed he's just as dead as though the law permitted it. I'm afraid you haven't much of a case, but if you'll go to work and get twenty-five dollars together, I'll see what I can do for you. We may be able to pull a case through on the ground of extreme cruelty. I might even start the case if you brought in ten dollars."

Wellington went away sorrowfully. The laws of Ohio were very little more satisfactory than those of North Carolina. And as for the ten dollars,—the lawyer might as well have told him to bring in the moon, or a deed for the Public Square. He felt very, very low as he hurried back home to supper, which he would have to go without if he were not on hand at the usual suppertime.

But just when his spirits were lowest, and his outlook for the future most hopeless, a measure of relief was at hand. He noticed, when he reached home, that Mrs. Braboy was a little preoccupied, and did not abuse him as vigorously as he expected after so long an absence. He also perceived the smell of strange tobacco in the house, of a better grade than he could afford to use. He thought perhaps someone had come in to see about the washing; but he was too glad of a respite from Mrs. Braboy's rhetoric to imperil it by indiscreet questions.

Next morning she gave him fifty cents.

"Braboy," she said, "ye've be'n helpin' me nicely wid the washin', an' I'm going ter give ye a holiday. Ye can take yer hook an' line an' go fishin' on the breakwater. I'll fix ye a lunch, an' ye needn't come back till night. An' there's half a dollar; ye can buy yerself a pipe er terbacky. But be careful an' don't waste it," she added, for fear she was overdoing the thing.

Uncle Wellington was overjoyed at this change of front on the part of Mrs. Braboy; if she would make it permanent he did not see why they might not live together very comfortably.

The day passed pleasantly down on the breakwater. The weather was agreeable, and the fish bit freely. Toward evening Wellington started home with a bunch of fish that no angler need have been ashamed of. He looked forward to a good warm supper; for even if something should have happened during the day to alter his wife's mood for the worse, any ordinary variation would be more than balanced by the substantial addition of food to their larder. His mouth watered at the thought of the finny beauties sputtering in the frying pan.

He noted, as he approached the house, that there was no smoke coming from the chimney. This only disturbed him in connection with the matter of supper. When he entered the gate he observed further that the window shades had been taken down.

"'Spec' de ole 'oman's been housecleanin'," he said to himself. "I wonder she didn' make me stay an' he'p 'er."

He went round to the rear of the house and tried the kitchen door. It was locked. This was somewhat of a surprise, and disturbed still further his expectations in regard to supper. When he had found the key and opened the door, the gravity of his next discovery drove away for the time being all thoughts of eating.

The kitchen was empty. Stove, table, chairs, washtubs, pots and pans, had vanished as if into thin air.

"Fo' de Lawd's sake!" he murmured in open-mouthed astonishment.

He passed into the other room,—they had only two,—which had served as bedroom and sitting room. It was as bare as the first, except that in the middle of the floor were piled uncle Wellington's clothes. It was not a large pile, and on the top of it lay a folded piece of yellow wrapping paper.

Wellington stood for a moment as if petrified. Then he rubbed his eyes and looked around him.

"W'at do dis mean?" he said. "Is I er-dreamin', er does I see w'at I 'pears ter see?" He glanced down at the bunch of fish which he still held. "Heah's de fish; heah's de house; heah I is; but whar's de ole 'oman, an' whar's de fu'niture? *I can't figure out w'at dis yer all means.*"

He picked up the piece of paper and unfolded it. It was written on one side. Here was the obvious solution of the mystery,—that is, it would have been obvious if he could have read it; but he could not, and so his fancy continued to play upon the subject. Perhaps the house had been robbed, or the furniture taken back by the seller, for it had not been entirely paid for.

Finally he went across the street and called to a boy in a neighbor's yard.

"Does you read writin', Johnnie?"

"Yes, sir, I'm in the seventh grade."

"Read dis yer paper fuh me."

The youngster took the note, and with much labor read the following:—

Mr. Braboy:

In lavin' ye so suddint I have ter say that my first husban' has turned up unixpected, having been saved onbeknownst ter me from a wathry grave an' all the money wasted I spint fer masses fer ter rist his sole an' I wish I had it back I feel it my dooty ter go an' live wid 'im again. I take the furnacher because I bought it yer close is yors I leave them and wishin' yer the best of luck I remane oncet yer wife but now agin

Mrs. Katie Flannigan.

N.B. I'm lavin town terday so it won't be no use lookin' fer me.

On inquiry uncle Wellington learned from the boy that shortly after his departure in the morning a white man had appeared on the scene, followed a little later by a moving van, into which the furniture had been loaded and carried away. Mrs. Braboy, clad in her best clothes, had locked the door, and gone away with the strange white man.

The news was soon noised about the street. Wellington swapped his fish for supper and a bed at a neighbor's, and during the evening learned from several sources that the strange white man had been at his house the afternoon of the day before. His neighbors intimated that they thought Mrs. Braboy's departure a good riddance of bad rubbish, and Wellington did not dispute the proposition.

Thus ended the second chapter of Wellington's matrimonial experiences. His wife's departure had been the one thing needful to convince him, beyond a doubt, that he had been a great fool. Remorse and homesickness forced him to the further conclusion that he had been knave as well as fool, and had treated aunt Milly shamefully. He was not altogether a bad old man, though very weak and erring, and his better nature now gained the ascendency. Of course his disappointment had a great deal to do with his remorse; most people do not perceive the hideousness of sin until they begin to reap its consequences. Instead of the beautiful Northern life he had dreamed of, he found himself stranded, penniless, in a strange land, among people whose sympathy he had forfeited, with no one to lean upon, and no refuge from the storms of life. His outlook was very dark, and there sprang up within him a wild longing to get back to North Carolina,—back to the little whitewashed cabin, shaded with china and mulberry trees; back to the woodpile and the garden; back to the old cronies with whom he had swapped lies and tobacco for so many years. He longed to kiss the rod of aunt Milly's domination. He had purchased his liberty at too great a price.

The next day he disappeared from Groveland. He had announced his departure only to Mr. Johnson, who sent his love to his relations in Patesville.

It would be painful to record in detail the return journey of uncle Wellington—Mr. Braboy no longer—to his native town; how many weary miles he walked; how many times he risked his life on railroad tracks and between freight cars; how he depended for sustenance on the grudging hand of backdoor charity. Nor would it be profitable or delicate to mention any slight deviations from the path of rectitude, as judged by conventional standards, to which he may occasionally have been driven by a too insistent hunger; or to refer in the remotest degree to a compulsory sojourn of thirty days in a city where he had no references, and could show no visible means of support. True charity will let these purely personal matters remain locked in the bosom of him who suffered them.

IV

Just fifteen months after the date when uncle Wellington had left North Carolina, a weather-beaten figure entered the town of Patesville after nightfall, following the railroad track from the north. Few would have recognized in the hungry-looking old brown tramp, clad in dusty rags and limping along with bare feet, the trim-looking middle-aged mulatto who so few months before had taken the train from Patesville for the distant North; so, if he had but known it, there was no necessity for him to avoid the main streets and sneak around by unfrequented paths to reach the old place on the other side of the town. He encountered nobody that he knew, and soon the familiar shape of the little cabin rose before him. It stood distinctly outlined against the sky, and the light streaming from the half-opened shutters showed it to be occupied. As he drew nearer, every familiar detail of the place appealed to his memory and to his affections, and his heart went out to the old home and the old wife. As he came nearer still, the odor of fried chicken floated out upon the air and set his mouth to watering, and awakened unspeakable longings in his half-starved stomach.

At this moment, however, a fearful thought struck him; suppose the old woman had taken legal advice and married again during his absence? Turnabout would have been only fair play. He opened the gate softly, and with his heart in his mouth approached the window on tiptoe and looked in.

A cheerful fire was blazing on the hearth, in front of which sat the familiar form of aunt Milly—and another, at the sight of whom uncle Wellington's heart sank within him. He knew the other person very well; he had sat there more than once before uncle Wellington went away. It was the minister of the church to which his wife belonged. The preacher's former visits, however, had signified nothing more than pastoral courtesy, or appreciation of good eating. His presence now was of serious portent; for Wellington recalled, with acute alarm, that the elder's wife had died only a few weeks before his own departure for the North. What was the occasion of his presence this evening? Was it merely a pastoral call? or was he courting? or had aunt Milly taken legal advice and married the elder?

Wellington remembered a crack in the wall, at the back of the house, through which he could see and hear, and quietly stationed himself there.

"Dat chicken smells mighty good, Sis' Milly," the elder was saying; "I can't fer de life er me see why dat lowdown husban' er yo'n could ever run away f'm a cook like you. It's one er de beatenis' things I ever heared. How he could lib wid you an' not 'preciate you *I* can't understan', no indeed I can't."

Aunt Milly sighed. "De trouble wid Wellin'ton wuz," she replied, "dat he didn' know when he wuz well off. He wuz alluz wishin' fer change, er studyin' 'bout somethin' new."

"Ez fer me," responded the elder earnestly, "I likes things what has be'n prove' an' tried an' has stood de tes', an' I can't 'magine how anybody could spec' ter fin' a better housekeeper er cook dan you is, Sis' Milly. I'm a-gittin' mighty lonesome sence my wife died. De Good Book say it is not good fer man ter lib alone, en it 'pears ter me dat you an' me mought git erlong tergether monst'us well."

Wellington's heart stood still, while he listened with strained attention. Aunt Milly sighed.

"I ain't denyin', elder, but what I've be'n kinder lonesome myse'f fer quite a w'ile, an' I doan doubt dat w'at de Good Book say 'plies ter women as well as ter men."

"You kin be sho' it do," averred the elder, with professional authoritativeness; "yas 'm, you kin be cert'n sho'."

"But, of co'se," aunt Milly went on, "havin' los' my ole man de way I did, it has tuk me some time fer ter git my feelin's straighten' out like dey oughter be."

"I kin 'magine yo' feelin's, Sis' Milly," chimed in the elder sympathetically, "w'en you come home dat night an' foun' yo' chist broke open, an' yo' money gone dat you had wukked an' slaved full f'm mawnin' 'tel night, year in an' year out, an' w'en you foun' dat no-'count nigger gone wid his clo's an' you lef' all alone in de worl' ter scuffle 'long by yo'self."

"Yas, elder," responded aunt Milly, "I wa'n't used right. An' den w'en I heared 'bout his goin' ter de lawyer ter fin' out 'bout a defoce, an' w'en I heared w'at de lawyer said 'bout my not bein' his wife 'less he wanted me, it made me so mad, I made up my min' dat ef he ever put his foot on my do'sill ag'in, I'd shet de do' in his face an' tell 'im ter go back whar he come f'm."

To Wellington, on the outside, the cabin had never seemed so comfortable, aunt Milly never so desirable, chicken never so appetizing, as at this moment when they seemed slipping away from his grasp forever.

"Yo' feelin's does you credit, Sis' Milly," said the elder, taking her hand, which for a moment she did not withdraw. "An' de way fer you ter close yo' do' tightes' ag'inst 'im is ter take me in his place. He ain' got no claim on you no mo'. He tuk his ch'ice 'cordin' ter w'at de lawyer tol' 'im, an' 'termine' dat he wa'n't yo' husban'. Ef he wa'n't yo' husban', he had no right ter take yo' money, an' ef he comes back here ag'in you kin hab 'im tuck up an' sent ter de penitenchy fer stealin' it."

Uncle Wellington's knees, already weak from fasting, trembled violently beneath him. The worst that he had feared was now likely to happen. His only hope of safety lay in flight, and yet the scene within so fascinated him that he could not move a step.

"It 'u'd serve him right," exclaimed aunt Milly indignantly, "ef he wuz sent ter de penitenchy fer life! Dey ain't nuthin' too mean ter be done ter 'im. What did I ever do dat he should use me like he did?"

The recital of her wrongs had wrought upon aunt Milly's feelings so that her voice broke, and she wiped her eyes with her apron.

The elder looked serenely confident, and moved his chair nearer hers in order the better to play the role of comforter. Wellington, on the outside, felt so mean that the darkness of the night was scarcely sufficient to hide him; it would be no more than right if the earth were to open and swallow him up.

"An' yet aftuh all, elder," said Milly with a sob, "though I knows you is a better man, an' would treat me right, I wuz so use' ter dat ole nigger, an' libbed wid 'im so long, dat ef he'd open dat do' dis minute an' walk in, I'm feared I'd be foolish ernuff an' weak ernuff to forgive 'im an' take 'im back ag'in."

With a bound, uncle Wellington was away from the crack in the wall. As he ran round the house he passed the woodpile and snatched up an armful of pieces. A moment later he threw open the door.

"Ole 'oman," he exclaimed, "here's dat wood you tol' me ter fetch in! Why, elder," he said to the preacher, who had started from his seat with surprise, "w'at's yo' hurry? Won't you stay an' hab some supper wid us?"

(1889)

The Apostate of Chego-Chegg

Abraham Cahan

I

"So this is America, and I am a Jewess no longer!" brooded Michalina, as she looked at the stretch of vegetable gardens across the road from the threshold where she sat. "They say farmhands work shorter hours on Saturdays, yet God knows when Wincas will get home." Her slow, black eyes returned to the stocking and the big darning needle in her hands.

She was yearning for her Gentile husband and their common birthplace, and she was yearning for her father's house and her Jewish past. Wincas kept buzzing in her ear that she was a Catholic, but he did not understand her. She was a *meshumedeste*—a convert Jewess, an apostate, a renegade, a traitoress, something beyond the vituperative resources of Gentile speech. The bonfires of the Inquisition had burned into her people a point of view to which Wincas was a stranger. Years of religious persecution and enforced clannishness had taught them to look upon the Jew who deserts his faith for that of his oppressors with a horror and a loathing which the Gentile brain could not conceive. Michalina's father had sat seven days shoeless on the ground, as for the dead, but death was what he naturally invoked upon the "defiled head," as the lesser of the two evils. Atheism would have been a malady; *shmad* (conversation to a Gentile creed) was far worse than death. Michalina felt herself burned alive. She was a meshumedeste. She shuddered to think what the word meant.

At first she seemed anxious to realize the change she had undergone. "You are a Jewess no longer—you are a Gentile woman," she would say to herself. But the words were as painful as they were futile, and she turned herself adrift on the feeling that she was the same girl as of old, except that something terrible had befallen her. "God knows where it will all end," she would whisper. She had a foreboding that something far more terrible, a great crushing blow that was to smite her, was gathering force somewhere.

Hatred would rise in her heart at such moments—hatred for her "sorceress of a stepmother," whose cruel treatment of Michalina had driven her into the arms of the Gentile lad and to America. It was owing to her that Rivka (Rebecca) had become Michalina, a meshumedeste.

The Long Island village (one of a dozen within half an hour's walk from one another) was surrounded by farms which yielded the Polish peasants their livelihood. Their pay was about a dollar a day, but potatoes were the principal part of their food, and this they got from their American employers free. Nearly every peasant owned a fiddle or a banjo. A local politician had humorously dubbed the settlement Chego-Chegg (this was his phonetic summary of the Polish language), and the name clung.

Wincas and Michalina had been only a few days in the place, and although they spoke Polish as well as Lithuanian, they were shy of the other peasants and felt lonely. Michalina had not seen any of her former coreligionists since she and her husband had left the immigrant station, and she longed for them as one for the first time in mid-ocean longs for a sight of land. She had heard that there were two Jewish settlements near by. Often she would stand gazing at the horizon, wondering where they might be; whereupon her vague image of them at once allured and terrified her.

The sun shone dreamily, like an old man smiling at his own drowsiness. It was a little world of blue, green, gray, and gold, heavy with sleep. A spot of white and a spot of red came gleaming down the road. Rabbi Nehemiah was on his way home from Greyton, where he had dined with the "finest house-holder" and "said some law" to the little congregation at the afternoon service. For it was Sabbath, and that was why his unstarched shirt collar was so fresh and his red bandana was tied around the waist of his long-skirted coat. Carrying things on the seventh day being prohibited, Rabbi Nehemiah *wore* his handkerchief.

The door of the general store (it was also the inn), overlooking the cross-roads from a raised platform, was wide open. A Polish peasant in American trousers and undershirt, but with a Warsaw pipe dangling from his mouth, sat on a porch, smoking quietly. A barefooted boy was fast asleep in the grass across the road, a soldier's cap by his side, like a corpse on the battlefield.

As Michalina glanced up the gray road to see if Wincas was not coming, her eye fell upon Rabbi Nehemiah. A thrill ran through her. She could tell by his figure, his huge white collar, and the handkerchief around his waist that he was a pious, learned Jew. As he drew near she saw that his face was overgrown with wisps of a silken beard of a yellowish shade, and that he was a man of about twenty-seven.

As he walked along he gesticulated and murmured to himself. It was one of his bickerings with Satan.

"It's labor lost, Mr. Satan!" he said, with a withering smile. "You won't catch me again, if you burst. Go try your tricks on somebody else. If you hope to get me among your regular customers you are a very poor businessman, I tell you that. Nehemiah is as clever as you, depend upon it. Go, mister, go!"

All this he said quite audibly, in his velvety, purring bass, which set one wondering where his voice came from.

As he came abreast of Michalina he stopped short in consternation.

"Woe is me, on the holy Sabbath!" he exclaimed in Yiddish, dropping his hands to his sides.

The color rushed to Michalina's face. She stole a glance at the Pole down the road. He seemed to be half asleep. She lowered her eyes and went on with her work.

"Will you not stop this, my daughter? Come, go indoors and dress in honor of the Sabbath," he purred on, with a troubled, appealing look.

"I don't understand what you say, sir," she answered, in Lithuanian, without raising her eyes.

The devout man started. "I thought she was a child of Israel!" he exclaimed, in his native tongue, as he hastily resumed his way. "Fie upon her! But what a pretty Gentile maiden!—just like a Jewess—" Suddenly he interrupted himself. "You are at it again, aren't you?" he burst out upon Satan. "Leave me alone, will you?"

Michalina's face was on fire. She was following the pious man with her glance. He was apparently going to one of those two Jewish villages. Every step he took gave her a pang, as if he were tied to her heart. As he disappeared on a side road behind some trees she hastily took her darning indoors and set out after him.

II

About three quarters of an hour had passed when, following the pious, little man, she came in sight of a new town that looked as if it had sprung up overnight. It was Burkdale, the newest offshoot of an old hamlet, and it owed its existence to the "Land Improvement Company," to the president of which, Madison Burke, it owed its name. Some tailoring contractors had moved their "sweatshops" here, after a prolonged strike in New York, and there were, besides, some fifty or sixty peddlers who spent the week scouring the island for custom and who came here for the two Sabbath days—their own and that of their Christian patrons. The improvised little town was lively with the whir of sewing machines and the many-colored display of shop windows.

As the man with the red girdle made his appearance, a large, stout woman in a black wig greeted him from across the street.

"Good Sabbath, Rabbi Nehemiah!" she called out to him, with a faint smile.

"A good Sabbath and a good year!" he returned.

Michalina was thrilled once more. She was now following close behind the pious man. She ran the risk of attracting attention, but she no longer cared. Seeing a boy break some twigs, Rabbi Nehemiah made a dash at him, as though to rescue him from death, and seizing him by the arms, he shook the sticks out of his hands. Then, stroking the urchin's swarthy cheeks, he said fondly:

"It is prohibited, my son. God will give one a lashing for desecrating the Sabbath. Oh, what a lashing!"

A sob rose to Michalina's throat.

A short distance farther on Rabbi Nehemiah paused to remonstrate with a group of young men who stood smoking cigarettes and chatting by a merchandise wagon.

"Woe! Woe! Woe!" he exclaimed. "Do throw it away, pray! Are you not children of Israel? Do drop your cigarettes."

"Rabbi Nehemiah is right," said a big fellow, with a wink, concealing his cigarette behind him. The others followed his example, and Rabbi Nehemiah, flushed with his easy victory, went on pleading for a life of piety and divine study. He spoke from the bottom of his heart, and his face shone, but this did not prevent his plea from being flavored with a certain humor, for the most part at his own expense.

"The world to come is the tree, while this world is only the shadow it casts," he said in his soft, thick voice. "Smoking on the Sabbath, staying away from the synagogue, backbiting, cheating in business, dancing with maidens, or ogling somebody else's wife—all this is a great pleasure, is it not? Well, the sages of this world, the dudes, the educated, and even a high-priced adornment like myself, think it is. We hunt for these delights. Behold, we have caught them. Close your fist tight! Hold the precious find with might and main, Rabbi Nehemiah! Presently, hard! The Angel of Death is coming. 'Please open your hand, Rabbi Nehemiah. Let us see what you have got.' Alas! It's empty, empty, empty—*Ai-ai!*" he suddenly shrieked in a frightened, piteous voice. While he was speaking the big fellow had stolen up behind him and clapped his enormous high hat over his eyes. The next moment another young man slipped up to Rabbi Nehemiah's side, snatched off his bandana, and set it on fire.

"Woe is me! Woe is me! On the holy Sabbath!" cried the devout man, in despair.

Michalina, who had been looking on at a distance, every minute making ready to go home, rushed up to Rabbi Nehemiah's side.

"Don't—pray don't!" she begged his tormentors, in Yiddish. "You know he did not touch you; why should you hurt him?"

A crowd gathered. The learned man was looking about him with a perplexed air, when along came Sorah-Elka, the bewigged tall woman who had saluted him a short while ago. The young men made way for her.

"What's the matter? Got a licking again?" she inquired, between a frown and a smile, and speaking in phlegmatic, articulate accents. Her smile was like her voice—pleasingly cold. She was the cleverest, the most pious, and the most ill-natured woman in the place. "Serves you right, Rabbi Nehemiah. You look for trouble and you get it. What more do you want? What did they do to him, the scamps?"

"Nothing. They only knocked his hat over his eyes. They were fooling," answered a little boy.

Sorah-Elka's humor and her calm, authoritative manner won Michalina's heart. Oh, if she were one of this Jewish crowd! She wished she could speak to them. Well, who knew her here? As to Rabbi Nehemiah, he did not seem to recognize her, so she ventured to say, ingratiatingly:

"He didn't do them anything. He only talked to them and they hit him on the head."

Many eyes were leveled at the stranger. The young fellow who had burned Rabbi Nehemiah's handkerchief was scanning her face.

Suddenly he exclaimed:

"I sha'n't live till next week if she is not the meshumedeste of Chego-Chegg! I peddle over there."

The terrible untranslatable word, the most loathsome to the Yiddish ear, struck Michalina cold. She wondered whether this was the great calamity which her heart had been predicting. Was it the beginning of her end? Rabbi Nehemiah recognized her. With a shriek of horror, and drawing his skirts about him, as for fear of contamination, he proceeded to describe his meeting with Michalina at the Polish village.

"What! This plague the meshumedeste who has a peasant for a husband!" said Sorah-Elka, as she swept the young woman with contemptuous curiosity. "May all the woes that are to befall me, you, or any good Jew—may they all strike the head of this horrid thing—fie upon her!" And the big woman spat with the same imperturbable smile with which she had drawled out her malediction.

Michalina went off toward Chego-Chegg. When the crowd was a few yards behind her somebody shouted:

"Meshumedeste! Meshumedeste!"

The children and some full-grown rowdies took up the cry:

"Meshumedeste! Meshumedeste! Meshumedeste!" they sang in chorus, running after her and pelting her with stones.

Michalina was frightened to death. And yet her pursuers and the whole Jewish town became dearer to her heart than ever. "Where have you been?" Wincas asked, shaking her furiously.

"Don't! Don't! People are looking!" she protested, in her quietly strenuous way.

The village was astir. Children were running about; women sat on the porches, gossiping; two fiddles were squeaking themselves hoarse in the tavern. A young negro, lank, tattered, and grinning, was twanging a banjo to a crowd of simpering Poles. He it was who got the peasants to forsake their accordions, or even fiddles, for banjos. He was the civilizing and Americanizing genius of the place, although he had learned to jabber Polish long before any of his pupils picked up a dozen English words.

"Tell me where you have been," raged Wincas.

"Suppose I don't? Am I afraid of you? I felt lonesome—so lonesome! I thought I would die of loneliness, so I went for a walk and lost my way. Are you satisfied?"

They went indoors, where their landlady had prepared for them a meal of herring, potatoes, and beef stew.

Half an hour later they were seated on the lawn, conversing in whispers amid the compact blackness of the night. The two tavern windows gleamed like suspended sheets of gold. Diving out of these into the sea of darkness was a frisky host of banjo notes.

"How dark is it!" whispered Michalina.

"Are you afraid of devils?"

"No—why?"

"I thought you might be," he said.

After a long pause he suddenly pointed at his heart.

"Does it hurt you?" he asked.

"What do you mean, darling?" she demanded, interlacing her fingers over his shoulder and peering into his beardless face.

"Something has got into me. It's right here. It's pulling me to pieces, Michalinka!"

"That's nothing," she said. "It's only homesickness. It will wear off."

Wincas complained of his employer, the queer ways of American farming, the tastelessness of American food.

"God has cursed this place and taken the life out of everything," he said. "I suppose it's all because the people here are so wicked. Everything looks as it should, but you just try to put it into your mouth, and you find out the swindle. Look here, Michalinka, maybe it is the Jewish god getting even on me?"

She was bent upon her own thoughts and made no reply. Presently she began to caress him as she would a sick baby.

"Don't worry, my love," she comforted him. "America is a good country. Everybody says so. Wait till we get used to it. Then you won't go, even if you are driven with sticks from here."

They sat mutely clinging to each other, their eyes on the bright tavern windows, when a fresh, fragrant breeze came blowing upon them. Wincas fell into inhaling it thirstily. The breeze brought his native village to his nostrils.

"Mi-Michalinka darling!" he suddenly sobbed out, clasping her to his heart.

III

When Michalina, pale, weak, and beautiful, lay in bed, and the midwife bade her look at her daughter, the young mother opened her flashing black eyes and forthwith shut them again. The handful of flesh and her own splitting headache seemed one and the same thing. After a little, her agonizing sleep was broken and her torpid gaze found the baby by the wall, she was overcome with terror and disgust. It was a *shikse* (Gentile girl), a heap of defilement. What was it doing by her side?

She had not nursed the baby a week before she grew attached to it. By the time little Marysia was a month old, she was dearer than her own life to her.

The little railroad station about midway between the two settlements became Michalina's favorite resort. Her neighbors she shunned. She had been brought up to look down upon their people as "a race like unto an ass." At home she could afford to like them. Now that she was one of them, they were repugnant to her. They, in their turn, often mocked her and called her "Jew woman." And so she would often go to spend an hour or two in the waiting room of the station or on the platform outside. Some of the passengers were Jews, and these would eye her curiously, as if they had heard of her. She blushed under their glances, yet she awaited them impatiently each time a train was due.

One morning a peddler, bending under his pack, stopped to look at her. When he had dropped his burden his face seemed familiar to Michalina. He was an insignificant little man, clean-shaven, with close-clipped yellowish hair, and he wore a derby hat and a sack coat.

All at once his face broke into a broad, affectionate smile.

"How do you do?" he burst out in a deep, mellow voice which she recognized instantly. "I once spoke to you in Chego-Chegg, do you remember? I see you are amazed to see me in a short coat and without beard and side-locks."

"You look ten years younger," she said in a daze of embarrassment.

"I am Rabbi Nehemiah no longer," he explained bashfully. "They call me Nehemiah the Atheist now."

"Another sinner!" Michalina thought, with a little thrill of pleasure.

Nehemiah continued, with a shamefaced smile:

"When my coat and my side-locks were long my sight was short, while now—why, now I am so saturated with wisdom that pious Jews keep away from me for fear of getting wet, don't you know? Well, joking aside, I had ears, but could not hear because of my ear-locks; I had eyes, and could not see because they were closed in prayer. Now I am cured of my idiocy. And how are you? How are you getting along in America?"

His face beamed. Michalina's wore a pained look. She was bemoaning the fall of an idol.

"I am all right, thank you. Don't the Burkdale people trouble you?" she asked, reddening violently.

"Men will be men and rogues will be rogues. Do you remember that Saturday? It was not the only beating I got, either. They regaled me quite often—the oxen! However, I bear them no ill will. Who knows but it was their cuffs and buffets that woke me up? The one thing that gives me pain is this: the same fellows who used to break my bones for preaching religion now beat me because I expose its idiocies. I am like the great rabbi who had once been a chief of highwaymen. 'What of it?' he used to say. 'I was a leader then, and a leader I am now.' I was whipped when I was Rabbi Nehemiah, and now that I am Nehemiah the Atheist I am whipped again. By the way, do you remember how they hooted you? There's nothing to blush about, missus. Religion is all humbug. There are no Jews and no Gentiles, missus. This is America. All are noblemen here, and all are brothers—children of one mother—Nature, dear little missus." The word was apparently a tidbit to his tongue. He uttered it with relish, peering admiringly into Michalina's face. "Go forth, dear little missus! Go forth, O thou daughter of Zion, and proclaim to all those who are groveling in the mire of Judaism—"

"S-s-s-sh!" she interrupted imploringly. "Why should you speak like that? Don't—oh, don't!"

He began a long and heated argument. She could not follow him.

Marysia was asleep in her arms, munching her little lips and smiling. As Michalina stole a glance at her, she could not help smiling, too. She gazed at the child again and again, pretending to listen. For the twentieth time she noticed that in the upper part of her face Marysia bore a striking resemblance to Wincas.

Michalina and Nehemiah often met. All she understood of his talk was that it was in Yiddish, and this was enough. Though he preached atheism, to her ear his words were echoes from the world of synagogues, rabbis, purified meat, blessed Sabbath lights. Another thing she gathered from his monologues was that he was a fellow outcast. Of herself she never spoke. Being a mystery to him made her a still deeper mystery to herself, and their secret interviews had an irresistible charm for her.

One day Michalina found him clean-shaven and in a new necktie.

"Good morning!" he said, with unusual solemnity. And drawing a big red apple from his pocket, he shamefacedly placed it in her hand.

"What was it you wanted to tell me?" she inquired, blushing.

"Oh, nothing. I meant it for fun. It's only a story I read. It's about a great man who was in love with a beautiful woman all his life. She was married to another man and true to him, yet the stranger loved her. His soul was bewitched. He sang of her, he dreamed of her. The man's name was Petrarca and the woman's was Laura."*

"I don't know what you mean by your story," she said, with an embarrassed shrug of her shoulders.

"How do you know it is only a story?" he rejoined, his eye on the glistening rail. "Maybe it is only a parable? Maybe you are Laura? Laura mine!" he whispered.

"Stop that!" she cried, with a pained gesture.

At that moment he was repulsive.

"Hush, don't eat your heart, little kitten. I was only joking."

IV

Michalina ventured to visit Burkdalc once again. This time she was not bothered. Only here and there someone would whisper, "Here comes the apostate of Chego-Chegg." Little by little she got to making the most of her purchases in the Jewish town. Wincas at first stormed, and asked whether it was true that

---

Petrarca, Laura: Petrarch (Francesco Petrarca, 1304–1374), the most famous early Italian sonnet writer, whose sonnets for Laura are among the best known courtly love poems. The Petrarchan Sonnet form is named for the sonnet structure he perfected.

the Jew had bedeviled his wife's heart; but before long she persuaded him to go with her on some of her shopping expeditions. Michalina even decided that her husband should learn to press coats, which was far more profitable than working on a farm; but after trying it for a few days, he stubbornly gave it up. The soil called him back, he said, and if he did not obey it, it might get square on him when he was dead and buried in it.

By this time they had moved into a shanty on the outskirts of the village, within a short distance from Burkdale.

At first Michalina forbade Wincas to write to his father, but he mailed a letter secretly. The answer inclosed a note from Michalina's father, in Yiddish, which Wincas, having in his ecstasy let out his secret, handed her.

> Your dear father-in-law [the old man wrote] goes about mocking me about you and his precious son. "Will you send her your love?" he asked. "Very well, I will," said I. And here it is, Rivka. May eighty toothaches disturb your peace even as you have disturbed the peace of your mother in her grave. God grant that your impure limbs be hurled from one end of the world to the other, as your damned soul will be when you are dead like a vile cur. Your dear father-in-law (woe to you, Rivka!) asks me what I am writing. "A blessing," say I. May similar blessings strew your path, accursed meshumedeste. That's all.

Nehemiah and Michalina had taken root in the little town as the representatives of two inevitable institutions. Burkdale without an atheist and a convert seemed as impossible as it would have been without a marriage-broker, a synagogue, or a bath house "for all daughters of Israel."

Nehemiah continued his frenzied agitation. Neglecting his business, half-starved, and the fair game of every jester, but plumed with some success, the zealot went on scouting religious ceremonies, denouncing rabbis, and preaching assimilation with the enlightened Gentiles. Nehemiah was an incurably religious man, and when he had lost his belief disbelief became his religion.

And so the two were known as the *appikoros* (atheist) and the meshumedeste. Between the two there was, however, a wide difference. Disclaim Judaism as Nehemiah would, he could not get the Jews to disclaim him; while Michalina was more alien to the Mosaic community than any of its Christian neighbors. With her child in her arms she moved about among the people of the place like a lone shadow. Nehemiah was a Jew who "sinned and led others to sin"; she was not a Jewess who had transgressed, but a living stigma, all the more accursed because she had once been a Jewess.

Some of the Jewish women were friendly to her. Zelda the Busybody exchanged little favors with her, but even she stopped at cooking utensils, for Michalina's food was *treife*** and all her dishes were contaminated. One day,

---

*Not prepared according to Mosaic law, proscribed; the opposite of *kosher*. [Cahan's note.]

when the dumpy little woman called at the lonely hovel, the convert offered her a wedge of her first lemon pie. It was Zelda who had taught her to make it, and in her exultation and shamefacedness Michalina forgot the chasm that separated her from her caller.

"Taste it and tell me what is wrong about it," she said, blushing.

Zelda became confused.

"No, thank you. I've just had dinner, as true as I'm living," she stammered.

The light in Michalina's eyes went out. For a moment she stood with the saucer containing the piece of pie in her hand. When the Burkdale woman was gone she threw the pie away.

She bought a special set of dishes which she kept *kosher*, according to the faith of the people of Burkdale. Sometimes she would buy her meat of a Jewish butcher, and, on coming home, she would salt and purify it. Not that she expected this to be set to her credit in the world to come, for there was no hope for her soul, but she could not help, at least, playing the Jewess. It both soothed and harrowed her to prepare food or to bless Sabbath light as they did over in Burkdale. But her Sabbath candles burned so stern, so cold, so unhallowed. As she embraced the space about them and with a scooping movement brought her hands together over her shut eyes and fell to whispering the benediction, her heart beat fast. She felt like a thief.

"Praised be Thou, O Lord, King of the world, who has sanctified us by Thy commandments and commanded us to kindle the light of Sabbath."

When she attempted to recite this she could not speak after the third word.

Michalina received another letter from her father. The old man's heart was wrung with compunction and yearning. He was panting to write to her, but, alas! Whoever wrote a meshumedeste except to curse her?

It is to gladden your treacherous heart that I am writing again [ran the letter]. Rejoice, accursed apostate, rejoice! We cannot raise our heads for shame, and our eyes are darkened with disgrace. God give that your eyes become so dark that they behold neither your cur of a husband nor your vile pup. May you be stained in the blood of your own heart even as you have stained the name of our family.

Written by me, who curse the moment when I became your father.

Michalina was in rage. "We cannot raise our heads"? Who are "we"? He and his sorceress of a wife? First she makes him drive his own daughter to "the impurity" of the Gentile faith, and then she gets him to nurse this unhappy child of his for the disgrace she brought on her head! What are they worrying about? Is it that they are afraid it will be hard for Michalina's stepsister to get a husband because there is a meshumedeste in the family? Ah, she is writhing and twitching with pain, the sorceress, isn't she? Writhe away, murderess! Let her taste some of the misery she has heaped on her stepdaughter. "Rejoice, apostate, rejoice!" Michalina did rejoice. She was almost glad to be a meshumedeste.

"But why should it have come out like this?" Michalina thought. "Suppose I had never become a meshumedeste, and Nehemiah, or some handsomer Jew, had married me at home . . . . Would not the sorceress and her daughter burst with envy! Or suppose I became a Jewess again, and married a pious, learned, and wealthy Jew who fainted with love for me, and my stepmother heard of it, and I sent my little brother lots of money—wouldn't she burst, the sorceress! . . . And I should live in Burkdale, and Sorah-Elka and the other Jews and Jewesses would call at my house, and eat, and drink. On Saturdays I should go to the synagogue with a big prayer book, and on meeting me on the road people would say, 'Good Sabbath!' and I should answer, 'A good Sabbath and a good year!'"

V

Spring was coming. The air was mild, pensive, yearning. Michalina was full of tears.

"Don't rail at the rabbis—don't!" she said, with unusual irritation, to Nehemiah at her house. "Do you think I can bear to hear it?"

She cried. Nehemiah's eyes also filled with tears.

"Don't, little kitten," he said; "I didn't mean to hurt you. Are you sorry you became a Christian?" he added, in an embarrassed whisper.

For the first time she recounted her story to him. When she had finished the atheist was walking up and down.

"*Ai-ai-ai! Ai-ai!*" All at once he stopped. "So it was out of revenge for your stepmother that you married Wincas!" he exclaimed. Then he dropped his voice to a shamefaced undertone. "I thought you had fallen in love with him."

"What's that got to do with him?" she flamed out.

His face changed. She went on:

"Anyhow, he is my husband, and I am his wife and a Gentile woman, an accursed soul, doomed to have no rest either in this world or in the other. May the sorceress have as much darkness on her heart as I have on mine!"

"Why should you speak like that, little kitten? Of course I am an atheist, and religion is humbug, but you are grieving for nothing. According to the Jewish law, you are neither his wife nor a Gentile woman. You are a Jewess. Mind, I don't believe in the Talmud; but, according to the Talmud, your marriage does not count. Yes, you are unmarried!" he repeated, noting her interest. "You are a maiden, free as the birds in the sky, my kitten. You can marry a Jew 'according to the laws of Moses and Israel,' and be happy."

His voice died away.

"Lau-au-ra!" he wailed, as he seized her hand and began to kiss its fingers.

"Stop—oh, stop! What has come to you!" she shrieked. Her face was crimson. After an awkward silence, she sobbed out: "Nobody will give me anything but misery—nobody, nobody, nobody! What shall I do? Oh, what shall I do?"

Under the pretense of consulting a celebrated physician, Michalina had obtained Wincas's permission to go to New York. In a secluded room, full of dust and old books, on the third floor of an Orchard street tenement house, she found a ray-bearded man with a withered face. Before him were an open folio and a glass half filled with tea. His rusty skullcap was pushed back on his head.

The blood rushed to her face as she stepped to the table. She could not speak.

"A question of law?" asked the rabbi. "Come, my daughter, what is the trouble?"

Being addressed by the venerable man as a Jewess melted her embarrassment and her fear into tears.

"I have married a Gentile," she murmured, with bowed head.

"A Gentile! Woe is me!" exclaimed the rabbi, with a look of dismay and pity.

"And I have been baptized, too."

Here an old bonnetless woman came in with a chicken. The rabbi was annoyed. After hastily inspecting the fowl, he cried:

"Kosher! Kosher! You may eat it in good health."

When the old woman was gone he leaped up from his seat and bolted the door.

"Well, do you want to do penance?" he demanded, adjusting his skullcap. She nodded ruefully.

"Well, where is the hindrance? Go ahead, my daughter; and if you do it from a pure heart, the Most High will help you."

"But how am I to become a Jewess again? Rabbi, a man told me I never ceased to be one. Is it true?"

"Foolish young woman! What, then, are you? A Frenchwoman? The God of Israel is not in the habit of refunding one's money. Oh, no! 'Once a Jew, forever a Jew'—that's the way he does business."

"But I am married to a Gentile," she urged, with new light in her black eyes.

"Married? Not in the eye of our faith, my child. You were born a Jewess, and a Jewess cannot marry a Gentile. Now, if your marriage is no marriage—what, then, is it? A sin! Leave the Gentile, if you want to return to God. Cease sinning, and live like a daughter of Israel. Of course—of course the laws of the land— of America—do you understand?—they look upon you as a married woman, and they must be obeyed. But the laws of our faith say you are not married, and were a Jew to put the ring of dedication on your finger, you would be his wife. Do you understand, my child?"

"And how about the baby, rabbi? Suppose I wanted to make a proselyte of her?"

"A proselyte! Your learning does not seem to go very far," laughed the old man. "Why, your little girl is even a better Jewess than you have been, for she has not sinned, while you have."

"But her father—"

"Her father! What of him? Did *he* go through the throes of childbirth when the girl was born to you? Don't be uneasy, my daughter. According to our faith, children follow their mother. You are a Jewess, and so is she. She is a pure child of Israel. What is her name? Marysia? Well, call her some Jewish name—say Mindele or Shayndele. What does it amount to?"

As Michalina was making her way down the dingy staircase, she hugged the child and kissed her convulsively.

"Sheindele! Sheindele! Pure child of Israel," she said between sobs, for the first time addressing her in Yiddish. "A Jewish girlie! A Jewish girlie!"

VI

The charitable souls who had joined to buy the steamship tickets were up with the larks. At seven o'clock Sorah-Elka's apartments on the second floor of a spick-and-span frame house were full of pious women come to behold their "good deed" in the flesh. It was the greatest event in the eventful history of Burkdale. Michalina, restored to her Hebrew name, was, of course, the center of attention. Sorah-Elka and Zelda addressed her in the affectionate diminutive; the other women, in the most dignified form of the name; and so "Rievele dear" and "Rieva, if you please" flew thick and fast.

Nehemiah kept assuring everybody that he was an atheist, and that it was only to humor Rebecca that he was going to marry her according to the laws of Moses and Israel. But then nobody paid any heed to him. The pious souls were all taken up with the young woman they were "rescuing from the impurity."

Rebecca was polite, grateful, smiling, and nervous. Sorah-Elka was hovering about, flushed and morose.

"You have kissed her enough," she snarled at Zelda. "Kisses won't take her to the ship. You had better see about the lemons. As long as the ship is in harbor I won't be sure of the job. For one thing, too many people are in the secret. I wish we were in New York, at least."

The preparations were delayed by hitch after hitch. Besides, a prosperous rescuer bethought herself at the eleventh hour that she had a muff, as good as new, which might be of service to Rebecca; and then another rescuer, as prosperous and as pious, remembered that her jar of preserved cherries would be a godsend to Rebecca on shipboard. Still, the train was due fully an hour later; the English steamer would not sail before two o'clock, so there was plenty of time.

As to Wincas, he had gone to work at five in the morning and would not be back before seven in the evening.

Zelda was frisking about with the little girl, whom she exultantly addressed as Shayndele; and so curious was it to call a former Gentile child by a Yiddish name that the next minute everybody in the room was shouting: "Shayndele, come to me!" "Shayndele, look!" "Shayndele going to London to be a pious Jewess!" or "Shayndele, a health to your head, arms, and feet!"

"Never fear, Nehemiah will be a good father to her, won't you, Nehemiah?" said one matron.

Suddenly a woman who stood by the window gave a start.

"Her husband!" she gasped.

There was a panic. Sorah-Elka was excitedly signing to the others to be cool. Rebecca, pale and wild-eyed, burst into the bedroom, whence she presently emerged on tiptoe, flushed and biting her lip.

"What can he be doing here at this hour? I told him I was going to the New York professor," she said under her breath. Concealing herself behind the window frame, she peeped down into the street.

"Get away from there!" whizzed Sorah-Elka, gnashing her teeth and waving her arms violently.

Rebecca lingered. She saw the stalwart figure of her husband, his long blond hair curling at the end, and his pale, oval face. He was trudging along aimlessly, gaping about him in a perplexed, forlorn way.

"He is wandering about like a cow in search of her calf," Michalina remarked, awkwardly.

"Let him go whistle!" snapped Sorah-Elka. "We shall have to tuck you away somewhere. When the coast is clear again, I'll take you to the other railroad station. Depend upon it, we'll get you over to New York and onboard the ship before his pumpkin-head knows what world he is in. But I said that too many people were in the secret."

Sorah-Elka was a fighter. She was mistaken, however, as to the cause of Winca's sudden appearance. Even the few Poles who worked in the Burkdale sweatshops knew nothing of the great conspiracy. Water and oil won't swap secrets even when in the same bottle. It was Michalina's manner during the last few days, especially on parting with him this morning, which had kindled suspicion in the peasant's breast. What had made her weep so bitterly, clinging to him and kissing him as he was leaving? As the details of it came back to him, anxiety and an overpowering sense of loneliness had gripped his heart. He could not go on with his work.

There was a cowardly stillness in Sorah-Elka's parlor. Nehemiah was rubbing his hands and gazing at Rebecca like a prisoner mutely praying for his life. Her eye was on the window.

"What can he be doing here at such an early hour?" she muttered, sheepishly. "Maybe he has lost his job."

"And what if he did? Is it any business of yours? Let him hang and drown himself!" declared Sorah-Elka.

"Why should you curse him like that? Where is his fault?" Rebecca protested feebly.

"Look at her—look at her! She *is* dead, stuck on the lump of uncleanliness, isn't she? Well, hurry up, Riebela darling. Zelda will see to the express. Come, Rievela, come!"

Rebecca tarried.

"What has got into you? Why don't you get a move on you? You know one minute may cost us the whole game."

There was a minute of suspense. All at once Rebecca burst out sobbing:

"I cannot! I cannot!" she said, with her fists at her temples. "Curse me; I deserve it. I know I am doomed to have no rest either in this world or in the other, but I cannot leave him—I cannot. Forgive me, Nehemiah, but I cannot. What shall I do? Oh, what shall I do?"

The gathering was dumbfounded. Sorah-Elka dropped her immense arms. For several moments she stood bewildered. Then she said:

"A pain on my head! The good women have spent so much on the tickets!"

"I'll pay it all back—every cent—every single cent of it," pleaded Michalina. Again her own Yiddish sounded like a foreign tongue to her.

"You pay back! From the treasures of your beggarly peasant husband, perhaps? May you spend on doctor's bills a thousand dollars for every cent you have cost us, plaguy meshumedeste that you are!"

A bedlam of curses let itself loose. Michalina fled.

"Let her go to all the eighty dark, bitter, and swampy years!" Sorah-Elka concluded, as the door closed upon the apostate. "A meshumedeste will be a meshumedeste."

(1899)

Maggie's Minstrel

Florence Converse

It was that latest of daylight hours, when all green things are greenest, before the sudden flushing of the afterglow startles the eyes upward. We were planting a tree.

The little white-haired genius of the garden pressed her rheumatic knees confidingly against the dewy bosom of mother earth and made wavering passes with a trowel. Christina held the watering pot absently, at the dribbling angle. The dribble dribbled down her gown; but I reflected that it was a wash-gown and turned my attention to more important matters. I was shuffling the leaves of the "Phaedrus," trying to find the prayer to Pan, for planting trees was to be a rite with us.* This was the first tree we had ever planted. Maggie, in everybody's light, in everybody's way, stood gripping the handle of the spade with both hands, one foot uplifted to force the edge through the sod. It was the wrong foot, but I did not know that till afterward, and neither did Maggie, although she was our cook.

We were all talking, not actually at once, but our remarks overlapped, anthem-fashion, and returned upon themselves, da capo, da capo.

Maggie was saying: "Is it here that you want it, Mrs. Hazeltine? Is it here? Is it here, then? Is it here?" Every time she said "Is it here?" she lifted the spade and her foot, and set them down in the place that interfered most effectively with the wanderings of the trowel.

Christina was saying: "It will never shade the back piazza—never in this world. Just consider. The sun sets over there. No, Mother, you should bring it at least four feet this way. I thought you meant it to shade the—"

Christina's mother, the genius before mentioned, was saying: "How can I see where I want to plant it, with Maggie directly in my light? Take the spade away. Do you want to cut off my fingers, Maggie? That is the third time. My dear, I know exactly where I wish to plant this tree. It will shade the piazza perfectly."

I was saying: "Why translation? Why don't we read it in the original Greek?"

Christina was continuing to say: "No, mother; it must be four feet this—"

Then a strain of music smote upon our ears, and we all looked up, to see the sky rosy west and east and overhead, and a young man leaning against the wild clematis vine that curtained the west piazza. He was playing on a little double pipe of the kind shepherds use in Sicily, and deep in his eyes glowed a smile, intimate, yet dreamily remote.

---

*Plato's the *Phaedrus*, with Socrates' famous invocation to Pan, the spirit of wild nature. Christina reads from Socrates' prayer later in the story.

"Pan!" said Christina, and "Orpheus!" said I; but Maggie: "An Eyetalian! My kitchen door's open!" Christina's mother whispered, " 'Sh, Maggie!"

Presently I began to wonder whether the newcomer had laid us all under a spell with his tender, melancholy piping and his merry, tender smile; for we did not say another word, and he piped and piped and smiled and smiled. Then on a sudden, with one last bird-like trill, he had taken the little pipe from his lips, thrust it into his coat pocket, drawn from beneath his arm a hitherto unguessed accordion, and was expelling therefrom a gusty succession of sounds that we later learned to interpret as "Yankee Doodle."

The spell was broken. Christina hurried toward him, pouring copious libations at every step; I could feel the water soaking through the soles of my thin slippers as I followed her.

Italy was our passion, the Italian immigrant our problem and our soul's brother. We reread "The Divine Comedy" once a year and the immigration laws once a month, sometimes oftener. We had translated into English the "Little Flowers of St. Francis" and three of Petrarch's sonnets, and into Italian the Declaration of Independence, Lincoln's speech at Gettysburg, and the law against spitting in public streets and vehicles. In winter we taught Italian classes at a social settlement. Christina had men in her classes, and she taught them English, and about Mazzini, and the evils of the "boss" system in municipal politics. My class was a mother's club, and the mothers all spoke dialects that I could not understand. I did not try to teach them English, but we smiled at one another a great deal, and said, *"Come sta?"* At Christmas I gave them statuettes of the Madonna. On the days when we did not go to the social settlement to teach, we had lessons in Italian at home, from educated, but starving, Italians, who really needed the money. One winter Christina had four teachers, all teaching her at once, but at different hours; and I had six. Christina had not so much time as I to take lessons; she was mastering the intricacies of the "boss" system.

In the intervals of teaching and being taught we served on committees, the functions of which were to restate, in terms of industry, charity, civics, literature, or arts, the problem of the Americanizing of the Italian immigrant.

There were inevitably moments of reaction, briefest flickers on the tip of passion's flame, in springtime; but the heart of our fires burned uniformly intense. April might overhear us murmuring against the monotony of *"Come sta?"* but June would surely find us reading Dante and preparing a course of lectures on Italian and American heroes of independence. What though this very spring, on leaving town, we had confided to each other guiltily that we feared we should not care if we never saw the face of the Italian immigrant again? Behold us now, after four weeks of mountain solitude, tripping over one another to greet him, chirping ecstatically, *"Come sta?"* and again *"Come sta?"* Our hearts were fluttering in pleasurable anticipation of the lines and gestures and cues in this little drama of getting acquainted; we knew them all by heart, even as we knew the third canto of the "Paradiso"; his glowing gratitude, his swift delight and tentative "You spick my langwidge?"; his flattering lapse into his native tongue; his wistful pleasure over the fact that we, too, had been in *Italia*—yes, even in *la bella Napoli.*

"*Come sta?*" we blithely prompted. But he did not take the cure. His dreamful, smiling gaze seemed to pass through us as we approached; he continued his barbaric, impassioned rendering of "Yankee Doodle." It is disconcerting, mysterious, not to be looked at by the person whom you address. Perhaps he was Pan, after all.

"*Come sta?*" we repeated, but with less assurance; and Christina added, "*Italiano, lei?*"

"Yankee Dodle" ended on a long, braying note as the unknown crushed the accordion against his heart.

"That one she is Italian?" he inquired, nodding beyond us.

"That one" was unmistakably Maggie, who, seeing the nod, came trundling across the little lawn. Maggie was round; there was a tremolo, as of a joggled dumpling, in all her motions.

We laughed. The blood of the Celt rioted merrily in Maggie's veins. We laughed, and shook our heads. How should we guess that there was a new play toward, and that to us had been assigned the minor parts? Enter Maggie, short and fat and middle-aged, with a grin. How could we dream of such a thing?

"Oh, well-a," he acquiesced enigmatically; and still his musing smile caressed the circularities of our handmaiden.

"He thought you were Italian, Maggie," said I, yielding to a mischievous impulse. But a second time our knowledge of human nature proved inadequate, for Maggie was pleased; her grin became ridiculously coy.

Months afterward, when we were still discussing cause and effect, Christina and I came to the conclusion that our own devotion to things Italian had imperceptibly served an educational purpose in undermining Maggie's native prejudice and preparing her for this psychological moment. Christina's mother, whose point of view is less Italianate than ours, inclined to believe that Maggie would have been quite as flattered if that delicately respectful yet ardently appreciative gaze had emanated from the eye of a Hottentot; but, as we pointed out, such emotional gradations are not native to the eyes, or the bosoms, of Hottentots.

"American born, I am," said Maggie to the minstrel, with her most affable intonation.

"Oh, well-a," he answered, still with that curious air of waiving all objections.

"Children! children! Are you going to plant this tree tonight?" called a brisk, high little voice from the other end of the lawn.

We looked irresolutely at Orpheus. Then Christina threw me a glance which conveyed the information that her purse was in the left-hand corner of her top bureau drawer, at the back.

"I will bring a light," I said. "It will be too dark by the time we want to read the prayer to Pan." I gracefully withdrew.

When I came out again the movement was da capo, and Christina was saying:

"No, Mother, you are mistaken. It must come at least four feet this way."

"As you have the spade, you may use it, Maggie," rejoined Mrs. Hazeltine. "It will save time. Right here."

I had brought out the majolica Cupid that sits above the stairs in the living room and lights us on our way to bed. He holds a poppy blossom in each hand, and in the blossoms we kept tall candles.

Christina applauded my inspiration joyously. The little flames trailed backward through the dusk as I walked; the hot wax dripped on my fingers. Maggie had once more set hand and foot to her task, and my arrival illumined her picturesque attitude.

"You will fall yourself over yourself," observed the minstrel. "It is not a way to dig the hole."

He laid one brown, thin hand quietly upon Maggie's two puffed, red ones, which grasped the spade, and for the first time his glance condescended to us.

"If I shall plant this tree?" he inquired. "It is permitted?"

"Oh, if you would!" we chorused—we three, for Maggie said nothing. In a sudden flaring of the Cupid-candles I was surprised to see that her face was crimson, and there was the strangest look in her eyes, as if she had had some sort of shock. It was a very young look, and helpless.

The stranger withdrew his hand from hers as casually as he had laid it there, and took possession of the spade. He must have been holding Maggie's hands in that absentminded fashion for as many as fifteen seconds.

"Don't drip the wax down my neck! Hold him lower! Hold him steady! Here, let me hold him!" expostulated Christina.

But I clung to the revealing torchbearer, and turned his light upon the serene face of the minstrel.

"If he were really Orpheus, for example," I mused, "his youth would make no difference; it would be only an illusion. Or is it Maggie's middle age that would be an illusion?"

"You are a gardener?" hazarded Christina's mother, following the motions of the spade with approving eye.

"No, Signora; I work in shoe factory, Haverhill, Mass-achu-setts."

"Then you are out of work?" asked Christina. "You are looking for something to do? Too bad!" Christina had sweetly sympathetic possibilities in her voice.

For a moment he stopped digging, and lifted his head with a reassuring smile.

"Ah, Signorina, it is summer," he said, and leaning on the spade, he let his eyes move contentedly along the line of penciled light that illumined the edges of the mountains against the dusking sky.

Christina and I exchanged glances of rapture. The situation was so poetic, so improvident, so familiarly Italian!

"I am Siciliano," he continued. "In my country we have mountains—" again his eye swept the undulating skyline—"very different," he added, with an apologetic smile.

"Mongibello," nodded Christina. "Yes, we know. Very different, very beautiful."

"Oh, this is pretty," he said resignedly. "I like this very well. Trees and much shade, and plenty little—br-rook. If I can see Mongibello up there,"—he pointed skyward, —"I will like this very well. But Mongibello stays in Sicilia. Oh, well a."

"Then why did you come to America if you were so happy in Sicily?" Christina pressed gravely.

"So happy, Signorina, yes—and so hungry!"

The poetry of his reply silenced us for the moment; but Christina's economic instincts quickly rallied.

"Yet when you have a good job in a shoe factory, you give it up," she admonished. "You will be just as hungry in America as in Sicily if you do not work."

His smile was careless.

"To be a little hungry in summer, Signorina, that makes not bad to me. *Ecco,* my dinner!" He pulled the musical pipe from his pocket and blew a minor scale. "Signorina, to eat the dead shoe leather in summer that slays the good appetite. To stay in the shoe factory that also is to starve." He threw down the spade. "*Ecco,* the hole, Signora!" He knelt, and began to examine the roots of the little pine tree carefully. I held the torchbearer lower.

"And what becomes of your wife and children while you're traipsin' through the country blowin' a whistle?" inquired Maggie, a curious, personal resentment in her tone.

He flung his head back, and the candlelight fell upon his face. Silent, teasing laughter spoke in his eyes as he looked up at Maggie.

"My wife and my children they are not become—yet," he replied. The conquering laughter endured on his lips, in his eyes. "I look for her when I walk on the road; I look for her behind a tree; I call her with my moosic, so."

He had the pipe out again, and was tootling imperatively at Maggie; his very eyes seemed to tootle. "I look for her when I come up this hill to this house." There was a sudden flash from those eyes, and then he lowered them. "I think I find her very soon now," he said, and he began to put the little tree in the hole.

Christina and I squeezed each other's hands. Christina was beginning to realize that here was a situation.

"Water!" said Mrs. Hazeltine.

We had left the can at the other side of the lawn; but when Maggie had brought it back, Christina found the "Prayer to Pan," and read it by the light of Cupid's candles; while first Maggie, and then the minstrel—because Maggie's hands were shaky, and she slopped the water—poured a libation about the roots of the little pine tree, and Christina's mother patted the grassy sods in place with loving, grubby fingers.

"Beloved Pan," intoned Christina, and the minstrel bared his head—"Beloved Pan, and all ye other gods who haunt this place, give me beauty in the inward soul; and may the outward and inward man be at one. May I reckon the wise to be the wealthy, and may I have such quantity of gold as none but the temperate can carry."

When she had come to the end, the minstrel made the sign of the cross upon his breast, and resumed his battered hat.

"Where is the purse?" whispered Christina. But I had forgotten the purse when I went into the house; it was still upstairs in the left-hand corner of Christina's top drawer, at the back. Mrs. Hazeltine made furtive dives in the direction of a pocket. There was a brief pause as we stood embarrassed about the tree. I thought of suggesting that we take hands and dance in a ring; but Maggie made a saner suggestion.

"Do you think perhaps he's not had his supper, Mrs. Hazeltine?" she remarked.

"Oh, I'm afraid you haven't!" cried Christina's mother, hospitably. "Won't you go with Maggie, now, and let her give you something?"

"*La signora e molto graziosa,*" he beamed, lapsing for the first time into his native tongue; "but I have here my supper, I do not need—" He drew from his pocket a newspaper parcel in which we divined an onion.

"There's some of that there macaroni, cooked Eyetalian fashion," observed Maggie, still addressing her remarks to Mrs. Hazeltine. "I could warm it up. I haven't had my own supper yet. He can set down with me, —I ain't particular, —unless he'd rather eat to himself."

The Italian took off his hat and held it against his heart, making a slight, but courtly, inclination, first toward Mrs. Hazeltine, then toward Maggie. His face was radiant with appreciation and delight.

"If I will be invited from Miss McGee, it is much pleased," he cried. "I come, sure!"

"Not McGee—Doyle," said Maggie, leading the way to the kitchen.

"He can't be more than twenty-five," I murmured irrelevantly.

"And Maggie is thirty-six," supplemented Christina.

"Don't be absurd, children," said her mother; "he'll be gone in an hour."

But it was nearer two hours before Maggie came into the living room to put away the silver and the glasses.

"Has Orpheus gone, Maggie?" Christina inquired, concealing her curiosity under a light carelessness of tone.

"His name, in American, is Humbug," said Maggie. "Did you ever? In Eyetalian it's Oom—something-or-other, like that Dutchman in South Africa."

"Humbert!" ejaculated Christina.

"You mean Herbert," said Maggie.

"Well, maybe it is. I'm sure I hope so."

It was always difficult to enlarge Maggie's vocabulary; hers was a provincial mind. She dismissed our etymological efforts with the remark that he said he was named after the King of Italy. "The one that died." Then she changed the subject.

"He says he ain't ett such macaroni not since he left Italy three years ago. Talk about blarney!"

We hastened to reinforce Umberto's praise; but from the expression of Maggie's face I presently inferred that we were speaking to deaf ears.

"He thinks he'll see if he can't get a job to the farm for a day or two, now it's haying," she resumed.

Christina and I exchanged glances of furtive delight. Christina's mother discoursed for three minutes impressively upon the text "A rolling stone gathers no moss." In her peroration she excused the minstrel on the ground that he was "only a boy."

Maggie examined a tumbler, holding it up to the light to discover traces of lint.

"Of course he's young," she admitted, "but he ain't what I should call a boy. And I don't know as I blame him for cuttin' loose summers. Other folks than him does it."

The thrust went home. Christina and I preserved a guilty silence, our eyes fixed upon the pages of our respective magazines. There was the soft click of the tumblers against the shelf, one, two, three, four, then a dry, explosive, laugh from Maggie, and she said:

"Where do you think he says he's going to sleep tonight? Under my window! Ain't he a fool!"

Before we could reply she had gone into the kitchen and shut the door. Even as we gazed at one another, somewhere from out in the summer darkness came a premonitory blast from an accordion, and the first words of "Santa Lucia" trolled forth in a young and operatic baritone.

He was not gone in an hour or in a day. At the end of the week he still lingered, haying when the weather permitted, weeding in the garden under the guidance of Mrs. Hazeltine, turning the ice cream freezer for Maggie. Evening inevitably found him sitting on the kitchen doorstep, playing softly on his little pipe, or waking the echoes with his accordion.

"Are we going to let this thing go on?" we hourly asked one another. Apparently we were.

"But how can I insult Maggie by suggesting that she is fool enough—" murmured Mrs. Hazeltine.

"Yet evidently she is," said I.

"Christina might speak to him," her mother suggested, faintheartedly.

"Warn him against trifling with Maggie's young affections?" cried Christina. "Oh, no, Mother, I really couldn't. But I will if I get a chance."

The chance, however, was slow in offering. Umberto, when in our presence, confined himself and us to general topic: *il giardina, le montagne, la musica, il pellegrinaggio*—our polite word for his vagabondage. It was not until the day after Maggie asked us about the olive trees that he broached the theme of marriage, and even then his meaning was veiled in allegory.

Maggie's interest in Italy and its products—chiefly, it must be confessed, its food products—had expanded more rapidly during these ten days of Umberto's dalliance than in all the years in which she had been our faithful servitor and family friend. She suggested that we import polenta. She mourned the fact that she had never tasted a fresh fig. She presented us with a savory new concoction which she called a "fritter mixture," a *frito misto*, indeed, but with none of the original ingredients. She abjured lard and clamored for olive oil.

"Did you ever see an olive tree?" she asked us one evening when she was putting away the silver.

"Yes, we had; in Italy, many times."

"What kind of a tree are they?" she pursued.

Christina got out our photographic records of Italian journeys and showed Maggie picture after picture of olive trees, —whole orchards hung and garlanded with grapevines, hillsides cloudy with the silver bloom of the young leaves, —and explained their shape, their coloring, their esthetic value in the landscape, their usefulness. She paused at last before a lovely picture of a single olive tree in fruit, with a laughing little boy up in the branches picking the olives.

"Don't you think they are beautiful trees, Maggie?" she asked.

But Maggie's reply was bewildering in its reticence.

"It's not for me to say," she answered primly. And after a moment: "Bert's awful fond of olive trees. You haven't got another print of that picture, have you, Miss Christina? One that you don't want?" It happened that Christina had, and she gave it to her gladly.

The next day the opportunity for which we waited came, and incidentally Maggie's reticence was explained. Umberto was watering the little pine tree he had planted two weeks before, and examining its needles and tips. Christina and I went down and stood beside him, watching him.

"You think it will live now, don't you, Umberto?" Christina asked.

"Sure!" said Umberto.

His face was more sober than usual, and he seemed absorbed in serious, even sad, thoughts. I had never seen him so subdued.

"You like trees, Umberto?" continued Christina.

"Yes, Signorina." He sat back on his heels and surveyed the little pine. I thought the conversation ended, and was about to return to the piazza and my book; but he spoke again, this time in Italian:

"That Margarita—resembles a tree. Do you know the olive tree, in la Sicilia, Signorina? Where I am born there are a great many. When I see Margarita, I think of that little tree of my country, with those ripe fruits for me. She tells me she is old, but I reply that I prefer them when they are not so young. They are more beautiful when they are old."

"But, Umberto," began Christina, gently, also speaking in Italian, "let us consider the transplanting of trees. It is not safe to try to take up a tree of—of—middle age by the roots and make for it a different life. This little pine tree, for example, is young—"

"And I am, am I not young, Signorina?" cried Umberto.

"But it is not you, Umberto, who resembles a tree."

"Oh, well," he exclaimed in English, springing to his feet; and then excitedly, once more in Italian: "I ask you, Signorina, what is young? What is old? Is it not America that is young—so very young? Yes? And Italy is the old one. And I— I am Italy! *Ecco!*"

What could we say? After all, we reflected, it was Maggie who must have the last word. We smiled, and shook our heads at him, and betook ourselves to the reperusal of the "Vita Nuova."

That night, from my north window, which commands the kitchen doorstep, I became aware that an Italian lesson was in progress. There was a moon, and Maggie had put out the light in the kitchen, and drawn her rocking chair to the open door; I could hear her creaking ponderously back and forth. Umberto sat below her on the doorstep.

"*Cara*," said Umberto, "that is dee-ar-r. But we have in Italian another word—*carina*; that is dee-ar-r, but it is a more little dee-ar-r, more close. You have not these little words in America."

"Yes, we have," interrupted Maggie. "We have dear, and we have dearie."

"Dee-ree," said Umberto.

"Curreener," said Maggie.

Whereupon Umberto gave a musical cry, sprang to his feet, raced across the yard to the pasture fence, singing madly as he went, and leaped the fence without touching his hand to the rail. Four times he bounded over the fence, back and forth, in the moonlight, singing little high whoops and trills. He was like a passion-drunk bird wooing its mate. I could hear the creak of Maggie's rocking chair and her slow chuckle.

"What did you do that for, Bert?" she asked amusedly when he came back to her, breathing hard.

"Oh, well-a," he cried, throwing out his arms and sinking down on the doorstep.

"It does me good, Bert, to see anybody so full of feelin' as you are," said Maggie.

"I will do you good always; but you will see," he exclaimed in a passionate whisper. He was kneeling on the step. There was a low protest from Maggie, then another sound, soft, something like the continuous chirping of birds at dawn, and the rocker creaked once extra loud.

I shut my north window, although the night was warm, and went into Christina's room, and woke her out of her first sleep.

In the morning Maggie came to us in the garden, where we were all three killing rose bugs. Her manner was embarrassed; she ran a dishtowel between her hands. My own hands trembled so that I lost three rose bugs, and Christina stopped hunting altogether. Only Mrs. Hazeltine continued her pursuit with undiminished vigilance.

"Bert says him and I have the names of the king of Italy that's dead, and the queen, only she's still livin'. Oomburto and Mergeriter. Eyetalians is very kind to their wives, ain't they?"

"Not always," said Mrs. Hazeltine, fishing four entangled rose bugs out of the heart of a rugosa, and grinding them beneath her heel.

"Then it's the women's fault, I guess," returned Maggie. "I don't believe from the way Bert talks that Eyetalian women has much sense."

Mrs. Hazeltine paused in her search for rose bugs, and delivered a brief dissertation upon the fiery tempers of Italians and the dissimilarities of race between the American and the Italian. She even went so far as to say that she thought an American woman should consider long and seriously before marrying an Italian, "or any foreigner," she added weakly, veering off from personalities.

Maggie laughed consciously, and switched her dishtowel twice before she said that nobody could accuse her of having been in a hurry to marry any man, whether he was a Rooshian or a Filipino.

We waited breathless. At least Christina and I were breathless; Christina's mother had returned to the slaughter of rose bugs. But even she jumped when the announcement came.

"Bert's gone," said Maggie.

"Gone!" we gasped.

"Yes, gone. I sent him away."

"You mean," faltered Mrs. Hazeltine, "that he's not coming back?"

"That's for him to find out," said Maggie. After a moment, during which she seemed to take counsel with herself, she continued: "I wouldn't want it to get about as I had said this, and I wouldn't say it to nobody but you, Mrs. Hazeltine, —and the young ladies, —but it seems like I had sort of went to Bert's head. It's his bein' an Eyetalian and fuller of feelin' than most. But I didn't think it was fair to him not to give him a chance to find out how he feels when he ain't here. Maybe he'll get over it."

She waited, wistfully expectant of the polite, reassuring word from us. But we could not say it.

"Bert swears he won't," Maggie continued presently. "He's very fiery. But, then, of course, he's very young."

The little white-haired genius of the place went to the spot where Maggie stood beside the piazza steps.

"I honor and respect you, Maggie," she said. "You are a brave, good woman."

"If he comes back—" began Maggie. "But what's the use of countin' your chickens before they're hatched?" she added. "And if he don't, why, just the same, I wouldn't have missed these last two weeks—not for a farm!"

The days passed. Maggie in the kitchen caroled "Santa Lucia," or crooned under her breath the vague melodies Umberto had played on his little pipe. When Sunday came she asked to be allowed to go to the nearest town, about ten miles away, for the consolations of religion. By rising at five o'clock and availing herself of an intricate combination of buggies, trolley cars, and excursion trains, she could attend the half-past-ten o'clock mass and return in time to set the table for supper.

Yes, ours were very minor parts. We were not even on the stage in the last act; we only curtseyed in the epilogue. For of course Maggie met Bert in town, and when she came home she was married. Bert, it appeared, had prepared himself with a marriage license the day after he left us, and had spent the interim filling the streets of that mountain town with sweet music and keeping on eye out for Maggie.

"And where is Bert now?" we asked when we had found our tongues.

"Oh, he 's went on to Haverhill in the excursion, to take up his job and hire a tenement. I told him I couldn't come until the middle of September, and I'd not have him round here makin' a laughin' stock of himself to the farm. He's took my picture with him—the one of the olive tree. You don't mind, do you, Miss Christina? Bert said to tell you that if he has a little olive orchard, he stays at home now and not make himself a pillygreenidjul any more. Them was his words as near as I could make out; maybe you know what he meant."

"Maggie my dear, I hope—we all hope—that you will be very happy," said Christina's mother, with perfunctory benevolence.

"But you think I won't," retorted Maggie, "and only because he 's eleven years younger than me. I tried to be fair to him—I tried."

"Dear Maggie—dear, dear Maggie, you were fair!" we said; and we all wept with her.

"If you don't mind," faltered Maggie, presently, "I'd like to have the prayer that's in the book you prayed out of the night you planted that little pine tree—the night Bert come. Bert has spoke more than once of that prayer. I hunted it up when you was out one day, and we ready it over till the meanin' begun to come, about bein' healthy and wealthy and wise, and havin' just enough money to keep a-goin'. Bert and me feel as if that prayer blessed our union," said Maggie.

Christina immediately copied for her on the typewriter the "Prayer to Pan" from the "Phaedrus."

"Bert says he's goin' to frame the picture of the olive tree," said Maggie, "and I guess I'll have him frame this prayer and hang it underneath."

(1914)

The Alien in the Melting Pot

Frederick J. Haskin

I am the immigrant.

Since the dawn of creation my restless feet have beaten new paths across the earth.

My uneasy bark has tossed on all seas.

My wanderlust was born of the craving for more liberty and a better wage for the sweat of my face.

I looked toward the United States with eyes kindled by the fire of ambition and heart quickened with newborn hope.

I approached its gates with great expectation.

I entered with fine hopes.

I have shouldered my burden as the American man of all work.

I contribute eighty-five percent of all the labor in the slaughtering and meat-packing industries.

I do seven-tenths of the bituminous coal mining.

I do seventy-eight percent of all the work in the woolen mills.

I contribute nine-tenths of all the labor in the cotton mills.

I make nine-twentieths of all the clothing.

I manufacture more than half the shoes.

I build four-fifths of all the furniture.

I make half of the collars, cuffs, and shirts.

I turn out four-fifths of all the leather.

I make half the gloves.

I refine nearly nineteen-twentieths of the sugar.

I make half of the tobacco and cigars.

And yet, I am the great American problem.

When I pour out my blood on your altar of labor, and lay down my life as a sacrifice to your god of toil, men make no more comment than at the fall of a sparrow.

But my brawn is woven into the warp and woof of the fabric of your national being.

My children shall be your children and your land shall be my land because my sweat and my blood will cement the foundations of the America of Tomorrow.

If I can be fused into the body politic, the Melting Pot will have stood the supreme test.

(c. 1923)

Chinaman, Laundryman

H. T. Tsiang

"Chinaman"!
"Laundryman"!
Don't call me "man"!
I am worse than a slave.

Wash! Wash!
Why can I wash away
The dirt of others' clothes
But not the hatred of my heart?
My skin is yellow,
Does my yellow skin color the clothes?
Why do you pay me less
For the same work?
Clever boss!
You know
How to scatter the seeds of hatred
Among your ignorant slaves

Iron! Iron!
Why can I smooth away
The wrinkles of others' dresses
But not the miseries of my heart?
Why should I come to America
To wash clothes?
Do you think "Chinamen" in China
Wear no dresses?
I came to America
Three days after my marriage.
When can I see her again?
Only the almighty "Dollar" knows!

Dry! Dry!
Why do clothes dry,
But not my tears?
I work
Twelve hours a day,

He pays
Fifteen hours a week.
My boss says,
"Chinaman,
Go back to China
If you don't feel satisfied!
There,
Unlimited hours of toil:
Two silver dollars a week,
If
You can find a job."
"Thank you, Boss!
For you remind me.
I know
Bosses are robbers
Everywhere!"

Chinese boss says:
"You Chinaman,
Me Chinaman
Come work for me—
Work for your fellow countryman!
By the way,
You 'Wong,' me 'Wong'—
Do we not belong to same family?
Ha! ha!
We are cousins!
Oh yes!
You 'Hai Shan,' me 'Hai Shan,'
Do we not come from same district?
O, come work for me;
I will treat you better!"
"GET away from here,
What is the difference,
When you come to exploit me?"

"Chinaman"!
"Laundryman"!
Don't call me "Chinaman"!
Yes, I am a "Laundryman"!
The workingman!
Don't call me "Chinaman"!
I am the Worldman

"The International Soviet
Shall be his human race"!*

"Chinaman"!
"Laundryman"!
All the workingmen!
Here is the brush
Made of Marxism.
Here is the soap
Made of Leninism.
Let us all
Wash with the blood!
Let us all
Press with the iron!
Wash!
Brush!
Dry!
Iron!
Then we shall have
A clean world.

(1928)

* *"The International Soviet / Shall be his human race!:* Lines are adapted from the English-language version of "The Internationale," the principal musical expression of solidarity with international socialism (often described as the anthem of socialist ideals): "'Tis the final conflict / Let each stand in his place. / The international working class / Shall be the human race."

Rickshaw Boy

H. T. Tsiang

What shall I do?
What shall I do?

Father, penniless! Rent? No.
He was a farmer, the year was bad, so
He killed himself a year ago.

Now soldiers come, the bugles blow,
Raping the women, you take them where you go!
O my mother, where do they keep you now?

Who can pay with father gone!
The landlord come, there is no one
Here but old, old folks with money gone!

The rich man smiles in garments of gold.
My elder sister but fifteen, must be sold.
The rich man cares for nothing—but women and gold.

Grandfather is too old to be a wage slave.
Grandmother stands near the edge of the grave.
No more firm-breasted sister of fifteen,
She is a concubine, though young and green.

What shall I do?
What shall I do?
Only one way:
I must leave today.

Farther than a horse can I move my legs,
Pulling the chaise I shall be a horse instead;
I shall not worry to earn my bread.

Ta! ta! ta! ta!
Pulling rickshaw!
How far, how far?
Way beyond the dimming star!

Ta! ta! ta! ta!
Pulling rickshaw!
How far, how far?
Till the moon has come and the sun has gone!

Ta! ta! ta! ta!
Pulling rickshaw!
The cruel wind ruffles my heavy hair!
The stormy rain washes my body in chilling air!

Ta! ta! ta! ta!
Pulling rickshaw!
On my back is my bed!
In the rickshaw is my shed!

Ta! ta! ta! ta!
Pulling rickshaw!
My silent sobs are bitter, and I run and run!
The rich man smiles merrily, and has lots of fun!

Ta! ta! ta! ta!
Pulling rickshaw!
I beg for one copper tip,
The rich man answers with a ruthless kick!

Ta! ta! ta! ta!
Pulling rickshaw!
North! east! south! west!
Is the grave the only place a workingman may rest?

Ta! ta! ta! ta!
Pulling rickshaw!
International Park, no dogs nor "Chinese" admitted,
None but rich "Chinese" may be permitted!

Ta! ta! ta! ta!
Pulling rickshaw!
O, I shall die!
Blood pouring from this mouth of mine,
I shall die in the street's wet slime!
O missionary, you whip me with an extra dime,
Rushing to the station to meet your loving boy on time!

O! father, in death you are wasted low,
O! mothers, who knows where you are now;
Sister, your misery is grandparents' woe.
Grandmother and father, you are not lonely in gloom,
For I still can feed you in my tomb.

O, horse, you are lucky! your master gives you care,
Sometimes he releases you in the fresh air,
O, motor car, you are lucky! Your master gives you care,
Sometimes he spends money for your repair.

O, rich man now you make me pull rickshaw,
Someday I will make you eat rickshaw!
O, fellow workingmen, only to you dare I cry!
How poor I die!
How poor I die!

O, workingman, you are rich men's fools!
Rich men use you for their tools!
O, workingmen, arise! Be no more fools!
O, workingmen, be nobody's tools!

(1928)

A Yellow Man and a White

Eleanor Gates

Fong Wu sat on the porch of his little square-fronted house, chanting into the twilight. Across his padded blouse of purple silk lay his *sam-yen* banjo. And as, from time to time, his hymn to the Three Pure Ones was prolonged in high, fine quavers, like the uneven, squeaky notes of a woman's voice, he ran his left hand up the slender neck of the instrument, rested a long nail of his right on its taut, snake's skin head, and lightly touched the strings; then in quick, thin tones, they followed the song to Sang-Ching.*

The warm shadows of a California summer night were settling down over the wooded hills and rocky gulches about Fong Wu's, and there was little but his music to break the silence. Long since, the chickens had sleepily sought perches in the hen yard, with its high wall of rooty stumps and shakes, and on the branches of the Digger pine that towered beside it. Up the dry creek bed, a mile away, twinkled the lights of Whiskeytown; but now sounds from the homes of the white people came down to the lonely Chinese. If his clear treble was interrupted, it was by the cracking of a dry branch as a cottontail sped past on its way to a stagnant pool, or it was by a dark-emboldened coyote, howling, dog-like, at the moon which, white as the snow that eternally coifs the Sierras, was just rising above their distant, cobalt line.

One year before, Fong Wu, heavily laden with his effect, had slipped out of the stage from Redding and found his way to a forsaken, ramshackle building below Whiskeytown. His coming had proved of small interest. When the news finally got about that "a monkey" was living in "Sam Kennedy's old place," it was thought, for a while, that laundrying, thereafter, would be cheaply done. This hope, however, was soon dispelled. For, shortly after his arrival, as Fong Wu asked at the grocery store for mail, he met Radigan's inquiry of "You do my washee, John?" with a grave shake of the head. Similar questions from others were met, later, in a similar way. Soon it became generally known that the "monkey at Sam Kennedy's" did not do washing; so he was troubled no further.

Yet, if Fong Wu did not work for the people of Whiskeytown, he was not, therefore, idle. Many a sunrise found him wandering through the chaparral thickets back of his house, digging here and there in the red soil for roots and herbs. These he took home, washed, tasted, and perhaps, dried. His mornings were mainly spent in cooking for his abundantly supplied table, in tending his

---

The Three Pure Ones: Trinity of the three highest deities in Taoism. *Sang-Ching (also Shang ch'ing):* the second of these deities, responsible for disseminating sacred texts to lesser gods and humans.

fowls and house, and in making spotless and ironing smooth various undergarments—generous of sleeve and leg.

But of an afternoon, all petty duties were laid aside, and he sorted carefully into place upon his shelves numerous little bunches and boxes of dried herbs and numerous tiny phials of pungent liquid that had come to him by post; he filled wide sheets of foolscap with vertical lines of queer characters and consigned them to big, plainly addressed, well-stamped envelopes; he scanned closely the last newspapers from San Francisco, and read from volumes in diverse tongues; and he pored over the treasured Taoist book, "The Road to Virtue."

Sunday was his one break in the week's routine. Then, the coolies who panned or cradled for gold in the tailings of nearby abandoned mines, gathered at Fong Wu's. On such occasions, there was endless, lively chatter, a steady exchange of barbering—one man scraping another clean, to be, in turn, made hairless in a broad band about the poll and on cheek and chin—and much consuming of tasty chicken, dried fish, pork, rice, and melon seeds. To supplement all this, Fong Wu recounted the news: the arrival of a consul in San Francisco; the raid on a slave- or gambling-den, the progress of a tong war under the very noses of the baffled police, and the growth of the Coast feeling against the continued, quiet immigration of Chinese. But of the social or political affairs of the Flowery Kingdom—of his own land beyond the sea, Fong Wu was consistently silent.

Added to his Sunday responsibilities as host and purveyor of news, Fong Wu had others. An ailing countryman, whether seized with malaria or suffering from an injury, found ready and efficient attention. The bark of dogwood, properly cooked, gave a liquid that killed the ague; and oil from a diminutive bottle, or a red powder whetted upon the skin with a silver piece, brought out the soreness of a bruise.

Thus, keeping his house, herb hunting, writing, studying, entertaining, doctoring, Fong Wu lived on at Whiskeytown.

Each evening, daintily manipulating ivory chopsticks, he ate his supper of rice out of a dragon-bordered bowl. Then, when he had poured tea, all gold-encrusted—a cluster of blossoms nodding in a vase at his shoulder, the while—he went out upon the porch of the square-fronted house.

And there, as now, a scarlet-buttoned cap on his head, his black eyes soft with dreaming, his richly wrought sandals tapping the floor in time, his long queue—a smooth, shining serpent—in thick coils about his tawny neck, Fong Wu thrummed gently upon the three-stringed banjo, and, in peace, chanted into the twilight.

Flying hoofs scattered the gravel on the strip of road before Fong Wu's. He looked through the gloom and saw a horse flash past, carrying a skirted rider toward Whiskeytown. His song died out. He let his banjo slip down until its round head rested between his feet. Then, he turned his face up the gulch.

Despite the dusk, he knew the traveler: Mrs. Anthony Barrett, who, with her husband, had recently come to live in a house near Stillwater. Every evening, when the heat was over, she went by, bound for the day's mail at the post office. Every evening, in the cool, Fong Wu saw her go, and sometimes she gave him a friendly nod.

Her mount was a spirited, mouse-dun mustang, with crop-ears, a roached mane, and the back markings of a mule. She always rode at a run, sitting with easy erectness. A wide army hat rested snugly on her fair hair, and shaded a white forehead and level-looking eyes. But notwithstanding the sheltering brim, on her girlish face were set the glowing, scarlet seals of wind and sun.

As he peered townward after her, Fong Wu heard the hurrying hoof beats grow gradually fainter and fainter—and cease. Presently the moon topped the pines on the foothills behind him, bathing the gulch in light. The road down which she would come sprang into view. He watched its furthest open point. In a few moments the hoof beats began again. Soon the glint of a light waist showed through the trees. Next, horse and rider rounded a curve at hand. Fong Wu leaned far forward.

And then, just as the mustang gained the strip of road before the square-fronted house, it gave a sudden, unlooked-for, outward leap, reared with a wild snort, and, whirling, dashed past the porch—riderless.

With an exclamation, Fong Wu flung his banjo aside and ran to the road. There under a Manzanita bush, huddled and still, lay a figure. He caught it up, bore it to the porch, and put it gently down.

A brief examination, made with the deftness practice gives, showed him that no bones were broken. Squatting beside the unconscious woman, he next played slowly with his long-nailed fingers upon her pulse. Its beat reassured him. He lighted a lamp and held it above her. The scarlet of her cheeks was returning.

The sight of her, who was so strong and active, stretched, weak and fainting, compelled Fong Wu into spoken comment. "The petal of a plum blossom," he said compassionately, in his own tongue.

She stirred a little. He moved back. As, reviving, she opened her eyes, they fell upon him. But he was half turned away, his face as blank and lifeless as a mask.

She gave a startled cry and sat up. "My hurtee?" she asked him, adopting pidgin English. "Me fallee off?"

Fong Wu rose. "You were thrown," he answered gravely.

She colored in confusion. "Pardon me," she said, "for speaking to you as if you were a coolie." Then, as she got feebly to her feet—"I believe my right arm is broken."

"I have knowledge of healing," he declared: "let me look at it." Before she could answer, he had ripped the sleeve away. "It is only a sprain," he said. "Wait." He went inside for an amber liquid and bandages. When he had laved the injured muscles, he bound them round.

"How did it happen?" she asked, as he worked. He was so courteous and professional that her alarm was gone.

"Your horse was frightened by a rattler in the road. I heard it whir."

She shuddered. "I ought to be thankful that I didn't come my cropper on it." She said, laughing nervously.

He went inside again, this time to prepare a cupful of herbs. When he offered her the draught, she screwed up her face over its nauseating fumes.

"If that acts as strongly as it tastes," she said, after she had drunk it, "I'll be well soon."

"It is to keep away inflammation."

"Oh! Can I go now?"

"Yes. But tomorrow return, and I will look at the arm." He took the lamp away and replaced his red-buttoned cap with a black felt hat. Then he silently preceded her down the steps to the road. Only when the light of her home shone plainly ahead of them, did he leave her.

They had not spoken on the way. But as he bowed a goodnight, she addressed him. "I thank you," she said. "And may I ask your name?"

"Kwa"—he began, and stopped. Emotion for an instant softened his impassive countenance. He turned away. "Fong Wu," he added, and was gone.

The following afternoon the crunch of cartwheels before the square-fronted house announced her coming. Fong Wu closed "The Book of Virtue," and stepped out upon the porch.

A white man was seated beside her in the vehicle. As she sprang from it, light-footed and smiling, and mounted the steps, she indicated him politely to the Chinese.

"This is my husband," she said. "I have told him how kind you were to me last night."

Fong Wu nodded.

Barrett hastened to voice his gratitude. "I certainly am very much obliged to you," he said. "My wife might have been bitten by the rattler, or she might have lain all night in pain if you hadn't found her. And I want to say that your treatment was splendid. Why, her arm hasn't swollen or hurt her. I'll be hanged if I can see—you're such a good doctor—why you stay in this—"

Fong Wu interrupted him. "I will wet the bandage with medicine," he said, and entered the house.

They watched him with some curiosity as he treated the sprain and studied the pulse. When he brought out her second cup of steaming herbs, Mrs. Barrett looked up at him brightly.

"You know we're up here for Mr. Barrett's health," she said. "A year or so after we were married, he was hurt in a railway collision. Since then, though his wounds healed nicely, he has never been quite well. Dr. Lord, our family physician, prescribed plenty of rough work, and a quiet place, far from the excitement of a town or city. Now, all this morning, when I realized how wonderful it was that my arm wasn't aching, I've been urging my husband—what do you suppose?—to come and be examined by you!"

Fong Wu, for the first time, looked fully at the white man, marking the sallow, clayey face, with its dry, lined skin, its lusterless eyes and drooping lids.

Barrett scowled at his wife. "Nonsense, dear," he said crossly; "you know very well that Lord would never forgive me."

"But Fong Wu might help you, Anthony," she declared.

Fong Wu's black eyes were still fixed searchingly upon the white man. Before their scrutiny, soul-deep, the other's faltered and fell.

"You might help him, mightn't you, Fong Wu?" Mrs. Barrett repeated.

An expression, curious, keen, and full of meaning, was the answer. Then, "I might if he—" Fong Wu said, and paused.

Past Mrs. Barrett, whose back was toward her husband, the latter had shot a warning glance. "Come, come, Edith," he cried irritably, "let's get home."

Mrs. Barrett emptied her cup bravely. "When shall we call again?" she asked.

"You need not come again," Fong Wu replied. "Each day you have only to dampen the bandages from these." He handed her a green-flowered box containing twelve tiny compartments; in each was a phial.

"And I shan't have to take any more of this—this awful stuff?" she demanded gaily, giving back the cup.

"No."

"Ah! And now, I want to thank you again, with all my heart. Here—" she reached into the pocket of her walking skirt—"here is something for your trouble." Two double-eagles lay on her open palm.

Fong Wu frowned at them. "I take no money," he said, a trifle gruffly. And as she got into the cart, he closed the door of his home behind him.

It was a week before Mrs. Barrett again took up her rides for the mail. When she did, Fong Wu did not fail to be on his porch as she passed. For each evening, as she cantered up the road, spurring the mustang to its best paces, she reined to speak to him. And he met her greetings with unaccustomed good humor.

Then she went by one morning before sunrise, riding like the wind. A little later she repassed, whipping her horse at every gallop. Fong Wu, called to his door by the clatter, saw that her face was white and drawn. At noon, going up to the post office, he heard a bit of gossip that seemed to bear upon her unwonted trip. Radigan was rehearsing it excitedly to his wife, and the Chinese busied himself with his mail and listened—apparently unconcerned.

"I c'n tell you she ain't afraid of anythin', that Mrs. Barrett," the postmaster was saying: "neither th' cayuse she rides or a critter on two legs. An' that fancy little drug clerk from 'Frisco got it straight from th' shoulder."

"S-s-sh!" admonished his wife, from the back of the office. "Isn't there someone outside?"

"Naw, just th' chink from Kennedy's. Well, as I remarked, she did jus' light into that dude. 'It was criminal!' she says, an' her eyes snapped like a whip; 'it was criminal! an' if I find out for sure that you are guilty, I'll put you where you'll never do it again.' Th' young gent smirked at her an' squirmed like a worm. 'You're wrong, Mrs. Barrett,' he says, lookin' like th' meek puppy he is, 'an' you'll have t' look some place else for th' person that done it.' But she wouldn't talk no longer—jus' walked out, as mad as a hornet."

"Well, well," mused Mrs. Radigan. "I wonder what 'twas all about. 'Criminal,' she said, eh? That's funny!" She walked to the front of the office and peeked through the wicket. But no one was loitering near except Fong Wu, and his face was the picture of dull indifference.

That night, long after the hour for Mrs. Barrett's regular trip, and long past the time for his supper song, Fong Wu heard slow, shuffling steps approach the house. A moment afterward, the knob of his door was rattled. He put out his light and slipped a knife into his loose sleeve.

After some fumbling and moving about on the porch, a man called out to him. He recognized the voice.

"Fong Wu! Fong Wu!" it begged. "Let me in. I want to see you; I want to ask you for help—for something I need. Let me in; let me in."

Fong Wu, without answering, relit his lamp, and, with the air of one who is at the same time both relieved and a witness of the expected, flung the door wide.

Then into the room, writhing as if in fearful agony, his hands palsied, his face a-drip and, except for dark blotches about the mouth, green-hued, his eyes wild and sunken, fell, rather than tottered, Anthony Barrett.

"Fong Wu," he pleaded from the floor at the other's feet, "you helped my wife, when she was sick, now help me. I'm dying! I'm dying. Give it to me, for God's sake! give it to me." He caught at the skirt of Fong Wu's blouse.

The Chinese retreated a little, scowling. "What do you want?" he asked.

A paroxysm of pain seized Barrett. He half rose and half stumbled forward. "You know," he panted, "you know. And if I don't have some, I'll die. I can't get it anywhere else. She's found me out, and scared the drug clerk. Oh, just a little, old man, just a little!" He sank to the floor again.

"I can give you nothing," said Fong Wu bluntly. "I do not keep—what you want."

With a curse, Barrett was up again. "Oh, you don't," he screamed, leering frenziedly. "You yellow devil! You almond-eyed pigtail! But I know you do! And I must have it. Quick! quick!" He hung, clutching, on the edge of Fong Wu's wide ironing table, an ashen wreck.

Fong Wu shook his head.

With a cry, Barrett came at him and seized his lean throat. "You damned high-binder!" he gasped. "You saddle-nosed monkey! You'll get me what I want or I'll give you away. Don't I know why you're up here in these woods, with your pretty clothes and your English talk? A-*ha!* You bet I do! You're hiding, and you're wanted."—he dropped his voice to a whisper—"the tongs would pay head-money for you. If you don't give it to me, I'll put every fiend in 'Frisco on your trail."

Fong Wu had caught Barrett's wrists. Now he cast him to one side. "Tongs!" he said with a shrug, as if they were beneath his notice. And "Fiends!" he repeated contemptuously, a taunt in his voice.

The white man had fallen prone and was groveling weakly. "Oh, I won't tell on you," he wailed imploringly. "I won't, I won't, Fong Wu; I swear it on my honor."

Fong Wu grunted and reached to a handy shelf. "I will make a bargain with you," he said craftily; "first, you are to drink what I wish."

"Anything! anything!" Barrett cried.

From a box of dry herbs, long untouched, the Chinese drew out a handful. There was no time for brewing. Outraged nature demanded instant relief. He dropped them into a bowl, covered them with water, and stirred swiftly. When the stems and leaves were broken up and well mixed, he strained a brown liquid from them and put it to the other's lips.

"Drink," he commanded, steadying the shaking head.

Barrett drank, unquestioning.

Instantly the potion worked. Calmed as if by a miracle, made drowsy to the point where speech was impossible, the white man, tortured but a moment before, tipped sleepily into Fong Wu's arms. The Chinese waited until a full effect was secured, when he lifted his limp patient to the blanket-covered ironing table. Then he went out for fuel, built a fire, and, humming softly—with no fear of waking the other—sat down to watch the steeping of more herbs.

What happened next at the square-fronted house was the unexpected. Again there was the sound of approaching footsteps, again someone gained the porch. But this time there was no pausing to ask for admission, there were no weak requests for aid. A swift hand felt for the knob and found it; a strong arm pushed at the unlocked door. And through it, bareheaded, with burning eyes and blanched cheeks, her heavy riding whip dangling by a thong from her wrist, came the wife of Anthony Barrett.

Just across the sill she halted and swept the dim room. A moment, and the burning eyes fell upon the freighted ironing table. She gave a piercing cry.

Fong Wu neither spoke nor moved.

After the first outburst, she was quiet—the quiet that is deliberative, threatening. Then she slowly closed her fingers about the whip butt. Fixing her gaze in passionate anger upon him, she advanced a few steps.

"So it was you," she said, and her voice was hollow.

To that he made no sign, and even his colorless face told nothing.

She came forward a little farther, and sucked in a long, deep breath. "You *dog* of a Chinaman!" she said at last, and struck her riding skirt.

Fong Wu answered silently. With an imperative gesture, he pointed out the figure on the ironing table.

She sprang to her husband's side and bent over him. Presently she began to murmur to herself. When, finally, she turned, there were tears on her lashes, she was trembling visibly, and she spoke in whispers.

"Was I wrong?" she demanded brokenly. "I *must* have been. He's not had it; I can tell by his quick, easy breathing. And his ear has a faint color. You are trying to help him! I know! I know!"

A gleaming white line showed between the yellow of Fong Wu's lips. He picked up a rude stool and set it by the table. She sank weakly upon it, letting the whip fall.

"Thank God! thank God!" she sobbed prayerfully, and buried her face in her arms.

Throughout the long hours that followed, Fong Wu, from the room's shadowy rear, sat watching. He knew sleep did not come to her. For now and then he saw her shake from head to heel convulsively, as he had seen men in his own country quiver beneath the scourge of bamboos. Now and then, too, he heard her give a stifled moan, like the protest of a dumb creature. But in no other ways did she bare her suffering. Quietly, lest she wake her husband, she fought out the night.

Only once did Fong Wu look away from her. Then, in anger and disgust his eyes shifted to the figure on the table. "The petal of a plum blossom"—he muttered in Chinese—"the petal of a plum blossom beneath the hoofs of a pig!" And again his eyes dwelt upon the grief-bowed wife.

But when the dawn came stealing up from behind the purple Sierras, and Mrs. Barrett raised her wan face, he was studiously reviewing his row of bottles, outwardly unaware of her presence.

"Fong Wu," she said, in a low voice, "when will he wake?"

"When he is rested; at sunrise, maybe, or at noon."

"And then?"

"He will be feeble. I shall give him more medicine, and he will sleep again."

He rose and busied himself at the fire. Soon he approached her, bringing the gold-incrusted teapot and a small, handleless cup.

She drank thirstily, filling and emptying the cup many times. When she was done, she made as if to go. "I shall see that everything is alright at home," she told him. "After that, I shall come back." She stooped and kissed her husband tenderly.

Fong Wu opened the door for her, and she passed out. In the road, unhitched, but waiting, stood the mustang. She mounted and rode away.

When she returned, not long afterward, she was a new woman. She had bathed her face and donned a fresh waist. Her eyes were alight, and the scarlet was again flaming in her cheeks. Almost cheerfully, and altogether hopefully, she resumed her post at the ironing table.

It was late in the afternoon before Barrett woke. But he made no attempt to get up, and would not eat. Fong Wu administered another dose of herbs, and without heeding his patient's expostulations. The latter, after seeking his wife's hand, once more sank into sleep.

Just before sunset, Fong Wu, who scorned to rest, prepared supper. Gratefully, Mrs. Barrett partook of some tender chicken and rice cakes. When darkness shut down, they took up their second long vigil.

But it was not the vigil of the previous night. She was able to think of other things than her husband's condition and the doom that, of a sudden, had menaced her happiness. Her spirits having risen, she was correspondingly impatient of a protracted, oppressive stillness, and looked about for an interruption, and for diversion. Across from her, a Celestial patrician in his blouse of purple silk and his red-buttoned cap, sat Fong Wu. Consumed with curiosity—now that she had time to observe him closely—she longed to lift the yellow, expressionless mask from his face—a face which might have patterned that of an Oriental sphinx. At midnight, when he approached the table to satisfy himself of Barrett's progress, and to assure her of it, she essayed a conversation.

Glancing up at his laden shelves, she said, "I have been noticing your medicines, and how many kinds there seem to be."

"For each ailment that is visited upon man, earth offers up a cure," he answered. "Life would be a mock could Death, unchallenged, take it."

"True. Have you found in the earth, then, the cure for each ailment of man?"

"For most, yes. They seek yet, where I learned the art of healing, an antidote for the cobra's bite. I know of no other they lack."

"Where you were taught they must know more than we of this country know."

Fong Wu gave his shoulders a characteristic shrug.

"But," she continued, "you speak English so perfectly. Perhaps you were taught that in this country."

"No—in England. But the other, I was not."

"In England! Well!"

"I went there as a young man."

"But these herbs, these medicines you have—they did not come from England, did they?"

He smiled. "Some came from the hills at our back." Then crossing to his shelves and reaching up, "This"—he touched a silk-covered package—"is from Sumbawa in the Indian Sea; and this"—his finger was upon the cork of a phial—"is from Feng-shan, Formosa; and other roots are taken in the winter from the lake of Ting-ting-hu, which is then dry; and still others come from the far mountains of Chamur."

"Do you know," Mrs. Barrett said tentatively, "I have always heard that Chinese doctors give horrid things for medicine—sharks' teeth, frogs' feet, lizards' tails, and—all sorts of dreadful things."

Fong Wu proffered no enlightenment.

"I am glad," she went on, "that I have learned better."

After a while she began again: "Doubtless there is other wonderful knowledge, besides that about doctoring, which Chinese gentlemen possess."

Fong Wu gave her a swift glance. "The followers of Laou-Tsze know many things," he replied, and moved into the shadows as if to close their talk.

Toward morning, when he again gave her some tea, she spoke of something that she had been turning over in her mind for hours.

"You would not take money for helping me when I was hurt," she said, "and I presume you will refuse to take it for what you are doing now. But I should like you to know that Mr. Barrett and I will always, always be your friends. If"—she looked across at him, no more a part of his rude surroundings than was she—"if ever there comes a time when we could be of use to you, you have only to tell us. Please remember that."

"I will remember."

"I cannot help but feel," she went on, and with a sincere desire to prove her gratitude, rather than to pry out any secret of his, "that you do not belong here—that you are in more trouble than I am. For what can a man of your rank have to do in a little town like this!"

He was not displeased with her. "The ancient sage," he said slowly, "mounted himself upon a black ox and disappeared into the western wilderness of Tibet. Doubtless others, too, seek seclusion for much thinking."

"But you are not the hermit kind," she declared boldly. "You belong to those who stay and fight. Yet here you are, separated from your people and your people's graves—alone and sorrowful."

"As for my living people, they are best without me; as for my people dead, I neither worship their dust nor propitiate devils. The wise one said: 'Why talk forever on of men who are long gone?'"

"Yet—" she persisted.

He left the stove and came near her. "You are a woman but you know much. You are right. My heart is heavy for a thing I cannot do—for the shattered dreams of the men of Hukwang." He beat his palms together noiselessly, and moved to and fro on soft sandals. "Those dreams were of a young China that was to take the place of the old—but that died unborn."

She followed his words with growing interest. "I have heard of those dreams," she answered: "they were called 'reform.'"

"Yes. And now all the dreamers are gone. They have voyaged to glean at Harvard, Yale, Cornell, and in the halls of Oxford. There were 'five loyal and six learned,' and they shed their blood at the Chen Chih Gate. One there was who died the death that is meted a slave at the court of the Son of Heaven. And one there was"—his face shrank up, as if swiftly aging; his eyes became dark, upturning slits; as one who fears pursuit he cast a look behind him—"and one there was who escaped beyond the blood-bathed walls of the Hidden City and gained the Sumatra Coast. Then, leaving Perak, in the Straits Settlements, he finally set foot upon a shore where men, without terror, may reach toward higher things."

"And was he followed?" she whispered, comprehending.

"He fled quietly, quietly. For long are the claws of the she-panther that is crouched on the throne of the Mings."

Both fell silent. The Chinese went back to the stove where the fire was dying. The white woman, wide awake, and lost in the myriad of scenes his tale had conjured, sat by the table, for once almost forgetful of her charge.

The dragging hours of darkness past, Anthony Barrett found sane consciousness. He was pale, yet strengthened by his long sleep, and he was hungry. Relieved and overjoyed, Mrs. Barrett ministered to him. When he had eaten and drunk, she helped him from the table to the stool, and thence to his feet. Her arm about him, she led him to the door. Fong Wu had felt his pulse and it had ticked back the desired message, so he was going home.

"Each night you are to come," Fong Wu said, as he bade them goodbye. "And soon, very soon, you may go from here to the place from which you came."

Mrs. Barrett turned at the door. A plea for pardon in misjudging him, thankfulness for his help, sympathy for his exile—all these shone from her eyes. But words failed her. She held out her hand.

He seemed not to see it; he kept his arms at his sides. A "dog of a Chinaman" had best not take a woman's hand.

She went out, guiding her husband's footsteps, and helped him climb upon the mustang from the height of the narrow porch. Then, taking the horse by the bridle, she moved away down the slope to the road.

Fong Wu did not follow, but closed the door gently and went back to the ironing table. A handkerchief lay beside it—a dainty linen square that she had left. He picked it up and held it before him by two corners. From it wafted a faint, sweet breath.

Fong Wu let it flutter to the floor. "The perfume of a plum petal," he said softly, in English; "the perfume of a plum petal."

(1905)

The Old Lamp

Catalina Páez

It was Mollie O'Brien who first broached the Settlement to Carmelina. Mollie O'Brien, whose mother scrubbed offices from dawn till dusk, while her father sojourned remote from the bosom of this family in a mysterious region denominated "the Island." For such as Mollie, gravitating between a lonely hearth and the seething maelstrom of the streets, the Settlement spread its nets. And for such as Mollie, acknowledged Carmelina, the Settlement has its advantages. But what need of Settlements had she—Carmelina—enthroned upon the stairs of her own vegetable cellar, sucking an orange from her own fruit stand, and rejoicing in a full complement of parents, to say nothing of Nonna—a very queen among grandmothers? Carmelina rested quite content with the cellar, the stand, and her family connection. For luxuries, she had Tomassino, the cat, all unsalable fruit, and an occasional fiesta at the church of San Bernardo, when there was praying, and brass bands, and incense, and confetti, and everyone blossomed like the rose in purple and complementary harmonies. And all this spelled happiness.

What more could one ask? Raiment sufficient to cover one, without the encumbrances of fashion; macaroni and polenta at stated intervals, plus risotto on the Sabbath; and, when the day was over, a snug corner on the mattress in the dark bedroom, with *mamaina*'s loving arms around her, *mamaina*'s soft Tuscan lullabies in her ears. Her *carissima mamaina*, Bianca. Bianca, so loving, so tender, so lavish with the polenta, so cautious with the customers! Bianca, whose kerchiefs were so beautifully gay, whose eyes so beautifully brown, whose coils and coils of shining braids the longest and thickest in the world! (Of that fact Carmelina was positive.) What a calamity to be afflicted with a mother whose hair, all gray and drab, hung in straggling wisps about her face; whose eyes, if eyes she had, were lost behind spectacles; who neither bargained nor bartered, but spent her days slopping around with buckets of water! Ugh! Carmelina hated water. No wonder Millie took to the Settlement! But again, what had the Settlements to offer one so felicitously circumstanced as she?

"A yard and a sand pile"? Pooh! She had a cellar and a pile of cabbages. "A lady who made things of clay, pigs and the like, and would teach one how"? Well, Bianca made things; things of straw, beautiful gleaming straw baskets and braid and fans. There was a certain little three-cornered basket she wove for no one but Carmelina; and when it came to the handle she tossed out a long strip for Carmelina to catch in her grimy little hands, and they two would weave together, both beginning in the middle, "Music at the Settlement?

Song?" Carmelina and Bianca sang, too, sang as they wove, a little song, Tuscan, like the mother, and the straw, and the pattern they were making.

> *"La violetta*
> *Che in sull' erbetta*
> *S'apre al mattin novella;*
> • *Di' non è cosa*
> *Tutta adorosa,*
> *Tutta leggiudra è bella?"*

And yet more settlement marvels? "A story hour"! "A story circle," drawn up, on little wooden chairs, about a "story lady," who recounted wonderful tales of "knights and heroes and fairyland"? No marvel there! Did she not also have stories? And what were circles and ladies and little wooden chairs compared to the joy of huddling beside Nonna on a potato sack, with Tomassino's soft fur tickling one's cheek, the earthly scents of vegetables delighting one's nose, and Nonna's sweet *patois* droning in one's ears? And what legend of knighthood could compare to hers of saints and miracles? What hero to Garibaldi?* What fairyland to Italy? Glorious, sunny Italy, where Vesuvio loomed grimly in the distance, and almond trees cast fragrance from the hillsides! Ah the trees! The trees! Carmelina had seen no tree since, a baby, she had entered the slums via Castle Garden; but Nonna kept them green and fragrant in her memory. Someday when Pietro and Bianca had garnered a harvest of *soldi* from the penny bananas and three-cent oranges, and the onions and cabbages of fluctuating value, she would again see Italy, and the almond flowers, and the trees! Meanwhile she mingled trees with her visions of Heaven, along with talking dolls and purple satin dresses. The trees were her final boast.

"I bet you don't have trees in your old fairyland!" she said largely.

Mollie betrayed some uncertainty. "But we have a beanstalk!" she hastened to proclaim. Then Mollie laid down her trump ace. "In the yard, at the Settlement, there is—a tree!"

Carmelina's orange rolled unheeded to her feet. "A tree!" she repeated. "A tree! A really, truly tree? I don't believe it! There ain't no trees in Rivington Street! There ain't no trees nowhere," she added sadly, "only Italy!"

At this Mollie, incensed by what she considered aspersions upon her veracity, took an indignant departure. Carmelina picked up her orange, but the fruit had lost its savor; the orange went into the gutter. Carmelina watched it float away upon a fetid stream, but her eyes saw only a vision of something green and shadowy. "A tree!" she murmured, as, from force of habit, she sank upon the curb and dabbled her toes in the languid current. The gutter, once so cool, today seemed merely slimy. Carmelina withdrew to the shady side of an ash

---

*Garibaldi: Giuseppe Garibaldi (1807–1882), Italian soldier famous for military actions that contributed to the unification of Italy.

barrel; but the barrel, like unto the land of Pharaoh, was corrupted by reason of a swarm of flies, and its shady side proved torrid. Through the glare came Carmelina's vision of something green, and shadowy. She mopped her brow upon her multicolored garment, then rose, and with her face toward Rivington street, issued her manifesto.

"I am going," she said, "to the tree!"

In this wise was Carmelina lured into the haunts of the Philistines.

Verily it was cool! It was green! It was shadowy! at first rapturous glance Carmelina could only clasp her hands in ecstasy; then she touched it, she smelled it, and finally sat down beneath it, her cheek pressed close to that delightful prickly bark. "I stay," she announced. At six o'clock a hollowness within called up visions of polenta—and home. Carmelina arose reluctantly, cast a quick glance about the now deserted yard, and, reaching up on tiptoe, broke off a leaf, just a tiny little leaf. The she fled homeward.

But the next morning the Settlement workers found her again knocking at their gates. The genial headworker smiled. A new lamb come into the fold! "I am glad to see you," she said, taking the unwashed hands in hers, "you are just in time for the singing." Carmelina pulled away her hands defiantly.

"I didn't come for no singin'," she muttered. "I can sing home! And I didn't come for no pigs, or stories, or sand piles; I don't care nothin' about them! I don't care nothin' about nothin'—only your *tree!*" and her eyes turned wistfully toward the yard.

It had not vanished overnight! Carmelina drew a sigh of relief, and settled down again with her cheek against the bark. And there she remained all the hot, sunny morning, untempted by even the allurements of the sand pile, which soon became a center of activity. But Carmelina was naturally a gregarious animal. She watched, and in her turn was watched. There came a sudden shower of sand, another, and another. Choking, blinded, she scooped up a yellow handful and hurled it back at Mollie O'Brien. Five minutes later she had a recognized place in the caravan which crossed and recrossed the sandy waste.

But at the story hour she balked again. "I can have stories home!" she reiterated, though Mollie fancied that the tone wavered. Carmelina made again for her tree and watched the caravan file into a big sunlit room; watched them assort themselves upon the circle of little chairs; and then watched their eager faces, upturned toward a central someone. How interested they looked! How happy! She could hear the pleasant rise and fall of a gentle voice. Was it a knight? she wondered, or a hero? Or could it be—the beanstalk? Concerning that beanstalk she had pondered deeply, having gathered from Mollie only so much that it was in some way akin to a tree. If so, the tale might prove not altogether unworthy of attention. Almost unbidden her feet strayed toward the door, across the threshold, nor stopped until they had reached the circumference of that magic circle. And all the while the gentle voice told on.

"And the princess looked out of the window at the wicked magician's beautiful new lamps which glittered and sparkled in the sunlight. 'How beautiful they are,' thought the princess, 'how much nicer than that ugly old lamp which my husband prizes so highly.' Then she went and took the old lamp, their faithful, trusty friend, and just because it wasn't in quite the latest style, and was a little worn and shabby from hard work—"

No beanstalk this in very truth. But how entrancing! Carmelina caught her breath and moved yet closer into the magic circle. Of a certainty there was entertainment here.

"And so the princess held up the old lamp, being careful to screen it from the view of any passersby, for she was terribly ashamed of its age and shabbiness, and—"

Carmelina shuddered; plainly catastrophe threatened. When the catastrophe occurred she shuddered again, but laughed and clapped her hands when came the final ever-enduring bliss.

"Tell us some more," commanded the circle, settling back expectantly upon their little wooden chairs. Carmelina slipped quietly into a vacant seat. "Yes," she breathed, "tell us some more."

And thus was Carmelina's subjugation made complete.

Thenceforth the gutter knew her no more, for the gutter came to be measured by Settlement standards, and was found lacking. To dabble therein was an offence against society, an offence to be expiated only by baptismal rites in the ancient manner—immersion complete, and in these times, frequent. After the first stormy protests, Carmelina submitted, since the way to godliness must ever be a watery one. And one not to be traveled without tribulation of spirit Carmelina discovered to her sorrow. The occasional tubbings at the Settlement being deemed insufficient, she was instructed as to ceremonies for the home, morning and evening observances never to be omitted. Thus Bianca, arising from her pallet in the gray dawn of an early morning, stepped into a gust of spray from the ancient watering pot, with which her daughter was besprinkling herself. "Ecco, she dreams!" cried the mother, shaking her offspring, and incidentally fresh showers from the watering can. "No," sputtered Carmelina, "I bathe," and she directed an icy stream down her shrinking back. Bianca raised her hands in horror. "Art thou mad?" she exclaimed. Then she confiscated the watering can and administered chastisement.

Carmelina crept shivering into her clothes; occasionally she sobbed, and later she choked over her polenta. All that day, and for many days thereafter, there were rancors in the vessel of her peace. She did not phrase her emotion, she did not try—the tragedies of childhood are oftenest inarticulate. Carmelina knew only that something had clouded her concept of her mother; she had been thwarted in pursuit of good—and by Bianca. She could not tell herself, because she could not know, that Bianca had crossed swords with her in a conflict ancient as the everlasting hills, and yet forever new; a conflict which began in Eden, and will end only when man, perfected, shall once more enter Eden; a conflict patricidal, in which the sons oppose the fathers, and daughters are arrayed against their mothers; the conflict between Tradition and Innovation—the battle of Progress and Prejudice—the war of Yesterday with Tomorrow.

The art and science of the bath proved to be the only required subject in the Settlement curriculum, and having mastered this, Carmelina found herself free to choose from among a host of electives, all of them delightful. The circle was omnipresent; reading circles, sewing circles, singing circles, story circles; and the circle was closely rivaled by the club—boys' clubs, girls' clubs, clubs athletic, clubs dramatic, clubs for work, and clubs for play. In addition there were field days, and museums, and classes, and lectures, and a new and wonderful occupation known as "arts and crafts," a fascinating diversion with clay, and paints, and colored papers. And in all these activities Carmelina was a large part. With Latin ardor and intemperance she entered into everything, and in everything was equally enthusiastic. She sang, acted, modeled, and debated; she engaged in feats of engineering on the sand pile, and in feats of daring on the horizontal bars; she visited parks and museums; and she listened to innumerable stories, of which she could never have too many, and to innumerable discourses, of which she could never have too few.

In the beginning she had regarded the discourse as a new and strange variety of fairy tale, compound of fancy and hyperbole, and had discovered with amazement that the speakers expected to be taken seriously. Then for a time she listened, as to the vagaries of a disordered mind. Surely sanity could never propound doctrines so astounding! The open window absurdity, for example! Open windows in mid-winter forsooth! And how were they going to keep out the cold? And how were they going to accomplish this nightly opening, anyway, with the windows nailed immovable from frost till spring (as all properly managed windows should be), and in the case of bedrooms, overhung with the family wardrobe? "Dark"? Of a surety they were dark. How otherwise, with a blank wall three feet away? But all bedrooms were dark, and it was well, since bedrooms were only meant for sleeping. So said Bianca, at any rate; and here Carmelina's logic ended. Not so the discourse, however. It proceeded with terrifying specifications to which Carmelina paid frightened heed. To the child of the tenements there is dread import in the word "consumption." So Carmelina listened. She knew about consumption. Yes. Consumption takes away one's brothers and sisters one by one, till there is no one left to play with but Mollie O'Brien and such like. And it was the dark bedrooms that did it? And the nailed-up windows? And consumption would take her, too, unless the windows were opened? Alas and alack! But it was Bianca who nailed the windows; it was Bianca who said that night air bred fevers! Bianca must be enlightened.

Bianca, however, repudiated enlightenment. Consumption, she asserted, was sent by an all-wise Providence, whereupon she crossed herself and promised a candle to Saint Joseph. And there the matter rested.

Little by little, constant exhortation wore away the stone of Carmelina's skepticism; little by little she accepted the one time heresies of the Settlement; little by little she exalted the ways of the Philistines. And little by little she learned to look with disfavor upon the things which had once spelled happiness. In the light of a new intelligence the cellar was revealed as damp, musty, filthy; Carmelina shuddered to think how it might reek with germs (the germ theory being her most recent acquisition). She shuddered also to consider the bacteria she must have consumed with the unsalable fruit, in the dark ages when she had consumed unsalable fruit; now she rejected it uncompromisingly, for she knew that therein lurked ptomaines. She knew likewise that Tomassino was mongrel, thieving, flea-infested. And Nonna was fat, toothless, dirty, shrill of voice, and her *patois* (for Nonna and Pietro having hailed from Naples, jabbered in dialect after the fashion of their kind) an abomination. It was some small satisfaction to realize that Bianca, at least, preserved uncorrupted her Tuscan purity of speech.

A satisfaction by no means unqualified, however; for Bianca's light burned low. Dimmer and dimmer grew the old lamp, fainter, and fainter its beam, until to Carmelina, dazzled by the glaring searchlight of Progress, it seemed scarcely to shine at all.

Settlement standards had dealt unkindly with Bianca. Bianca, so sparing of water, so cautious of air, so disdainful of germs and microbes! Bianca, who haggled disgracefully over the onions and cabbages; who wove color schemes that shrieked in discord; who, in housekeeping primitive as mother Eve's, defied every law of domestic science. Domestic Science—for the Settlement spelled it large—a fetish at whose shrine Carmelina burned tardy but increasingly abundant incense. And in the sanctuary of Domestic Science the old lamp flickered and went out. Carmelina made valiant effort to keep it aglow, but the old lamp refused its light to heresies. Vainly did Carmelina expound them as true beliefs, Bianca was not to be proselytized. So she clung to her sooty pots and kettles, her greasy skillets, her feather beds, unsheeted and unaired. And Carmelina, making disparaging contrast between these empiricisms and the shining patty-pans, the immaculate toy bedding of the Settlement junior housekeeping, clung to her theories, her science, her modern methods, and slopped around with buckets of water more diligently than Mrs. O'Brien in her most strenuous moments.

And day by day the conflict became more bitter, as day by day Tradition contested Innovation, and Progress combated Prejudice. And day by day Carmelina's heart grew heavier; day by day her discontent increased; day by day she came to despise the things which had once spelled happiness. How she despised them! The reeking stand; the festering cellar; the mangy Tomassino; the garrulous, unkempt Nonna! It seemed to Carmelina that she despised everything in her world that was not of the Settlement—everything except Bianca. One cannot despise that which one loves (and who does not love one's mother?), but one can be—alas, that it should be so!—one can be *ashamed* of her.

How much ashamed Carmelina never fully realized until that fatal day when Bianca appeared at the Settlement. How, whence, or why she came, always remained a mystery. Perhaps it was that latent spirit of adventure, common to all humanity, or a still more common human curiosity that sent her forth upon a voyage of discovery into the land of the Philistines. Or perhaps it was a motive more than human, that brooding instinct universal, which carries the mother hen, flapping and clacking, to the watery peril which has swallowed up her venturesome brood of ducklings.

Whatever that instinct, whatever the motive, Carmelina, skipping gaily down the corridor one August afternoon, suddenly started and stopped short. There, in the open doorway, silhouetted against the brilliant sunshine beyond, stood Bianca. Mystified, awed, she hesitated upon the threshold, every detail of face, form, and costume thrown into high relief; every detail accented by the gentle gloom, the soft wood tones of the Settlement interior. Carmelina, peering through the shadows, saw as she had never seen before. Never had Bianca's reds and purples appeared so redly red, so blatantly purple, as they did against these Settlement refinements of color: these tints of green, these hues of red dulled into delicate harmonies. Never had her dusk skin appeared so brown, so wrinkled, so greasy; her hands so rough and soiled; her feet so large and clumsy, as here in this temple of cleanliness and grooming. Never had her lack of grace and stature, her slouching gait been more apparent, as she lurched forward, walking much from the hips, in the manner of Tuscan women.

For a moment Carmelina felt her heart stand still; then it gave a great jump—right up into her throat, where it throbbed so vehemently that it made her feel frightened. There was no other way to account for her feeling so frightened. Assuredly she was not frightened of Bianca! Bianca would work her no harm! What harm *could* she work her bambina? Why Bianca had not even seen her! (of a sudden she became unaccountably grateful for the gloom and the shadows), need not see her if she but exercise caution! (she slipped back a pace or two farther into the gloom). And how was anyone to guess that Bianca belonged to her—to her with her clean face, her tidy hair, her spotless apron. Security was rendered doubly secure by Bianca's scanty English; she could never reveal herself with a vocabulary confined to the terms of barter. And with this sense of security, Carmelina realized that it was not harm she feared, but recognition, identification. How could she acknowledge a mother such as this before the immaculate, cultured women of the Settlement? How could she take her by the hand and lead her out among them, to flaunt her lack of all that they esteemed; to have her scorned—or pitied?

Her heart, pulsating there in her throat, would surely strangle her! She caught a tortured breath, and covering her face with her hands, sank into a dark corner behind the stairs.

She heard the hall door slam; and then during agonized centuries she heard the familiar slip-slapping of Pietro's castoff number sevens (Bianca never indulged herself in the luxury of new shoes); heard them pass down the hall, scrape upon a door sill, and thereafter shuffle slowly and less distinctly, with ever and anon a pause, filled in by little wordless Tuscan exclamations. Carmelina could picture her mother wandering about the library just beyond, inspecting, admiring, fingering; could picture her awe and astonishment at each new wonder—the library was full of wonders—and she could picture an upward glance, a swift gesture of reverence when she heard a quick, surprised: "Ecco, il Bambino!" Almost unconsciously, Carmelina, too, crossed herself there in her dark corner, for Bianca's exclamation brought to her vivid image of the Divine Mother and Her Inscrutable Son, who, in the room beyond, smiled out of a golden halo.

Bianca must have made long pause before Our Lady "of the Chair," for during many minutes neither speech nor motion broke the quiet of the library. Then all in a moment the silent room was animated with stir and bustle; a door opened, feet clattered, and voices were everywhere. Something thumped down upon the table, a soft, muffled thump, and Carmelina heard a rustling most familiar, and the voice of the headworker rising above the others.

"Well, then, I suppose there's nothing for me to do but send it back where it came from! But it seems to me that *some*one among you ought to know how to use it."

"It certainly isn't in *my* line," said the instructor of Domestic Science.

"Nor mine," added the expert in gymnastics.

"It seems to me," laughed the director of singing, "that it's up to the department of arts and crafts."

"The department of arts and crafts has limits to her capabilities," retorted the department's executive. "Just at present she handles drawing, painting, clay modeling, designing, cord and raffia; but she makes no pretence to omniscience, and in the matter upon the carpet, thinks it's decidedly up to somebody else."

"Who in every probability will have to be the expressman, since we all seem incompetent to manage the situation," finished the headworker. "I'm sorry, too. It's so much more practical than cord weaving, so much prettier than raffia." Again Carmelina heard that familiar rustling; and then she heard an ominous slip-slapping, even more familiar. She crept softly to the door and peeped through the crack into the library.

She saw the headworker and her principal assistants grouped about a table, upon which lay a pile of something smooth and yellow, something that ran into glistening strands through the fingers of the headworker as she held it up before her companions who were shaking puzzled heads. And moving toward them, from her unobserved station under the Madonna, was Bianca, hands outstretched, eyes alight, face aglow. "Like a musician reaching out for a violin," said the directory of singing in speaking of it later. "Or a sculptor, when his eyes behold a block of unchiseled marble," murmured she of the arts and crafts. Straight for the table headed Bianca, while the ladies stared and Carmelina stood aghast at such temerity.

"Why—why—what?—" began the headworker, and stopped to watch.

"I really believe she is going to do something with it!" exclaimed the expert in gymnastics, in an awestruck aside.

"Of course she is! Don't you see that she is setting the splints? My, look at her fingers fly!" The voice was that of the story lady. "How clever she must be! I always did admire people who could do things with their hands!"

"She's a perfect picture with that streak of vermilion against her tawny skin. I wonder if she would pose for me! And, girls, did you ever see such braids? I'd wager they're all her own, too!" and the little leader of arts and crafts ruefully patted a blond coronet, which, to Carmelina's eyes, seemed thicker than Bianca's.

"A picture." Bianca a picture! A picture of what? But the tone had denoted approval. And these other comments were all of them flattering! Bianca was "clever," and admired by the story lady. Carmelina's small brain reeled. Such a complexity of emotions as she had known during the past half-hour would have warranted disturbance of an older and wiser equilibrium than hers.

The comments continued to flow thick and fast, and with each comment Bianca's light flickered brighter, until at last the old lamp burst into a brilliant glow. And Bianca, all unconscious, uncomprehending, absorbed, wove on.

"Why, it's a fan!" cried the story lady, as the finished work was passed from hand to hand, "one of those lovely straw fans like that I brought from Tuscany last summer! Pauline never let me have a minute's peace until I gave it to her, and I've always wanted another one. Oh, I wish she'd show me how!"

"I wish she'd show us *all* how!" It was the headworker who spoke. "A class in basketry, girls! And then we could teach the children, and I wouldn't have to send the straw back. Can't somebody ask her? Can't *any*body talk to her?"

"*I* can."

The tone was proud, possessive. The ladies looked up, Bianca looked up, and Carmelina, with her clean face, her tidy hair, her spotless apron, stood forth in the doorway. She flashed Bianca a brilliant, happy smile, and Bianca flashed hers back.

"Ecco!" she cried, and held up that which she was weaving. It was a basket, a little three-cornered basket.

Then she gathered into her skilful fingers a handful of gleaming strands, and tossed out a long strip. Carmelina sprang forward, caught it dexterously, and thereafter they two wove together, both beginning in the middle. And as they wove, Carmelina's heart grew lighter than the straw and she broke into a little song, Tuscan, like her mother:

> "*La violetta*
> *Che in sull' erbetta*
> *S'apre al mattin novella;*
> *Di' non è cosa*
> *Tutta adorosa,*
> *Tutta leggiadra è bella?*"

And the Perfect Mother and her Perfect Child smiled down from a golden halo in silent benediction.

(1909)

Happiness

Carl Sandburg

I asked professors who teach the meaning of life to tell
 me what is happiness.
And I went to famous executives who boss the work of
 thousands of men.
They all shook their heads and gave me a smile as though
 I was trying to fool with them.
And then one Sunday afternoon I wandered out along
 the Desplaines river
And I saw a crowd of Hungarians under the trees with
 their women and children and a keg of beer and an
 accordion.

(1916)

PART IV

The Cultural Pluralism Debate

As the introduction to the previous part discusses, the popular metaphor of the United States as a melting pot of races and ethnicities took hold in the era as an argument for incorporating immigrant cultures into a unified American identity of the future. This part features works that emphasize cultural pluralism as an alternative to the melting pot vision of national identity (as well as to complete assimilation to Anglo-American culture). One of the most common conceptions of cultural pluralism of our own era is the salad bowl metaphor, which, in debates over multiculturalism, is used in contrast to the potential homogeneity of the melting pot. This analogy characterizes the United States as a pluralist tossed salad, as it were, of discreet identities that retain their distinctive flavors rather than melt together as they are mixed. Still, as the texts in this part illustrate, the 1870–1930 period offers us even more nuanced ways to think about the origins of cultural pluralism in U.S. immigration debates.

Popular literature of the period suggests that pluralism was, paradoxically, both self-evident and virtually indefinable. That the nation was pluralist was evident to those calling for immigrants to assimilate or to "melt" into the melting pot, since both of these actions need at least one other ethnic group to exist at all. Regarding the difficulty of defining cultural pluralism, socio-linguist Nicholas Rescher explains that pluralism represents a contradictory "harmony" of "dissensus" rather than consensus, one in which competing cultures and ideas are challenged "to function effectively even in the presence of dissensus."[1] As the works in this part demonstrate, the challenge of cultural pluralism in the Progressive Era was imagining how to sustain a harmony of dissensus by preserving ethnic cultures—but without sacrificing the goal of "becoming American."

To illustrate how advocates of cultural pluralism and those favoring the melting pot envisioned competing definitions of American identity, we can contrast two issues of *The Czechoslovak Review*. This was a Chicago-based, English-language journal for a mixed audience of natives and immigrant Czechs. In the June 1919 issue, Joseph Štýbr explained that the goal of the Czech community in the United States was to hasten the "amalgamation of the foreigner." (This essay leads our part on the melting pot.) Štýbr, an immigrant himself, asserted that immigration necessarily entails a process whereby new arrivals gradually lose their native identities as they merge into the melting pot; and over generations, Štýbr explained, immigrants expunge their previously hyphenated identity for a new, homogeneous American identity.[2] However, in 1922, just three years later, *The Czechoslovak Review* offered a more optimistic account of preserving ethnic distinctiveness in E. F. Prantner's "Young America's Attitude to Immigrant Ancestry." In this lecture, originally given to the Czechoslovak Students Club of Pittsburgh, he argued that the melting pot was not a national end-goal but, rather, just a transitional state toward an inevitable, and preferable, cultural pluralism. Prantner even brought restrictionism into the mix, arguing that Czech immigrants were "confronted with the ever-increasing tendency demanding further restrictions on the in-flow of immigrants; and . . . we observe the

279

rapidly waning influence of the Bohemians and Slovaks, as groups, in our public affairs." In light of increasing pressures to limit the flow of immigration into the United States, and diminished agency on the part of those already within the United States, Prantner suggested that the "responsibility" of the new generation of Czech immigrants and descendants was "to preserve in this land of wonderful opportunities the memory of your Czechoslovak forefathers who pioneered in commerce and industry, each according to his ability, and who helped to build up and defend this great Democratic Commonwealth." Crucially, Prantner argued for an assertion of Czech identity that was a hybrid of an Old World past and contemporary immigrant present. Czechs were to see their history as, paradoxically, both uniquely Czech and uniquely American: "I want you to regard your [Czech] ancestors with that same high degree of pride with which the descendants of the Mayflower pilgrims worship their ancestors. The Mayflower immigrants were no better than your immigrant forefathers."[3]

Such an approach would unite young Czech descendants of recent immigrants with, in Prantner's words, the "Sons and Daughters of the American Revolution." In contrast to Theodore Roosevelt's urging that Old World ethnic identities be abolished in favor of Anglo-Saxonism (see Part II), Prantner suggested that amid the parallel forces of restriction legislation and waning immigrant influence, the solution is cultural pluralism. In this model, new identities are superimposed on native culture; this mode of pluralism is, for Prantner, a privilege afforded to naturalized immigrants. He argued, "You have every right to do that, for your people have always acquitted themselves nobly both in peace and in war." In an environment in which immigrants were urged to conform to the cultural norms of their new land—or "melt" into it, as Štýber had advocated—Prantner implored the sons and daughters of immigrants to "learn to sing the dear old folk songs" of Czechoslovakia because "they are veritable treasures in themselves."[4] Interestingly, Prantner's essay appeared alongside a decidedly nationalist Czech poem, "Kosmic Songs," translated into English by Štýber.

Much as *The Czechoslovak Review* gave voice to opposing views regarding preserving ethnic distinctiveness, this part offers works that both endorse and refute pluralism as a viable conceptual framework for national identity formation. Indeed, Prantner's essay and Štýber's translation of Czech nationalist poetry should not suggest that, somehow after World War I, assimilation failed and pluralism rose in public approval. Instead, in these debates over immigration, the lines of debate overlapped rather than fell into easily charted waves of ascendency and decline. Still, even with the emphasis on cultural difference in these works, pluralism often figures as a threat to be "cured" by restriction legislation or by immigrant absorption into the national culture.

This part opens with two essays that are among the most famous efforts in the period to define the very term *pluralism*: Horace Kallen's "Democracy Versus the Melting-Pot" and Randolph Bourne's "Trans-National America." Inverting the widespread idea that pluralism is a transitional state toward assimilation, Kallen characterizes assimilation as the process by which immigrants gain a foothold in the culture until "a process of dissimilation begins," one that leads to their passage into an eventual pluralist identity. The dominant image of the melting pot becomes, for Kallen, the image of the orchestra, where the "harmony and dissonances and discords" played by all ethnic identities become the "symphony of civilization." Unlike traditional symphonies, which are written before they are played, this symphony of civilization is, as Kallen describes, a composition played as it is written. This improvisatory quality is both the threat and sustenance of Kallen's cultural pluralism. Bourne, too, argues that assimilation is only a stage toward an eventual cultural pluralism. His reconception of U.S. culture as a loose federation of cultures empties Anglo-Saxonism of its claims to dominance at the same time that it opens the door for new arrivals to assert the legitimacy of the cultural practices they brought to this country. Bourne writes, "The non-English American can scarcely be blamed if he sometimes thinks of the Anglo-Saxon predominance in America as little more than a predominance of priority. The Anglo-Saxon was merely the first immigrant, the first to found a colony." Bourne's solution, a transnational tapestry of many different cultures asserting themselves at once, resembles Kallen's vision of cultural pluralism in the authority it bestows upon immigrant otherness. As does Kallen, Bourne sees the task of the future as a harmonization of cultural difference. For Bourne, however, dissonance and discord is a less viable option, and in this way his transnationalism asserts the primacy of cultural unity in his conception of national identity.

The selections that follow Kallen and Bourne illustrate that three different modes of pluralism emerged during this period, which we term *orientalist, romanticist,* and *palimpsestic* pluralism. The first of these modes, which borrows from Edward Said's usage of the term *orientalist* in postcolonial studies, construes newly arrived immigrants as exotic others. The sheer numbers and seemingly self-sufficient communities of these immigrants are seen as threats to the primacy of Anglo-Saxon nativism as the standard for American identity. To retain this primacy, orientalist pluralism exaggerates the differences between native born U.S. citizens and immigrants, painting immigrant cultural practices as unusual and even less-than-civilized manifestations of difference. Works by Dorothy Dudley, Max Michelson, and Robert Haven Schauffler demonstrate how pluralism could exoticize immigrants rather than portray them as distinct people in their own right. For instance, Schauffler's narrator deploys an exotic conception of immigrants in order to strengthen the authority of Anglo-Saxon cultural identity. His idealization of New York's immigrant neighborhoods prompts his father to threaten to withhold the narrator's inheritance. Eventually, the narrator's "slumming" with colorful immigrants acts as a vaccine, enticing the narrator into precisely the restraint needed for him to develop into a twentieth-century Anglo-Saxon man—and to ensure the continued dominance of what he describes as New York's "Great White Way" into the next generation.

At this time, a romanticist school of pluralism also emerged, in which writers valorized new immigrant otherness as a means of fortifying an idealized version of the dominant culture. Maria Moravsky, for instance, introduced the idea that cultural pluralism can be defined by powerful assertions of difference that should be incorporated into the nation to strengthen its dominant culture. National identity for Moravsky was always a hyphenated one; her hyphenation tolerated and even celebrated a messy superimposition of both native and immigrant cultural practices. Romantic pluralists such as Moravsky conceived of a national identity that called for the preservation of immigrant cultures without the depredation of Anglo-Saxon cultural authority. Like adherents of the melting pot vision and assimilationists, those advocating romantic pluralism favored an absorption of the immigrant into a unified national identity; but, unlike the others, romantic pluralists did not favor the erasure of the ethnic cultures that came with immigration. The struggle to carve a space for oneself in such highly negotiated modes of identity formation is dramatized in the poems that follow by anonymous Cantonese writers from San Francisco's Chinatown. Read together, these three poems demonstrate how the romanticist pluralism of Moravsky did not always work in practice—as in Chinese immigrant communities, where U.S. cultural practices of divorce and unrestrained marital choice were so "extreme" that the poet's "worn writing brush cannot reveal them all." Even though orientalist and romanticist strains of pluralism differed in the cultural authority they ascribed to immigrants, both sought to contain new immigrants by objectifying them as a force that threatened (orientalist pluralism) or might revivify (romantic pluralism) the dominant social order.

The tension between everyday practices of pluralism and the demand for cultural unity is evident in the stories by Bruno Lessing and Margherita Arlina Hamm. Each cautions that the most difficult experience for immigrants is the creation of a pluralist identity that is not a transitional stage toward assimilation but instead an identity in its own right that can strengthen the nation's dominant cultural practices. In the conflict between nativist Christianity and immigrant Hebraic prophecy in "Unconverted," Lessing emphasizes how religion can be the locus for the assertion of romantic pluralism. The central conflict of the story, Reverend Gillespie's efforts to convert Jewish immigrants to Christianity, also illustrates the divisions between romantic pluralism and the subjugation model of assimilation we discussed in Part II. The conversion in Lessing's story is not a religious one; instead, it is a transformation from fervent assimilationism, represented by Reverend Gillespie, to a romantic pluralism whose confluence of native-born Christianity and immigrant Judaism can strengthen the nation's spiritual identity even in the midst of the economic panic that serves as the story's historical context. In Hamm's story of the collision of religious and ethnic identities, pluralism could seem poised between the orientalist and romanticist visions. To be sure, Hamm's tale of Kalaun, a circus elephant trainer in Egypt before immigrating to the United States, does not eschew the exotic in its portrayals of immigrant family life. At the same time, Hamm renders a cautionary tale of pluralism in which newly arrived immigrants are potentially worthy contributors to the nation's development, provided that their cultural practices are adopted with restraint.

In contrast to those advocating containment, a third mode of pluralism asserted that new immigrant cultural practices could coexist with those of nativists. This coexistence between dissimilar cultures was conceived in the same way that, for example, two different texts can exist together in simultaneity on the same page or parchment as a palimpsest. A palimpsest is a manuscript page or parchment in which the original writing has been rubbed off or erased to make room for a new piece of writing; however, the original text is not fully effaced, and what remains is a superimposition of both the original and the new text on one another. The palimpsest produces a semantic uncertainty because multiple written texts, and sometimes multiple languages, are overlaid on one another. Because of this semantic and linguistic clashing, the palimpsest has been a popular metaphor for the reading and writing processes over the years, especially recently, with the rise of postmodernist studies.[5]

This mode of cultural pluralism conceived U.S. identity in terms of the clash and uncertainty of the palimpsest—immigrants and natives superimposed on one another—rather than in terms of the cultural unities presumed by restrictionism, assimilationism, or the melting pot. The "Babel of voices" that is central, for instance, to Lucille Baldwin Van Slyke's "The Tooth of Antar" understandably overwhelms Nazileh, a young Syrian immigrant in Brooklyn. At the same time, Nazileh's Babel is a superimposition of immigrant and native-born cultures in which many ethnicities coexist without the need to resolve their cultural cacophony. Nazileh ensures the retention of Old World culture in a pluralist landscape in which German, Syrian, and native-born cultural practices are asserted simultaneously. Nazileh's experiences demonstrate a mode of pluralism in which the dominance of any one ethnicity within this cultural clash is situational rather than at all times the privilege of the native-born. Indeed, her revival of Syrian custom for a new generation of immigrants occurs in a Babel that at any moment can be both loud and "faint and far away." The final story in this part, Myra Kelly's "H.R.H., the Prince of Hester Street," imagines an ambitious pluralist future in which multiple, clashing modes of ethnic identity are overlaid on each other as in a palimpsest. This vision of cultural pluralism revisits the pressures in Kallen's and Bourne's pieces that open this part, without quite solving the problems they take up. In Kelly's story, language and writing become the place where pluralism is favored over orientalist dominance and romanticist cultural enrichment. In closing with Kelly's story, this part emphasizes how the challenge of pluralism is also the challenge of accepting cultural ambiguities without fully resolving them—in a world, such as Kelly's classroom, where immigrants occupy the same physical space but entirely different figural spaces and differing levels of cultural authority.

Notes

1. Nicholas Rescher, *Pluralism: Against the Demand for Consensus* (Oxford: Clarendon, 1993), 105.
2. Joseph Štýbr, "Americanization," *The Czechoslovak Review* (June 1919): 153–154.
3. E. F. Prantner, "Young America's Attitude to Immigrant Ancestry," *The Czechoslovak Review* (April 1922): 92.
4. Ibid., 93.
5. Probably one of the more famous examples of the palimpsest in Western literature is Cicero's *De Republica,* most of which was discovered as a palimpsest in the Vatican Library in 1822. It had been erased partially so that a commentary by Augustine on the psalms could be written over it. The palimpsest also is deployed as an analogy in fields other than literature. In architecture, for instance, a palimpsest refers to an image or shadow of what once had stood in a physical environment, such as the paint boundaries that indicate where stairs once had been located, or dust lines that show where objects such as appliances or furniture once stood.

Democracy Versus the Melting-Pot:
A Study of American Nationality

Horace M. Kallen

Part One

It was, I think, an eminent lawyer who, backed by a ripe experience of inequalities before the law, pronounced our Declaration of Independence to be a collection of "glittering generalities." Yet it cannot be that the implied slur was deserved. There is hardly room to doubt that the equally eminent gentlemen over whose signatures this orotund synthesis of the social and political philosophy of the eighteenth century appears conceived that they were subscribing to anything but the dull and sober truth when they underwrote the doctrine that God had created all men equal and had endowed them with certain inalienable rights, among these being life, liberty, and the pursuit of happiness. That this doctrine did not describe a condition, that it even contradicted conditions, that many of the signatories owned other men and bought and sold them, that many were eminent by birth, many by wealth, and only a few by merit—all this is acknowledged. Indeed, they were aware of these inequalities; they would probably have fought their abolition. But they did not regard them as incompatible with the Declaration of Independence. For to them the Declaration was neither a pronouncement of abstract principles nor an exercise in formal logic. It was an instrument in a political and economic conflict, a weapon of offense and defense. The doctrine of "natural rights" which is its essence was formulated to shield social orders against the aggrandizement of persons acting under the doctrine of "divine right": its function was to afford sanction for refusing customary obedience to traditional superiority. Such also was the function of the Declaration. Across the water, in England, certain powers had laid claim to the acknowledgment of their traditional superiority to the colonists in America. Whereupon the colonists, through their representatives, the signatories to the Declaration, replied that they were quite as good as their traditional betters, and that no one should take from them certain possessions which were theirs.

Today the descendants of the colonists are reformulating a declaration of independence. Again, as in 1776, Americans of British ancestry find that certain possessions of theirs, which may be lumped under the word "Americanism," are in jeopardy. This is the situation which Mr. Ross's book, in common with many others, describes.* The danger comes, once more, from a

---

*E. A. Ross, sociologist and Kallen's colleague at the University of Wisconsin, whose book *The Old World in the New: The Significance of Past and Present Immigration to the American People* argued that the "new immigrants" of the late nineteenth and early twentieth century were inferior races when compared to the

force across the water, but the force is this time regarded not as superior, but as inferior. The relationships of 1776 are, consequently, reversed. To conserve the inalienable rights of the colonists of 1776, it was necessary to declare all men equal; to conserve the inalienable rights of their descendants in 1914, it becomes necessary to declare all men unequal. In 1776 all men were as good as their betters; in 1914 men are permanently worse than their betters. "A nation may reason," writes Mr. Ross, "why burden ourselves with the rearing of children? Let them perish unborn in the womb of time. The immigrants will keep up the population. A people that has no more respect for its ancestors and no more pride of race than this deserves the extinction that surely awaits it."

I

Respect for ancestors, pride of race! Time was when these would have been repudiated as the enemies of democracy, as the antithesis of the fundamentals of our republic, with its belief that "a man's a man for a' that." And now they are being invoked in defense of democracy, against the "melting pot," by a sociological protagonist of the "democratic idea"! How conscious their invocation is cannot be said. But that they have unconsciously colored much of the social and political thinking of this country from the days of the Cincinnati on, seems to me unquestionable, and even more unquestionable that this apparently sudden and explicit conscious expression of them is the effect of an actual, felt menace. Mr. Ross, in a word, is no voice crying in a wilderness. He simply utters aloud and in his own peculiar manner what is felt and spoken wherever Americans of British ancestry congregate thoughtfully. He is the most recent phase of the operation of these forces in the social and economic history of the United States; a voice and instrument of theirs. Being so, he has neither taken account of them nor observed them, but has reacted in terms of them to the social situation which constitutes the theme of his book. The reaction is secondary, the situation is secondary. The standards alone are really primary and, perhaps, ultimate. Fully to understand the place and function of "the old world in the new," and the attitude of the "new world" towards the old, demands an appreciation of the influence of these primary and ultimate standards upon all the peoples who are citizens of the country.

II

In 1776 the mass of white men in the colonies were actually, with respect to one another, rather free and rather equal. I refer, not so much to the absence

---

"old immigrants" of the mid-nineteenth century, and that this "new immigration" was a threat to Anglo-Saxon cultural authority.

of great differences in wealth, as to the fact that the whites were *like-minded*. They were possessed of ethnic and cultural unity; they were homogenous with respect to ancestry and ideals. Their century-and-a-half-old tradition as Americans was continuous with their immemorially older tradition as Britons. They did not, until the economic-political quarrel with the mother country arose, regard themselves as other than Englishmen, sharing England's dangers and England's glories. When the quarrel came they remembered how they had left the mother country in search of religious liberty for themselves; how they had left Holland, where they had found this liberty, for fear of losing their ethnic and cultural identity, and what hardships they had borne for the sake of conserving both the liberty and the identity. Upon these they grafted that political liberty the love of which was innate, perhaps, but the expression of which was occasioned by the economic warfare with the merchants of England. This grafting was not, of course, conscious. The continuity established itself rather as a mood than as an articulate idea. The economic situation was only an occasion, and not a cause. The cause lay in the homogeneity of the people, their like-mindedness, and in their self-consciousness.

Now, it happens that the preservation and development of any given type of civilization rests upon these two conditions—like-mindedness and self-consciousness. Without their art, literature—culture in any of its nobler forms—is impossible: and colonial America had a culture—chiefly New England—but representative enough of the whole British-American life of the period. Within the area of what we now call the United States this life was not, however, the only life. Similarly animated groups of Frenchmen and Germans, in Louisiana and Pennsylvania, regarded themselves as the cultural peers of the British, and because of their own common ancestry, their like-mindedness and self-consciousness, they have retained a large measure of their individuality and spiritual autonomy to this day, after generations of unrestricted and mobile contact and a century of political union with the dominant British populations.

In the course of time the state, which began to be with the Declaration of Independence, became possessed of all the United States. French and Germans in Louisiana and Pennsylvania remained at home; but the descendants of the British colonists trekked across the continent, leaving tiny self-conscious nuclei of population in their wake, and so established ethnic and cultural standards for the whole country. Had the increase of these settlements borne the same proportion to the unit of population that it bore between 1810 and 1820, the Americans of British stock would have numbered today over 100,000,000. The inhabitants of the country do number over 100,000,000; but they are not the children of the colonists and the pioneers; they are immigrants and the children of immigrants, and they are not British, but of all the other European stocks.

First came the Irish, integral to the polity of Great Britain, but ethnically different, Catholic in religion, fleeing from economic and political oppression, and—self-conscious and rebellious. They came seeking food and freedom, and revenge against the oppressors on the other side. Their area of settlement is chiefly the East. There they were not met with open arms. Historically only semi-alien, their appearance aroused, nonetheless, both fear and active opposition. Their diversity in religion was outstanding, their gregarious politics disturbing. Opposition, organized, religious, political, and social, stimulated their natural gregariousness into action. They organized, in their turn, religiously and politically. Slowly they made their way, slowly they came to power, establishing themselves in many modes as potent forces in the life of America. Mr. Ross thinks that they have their virtue still to prove; how he does not say. To the common sense of the country they constitute an approved ethnic unity of the white American population.

Behind the Irish came the great mass of the Germans, quite diverse in speech and customs, culturally and economically far better off than the Irish, and self-conscious, as well through oppression and political aspiration as for these other reasons. They settled inland, over a stretch of relatively continuous territory extending from western New York to the Mississippi, from Buffalo to Minneapolis, and from Minneapolis to St. Louis. Spiritually, these Germans were more akin to the American settlers than the Irish, and, indeed, although social misprision pursued them also, they were less coldly received and with less difficulty tolerated. As they made their way, greater and greater numbers of the peasant stock joined them in the Western nuclei of population, so that between the Great Lakes and the Mississippi Valley they constitute the dominant ethnic type. Beyond them, in Minnesota, their near neighbors, the Scandinavians, prevail, and beyond these, in the mountain and mining regions, the central and eastern and southern Europeans—Slavs of various stocks, Magyars, Finns, Italians. Beyond the Rockies, cut off from the rest of the country by this natural barrier, a stratum of Americans of British ancestry balances the thinnish stratum on the Atlantic sea coast; flanked on the south by Latins and scattering groups of Asiatics, and on the north by Scandinavians. The distribution of the population upon the two coasts is not dissimilar; that upon the Atlantic littoral is only less homogenous. There French-Canadians, Irish, Italians, Slavs, and Jews alternate with the American population and each other, while in the West the Americans lie between and surround the Italians, Asiatics, Germans, and Scandinavians.

Now, of all these immigrant peoples the greater part are peasants, vastly illiterate, living their lives at fighting weight, with a minimum of food and a maximum of toil. Mr. Ross thinks that their coming to America was determined by no spiritual urge; only the urge of steamship agencies and economic need or greed. However generally true this opinion may be, he ignores, curiously enough, three significant and one notable exception to it. The significant exception are the Poles, the Finns, the Bohemians—the subjugated Slavic nationalities generally. Political and religious and cultural persecution plays no small role in the movement of the masses of them. The notable exception is the Jews. The Jews come far more with the attitude of the earliest settlers than any of the other peoples; for they more than any other present-day immigrant group are in flight from persecution and disaster; in search of economic opportunity, liberty of conscience, civic rights. They have settled chiefly in the Northeast, with New York City as the center of greatest concentration. Among them, as among the Puritans, the Pennsylvania Germans, the French of Louisiana, self-consciousness and like-mindedness are intense and articulate. But they differ from the subjugated Slavic peoples in that the latter look backward and forward to *actual*, even if enslaved homelands; the Jews, in the mass, have thus far looked to America as their home land.

In sum, when we consider that portion of our population which has taken root, we see that it has not stippled the country in small units of diverse ethnic groups. It forms rather a series of stripes or layers of varying sizes, moving east to west along the central axis of settlement, where towns are thickest; *i.e.*, from New York and Philadelphia, through Chicago and St. Louis, to San Francisco and Seattle. Stippling is absent even in the towns, where the variety of population is generally greater. Probably 90 percent of that population is either foreign-born or of foreign stock; yet even so, the towns are aggregations, not units. Broadly divided into the sections inhabited by the poor, this economic division does not abolish, it only crosses, the ethnic one. There are rich and poor little Italys, Irelands, Hungarys, Germanys, and rich and poor little Ghettoes. The *common* city life, which depends upon like-mindedness, is not inward, corporate, and inevitable, but external, inarticulate, and incidental, a reaction to the need of amusement and the need of protection, not the expression of a unity of heritage, mentality and interest. Politics and education in our cities thus present the phenomenon of ethic compromises not unknown in Austria-Hungary; concessions and appeals to "the Irish vote," "the Jewish vote," "the German vote"; compromise school committees where members represent each ethnic faction, until, as in Boston, one group grows strong enough to dominate the entire situation.

South of Mason and Dixon's line the cities exhibit a greater homogeneity. Outside of certain regions in Texas the descendants of the native white stock, often degenerate and backward, prevail among the whites, but the whites as a whole constitute a relatively weaker proportion of the population. They live among nine million negroes, whose own mode of living tends, by its mere massiveness, to standardize the "mind" of the proletarian South in speech, manner, and the other values of social organization.

III

All the immigrants and their offspring are in the way of becoming "Americanized," if they remain in one place in the country long enough—say, six or seven years. The general notion, "Americanization," appears to denote the adoption of English speech, of American clothes and manners, of the

American attitude in politics. It connotes the fusion of the various bloods, and a transmutation by "the miracle of assimilation" of Jews, Slavs, Poles, Frenchmen, Germans, Hindus, Scandinavians into beings similar in background, tradition, outlook, and spirit to the descendants of the British colonists, the Anglo-Saxon stock. Broadly speaking, the elements of Americanism are somewhat external, the effect of environment; largely internal, the effect of heredity. Our economic individualism, our traditional laissez-faire policy, is largely the effect of environment: where nature offers more than enough wealth to go round, there is no immediate need for regulating distribution. What poverty and unemployment exist among us is the result of unskilled and wasteful social housekeeping, not of any actual natural barrenness. And until the disparity between our economic resources and our population becomes equalized, so that the country shall attain an approximate economic equilibrium, this will always be the case. With our individualism go our optimism and our other "pioneer" virtues: they are purely reactions to our unexploited natural wealth, and, as such, moods which characterize all societies in which the relation between population and resource is similar. The predominance of the "new freedom" over the "new nationalism" is a *potent* political expression of this relationship, and the overwhelming concern of both novelties with the economic situation rather than with the cultural or spiritual is a still stronger one. That these last alone justify or condemn this or that economic condition or program is a commonplace: "by their fruits shall ye know the soils and the roots."

The fruits in this case are those of New England. Eliminate from our roster Whittier, Longfellow, Lowell, Hawthorne, Emerson, Howells, and what have we left? Outstanding are Poe and Whitman, and the necromantic mysticism of the former is only a sick-minded version of the naturalistic mysticism of the latter, while the general mood of both is that of Emerson, who in his way expresses the culmination of that movement in mysticism from the agonized conscience of colonial and Puritan New England—to which Hawthorne gives voice—to serene and optimistic assurance. In religion this spirit of Puritan New England non-conformity culminates similarly: in Christian Science when it is superstitious and magical; in Unitarianism when it is rationalistic; in both cases, over against the personal individualism, there is the cosmic unity. For New England, religious, political, and literary interests remained coordinate and indivisible; and New England gave the tone to and established the standards for the rest of the American state. Save for the very early political writers, the "solid South" remains unexpressed, while the march of the pioneer across the continent is permanently marked by Mark Twain for the Middle West, and by Bret Harte for the Pacific slope. Both these men carry something of the tone and spirit of New England, and with them the "great tradition" of America, the America of the "Anglo-Saxon," comes to an end. There remains nothing large or significant that is unexpressed, and no unmentioned writer who is so completely representative.

The background, tradition, spirit, and outlook of the whole of the America of the "Anglo-Saxon," then, find their spiritual expression in the New England school, Poe, Whitman, Mark Twain, Bret Harte. They realize an individual who has passed from the agonized to the optimistic conscience, a person of the solid and homely virtues tempered by mystic certainty of his destiny, his election, hence always ready to take risks, and always willing to face dangers. From the agony of Arthur Dimmesdale to the smug industrial and social rise of Silas Lapham, from the irresponsible kindliness of Huck Finn to the "Luck of Roaring Camp," the movement is the same, though on different social levels. In regions supernal its coordinate is the movement from the God of Jonathan Edwards to the Oversoul of Emerson and the Divinity of Mrs. Eddy. It is summed up in the contemporary representative "average" American of British stock—an individualist, English-speaking, interested in getting on, kind, neighborly, not too scrupulous in business, indulgent to his women, optimistically devoted to laissez-faire in economics and politics, very respectable in private life, tending to liberalism and mysticism in religion, and moved, where his economic interests are unaffected, by formulas rather than ideas. He typifies the aristocracy of America. From among his fellows are recruited her foremost protagonists in politics, religion, art and learning. He constitutes, by virtue of being heir of the oldest *rooted* economic settlement and spiritual tradition of the white man in America, the measure and the standard of Americanism that the newcomer is to attain.

Other things being equal, a democratic society which should be a realization of the assumptions of the Declaration of Independence, supposing them to be true, would be a leveling society such that all persons become alike, either on the lowest or the highest plane. The outcome of free social contacts should, according to the laws of imitation, establish "equality" on the highest plane; for imitation is of the higher by the lower, so that the cut of a Paris gown at $1000 becomes imitated in department stores at $17.50, and the play of the rich becomes the vice of the poor. This process of leveling up through imitation is facilitated by the so-called "standardization" of externals. In these days of ready-made clothes, factory-made goods, refrigerating plants, it is almost impossible that the mass of the inhabitants of this country should wear other than uniform clothes, use other than uniform furniture or utensils, or eat anything but the same kind of food. In these days of rapid transit and industrial mobility it must seem impossible that any stratification of population should be permanent. Hardly anybody seems to have been born where he lives, or to live where he has been born. The teetering of demand and supply in industry and commerce keeps large masses of population constantly mobile; so that many people no longer can be said to have homes. This mobility reinforces the use of English—for a *lingua franca*, intelligible everywhere, becomes indispensable—by immigrants. And ideals that are felt to belong with the language tend to become "standardized," widespread, uniform, through the devices of the telegraph and the telephone, the syndication of "literature," the cheap newspaper and the cheap novel, the vaudeville circuit, the "movie," and the star system. Even more significantly, mobility leads to the propinquity of the different stocks, thus promoting intermarriage and pointing to the coming of a new "American race"—a blend of at least all the European stocks (for there seems to be some difference of opinion as to whether negroes should constitute an element in this blend) into a newer and better being whose qualities and ideals shall be the qualities and ideals of the contemporary American of British ancestry. Apart from the unintentional impulsion towards this end, of the conditions I have just enumerated, there exists the instrument especially devised for this purpose which we call the public school—and to some extent there is the State university. That the end has been and is being attained, we have the biographical testimony of Jacob Riis, of [Edward] Steiner, and of Mary Antin—a Dane and two Jews, intermarried, assimilated even in religion, and more excessively self-consciously American than the Americans. And another Jew, Mr. Israel Zangwill, of London, profitably promulgates it as a principle and an aspiration, to the admiring approval of American audiences, under the device, "the melting pot."

IV

All is not, however, fact, because it is hope; nor is the biography of an individual, particularly of a literary individual, the history of a group. The Riises and the Steiners and Antins protest too much, they are too self-conscious and self-centered, their "Americanization" appears too much like an achievement, a *tour de force*, too little like a growth. As for Zangwill, at best he is the obverse of Dickens, at worst he is a Jew making a special plea. It is the work of the Americanized writers that is really significant, and in that one senses, underneath the excellent writing, a dualism and the strain to overcome it. The same dualism is apparent in different form among the Americans, and the strain to overcome it seems even stronger. These appear to have been most explicit at the high-water marks of periods of immigration: the Know-Nothing party was one early expression of it; the organization, in the '80s, of the patriotic societies—The Sons and the Daughters of the American Revolution, later on of the Colonial Dames, and so on—another. Since the Spanish War it has shown itself in the continual, if uneven, growth of the political conscience, first as a muckraking magazine propaganda, than as a nationwide attack on the corruption of politics by plutocracy, finally as the altogether respectable and evangelical progressive party, with its slogan of "Human rights against property rights."

In this process, however, the non-British American or Continental immigrant has not been a fundamental protagonist. He has been an occasion rather than a force. What has been causal has been "American." Consider the personnel and history of the Progressive party by way of demonstration: it is composed largely of the professional groups and of the "solid" and "upper" middle class; as a spirit it has survived in Kansas, which by an historic accident happens to be the one Middle Western State predominately Yankee; as a victorious party it has survived in California, one of the few States outstandingly "American" in population. What is significant in it, as in every other form of the political conscience, is the fact that it is a response to a feeling of "something out of gear," and naturally the attention seeks the cause, first of all, outside of the self, not within. Hence the interest in economic-political reconstruction. But the maladjustment in that region is really external. And the political conscience is seeking by a mere change in outward condition to abolish an inward disparity. "Human rights versus property rights" is merely the modern version of the Declaration of Independence, still assuming that men are men merely, as like as marbles and destined under uniformity of conditions to uniformity of spirit. The course of our economic history since the Civil War shows aptly enough how shrewd were, other things being equal, Marx's generalizations concerning the tendencies of capital towards concentration in the hands of a few. Attention consequently has fixed itself more and more upon the equalization of the distribution of wealth—not socialistically, of course. And this would really abolish the dualism if the economic dualism of rich and poor were the fundamental one. It happens merely that it isn't.

The Anglo-Saxon American, constituting as he does the economic upper class, would hardly have reacted to economic disparity as he has if that had been the only disparity. In point of fact it is the ethnic disparity that troubles him. His activity as entrepreneur has crowded our cities with progressively cheaper laborers of Continental stock, all consecrated to the industrial machine, and towns like Gary, Lawrence, Chicago, Pittsburgh, have become industrial camps of foreign mercenaries. His undertakings have brought into being the terrible autocracies of Pullman and of Lead, North Dakota. They have created a mass of casual laborers numbering 5,000,000, and work-children to the number of 1,500,000 (the latter chiefly in the South, where the purely "American" white predominates). They have done all this because the greed of the entrepreneur has displaced high-demanding labor by cheaper labor, and has brought into being the unnecessary problem of unemployment. In all things greed has set the standard, so that the working ideal of the people is to get rich, to live, and to think as the rich, to subordinate government to the service of wealth, making the actual government "invisible." *Per contra* it has generated "labor unrest," the I.W.W.,* the civil war in Colorado.†

---

*I.W.W.: International Workers of the World, also known as the Wobblies, an international labor union founded in Chicago in 1905.

†*"the civil war in Colorado"*: Most likely refers to early twentieth-century labor battles in Colorado's mining communities. Many of Kallen's readers would have remembered the recent Colorado Coal Strike of 1913–1914, and specifically the 1914 Ludlow Massacre in Ludlow, Colorado. On April 20, 1914, the Colorado National Guard fired on 1,200 striking miners and their families living in a Ludlow tent city. Six miners and union officials were killed in the fighting that ensued, along with two women, twelve children, and one National Guardsman.

Because the great mass of the laborers happen to be of Continental and not British ancestry, and because they are latecomers, Mr. Ross blames them for this perversion of our public life and social ideals. Ignoring the degenerate farming stock of New England, the "poor whites" of the South, the negroes, he fears the anthropological as well as the economic effects of the "fusion" of these Continental Europeans, Slavs, and Italians and Jews, with the native stock, and grows anxious over the fate of American institutions at their hands. Nothing could better illustrate the fact that the dualism is primarily ethnic and not economic. Under the laissez-faire policy, the economic process would have been the same, of whatever race the rich, and whatever race the poor. Only race prejudice, primitive, spontaneous, and unconscious, could have caused a trained economist to ignore the so obvious fact that in a capitalist industrial society labor is useless and helpless without capital; that hence the external dangers of immigration are in the greed of the capitalist and the indifference of the Government. The restriction of immigration can naturally succeed only with the restriction of the entrepreneur's greed, which is its cause. But the abolition of immigration and the restoration of the supremacy of "human rights" over "property rights" will not abolish the fundamental ethnic dualism; it may aggravate it.

The reason is obvious. That like-mindedness in virtue of which men are as nearly as is possible in fact "free and equal" is not primarily the result of a constant set of external conditions. Its pre-potent cause is an intrinsic similarity which, for America, has its roots in that ethnic and cultural unity of which our fundamental institutions are the most durable expression. Similar environments, similar occupations, do, of course, generate similarities: "American" is an adjective of similarity applied to Anglo-Saxons, Irish, Jews, Germans, Italians, and so on. But the similarity is one of place and institution, acquired, not inherited, and hence not transmitted. Each generation has, in fact, to become "Americanized" afresh, and, withal, inherited nature has a way of redirecting nurture, of which our public schools give only too much evidence. If the inhabitants of the United States are stratified economically as "rich" and "poor," they are stratified ethnically as Germans, Scandinavians, Jews, Irish, and although the two stratifications cross more frequently than they are coincident, they interfere with each other far less than is hopefully supposed. The history of the "International" in recent years, the present debacle in Europe, are indications of how little "class-consciousness" modifies national consciousness. To the dominant nationality in American nationality, in the European sense, has had no meaning; for it had set the country's standards and had been assimilating others to itself. Now that the process seems to be slowing down, it finds itself confronted with the problem of nationality, just as do the Irish, the Poles, the Bohemians, the Czechs, and the other oppressed nationalities in Europe. "We are submerged," writes a great American man of letters, who has better than any one I know interpreted the American spirit to the world, "we are submerged beneath a conquest so complete that the very name of us means something not ourselves . . . I feel as I should think an Indian might feel, in the face of ourselves that were."

The fact is that similarity of class rests upon no inevitable external condition, while similarity of nationality is inevitably intrinsic. Hence the poor of two different peoples tend to be less like-minded than the poor and the rich of the same peoples. At his core no human being, even in a "state of nature," is a mere mathematical unit of action like the "economic man." Behind him in time and tremendously in him in quality are his ancestors; around him in space are his relatives and kin, looking back with him to a remoter common ancestry. In all these he lives and moves and has his being. They constitute his, literally, *natio*, and in Europe every inch of his non-human environment wears the effects of their action upon it and breathes their spirit. The America he comes to, beside Europe, is nature virgin and inviolate; it does not guide him with ancestral blazings; externally he is cut off from the past. Not so internally: whatever else he changes, he cannot change his grandfather. Moreover, he comes rarely alone; he comes companioned with his fellow nationals; and he comes to no strangers, but to kin and friend who have gone before. If he is able to excel, he soon achieves a local habitation. There he encounters the native American to whom he is a Dutchman, a Frenchy, a Mick, a wop, a dago, a hunky, or a sheeny, and he encounters these others who are unlike him, dealing with him as a lower and outlandish creature. Then, be he even the rudest and most primeval peasant, heretofore totally unconscious of his nationality, of his categorical difference from other men, he must inevitably become conscious of it. Thus, in our industrial and congested towns where there are real and large contacts between immigrant nationalities the first effect appears to be an intensification of spiritual dissimilarities, always to the disadvantage of the dissimilarities.

The second generation, consequently, devotes itself feverishly to the attainment of similarity. The older social tradition is lost by attrition or thrown off for advantage. The merest externals of the new one are acquired—via the public school. But as the public school imparts it, or as the settlement imparts it, it is not really a life, it is an abstraction, an arrangement of words: as an historic fact, a democratic ideal of *life*, it is not realized at all. At best and at worst—now that the captains of industry are becoming disturbed by the mess they have made, and "vocational training" is becoming part of the educational program—the prospective American learns a trade, acquiring at his most impressionable age the habit of being a cog in the industrial machine. And this he learns, moreover, from the sons and daughters of earlier immigrants, themselves essentially uneducated and nearly illiterate, with what spontaneity and teaching power they have squeezed out in the "normal" schools by the application of that Pecksniffian "efficiency"-press called pedagogy.

But life, the expression of emotion and realization of desire, the prospective American learns from the yellow press, which has set itself explicitly the task of appealing to his capacities. He learns of the wealth, the luxuries, the extravagances, and the immoralities of specific rich persons. He learns to want to be like them. As that is impossible in the mass, their amusements become his crimes or vices. Or suppose him strong enough to emerge from the proletarian into the middle class, to achieve economic competence and social respectability. He remains still the Slav, the Jew, the German, or the Irish citizen of the American commonwealth. Again, in the mass, neither he nor his children nor his children's children lose their ethnic individuality. For marriage is determined by sexual selection and by propinquity, and the larger the town, the lesser the likelihood of mixed marriage. Although the gross number of such marriages is greater than it was fifty years ago, the relative proportions, in terms of variant units of population, tends, I think, to be significantly less. As the stratification of the towns echoes and stresses the stratification of the country as a whole, the likelihood of a new "American" race is remote enough, and the fear of it unnecessary. But equally remote also is the possibility of a universalization of the inwardness of the old American life. Only the externals succeed in passing over.

It took over two hundred years of settled life in one place for the New England school to emerge, and it emerged in a community in which likemindedness was very strong, and in which the whole ethnic group performed all the tasks, economic and social, which the community required. How when ethnic and industrial groups are coincident? For there is a marked tendency in this country for the industrial and social stratification to follow ethnic lines. The first comers in the land constitute its aristocracy, are its chief protagonists of the pride of blood as well as of the pride of self, its formers and leaders of opinion, the standardizers of its culture. Primacy in time has given them primacy in status, like all "first-born," so that what we call the tradition and spirit of America is theirs. The non-British elements of the population are practically voiceless, but they are massive, "barbarian hordes," if you will, and the effect, the unconscious and spontaneous effect of their pressure, has been the throwing back of the Anglo-American upon his ancestry and ancestral ideals. This has taken two forms: (1) the "patriotic" societies—not, of course, the Cincinnati or the Artillery company, but those that have arisen with the great migrations, the Sons and Daughters of the American Revolution, the Colonial Dames; and (2) the specific clan or tribal organizations consisting of families looking back to the same colonial ancestry—the societies of the descendants of John Alden, etc., etc. The ancient hatred for England is completely gone. Wherever possible, the ancestral line is traced across the water to England; old ancestral homes are bought; and those of the forebears of national heroes like John Harvard or George Washington become converted into shrines. More and more public emphasis has been placed upon the unity of the English and American stock—the common interests of the "Anglo-Saxon" nations, and of "Anglo-Saxon" civilization, the unity of the political, literary, and social tradition. If all that is not ethnic nationality returned to consciousness, what is it?

Next in general estimation come the Germans and Irish, with the Jews a close third, although the position of the last involves some abnormalities. Then come the Slavs and Italians and other central and south Europeans; finally the Asiatics.

The Germans, as Mr. Ross points out, have largely a monopoly of brewing and baking and cabinet making. The Irish shine in no particular industries unless it be those carried on by municipalities and public service corporations. The Jews mass in the garment-making industries, tobacco manufacture, and in the "learned professions." The Scandinavians appear to be on the same level as the Jews in the general estimation, and going up. They are farmers, mostly, and out-door men. The Slavs are miners, metalworkers, and packers. The Italians tend to fall with the Negroes into the "pick and shovel brigade." Such a countrywide and urban industrial and social stratification is no more likely than the geographi-cal and sectional stratification to facilitate the coming of the "American race"! And as our political and "reforming" action is directed upon symptoms rather than fundamental causes, the stratification, as the country moves towards the in-evitable equilibrium between wealth and population, will tend to grow more rigid rather than less. Thus far the pressure of immigration alone has kept the strata from hardening. Eliminate that, and we may be headed for a caste system based on ethnic diversity and mitigated to only a negligible degree by economic differences.

Part Two

V

The array of forces for and against that like-mindedness which is the stuff and essence of nationality aligns itself as follows: For it make social imitation of the upper by the lower classes, the facility of communications, the national pastimes of baseball and motion picture, the mobility of population, the cheapness of printing, and the public schools. Against it make the primary ethnic differences with which the population starts, its stratification over an enormous extent of country, its industrial and economic stratification. We are an English-speaking country, but in no intimate and inevitable way, as is New Zealand and Australia, or even Canada. English is to us what Latin was to the Roman provinces and to the Middle Ages—the language of the upper and dominant class, the vehicle and symbol of culture: for the masses of our population it is a sort of Esperanto or Ido, a *lingua franca* necessary less in the spiritual than the economic contacts of the daily life. This mass is composed of elementals, peasants—Mr. Ross speaks of them menacing American life with "peasantism"—the proletarian founda-tion material of all forms of civilization. Their self-consciousness as groups is comparatively weak. This is a factor that favors their "assimilation," for the more cultivated a group is, the more it is aware of its individuality, and the less willing it is to surrender that individuality. One need think only of the Puritans them-selves, leaving Holland for fear of absorption into the Dutch population; of the Creoles and Pennsylvania Germans of this country, or of the Jews, anywhere. In his judgment of the assimilability of various stocks Mr. Ross neglects this important point altogether, probably because his attention is fixed on existing contrasts rather than potential similarities. Peasants, however, having nothing much to surrender in taking over a new culture, feel no necessary break, and find the transition easy. It is the shock of confrontation with other ethnic groups and the feeling of aliency that generates in them an intenser self-consciousness, which then militates against Americanization in spirit by reinforcing the two factors to which the spiritual expression of the proletarian has been largely confined. These factors are language and religion. Religion is, of course, no more a universal than language. The history of Christianity makes evident enough how religion is modified, even inverted, by race, place, and time. It becomes a principle of separation, often the sole repository of the national spirit, almost always the conservatory of the national language and of the tradition that is passed on with the language to succeeding generations. Among immigrants, hence, religion and language tend to be coordinate: a single expression of the spontaneous and instinctive mental life of the masses, and the primary inward factors making against assimilation. Mr. Ross, I note, tends to grow shrill over the competition of the parochial school with the public school, at the same time that he belittles the fact "that on Sundays Norwegian is preached in more churches in America than in Norway."

And Mr. Ross's anxiety would, I think, be more justified were it not that religion in these cases always does more than it intends. For it conserves the inward aspect of nationality rather than mere religion, and tends to become the center of exfoliation of a higher type of personality among the peasants in the natural terms of their own *natio*. This *natio*, reaching consciousness first in a reaction against America, then as an effect of the competition with Americanization, assumes spiritual forms other than religious: the parochial school, to hold its own with the public school, gets secularized while remaining national. *Natio* is what underlies the vehemence of the "Americanized" and the spiritual and political unrest of the Americans. It is the fundamental fact of American life today, and in the light of it Mr. Wilson's resentment of the "hyphenated" American is both righteous and pathetic. But a hyphen attaches, in things of the spirit, also to the "pure" English American. His cultural mastery tends to be retrospective rather than prospective. At the present time there is no dominant American mind. Our spirit is inarticulate, not a voice, but a chorus of many voices each singing a rather different tune. How to get order out of this cacophony is the question for all those who are concerned about those things which alone justify wealth and power, concerned about justice, the arts, literature, philosophy, science. What must, what *shall* this cacophony become—a unison or a harmony?

For decidedly the older America, whose voice and whose spirit was New England, is gone beyond recall. Americans still are the artists and thinkers of the land, but they work, each for himself, without common vision or ideals. The older tradition has passed from a life into a memory, and the newer one, so far as it has an Anglo-Saxon base, is holding its own beside more formidable rivals, the expression in appropriate form of the national inheritances of the various populations concentrated in the various States of the Union, populations of whom their national self-consciousness is perhaps the chief spiritual asset. Think of the Creoles in the South and the French-Canadians in the North, clinging to French for so many generations and maintaining, however weakly, spiritual and social contacts with the mother-country; of the Germans, with their *Deutschthum*, their *Mannerchore, Turnvereine*, and *Schutzenfeste*; of the universally separate Jews; of the intensely nationalistic Irish; of the Pennsylvania Germans; of the indomitable Poles, and even more indomitable Bohemians; of the 30,000 Belgians in Wisconsin, with their "Belgian" language, a mixture of Walloon and Flemish welded by reaction to a strange social environment. Except in such cases as the town of Lead, South Dakota, the great ethnic groups of proletarians, thrown upon themselves in a new environment, generate from among themselves the other social classes which Mr. Ross misses so sadly among them: their shopkeepers, their physicians, their attorneys, their journalists, and their national and political leaders, who form the links between them and the greater American society. They develop their own literature, or become conscious of that of the mother-country. As they grow more prosperous and "Americanized," as they become free from the stigma of "foreigner," they develop group self-respect: the "wop" changes into a proud Italian, the "hunky" into an intensely nationalist Slav. They learn, or they recall, the spiritual heritage of their nationality. Their cultural abjectness gives way to cultural pride and the public schools, the libraries, and the clubs become beset with demands for texts in the national language and literature.

The Poles are an instance with dwelling upon. Mr. Ross's summary of them is as striking as it is premonitory. There are over a million of them in the country, a backward people, prolific, brutal, priest-ridden—a menace to American institutions. Yet the urge that carries them in such numbers to America is not unlike that which carried the Pilgrim Fathers. Next to the Jews, whom their brethren in their Polish home are hounding to death, the unhappiest people in Europe, exploited by both their own upper classes and the Russian conqueror, they have resisted extinction at a great cost. They have clung to their religion because it was a mark of difference between them and their conquerors; because they love liberty, they have made their language of literary importance in Europe. Their aspiration, impersonal, disinterested, as it must be in America, to free Poland, to conserve the Polish spirit, is the most hopeful and American thing about them—the one thing that stands actually between them and brutalization through complete economic degradation. It lifts them higher than anything that, in fact, America offers them. The same thing is true for the Bohemians, 17,000 of them, workingmen in Chicago, paying a proportion of their wage to maintain schools in the Bohemian tongue and free thought; the same thing is true of many other groups.

How true it is may be observed from a comparison of the vernacular dailies and weeklies with the yellow American press which is concocted expressly for the great American masses. The content of the former, when the local news is deducted, is a mass of information, political, social, scientific; often translations into the vernacular of standard English writing, often original work of high literary quality. The latter, when the news is deducted, consists of the sporting page and the editorial page. Both pander rather than awaken, so that it is no wonder that in fact the intellectual and spiritual pabulum of the great masses consists of the vernacular papers in the national tongue. With them go also the vernacular drama, and the thousand and one other phenomena which make a distinctive culture, the outward expression of that fundamental like-mindedness wherein men are truly "free and equal." This, beginning for the dumb peasant masses in language and religion, emerges in the other forms of life and art and tends to make smaller or larger ethnic groups autonomous, self-sufficient, and reacting as spiritual units to the residuum of America.

What is the cultural outcome likely to be, under these conditions? Surely not the melting pot. Rather something that has become more and more distinct in the changing State and city life of the last two decades, and which is most articulate and apparent among just those peoples whom Mr. Ross praises most—the Scandinavians, the Germans, the Irish, the Jews.

It is in the area where Scandinavians are most concentrated that Norwegian is preached on Sunday in more churches than in Norway. That area is Minnesota, not unlike Scandinavia in climate and character. There, if the newspapers are to be trusted, the "foreign language" taught in an increasingly larger number of high schools is Scandinavian. The Constitution of the State resembles in many respects the famous Norwegian Constitution of 1813. The largest city has been chosen as the "spiritual capital," if I may say so, the seat of the Scandinavian "house of life," which the Scandinavian Society in America is reported to be planning to build as a center from which there is to spread through the land Scandinavian culture and ideals.

The eastern neighbor of Minnesota is Wisconsin, a region of great concentration of Germans. It is merely a political accident that the centralization of State authority and control has been possible there to a degree heretofore unknown in this country? That the Socialist organization is the most powerful in the land, able under ordinary conditions to have elected the Mayor of a large city and a Congressman, and kept out of power only by the coalition of other parties? That German is the overwhelmingly predominant "foreign language" in the public schools and in the university? Or that the fragrance of *Deutschthum* pervades the life of the whole State? The earliest German immigrants to America were group conscious to a high degree. They brought with them a cultural tradition and political aspiration. They wanted to found a State. If a State is to be regarded as a mode of life of the mind, they have succeeded. Their language is the predominant "foreign" one throughout the Middle West. The teaching of it is required by law in many places, southern Ohio and Indianapolis, for example. Their national institutions, even to cooking, are as widespread as they are. They are organized into a great national society, the German-American Alliance, which is dedicated to the advancement of German culture and ideals. They encourage and make possible a close and more intimate contact with the fatherland. They endow Germanic museums, they encourage and provide for exchange professorships, erect monuments to German heroes, and disseminate translations of the German classics. And there are, of course, the very excellent German vernacular press, the German theatre, the German club, the German organization of life.

Similar are the Irish, living in strength in Massachusetts and New York. When they began to come to this country they were far less well off and far more passionately self-conscious than the Germans. For numbers of them America was and has remained just a center from which to plot for the freedom of Ireland. For most it was an opportunity to escape both exploitation and starvation. The way they made was made against both race and religious prejudice: in the course of it they lost much that was attractive as well as much that was unpleasant. But Americanization brought the mass of them also spiritual self-respect, and their growing prosperity both here and in Ireland is what lies behind the more inward phases of Irish Nationalism—the Gaelic movement, the Irish theater, the Irish Art Society. I omit consideration of such organized bodies as the Ancient Order of Hibernians. All these movements alike indicate the conversion of the negative nationalism of the hatred of England to the position nationalism of the loving care and development of the cultural values of the Celtic spirit. A significant phase of it is the voting of Irish history into the curriculum of the high schools of Boston. In sum, once the Irish body had been fed and erected, the Irish mind demanded and generated its own peculiar form of self-realization and satisfaction.

And, finally, the Jews. Their attitude towards America is different in a fundamental respect from that of other immigrant nationalities. They do not come to the United States from truly native lands, lands of their proper *natio* and culture. They come from lands of sojourn, where they have been for ages treated as foreigners, at most as semi-citizens, subject to disabilities and persecutions. They come with no political aspirations against the peace of other states such as move the Irish, the Poles, the Bohemians. They come with the intention to be completely incorporated into the body politic of the state. They alone, as Mr. H.G. Wells notes, of all the immigrant peoples have made spontaneously conscious and organized efforts to prepare themselves and their brethren for the responsibilities of American citizenship. There is hardly a considerable municipality in the land, where Jews inhabit, that has not its Hebrew Institute, or its Educational Alliance, or its Young Men's Hebrew Association, or its Community House, especially dedicated to the task. They show the highest percentage of naturalization, according to Mr. Ross's tables, and he concedes that they have benefitted politics. Yet of all self-conscious peoples they are the most self-conscious. Of all immigrants they have the oldest civilized tradition, they are longest accustomed to living under law, and are at the outset the most eager and the most successful in eliminating the external differences between themselves and their social environment. Even their religion is flexible and accommodating, as that of the Christian sectories is not, for change involves no change in doctrine, only in mode of life.

Yet, once the wolf is driven from the door and the Jewish immigrant takes his place in our society a free man and an American, he tends to become all the more a Jew. The cultural unity of his race, history and background is only continued by the new life under the new conditions. Mr. H.G. Wells calls the Jewish quarter in New York a city within a city, and with more justice than other quarters because, although it is far more in tune with Americanism than the other quarters, it is also far more autonomous in spirit and self-conscious in culture. It has its sectaries, its radicals, its artists, its literati; its press, its literature, its theater, its Yiddish and its Hebrew, its Talmudical colleges and its Hebrew schools, its charities and its vanities, and its coordinating organization, the Kehilla, all more or less duplicated wherever Jews congregate in mass. Here not religion alone, but the whole world of radical thinking, carries the mother-tongue and the father-tongue, with all that they imply. Unlike the parochial schools, their separate schools, being national, do not displace the public schools; they supplement the public schools. The Jewish ardor for pure learning is notorious. And, again, as was the case with the Scandinavians, the Germans, the Irish, democracy applied to education has given the Jews their will that Hebrew shall be coordinate with French and German in the regent's examination. On a national scale of organization there is the American Jewish committee, the Jewish Historical Society, the Jewish Publication Society. Rurally, there is the model Association of Jewish Farmers, with their cooperative organization for agriculture and for agricultural education. In sum, the most eagerly American of the immigrant groups are also the most autonomous and self-conscious in spirit and culture.

VI

Immigrants appear to pass through four phases in the course of being Americanized. In the first phase they exhibit economic eagerness, the greed of the unfed. Since external differences are a handicap in the economic struggle, they "assimilate," seeking thus to facilitate the attainment of economic independence. Once the proletarian level of such independence is reached, the process of assimilation slows down and tends to come to a stop. The immigrant group is still a national group, modified, sometimes improved, by environmental influences, but otherwise a solitary spiritual unit, which is seeking to find its way out on its own social level. This search brings to light permanent group distinctions, and the immigrant, like the Anglo-Saxon American, is thrown back upon himself and his ancestry. Then a process of dissimilation begins. The arts, life, and ideals of the nationality become central and paramount; ethnic and national differences change in status from disadvantages to distinctions. All the while the immigrant has been using the English language and behaving like an American in matters economic and political, and continues to do so. The institutions of the Republic have become the liberating cause and the background for the rise of the cultural consciousness and social autonomy of the immigrant Irishman, German, Scandinavian, Jew, Pole, or Bohemian. On the whole, Americanization has not repressed nationality. Americanization has liberated nationality.

Hence, what troubles Mr. Ross and so many other Anglo-Saxon Americans is not really inequality; what troubles them is *difference*. Only things that are alike in fact and not abstractly, and only men that are alike in origin and in spirit and not abstractly, can be truly "equal" and maintain that inward unanimity of action and outlook which make a national life. The writers of the Declaration of Independence and of the Constitution were not confronted by the practical fact of ethnic dissimilarity among the whites of the country. Their descendants are confronted with it. Its existence, acceptance, and development provide one of the inevitable consequences of the democratic principle on which our theory of government is based, and the result at the present writing is to many worthies very unpleasant. Democratism and the Federal principle have worked together with economic greed and ethnic snobbishness to people the land with all the nationalities of Europe, and to convert the early American nation into the present American state. For in effect we are in the process of becoming a true federal state, such a state as men hope for as the outcome of the European war, a great republic consisting of a federation or commonwealth of nationalities.

Given, in the economic order, the principle of laissez-faire applied to a capitalistic society, in contrast with the manorial and guild systems of the past and the Socialist utopians of the future, the economic consequences are the same, whether in America, full of all Europe, or in England, full of the English, Scotch, and Welsh. Given, in the political order, the principle that all men are equal and that each, consequently, under the law at least, shall have the opportunity to make the most of himself, the control of the machinery of government by the plutocracy is a foregone conclusion. Laissez-faire and unprecedently bountiful natural resources have turned the mind of the state to wealth alone, and in the haste to accumulate wealth considerations of human quality have been neglected and forgotten, the action of government has been remedial rather than constructive, and Mr. Ross's "peasantism," i.e. the growth of an expropriated, degraded industrial class, dependent on the factory rather than on land, has been rapid and vexatious.

The problems which these conditions give rise to are important, but not primarily important. Although they have occupied the minds of all our political theorists, they are problems of means, of instruments, not of ends. They concern the conditions of life, not the *kind of life*, and there appears to have been a general assumption that only one kind of human life is possible in America. But the same democracy which underlies the evils of the economic order underlies also the evils—and the promise—of the ethnic order. Because no individual is merely an individual, the political autonomy of the individual has meant and is beginning to realize in these United States the spiritual autonomy of the group. The process is as yet far from fruition. We are, in fact, at the parting of the ways. A genuine social alternative is before us, either of which parts we may realize if we will. In social construction the will is father to the fact, for the fact is nothing more than the concord or conflict of wills. What do we *will* to make of the United States—a unison, singing the old Anglo-Saxon theme "America," the America of the New England school, or a harmony, in which that theme shall be dominant, perhaps, among others, but one among many, not the only one?

The mind reverts helplessly to the historic attempts at unison in Europe— the heroic failure of the pan-Hellenists, of the Romans, the disintegration and the diversification of the Christian Church, for a time the most successful unison in history; the present day failures of Germany and of Russia. Here, however, the whole social situation is favorable, as it has never been at any time elsewhere— everything is favorable but the basic law of America itself, and the spirit of American institutions. To achieve unison—it can be achieved—would be to violate these. For the end determines the means, and this end would involve no other means than those used by Germany in Poland, in Schleswig-Holstein, and Alsace-Lorraine; by Russia in the Pale, in Poland, in Finland. Fundamentally it would require the complete nationalization of education, the abolition of every form of parochial and private school, the abolition of instruction in other tongues than English, and the concentration of the teaching of history and literature upon the English tradition. The other institutions of society would require treatment analogous to that administered by Germany to her European acquisitions. And all of this, even if meeting with no resistance, would not completely guarantee the survival as a unison of the older Americanism. For the program would be applied to diverse ethnic types, and the reconstruction that, with the best will, they might spontaneously make of the tradition would more likely than not be a far cry from the original. It is already.

The notion that the program might be realized by radical and even enforced miscegenation, by the creation of the melting pot by law, and thus the development of the new "American race," is, as Mr. Ross points out, as mystically optimistic as it is ignorant. In historic times, so far as we know, no new ethnic types have originated, and what we know of breeding gives us no assurance of the disappearance of the old types in favor of the new, only the addition of a new type, if it succeeds in surviving, to the already existing older ones. Biologically, life does not unify; biologically, life diversifies; and it is sheer ignorance to apply social analogies to biological processes. In any event, we know what the qualities and capacities of existing types are; we know how by education to do something towards the repression of what is evil in them and the conservation of what is good. The "American race" is a totally unknown thing; to presume that it will be better because (if we like to persist in the illusion that it is coming) it will be later, is no different from imagining that, because contemporary, Russia is better than ancient Greece. There is nothing more to be said to the pious stupidity that identifies recency with goodness. The unison to be achieved cannot be a unison of ethnic types. It must be, if it is to be at all, a unison of social and historic interests, established by the complete cutting off of the ancestral memories of our populations, the enforced, exclusive use of the English language and English and American history in the schools and in the daily life.

The attainment of the other alternative, a harmony, also requires concerted public action. But the action would do no violence to our fundamental law and the spirit of our institutions, nor to the qualities of men. It would seek simply to eliminate the waste and the stupidity of our social organization, by way of freeing and strengthening the strong forces already in operation. Starting with our existing ethnic and cultural groups, it would seek to provide conditions under which each may attain the perfection that is proper to its kind. The provision of such conditions is the primary intent of our fundamental law and the function of our institutions. And the various nationalities which compose our commonwealth must first of all learn this fact, which is perhaps, to most minds, the outstanding ideal content of "Americanism"— that democracy means self-realization through self-control, self-government, and that one is impossible without the other. For the application of this principle, which is realized in a harmony of societies, there are European analogies also. I omit Austria and Turkey, for the union of nationalities is there based more on inadequate force than on consent, and the form of their organization is alien to ours. I think of England and of Switzerland. England is a state of four nationalities—the English, Welsh, Scotch, and Irish (if one considers the Empire, of many more), and while English history is not unmarred by attempts at unison, both the home policy and the imperial policy have, since the Boer War, been realized more and more upon the voluntary and autonomous cooperation of the component nationalities. Switzerland is a state of three nationalities, a republic as the United States is, far more democratically governed, concentrated in an area not much different in size, I suspect, from New York City, with a population not far from it in total. Yet Switzerland has the most loyal citizens in Europe. Their language, literary and spiritual traditions are on the one side German, on another Italian, on a third side French. And in terms of social organization, of economic prosperity, of public education, of the general level of culture, Switzerland is the most successful democracy in the world. It conserves and encourages individuality.

The reason lies, I think, in the fact that in Switzerland the conception of "natural rights" operates, consciously or unconsciously, as a generalization from the unalterable data of human nature. What is inalienable in the life of mankind is its intrinsic positive quality—its psychophysical inheritance. Men may change their clothes, their politics, their wives, their religions, their philosophies, to a greater or lesser extent: they cannot change their grandfathers. Jews or Poles or Anglo-Saxons, would have to cease to be. The selfhood which is inalienable in them, and for the realization of which they require "inalienable" liberty, is ancestrally determined, and the happiness which they pursue has its form implied in ancestral endowment. This is what, actually, democracy in operation assumes. There are human capacities which it is the function of the state to liberate and to protect; and the failure of the state as a government means its abolition. Government, the state, under the democratic conception, is merely an instrument, not an end. That it is often an abused instrument, that it is often seized by the powers that prey, that it makes frequent mistakes and considers only secondary ends, surface needs, which vary from moment to moment, is, of course, obvious; hence our social and political chaos. But that it is an instrument, flexibly adjustable to changing life, changing opinion, and the needs, our whole electoral organization and party system declare. And as intelligence and wisdom prevail over "politics" and special interests, as the steady and continuous pressure of the inalienable qualities and purposes of human groups more and more dominate the confusion of our common life, the outlines of a possible great and truly democratic commonwealth become discernible.

Its form is that of the Federal republic; its substance a democracy of nationalities, cooperating voluntarily and autonomously in the enterprise of self-realization through the perfection of men according to their kind. The common language of the commonwealth, the language of it great political tradition, is English, but each nationality expresses its emotional and voluntary life in its own language, in its own inevitable aesthetic and intellectual forms. The common life of the commonwealth is politico-economic, and serves as the foundation and background for the realization of the distinctive individuality of each *natio* that composes it. Thus "American civilization" may come to mean the perfection of the cooperative harmonies of "European civilization," the waste, the squalor, and the distress of Europe being eliminated—a multiplicity in a unity, an orchestration of mankind. As in an orchestra, every type of instrument has its specific timbre and tonality, founded in its substance and form; as every type has its appropriate theme and melody in the whole symphony, so in society each ethnic group is the natural instrument, its spirit and culture are its theme and melody, and the harmony and dissonances and discords of them all make the symphony of civilization, with this difference: a musical symphony is written before it is played; in the symphony of civilization the playing is the writing, so that there is nothing so fixed and inevitable about its progressions as in music, so that within the limits set by nature they may vary at will, and the range and variety of the harmonies may become wider and richer and more beautiful.

But the question is, do the dominant classes in America want such a society?

(1915)

Trans-National America

Randolph Bourne

I

No reverberatory effect of the great war has caused American public opinion more solicitude than the failure of the "melting pot." The discovery of diverse nationalistic feelings among our great alien population has come to most people as an intense shock. It has brought out the unpleasant inconsistencies of our traditional beliefs. We have had to watch hard-hearted old Brahmins virtuously indignant at the spectacle of the immigrant refusing to be melted, while they jeer at patriots like Mary Antin who write about our "forefathers." We have had to listen to publicists who express themselves as stunned by the evidence of vigorous traditionalistic and cultural movements in this country among Germans, Scandinavians, Bohemians and Poles, while in the same breath they insist that the alien shall be forcibly assimilated to that Anglo-Saxon tradition which they unquestionably label "American."

As the unpleasant truth has come upon us that assimilation in this country was proceeding on lines very different from those we had marked out for it, we found ourselves inclined to blame those who were thwarting our prophecies. The truth became culpable. We blamed the war, we blamed the Germans. And then we discovered with a moral shock that these movements had been making great headway even before the war even began. We found that the tendency, reprehensible and paradoxical as it might be, has been for the national clusters of immigrants, as they became more and more firmly established and more and more prosperous, to cultivate more and more assiduously the literatures and cultural traditions of their homelands. Assimilation, in other words, instead of washing out the memories of Europe, made them more and more intensely real. Just as these clusters became more and more objectively American, did they become more and more German or Scandinavian or Bohemian or Polish.

To face the fact that our aliens are already strong enough to take a share in the direction of their own destiny, and that the strong cultural movements represented by the foreign press, schools, and colonies are a challenge to our facile attempts, is not, however, to admit the failure of Americanization. It is not to fear the failure of democracy. It is rather to urge us to an investigation of what Americanism may rightly mean. It is to ask ourselves whether our ideal has been broad or narrow—whether perhaps the time has not come to assert a higher ideal than the "melting-pot." Surely we cannot be certain of our spiritual democracy when, claiming to melt the nations within us to a comprehension of our free and democratic institutions, we fly into panic at the first sign of their own will and tendency. We act as if we wanted Americanization to take place only on our own terms, and not by the consent of the governed. All our elaborate machinery of settlement and school and union, of social and political naturalization, however will move with friction just in so far as it neglects to take into account this strong and virile insistence that America shall be what the immigrant will have a hand in making it, and not what a ruling class, descendant of those British stocks which were the first permanent immigrants, decide that America shall be made. This is the condition which confronts us, and which demands a clear and general readjustment of our attitude and our ideal.

Mary Antin is right when she looks upon our foreign-born as the people who missed the Mayflower and came over on the first boat they could find. But she forgets that when they did come it was not upon other Mayflowers, but upon a "Maiblume," a "Fleur de Mai," a "Fior di Maggio," a "Majblomst." These people were not mere arrivals from the same family, to be welcomed as understood and long-loved, but strangers to the neighborhood, with whom a long process of settling down had to take place. For they brought with them their national and racial characters, and each new national quota had to wear slowly away the contempt with which its mere alienness got itself greeted. Each had to make its way slowly from the lowest strata of unskilled labor up to a level where it satisfied the accredited norms of social success.

We are all foreign-born or the descendants of foreign-born, and if distinctions are to be made between us they should rightly be on some other ground than indigenousness. The early colonists came over with motives no less colonial than the later. They did not come to be assimilated in an American melting pot. They did not come to adopt the culture of the American Indian. They had not the smallest intention of "giving themselves without reservation" to the new country. They came to get freedom to live as they wanted. They came to escape from the stifling air and chaos of the old world; they came to make their fortune in a new land. They invented no new social framework. Rather they brought over bodily the old ways to which they had been accustomed. Tightly concentrated on a hostile frontier, they were conservative beyond belief. Their pioneer daring was reserved for the objective conquest of material resources. In their folkways, in their social and political institutions, they were, like every colonial people, slavishly imitative of the mother-country. So that, in spite of the "Revolution," our whole legal and political system remained more English than the English, petrified and unchanging, while in England law developed to meet the needs of the changing times.

It is just this English-American conservatism that has been our chief obstacle to social advance. We have needed the new peoples—the order of the German and Scandinavian, the turbulence of the Slav and Hun—to save us from our own stagnation. I do not mean that the illiterate Slav is now the equal of the New Englander of pure descent. He is raw material to be educated, not into a New Englander, but into a socialized American along such lines as those thirty nationalities are being educated in the amazing schools of Gary. I do not believe that this process is to be one of decades of evolution. The spectacle of Japan's sudden jump from medievalism to post-modernism should have destroyed that superstition. We are not dealing with individuals who are to "evolve." We are dealing with their children, who, with that education we are about to have, will start level with all of us. Let us cease to think of ideals like democracy as magical qualities inherent in certain peoples. Let us speak, not of inferior races, but of inferior civilizations. We are all to educate and to be educated. These peoples in America are in a common enterprise. It is not what we are now that concerns us, but what this plastic next generation may become in the light of a new cosmopolitan idea.

We are not dealing with static factors, but with fluid and dynamic generations. To contrast the older and the newer immigrants and see the one class as democratically motivated by love of liberty, and the other by mere money-getting, is not to illuminate the future. To think of earlier nationalities as culturally assimilated to America, while we picture the later as a sodden and resistive mass, makes only for bitterness and misunderstanding. There may be a difference between these earlier and these later stocks, but it lies neither in motive for coming nor in strength of cultural allegiance to the homeland. The truth is that no more tenacious cultural allegiance to the mother country has been shown by any alien nation than by the ruling class of Anglo-Saxon descendants in these American States. English snobberies, English religion, English literary styles, English literary reverences and canons, English ethics, English superiorities, have been the cultural food that we have drunk in from our mother's breasts. The distinctively American spirit pioneer, as distinguished from the reminiscently English that appears in Whitman and Emerson and James, had had to exist on sufferance along side of this other cult, unconsciously belittled by our cultural makers of opinion. No country has perhaps had so great indigenous genius which had so little influence on the country's traditions and expressions. The unpopular and dreaded German-American of the present day is a beginning amateur in comparison with those foolish Anglophiles of Boston and New York and Philadelphia whose reversion to cultural type sees uncritically in England's cause the cause of Civilization, and, under the guise of ethical independence of thought, carries along European traditions which are no more "American" than the German categories themselves.

It speaks well for German-American innocence of heart or else for its lack of imagination that it has not turned the hyphen stigma into a "Tu quoque!" If there were to be any hyphens scattered about, clearly they should be affixed to those English descendants who had had centuries of time to be made American where the German had had only half a century. Most significantly has the war brought out of them this alien virus, showing them still loving English things, owing allegiance to the English Kultur, moved by English shibboleths and prejudice. It is only because it has been the ruling class in this country that bestowed the epithets that we have not heard copiously and scornfully of "hyphenated English-Americans." But even our quarrels with England have had the bad temper, the extravagance, of family quarrels. The Englishman of today nags us and dislikes us in that personal, peculiarly intimate way in which he dislikes the Australian, or as we may dislike our younger brothers. He still thinks of us incorrigibly as "colonials." America—official, controlling, literary, political America—is still, as a writer recently expressed it, "culturally speaking, a self-governing dominion of the British Empire."

The non-English American can scarcely be blamed if he sometimes thinks of Anglo-Saxon predominance in America as little more than a predominance of priority. The Anglo-Saxon was merely the first immigrant, the first to found a colony. He has never really ceased to be the descendant of immigrants, nor has he ever succeeded in transforming that colony into a real nation, with a tenacious, richly woven fabric of native culture. Colonials from the other nations have come and settled down beside him. They found no definite native culture which should startle them out of their colonialism, and consequently they looked back to their mother-country, as the earlier Anglo-Saxon immigrant was looking back to his. What has been offered the newcomer has been the chance to learn English, to become a citizen, to salute the flag. And those elements of our ruling classes who are responsible for the public schools, the settlements, all the organizations for amelioration in the cities, have every reason to be proud of the care and labor which they have devoted to absorbing the immigrant. His opportunities the immigrant has taken too gladly, with almost a pathetic eagerness to make his way in the new land without friction or disturbance. The common language has made not only for the necessary communication, but for all the amenities of life.

If freedom means the right to do pretty much as one pleases, so long as one does not interfere with others, the immigrant has found freedom, and the ruling element has been singularly liberal in its treatment of the invading hordes. But if freedom means a democratic cooperation in determining the ideals and purposes and industrial and social institutions of a country, then the immigrant has not been free, and the Anglo-Saxon element is guilt of just what every dominant race is guilty of in every European country: the imposition of its own culture upon the minority peoples. The fact that this imposition has been so mild and, indeed, semi-conscious does not alter its quality. And the war has brought out just the degree to which that purpose of "Americanizing," that is, "Anglo-Saxonizing," the immigrant has failed.

For the Anglo-Saxon now in his bitterness to turn upon the other peoples, talk about their "arrogance," scold them for not being melted in a pot which never existed, is to betray the unconscious purpose which lay at the bottom of his heart. It betrays too the possession of a racial jealousy similar to that of which he is now accusing the so-called "hyphenates." Let the Anglo-Saxon be proud enough of the heroic toil and heroic sacrifices which molded the nation.

But let him ask himself, if he had had to depend on the English descendants, where he would have been living today. To those of us who see in the exploitation of unskilled labor the strident red *leit-motif* of our civilization, the settling of the country presents a great social drama as the waves of immigration broke over it.

Let the Anglo-Saxon ask himself where he would have been if these races had not come? Let those who feel the inferiority of the non-Anglo-Saxon immigrant contemplate that region of the States which has remained the most distinctively "American," the South. Let him ask himself whether he would really like to see the foreign hordes Americanized into such an Americanization. Let him ask himself how superior this native civilization is to the great "alien" states of Wisconsin and Minnesota, where Scandinavians, Poles, and Germans have self-consciously labored to preserve their traditional culture, while being outwardly and satisfactorily American. Let him ask himself how much more wisdom, intelligence, industry and social leadership has come out of these alien states than out of all the truly American ones. The South, in fact, while this vast Northern development has gone on, still remains an English colony, stagnant and complacent, having progressed scarcely beyond the early Victorian era. It is culturally sterile because it has had no advantage of cross-fertilization like the Northern states. What has happened in states such as Wisconsin and Minnesota is that strong foreign cultures have struck root in a new and fertile soil. America has meant liberation, and German and Scandinavian political ideas and social energies have expanded to a new potency. The process has not been at all the fancied "assimilation" of the Scandinavian or Teuton. Rather has it been a process of their assimilation of us—I speak as an Anglo-Saxon. The foreign cultures have not been melted down or run together, made into some homogeneous Americanism, but have remained distinct but cooperating to the greater glory and benefit, not only of themselves but of all the native "Americanism" around them.

What we emphatically do not want is that these distinctive qualities should be washed out into a tasteless, colorless fluid of uniformity. Already we have far too much of this insipidity, masses of people who are cultural half-breeds, neither assimilated Anglo-Saxons nor nationals of another culture. Each national colony in this country seems to retain in its foreign press, its vernacular literature, its schools, its intellectual and patriotic leaders, a central cultural nucleus. From this nucleus the colony extends out by imperceptible gradations to a fringe where national characteristics are all but lost. Our cities are filled with these half-breeds who retain their foreign names but have lost the foreign savor. This does not mean that they have actually been changed into New Englanders or Middle Westerners. It does not mean that they have been really Americanized. It means that, letting slip from them whatever native culture they had, they have substituted for it only the most rudimentary American—the American culture of the cheap newspaper, the "movies," the popular song, the ubiquitous automobile. The unthinking who survey this class call them assimilated, Americanized. The great American public school has done its work. With these people our institutions are safe. We may thrill with dread at the aggressive hyphenate, but this tame flabbiness is accepted as Americanization. The same molders of opinion whose ideal is to melt the different races into Anglo-Saxon gold hail this poor product as the satisfying result of their alchemy.

Yet a truer cultural sense would have told us that it is not the self-conscious cultural nuclei that sap at our American life, but these fringes. It is not the Jew who sticks proudly to the faith of his fathers and boasts of that venerable culture of his who is dangerous to America, but the Jew who has lost the Jewish fire and become a mere elementary grasping animal. It is not the Bohemian who supports the Bohemian schools in Chicago whose influence is sinister, but the Bohemian who has made money and has got into ward politics. Just so surely as we tend to disintegrate these nuclei of nationalistic culture do we tend to creat hordes of men and women without a spiritual country, cultural outlaws, without taste, without standards but those of the mob. We sentence them to live on the most rudimentary planes of American life. The influences at the centre of the nuclei are centripetal. They make for the intelligence and the social values which mean an enhancement of life. And just because the foreign-born retains this expressiveness is he likely to be a better citizen of the American community. The influences at the fringe, however, are centrifugal, anarchical. They make for detached fragments of peoples. Those who came to find liberty achieve only license. They become the flotsam and jetsam of American life, the downward undertow of our civilization with its leering cheapness and falseness of taste and spiritual outlook, the absence of mind and sincere feeling which we see in our slovenly towns, our rapid moving pictures, our popular novels, and in the vacuous faces of the crowds on the city street. This is the cultural wreckage of our time, and it is from the fringes of the Anglo-Saxon as well as the other stocks that it falls. America has as yet no impelling integrating force. It makes too easily for this detritus of cultures. In our loose, free country, no constraining national purpose, no tenacious folk tradition and folk style hold the people to a line.

The war has shown us that not in any magical formula will this purpose be found. No intense nationalism of the European plan can be ours. But do we not begin to see a new and more adventurous ideal? Do we not see how the national colonies in America, deriving power from the deep cultural heart of Europe and yet living here in mutual toleration, freed from the age-long tangles of races, creeds, and dynasties, may work out a federated ideal? America is transplanted Europe, but a Europe that has not been disintegrated and scattered in the transplanting as in some Dispersion. Its colonies live here inextricably mingled, yet not homogeneous. They merge but they do not fuse.

America is a unique sociological fabric, and it bespeaks poverty of imagination not to be thrilled at the incalculable potentialities of so novel a union of men. To seek no other goal than the weary old nationalism, belligerent, exclusive, inbreeding, the poison of which we are witnessing now in Europe, is to make patriotism a hollow sham, and to declare that, in spite of our boastings, America must ever be a follower and not a leader of nations.

II

If we come to find this point of view plausible, we shall have to give up the search for our native "American" culture. With the exception of the South and that New England which, like the Red Indian, seems to be passing into solemn oblivion, there is no distinctively American culture. It is apparently our lot rather to be a federation of cultures. This we have been for half a century, and the war has made it evermore evident that this is what we are destined to remain. This will not mean, however, that there are not expressions of indigenous genius that could not have sprung from any other soil. Music, poetry, philosophy, have been singularly fertile and new. Strangely enough, American genius has flared forth just in those directions which are least [understood] of the people. If the American note is bigness, action, the objective as contrasted with the reflective life, where is the epic expression of this spirit? Our drama and our fiction, the peculiar fields for the expression of action and objectivity, are somehow exactly the fields of the spirit which remain poor and mediocre. American materialism is in some way inhibited from getting into impressive artistic form its own energy with which it bursts. Nor is it any better in architecture, the least romantic and subjective of all the arts. We are inarticulate of the very values which we profess to idealize. But in the finer forms—music, verse, the essay, philosophy—the American genius puts forth work equal to any of its contemporaries. Just in so far as our American genius has expressed the pioneer spirit, the adventurous, forward-looking drive of a colonial empire, is it representative of that whole—America of the many races and peoples, and not of any partial or traditional enthusiasm. And only as that pioneer note is sounded can we really speak of the American culture. As long as we thought of Americanism in terms of the "melting pot," our American cultural tradition lay in the past. It was something to which the new Americans were to be molded. In the light of our changing ideal of Americanism, we must perpetrate the paradox that our American cultural tradition lies in the future. It will be what we all together make out of this incomparable opportunity of attacking the future with a new key.

Whatever American nationalism turns out to be, it is certain to become something utterly different from the nationalisms of twentieth-century Europe. This wave of reactionary enthusiasm to play the orthodox nationalistic game which is passing over the country is scarcely vital enough to last. We cannot swagger and thrill to the same national self-feeling. We must give new edges to our pride. We must be content to avoid the unnumbered woes that national patriotism has brought in Europe, and that fiercely heightened pride and self-consciousness. Alluring as this is, we must allow our imaginations to transcend this scarcely veiled belligerency. We can be serenely too proud to fight if our pride embraces the creative forces of civilization which armed contest nullifies. We can be too proud to fight if our code of honor transcends that of the schoolboy on the playground surrounded by his jeering mates. Our honor must be positive and creative, and not the mere jealous and negative protectiveness against metaphysical violations of our technical rights. When the doctrine is put forth that in one American flows the mystic blood of all our country's sacred honor, freedom, and prosperity, so that an injury to him is to be the signal for turning our whole nation into that clan-feud of horror and reprisal which would be war, then we find ourselves back among the musty schoolmen of the Middle Ages, and not in any pragmatic and realistic America of the twentieth century.

We should hold our gaze to what America has done, not what medieval codes of dueling she has failed to observe. We have transplanted European modernity to our soil, without the spirit that inflames it and turns all its energy into mutual destruction. Out of these foreign peoples there has somehow been squeezed the poison. An American, "hyphenated" to bitterness is somehow non-explosive. For, even if we all hark back in sympathy to a European nation, even if the war has set every one vibrating to some emotional string twanged on the other side of the Atlantic, the effect has been one of almost dramatic harmlessness.

What we have really been witnessing, however unappreciatively, in this country has been a thrilling and bloodless battle of Kulturs. In that arena of friction which has been the most dramatic—between the hyphenated German-American and the hyphenated English-American—there have emerged rivalries of philosophies which show up deep traditional attitudes, points of view which accurately reflect the gigantic issues of the war. American has mirrored the spiritual issues. The vicarious struggle has been played out peacefully here in the mind. We have seen the stout resistiveness of the old moral interpretation of history on which Victorian England thrived and made itself great in its own esteem. The clean and immensely satisfying vision of the war as a contest between right and wrong; the enthusiastic support of the Allies as the incarnation of virtue on a rampage; the fierce envisaging of their selfish national purposes as the ideals of justice, freedom and democracy—all this has been thrown with intensest force against the German realistic interpretations in terms of the struggle for power and the virility of the integrated State. America has been the intellectual battleground of the nations.

The failure of the melting pot, far from closing the great American democratic experiment, means that it has only just begun. Whatever American nationalism turns out to be, we see already that it will have color richer and more exciting than our ideal has hitherto encompassed. In a world which has dreamed of internationalism, we find that we have all unawares been building up the first international nation. The voices which have cried for a tight and jealous nationalism of the European pattern are failing. From that ideal, however valiantly and disinterestedly it has been set for us, time and tendency have moved us further and further away. What we have achieved has been rather a cosmopolitan federation of national colonies, of foreign cultures, from whom the sting of devastating competition has been removed.

America is already the world-federation in miniature, the continent where for the first time in history has been achieved that miracle of hope, the peaceful living side by side, with character substantially preserved, of the most heterogeneous peoples under the sun. Nowhere else has such contiguity been anything but the breeder of misery. Here, notwithstanding our tragic failures of adjustment, the outlines are already too clear not to give us a new vision and a new orientation of the American mind in the world.

III

It is for the American of the younger generation to accept this cosmopolitanism, and carry it along with self-conscious and fruitful purpose. In his colleges, he is already getting, with the study of modern history and politics, the modern literatures, economic geography, the privilege of a cosmopolitan outlook such as the people of no other nation of today in Europe can possibly secure. If he is still a colonial, he is no longer the colonial of one partial culture, but of many. He is a colonial of the world. Colonialism has grown into cosmopolitanism, and his motherland is no one nation, but all who have anything life enhancing to offer to the spirit. That vague sympathy which the France of ten years ago was feeling for the world—a sympathy which was drowned in the terrible reality of war—may be the modern American's, and that in a positive and aggressive sense. If the American is parochial, it is in sheer wantonness or cowardice. His provincialism is the measure of his fear of bogies or the defect of his imagination.

Indeed, it is not uncommon for the eager Anglo-Saxon who goes to a vivid American university today to find his true friends not among his own race but among the acclimatized German or Austrian, the acclimatized Jew, the acclimatized Scandinavian or Italian. In them he finds the cosmopolitan note. In these youths, foreign-born or the children of foreign-born parents, he is likely to find many of his old inbred morbid problems washed away. These friends are oblivious to the repressions of that tight little society in which he so provincially grew up. He has a pleasurable sense of liberation from the stale and familiar attitudes of those whose ingrowing culture has scarcely created anything vital for his America of today. He breathes a larger air. In his new enthusiasms for continental literature, for unplumbed Russian depths, for French clarity of thought, for Teuton philosophies of power, he feels himself citizen of a larger world. He may be absurdly superficial, his outward-reaching wonder may ignore all the still and homelier virtues of his Anglo-Saxon home, but he has at least found the clue to that international mind which will be essential to all men and women of goodwill if they are ever to save this Western world of ours from suicide. His new friends have gone through a similar revolution. America has burned most of the baser metal also from them. Meeting now with this common American background, all of them may yet retain that distinctiveness of their native culture and their national spiritual slants. They are more valuable and interesting to each other for being different, yet that difference could not be creative were it not for this new cosmopolitan outlook which America has given them and which they all equally possess.

A college where such a spirit is possible even to the smallest degree, has within itself already the seeds of this international intellectual world of the future. It suggests that the contribution of America will be an intellectual internationalism which goes far beyond the mere exchange of scientific ideas and discoveries and the cold recording of facts. It will be an intellectual sympathy which is not satisfied until it has got at the heart of the different cultural expressions, and felt as they feel. It may have immense preferences, but it will make understanding and not indignation its end. Such a sympathy will unite and not divide. Against the thinly disguised panic which calls itself "patriotism" and the thinly disguised militarism which calls itself "preparedness" the cosmopolitan idea is set. This does not mean that those who hold it are for a policy of drift. They, too, long passionately for an integrated and disciplined America. But they do not want one which is integrated only for domestic economic exploitation of the workers or for predatory economic imperialism among the weaker peoples. They do not want one that is integrated by coercion or militarism, or for the truculent assertion of a medieval code of honor and of doubtful rights. They believe that the most effective integration will be one which coordinates the diverse elements and turns them consciously toward working out together the place of America in the world situation. They demand for integration a genuine integrity, a wholeness and soundness of enthusiasm and purpose which can only come when no national colony within our America feels that it is being discriminated against or that its cultural case is being prejudged. This strength of cooperation, this feeling that all who are here may have a hand in the destiny of America, will make for a finer spirit of integration than any narrow "Americanism" or forced chauvinism. In this effort we may have to accept some form of that dual citizenship which meets with so much articulate horror among us. Dual citizenship we may have to recognize as the rudimentary form of that international citizenship to which, if our words mean anything, we aspire. We have assumed unquestioningly that mere participation in the political life of the United States must cut the new citizen off from all sympathy with his old allegiance. Anything but a bodily transfer of devotion from one sovereignty to another has been viewed as a sort of moral treason against the Republic. We have insisted that the immigrant whom we welcomed escaping from the very exclusive nationalism of his

European home shall forthwith adopt a nationalism just as exclusive, just as narrow, and even less legitimate because it is founded on no warm traditions of his own. Yet a nation like France is said to permit a formal and legal dual citizenship even at the present time. Though a citizen of hers may pretend to cast off his allegiance in favor of some other sovereignty, he is still subject to her laws when he returns. Once a citizen, always a citizen, no matter how many new citizenships he may embrace. And such a dual citizenship seems to us sound and right. For it recognizes that, although the Frenchman may accept the formal institutional framework of his new country and indeed become intensely loyal to it, yet his Frenchness he will never lose. What makes up the fabric of his soul will always be of his Frenchness, so that unless he becomes utterly degenerate he will always to some degree dwell still in his native environment.

Indeed, does not the cultivated American who goes to Europe practice a dual citizenship, which, if not formal, is no less real? The American who lives abroad may be the least expatriate of men. If he falls in love with French ways and French thinking and French democracy and seeks to saturate himself with the new spirit, he is guilty of at least a dual spiritual citizenship. He may be still American, yet he feels himself through sympathy also a Frenchman. And he finds that this expansion involves no shameful conflict within him, no surrender of his native attitude. He has rather for the first time caught a glimpse of the cosmopolitan spirit. And after wandering about through many races and civilizations he may return to America to find them all here living vividly and crudely, seeking the same adjustment that he made. He sees the new peoples here with a new vision. They are no longer masses of aliens, waiting to be "assimilated," waiting to be melted down into the indistinguishable dough of Anglo-Saxonism. They are rather threads of living and potent cultures, blindly striving to weave themselves into a novel international nation, the first the world has seen. In an Austria-Hungary or a Prussia the stronger of these cultures would be moving instinctively to subjugate the weaker. But in America those wills-to-power are turned in a different direction into learning how to live together.

Along with dual citizenship we shall have to accept, I think, that free and mobile passage of the immigrant between America and his native land again which now arouses so much prejudice among us. We shall have to accept the immigrant's return for the same reason that we consider justified our own flitting about the earth. To stigmatize the alien who works in America for a few years and returns to his own land, only perhaps to seek American fortune again, is to think in narrow nationalistic terms. It is to ignore the cosmopolitan significance of this migration. It is to ignore the fact that the returning immigrant is often a missionary to an inferior civilization.

This migratory habit has been especially common with the unskilled laborers who have been pouring into the United States in the last dozen years from every country in southeastern Europe. Many of them return to spend their earnings in their own country or to serve their country in war. But they return with an entirely new critical outlook, and a sense of the superiority of American organization to the primitive living around them. This continued passage to and fro has already raised the material standard of living in many regions of these backward countries. For these regions are thus endowed with exactly what they need, the capital for the exploitation of their natural resources, and the spirit of enterprise. America is thus educating these laggard peoples from the very bottom of society up, awakening vast masses to a newborn hope for the future. In the migratory Greek, therefore, we have not the parasitic alien, the doubtful American asset, but a symbol of that cosmopolitan interchange which is coming, in spite of all war and national exclusiveness.

Only America, by reason of the unique liberty of opportunity and traditional isolation for which she seems to stand, can lead in this cosmopolitan enterprise. Only the American—and in this category I include the migratory alien who has lived with us and caught the pioneer "spirit and a sense of new social vistas—has the chance to become that citizen of the world. America is coming to be, not a nationality but a transnationality, a weaving back and forth, with the other lands, of many threads of all sizes and colors. Any movement which attempts to thwart this weaving, or to dye the fabric any one color, or disentangle the threads of the strands, is false to this cosmopolitan vision. I do not mean that we shall necessarily glut ourselves with the raw product of humanity. It would be folly to absorb the nations faster than we could weave them. We have no duty either to admit or reject. It is purely a question of expediency. What concerns us is the fact that the strands are here. We must have a policy and an ideal for an actual situation. Our question is: What shall we do with our America? How are we likely to get the more creative America by confining our imaginations to the ideal of the melting pot, or broadening them to some such cosmopolitan conception as I have been vaguely sketching?

The war has shown America to be unable, though isolated geographically and politically from a European world situation, to remain aloof and irresponsible. She is a wandering star in a sky dominated by two colossal constellations of states. Can she not work out some position of her own, some life of being in, yet not quite of, this seething and embroiled European world? This is her only hope and promise. A trans-nationality of all the nations, it is spiritually impossible for her to pass into the orbit of any one. It will be folly to hurry herself into a premature and sentimental nationalism, or to emulate Europe and play fast and loose with the forces that drag into war. No Americanization will fulfill this vision which does not recognize the uniqueness of this trans-nationalism of ours. The Anglo-Saxon attempt to fuse will only create enmity and distrust. The crusade against "hyphenates" will only inflame the partial patriotism of trans-nationals, and cause them to assert their European traditions in strident and unwholesome ways. But the attempt to weave a wholly novel international nation out of our chaotic America will liberate and harmonize the creative power of all these peoples and give them the new spiritual citizenship, as so many individuals have already been given, of a world.

Is it a wild hope that the undertow of opposition to metaphysics in international relations, opposition to militarism, is less a cowardly provincialism than a groping for this higher cosmopolitan ideal? One can understand the irritated restlessness with which our proud pro-British colonists contemplate a heroic conflict across the seas in which they have no part. It was inevitable that our necessary inaction should evolve in their minds into the bogey of national shame and dishonor. But let us be careful about accepting their sensitiveness as final arbiter. Let us look at our reluctance rather as the first crude beginnings of assertion on the part of certain strands in our nationality that they have a right to a voice in the construction of the American ideal. Let us face realistically the America we have around us. Let us work with the forces that are at work. Let us make something of this trans-national spirit instead of outlawing it. Already we are living this cosmopolitan America. What we need is everywhere a vivid consciousness of the new ideal. Deliberate headway must be made against the survivals of the melting pot ideal for the promise of American life.

We cannot Americanize America worthily by sentimentalizing and moralizing history. When the best schools are expressly renouncing the questionable duty of teaching patriotism by means of history, it is not the time to force shibboleth upon the immigrant. This form of Americanization has been heard because it appealed to the vestiges of our old sentimentalized and moralized patriotism. This has so far held the field as the expression of the new American's new devotion. The inflections of other voices have been drowned. They must be heard. We must see if the lesson of the war has not been for hundreds of these later Americans a vivid realization of their transnationality, a new consciousness of what America meant to them as a citizenship in the world. It is the vague historic idealisms which have provided the fuel for the European flame. Our American ideal can make no progress until we do away with this romantic gilding of the past.

All our idealism must be those of future social goals in which all can participate, the good life of personality lived in the environment of the Beloved Community. No mere doubtful triumphs of the past, which redound to the glory of only one or our trans-nationalities, can satisfy us. It must be a future America, on which all can unite, which pulls us irresistibly toward it, as we understand each other more warmly.

To make real this striving amid dangers and apathies is work for a younger intelligentsia of America. Here is an enterprise of integration into which we can all pour ourselves, of a spiritual welding which should make us, if the final menace ever came, not weaker, but infinitely strong.

(1916)

Introduction

Dmytro Zakharchuk

Zakharchuk wrote the following introduction for his second book of poems.

This is a small book of simple verses written in a foreign language. These words are filled with memories and love for my motherland and the village where I was born.

All these poems were written here—overseas, and almost all were published in Ukrainian magazines. I have assembled them in order to publish this small book. I do not expect to have many buyers because most Ukrainians do not desire to read books, even those written by the best authors.

I still have hope, and have published these few hundred volumes on my own expense because I would like those here in a foreign land to love their place of birth.

Parents should give this book to their children so that they can learn how wonderful and magical our homeland is far away over the sea. Every home should have this book because it is only with books that we can fight and prevent a decline in our culture. Children, born here, bit by bit feel ashamed of their wonderful Ukrainian language. They change their names because they think their parents come from distant strange places, and only America is good.

This is not so. That is why these verses will show them clearly that Ukraine is a beautiful land with a wonderful language, songs and everything else that is Ukrainian.

(1934)

Foreign Country

Dmytro Zakharchuk

He went overseas looking for a better future. He worked and saved money for his return home.

Once he fell in love with a nice girl born in the United States. They loved each other. He thought he would be happy only with her. Many years went by. When he returned from work his children would come to him and say Tata, Tata! More years went by. The children grew and went their own way. His wife died and he was laid off from work because he was too old.

His own house was taken from him by the mortgage company even though he worked for the house all his life. He ended without one cent. One day he looked at the sunrise and saw his native land. The sun kissed his grey hair and he remembered everything and became homesick. He decided to go there no matter what the price.

So he came back to his own land, to his home village. He knew everything—hills, valleys, fields. He returned to his village and said thanks to God for allowing him to live on his home land for his last days.

And now he lives and remembers the foreign land. What of his children? They forgot him. Only his land makes him happy.

There are many like him in foreign lands.

(1934)

Paderewski

Dorothy Dudley

Chicago: February sixth, 1916

Let the sun weep and the moon shed tears—
A sun god is ravaged,
Poland dying, and cold.

"We saw babies sucking beet roots,
Wrapped in rags;
Starvation, ruin, mould."

Let great elegance weep, fierceness and pride:
There, in front of Poland's flag,
Paderewski, passionate, cold.

And the light flamed of Poland's years.
And Chopin from her crags—
A clear proud story told.

Let the sun weep and the moon his bride:
Great art is ravaged,
Poland desolate and cold.

(1917)

Paderewski: Ignacy Jan Paderewski (1860–1941), Polish composer, musician, and diplomat. Paderewski was prime minister of Poland from November 1918 to January 1919, afterward becoming Poland's ambassador to the League of Nations.

A Polish Girl

Max Michelson

You carry the dishes in your hands
But your thoughts are elsewhere:

As if you inwardly knew
That in your kisses is the glow
Of Sobietsky* and the heroes;

That your body has the pungent taste
Which the willow-tree and the rose
Perhaps feel in the soil;

And that your hair carries the fragrance
Of the willow and the rose itself.

(1917)

*Sobietsky: Likely Jan Sobieski (1629–1696), renowned military commander and king of Poland and grand
duke of Lithuania from 1674 until his death.

The Island of Desire

Robert Haven Schauffler

The day tulips first bloomed in Union Square I solemnly swore to keep in their general vicinity. For I knew that after their advent the periphery of Manhattan was no place for people like me—especially West Street.

Where the sea-dogs rolled, like so many groundswells, past windows full of oilskins and little Metropolitan Towers in mother-of-pearl, celluloid collars in soak, and open-work plates decorated with the flags of all nations intertwined; where cabs bursting with luggage marked WANTED! galloped up to the docks at the last second with their anxious occupants hanging half out of the windows, as palpably outward bound as their luggage—where these things were in evidence was a dangerous place for Grant Winecoop.

It was dangerous for me because I had already hung out of those same cab windows too often for my own welfare. The location of my rooms is to blame for this fact. For Washington Square is too near Greenwich Village, which in turn is much too near West Street, which in its turn is too inhumanly near Europe.

Since leaving college I had half a dozen times been on the point of really making good in business. And each time the same thing had happened.

Over beyond where Fourth Street gets lost and runs into Twelfth Street I had been taking an innocent sunset stroll, trying to ignore the still, small voice that—night and day in springtime—never stops calling to me from somewhere out beyond Sandy Hook. And then all at once something had chimed in with that voice; it might have been only some important little tug with the catarrh, or the almost audible smell of a tarred rope, or an Italian longshoreman footing a tarantella on a holystoned deck. But suddenly the voice had swelled into irresistibility, and before I knew it I had found myself hanging out of a cab window.

The trouble was that my family was distinctly unsympathetic about these travels of mine. I suppose it is because they have never been "Hull down on the trail of rapture" themselves.

In fact, I had such a bad time with my father after the fifth trip that I held out against the sixth for three springs. And then when I finally found myself gliding out from Hoboken's Elysian Fields, I swore a sturdy oath never to return.

Of course I had to break it, though. There's something about Europe one can't stand more than so many months at a time. It's the men, I guess.

Well, when I got home last fall, there was such a serious ruction, and father demonstrated so irrefutably that he would cut me off with a lead quarter if I left again before I had made good, that I resolved then and there not only to keep to the central portion of the island as soon as tulips bloomed in Union Square, but also to stick exclusively to business and the serious side of life, and cut out the Princeton Club and the gang.

I soon found out, though, that this wasn't enough to do. I should have put atropine into my eyes and bought a pair of scientific ear-tabs such as old Herbert Spencer used to produce from his pocket and clap on at table whenever his fair neighbor's conversation bored him and he wished to meditate.

This is how I fell. On an April Friday afternoon I was keeping my vow by riding on the Broadway car, and fighting the still, small voice by reflecting on the sublimity of the Lincoln monument near Dead Man's Curve, when the power gave out and the car obligingly stopped where I could enjoy the sunset down the length of Thirteenth Street. As I looked the golden west was blotted by an even fairer vision. The funnels of a huge ocean liner swung across the street end.

The blood began roaring in my ears somewhat (I realized it afterwards) as the surf roars along the coast of the Riviera. My fingers unconsciously crushed flat—and ruined—the roll of music I was taking home on approval. And the other passengers were already beginning to eye me with curiosity or concern when I pulled myself together, made for the door, and dashed away from that terribly alluring sight.

To shake off the spell of those funnels required a regular campaign of oblivion including dinner at Rector's, a little tour through the land of vaudeville, a game of squash with the marker at the Athletic club, and a Turkish bath.

This course of treatment was so effective that, when I came to retire, the funnels had lost their clear-cut, compelling outlines on the ground glass of my mental camera. I even sneered at them as at so many Harlem factory chimneys, and lay down glorying in the sturdy Anglo-Saxon fortitude of my character.

The next moment it was morning and I was sitting up, sleepy but tingling with excitement. My blood was beginning again to imitate the Riviera surf. What was that loud, hoarse wail floating across the city?

All at once the conscious part of me recognized it, and knew as well that endurance had at last been strained to the snapping point.

I made a leap to the floor, pulled a steamer trunk out from under the bed, and began throwing things into it.

There was a knock, and Lyall came in. I was hardly surprised. For Lyall is the man with the sixth sense. He always knows when anything unusual is happening to a fellow and is always on hand. If you have neuralgia or a hopeless passion, if you need a loan or are thinking for any reason of throwing yourself in front of a subway train, Lyall will turn up within the half-hour and set you straight. Or if Helen of Troy has just accepted you under pledges of profound secrecy, or if your Western aunt has left you fifty thousand only ten minutes ago, Lyall will be on hand to dine you and wine you in the one case, or, in the other, to levy a fat subscription for that Goodwill House of his that he runs down somewhere in the slums.

"What are you going to do?" asked Lyall, though perfectly aware all the time what I was going to do.

" 'I am fevered with the sunrise,' " I misquoted,

> 'I am fretful with the bay,
> For the wander-thirst is on me
> And my soul is in Cathay.' "*

"Oh, yes," he laughed; "I know all about that 'schooner in the offing with her topsails shot with fire; and your heart has gone aboard her for the Islands of Desire,' eh? Yes, my boy; but how about your father?"

"Confound you, Lyall!" I exclaimed. "How can I think about father with that thing in my ears?"

I nodded in the direction of the river, where the liner that had waked me with its hoarse bass voice was still roaring admonition to men to go ashore if they did not wish to go abroad.

Lyall at once adopted a different tack.

"Well, then, what particular islands of desire may you be bound for?"

"Greece first," I answered, luxuriously. "Then Brindisi and slowly up through the 'Boot' to my beloved Slavic countries. I guess it'll be mostly Bohemia this time."

"My dear Winecoop"—his voice took on its most persuasive quality— "what is it you're after over there, anyway? Because if it's painting and sculpture and architecture, are you sure you quite realize what we are beginning to do in that line ourselves? For instance, have you been up to the Metropolitan or the new cathedral lately?"

I thought a little before replying. "No, Lyall, it's not so much the art I crave. I suppose it's more the people themselves, with their mysterious charm, their indefinable atmosphere— the romantic humans in their real settings."

All at once Lyall looked relieved.

"Oh, that's it? Well, then, I can cure you."

"Of what?"

"Why, of this *Wanderlust*, of course. I'll write you out a prescription now, and inside of twenty-four hours you'll be a well man."

"Canst thou minister to a mind diseased?" I sneered.

"Certainly," said Lyall.

I laughed, and went on packing. My visitor seized me by the shoulder so that it hurt.

---

*These lines are from Richard Hovey's 1896 poem, "The Sea Gypsy." The first line, misquoted here by Winecoop, reads: "I am fevered with the sunset." The title of Schauffler's story adapts the second stanza of Hovey's poem: "There's a schooner in the offing, / With her topsails shot with fire, / And my heart has gone aboard her / For the Islands of Desire."

"But I mean it. I'm in dead earnest. What'll become of Goodwill House if your father cuts you off with a lead quarter, I should like to know? Besides," he added, relapsing into the persuasive tone, "even if you're going in spite of me, my course of treatment won't delay you an hour. You can't possibly get a southern route boat before tomorrow. Besides, if you're stubborn, you'll never know what you missed. Now, I'll give you till the middle of the afternoon to pack."

The fellow certainly knew how to tickle my not inconsiderable bump of curiosity.

"Well," I grunted, "if it won't delay me."

At that the fellow actually sat down as gravely authoritative as any M.D. who ever prescribed bread pills for an imaginary neur-aesthete, pulled out his notebook, scribbled a sheetful, tore it off, and handed it over.

I saw only a jumble of names and numbers. The directions at the bottom ran: "Take Saturday after midday meal. Shake (yourself free of provincialism) before using."

That afternoon I took the Subway to Brooklyn Bridge, threaded my way through the drunken sailors of Park Row, doubled into the narrow squalor of Roosevelt Street, and, with a pitying laugh at my absent physician and a glance at his scrawl, began searching unwillingly for the first ingredient of the prescription, which was "No. 601."

Then something happened. A woman in a drab shawl passed. I first noticed her fixed eyes, so aggressively, orientally ignoring the very existence of all beings of the other sex; then the shawl half drawn across the lower face, suggesting past ages of harem discipline; and, above, the level, divinely molded brow of a marble Pallas Athene. She went her way, cold, immobile; but in a flash I was wandering again about the streets of modern Athens, alone, rather homesick, and marveling at this race of magnificent women who walked abroad less humanly than a race of nuns.

No. 601, according to the Greek letters on the glass, proved to be the Café Sophocles. There was something very like a sensation inside when I opened the door.

Half a dozen handsome youths were sitting around the stove smoking water pipes. At my entrance they broke off their merry chatter as if startled, and eyed me as though among Americans I were the first that had ever burst into that tranquil haven of the new Hellas. And they were no more surprised than I, who had never dreamed before my first delighted glance around their café that the authentic atmosphere of Socrates's land could ever thus be translated overseas. But I knew enough to pay no more attention to them than the Pallas outside had paid to me, and under this treatment they slowly recovered their normal tone.

Meanwhile I focused on the cup of real Turkish coffee and the delicious, familiar confection impaled in the Greek fashion on a long spit. And these took me back at once to the busy sidewalk cafés of Hermes Street.

Cigarettes followed, of a savor that Fifth Avenue has never attained. Nor had I, either, since my last dip in the waters of Corfu. I remembered how I had dived into that crystalline harbor of the Phaeacians in honor of the crafty Ulysses and his record swim, and my regret that the white-armed Nausicaa had not had a fragrant packet of them to offer the hero after his rub down, and perchance light one for him between her own dainty lips. All this came back at the first puff.

On the walls of the Café Sophocles hung a large photograph of the poor old Parthenon (what the Turks and their internal powder have left of it), and another one of a rare bronze I knew in the Naples Museum, which happened to be a surprising likeness of the waiter. Three of the lovely long necked lutes called *mpouzouki* hung over a rack stuck full of letters with Greek stamps waiting for the habitués of the place.

A young fellow who was twin brother of the Hermes of Praxiteles began a game of cards with the living image of the Discobolus. As he studied his hand he hummed himself a plaintive old folk song that I had once heard a shepherd playing on a yellow reed while his goats cropped among the fallen columns of Olympia. And all at once the Café Sophocles was filled with the same happy tranquility that I had breathed one morning of sunshine and light airs while wandering in the olive groves of Academe.

Delightedly I realized that these young gods were forgetting my nationality and losing the constraint which the intrusion had brought into this home of theirs.

Presently one of them made a friendly advance. Before falling back on English I used up my small Greek vocabulary on him. The rest looked up pleased. Cigarette cases flashed generously out.

"Had I, then, an interest in things Grecian?"

"Yes, indeed! The more for having been in their land."

"When was that?"

"In 1906."

"To attend the Olympic Games?"

"Yes."

The circle around the fire was visibly commoved. The Discobolus forced his chair upon me. The waiter, unbidden, hastened for a second cup of coffee. The Hermes introduced himself as one of the 1906 Marathon runners.

There followed an hour of Pindaric reminiscences.

Then I rose and put the long-necked lute into the hands of the Discobolus with an entreaty, and he tuned it up with an almost religious solemnity while the rest hushed their talk. After a patient search through his pockets for a quill as plectrum, he struck up, over a drone bass, a wild, minor air, strong with the strength of his native Spartan hills, and sad with the sadness of those remembering vanished happiness in an unhappy time.

At that I gripped each brown hand and left in haste. My one idea was to make for the shipping offices on lower Broadway before they closed. I though of Lyall with a sneer. What sort of a fiery and inflaming drink was this that he had prescribed for my fever?

I snatched the prescription from my pocket to tear it up, when these words caught my eye: "Stroll slowly up Mulberry Street to Grand."

Then I remembered promising my friend to taste his draught to the dregs, and turned reluctantly into the din and the foul tawdriness of the new Italy. Roosevelt Street had been almost as quiet, as discreetly reserved, as the summit of the Acropolis. Now Mulberry Street rang with the joyous din of the Roman Corso in carnival time.

In the small triangle of park this uproar melted by degrees into the *dolce far niente*—the "sweet do nothing"—which the warm south takes like a bromo-seltzer after its daily emotional debauch.

The feline luxury of these folk as they basked in the strong sunlight took me back to certain wonderful afternoons on the Spanish Steps and along the verges of the Bay of Naples, with old Vesuvius smoking lazily beyond the dancing blue waves.

An aged ruffian approached, peddling those long, thin black cigars with straws inside them which you light yesterday and throw away tomorrow. For old sake's sake I let him sell me one.

I strolled up a street filled with a thousand satisfying reminders of the magic land. The wordless bargaining over the prismatic pushcarts made me feel again like a child—so keen was it, so superbly did those natural pantomimists carry it on by gesture and expression and pose.

There were tiny shops hung with paper holly that dealt in "Fruits of the Seas," such as prawns and periwinkles, and all kinds of curious shellfish. There were carts full of artichokes and red peppers. But, to my shame as an American, I found the most Italian touch of all in the little book stalls that were doing a brisk business in such literature as Dante and Hugo and the "Arabian Nights," Swift, Goethe, the Bible, and d'Annunzio.

To make themselves feel more thoroughly at home, the people had stuck up here and there branches of orange and lemon filled with the fresh fruit.

Three goats were devouring a felt hat on some basement steps. Queening it on the floor below sat a girl with flying fingers. She was brown and luring as a gypsy. A large black comb full of brilliants nearly covered the back of her head. Sitting there among the bright colored rags she was sorting, she looked like a fairy princess arranging her jewels and laces. And I felt like abasing myself before that daughter of a folk with a sense of beauty that could thus make squalor delightful and even thrilling.

Presently, before I knew it, Grand Street had come, and Lyall's prescription directed me to dine at the "Azure Grotto of Capri." (This, of course, is not its real name. It would never do to have it Americanized.)

I found it easily, and, after one suspicious glance around, stifled a sigh of pleasure and genuine relief. For in the New World this was the first Italian restaurant I had found that had apparently discovered neither America nor bohemia with a small b.

There sat the padrona at the receipt of custom, solemnly lighting a long cigar in a candle flame for the grizzled guest who leaned ingratiatingly over her counter in the true classical style. There was the single little mouse colored waiter running about among the tables as nimbly and silently as the little donkeys that pad the lanes of Florence on their mouse-like feet.

The padrona beamed upon me. Before I was well within the room the padrone, her spouse, wished me "Good appetite!" The little waiter performed amazing acrobatics about my table and chair, all expressive of the loftiest flights of the spirit of Italian hospitality.

Barely seated, I swallowed an orange cordial; then ladled out of a huge tureen a plate of exceedingly "busy" soup, which Hamilcare (for the waiter had already introduced himself) kindly sprinkled with grated Parmesan. There followed *tagliatalli*, the macaroni of the gods, decked with a delicious meat sauce and more Parmesan. Hard upon that came *scaloppini con Marsala*— minute veal cutlets translated into a higher sphere—and all this accompanied by real *vino de Vesuvio* out of a straw-covered flask.

Then for dessert a tall glass of *Zabbaione*, while the padrona arranged my cigar on the candle rack. For all these mercies my check declared that fifty-five cents were due.

I had forgotten about Lyall, but in fumbling after a nickel for the already grateful Hamilcare (it would have spoiled him to give him more) I drew out the prescription and read its last ingredient, a certain number on East Seventy-fourth Street.

Still lost in the spell of Italy, I wandered towards the Bowery, stopping a moment to see the devoted crowds festooning the houses of Elizabeth Street, arching the roadway with red and white and green bunting, and building wayside shrines here and there for the coming *festa*.

Even the brutal Yankee realism of the Elevated could not shake me out of my reverie. I glowed to think that the dear Italians could make themselves so very much at home in my country—could actually charm one of their hosts, by their magic arts, to fly in spirit across the foam, if only for an hour, and so gain respite from the *Wanderlust* that had been consuming him.

For, as I suddenly realized, the dull ache of the disease was unmistakably better. In fact, for the last couple of hours I had been as unconscious of it as if climbing the olive slopes above Amalfi, or loafing against Giotto's Tower, or watching the gleam of pale St. Peter's dome across the moldering aqueducts that dot the Campagna.

"Seventy-six!" yelled the guard, and, still in a daze, I climbed to the pavement and went a full block before awaking with a start, not to Italy this time, nor Greece, nor even America, but to the country of Dvorák and Smetana and Huss.

A Bohemian funeral was coming up Second Avenue. First of all was an open barouche overflowing with floral crosses and anchors; then a band, the men pacing slowly and playing, as if they really felt it, a mighty, somber march filled with the lustrous melancholy of Slavonic lands. Then a white hearse escorted by a troop of little flower girls in white, and followed by a company of patriot athletes with the festively colored scarfs of the Sokols across their breasts and the red and white banners of Bohemia floating aloft. Last of all rumbled a single hack with shades lifted just enough to reveal a mother's face, tear-drenched, convulsed, wholly given up to such an abandon as the undemonstrative Slavs yields to only in the few supreme moments of life.

With that stately, tragic music still in my ears, I sought the given number and mounted two flights of stairs to find a large hall filled with dancers in mellow Old World costumes. I stared around in astonishment. This was no other than a Slavonic village green in festival time. Lyall had sent me to the famous Bohemia Peasant Ball!

How charmingly familiar the girls' scarlet stockings and low slippers looked beneath the short petticoats of infinite plaits, overlaid with rainbow aprons! How spirited the embroidered shirts of the men and their gaily braided trousers tucked into the high boots! And everywhere were those touches of clear, bright red which the Slav best knows how to use.

I went up into the deserted gallery as the music stopped and the parading began without which no Slavonic function is complete.

The floor was cleared by two cavaliers who sidled their dummy horses cleverly against the crowd. First came the priest with his acolyte, as in all village processions; then the fat matchmakers under his red umbrella, paired with the village notary, his quill over his ear and his inkpot slung about his neck; the ubiquitous Slovak tinker followed, and the chimneysweep with ladder and scraper; after them the Jewish peddler from across the border in a flowing kaftan, with his basket of knickknacks; and, last of all, the night watchman, with halberd and lantern and long porcelain pipe.

As for me up there in the gallery, I was rapt away into the very heart of Bohemia among its strange, proud, stolid, gloomy people, apparently so cold and dull and sullen, yet full in the depths of them of color and fire, of music passionate poetry—people that blossom out so touchingly in response to a little human tenderness, much as the colors of the opal blossom brighter for the warmth of the human hand.

As I sat there the wonder of the day began to dawn on me. Since plunging into Roosevelt Street it was as if I had been borne constantly farther and farther from any America that I had ever known. I began to feel almost like a stranger in some forgotten corner of the Old World, with months between himself and the group of friendly handkerchiefs that had once fluttered him farewell from the pier-head.

Slowly the illusion grew stronger, sharper. As I gazed down at the strange costumes, the high cheekbones, the small, heavy eyes of those foreign men, an obscure impulse seized me and hurried me out into the street and westward to the park, and set me strolling down Fifth Avenue under the young April moon.

That was a stroll to dream about. For, somehow or other, my vision seemed strangely fresh. The spires of St. Patrick's had never soared so airily for me as in that glowing sky, flushed with the weekend flare of the Great White Way. Nor had the Library ever seemed as noble, nor the Metropolitan Tower as mighty.

Down by Twenty-first Street I caught sight of the old "gang" I had long shunned, straggling home from the Princeton Club. And they, too, seemed positively glorified in my eyes.

I rushed up to them and began shaking hands all around, with heart in each grip. Lyall was with them, and his hand I wrung particularly hard. It was a delight to see and feel such strong, virile, clean young fellow creatures and to talk their language.

"*Hel*lo, where'd you drop from?" they greeted me.

"Where you been keeping yourself?"

"Been on another of your little trips abroad?"

"That's what I have," I answered, and sped a grateful look at Lyall. "It was a corking trip, too. But you've no idea how glad I am to be back!"

(1912)

The Greenhorn in America

Maria Moravsky

"Oh, I cannot live here, I am always late! Everybody runs ahead! The crowd on the street is so restless! Why are they hurrying so?"

This is the first complaint which hospitable America hears from the Russian immigrant. We are a slow, quiet nation. One of our national stories illustrates this.

"Ivan, Ivan," says the mistress to her servant, "give a handful of hay to the horses, and take a rest."

After two hours she calls again,—

"Ivan, Ivan, shut the door of the hall, and take a rest."

Three hours later.—

"Ivan, look at the church clock, and tell me what time it is, and take a rest."

The Russian people have a contemplative soul and are rather lazy. We are nearer to primitive life, when man worked as much as was absolutely necessary to cover his important needs when he ate, slept, hunted, picked flowers, and had nothing more to do. The sweet remembrance of that plain life lives in the half-oriental soul of the Russian people, and its traditions are potent.

When a few Europeanized Russian manufacturers tried to transplant Taylor's system into their country, there resulted innumerable strikes, and the poor bosses, who were too advanced for our labor environment, were carried out of the factories on wheelbarrows.*

Such a shame!

The circumstances under which the workingmen of Russia can work are usually as follows:—

They come to the shop or factory half an hour late; and sometimes after a family holiday the delay is greater. At other times, after they have been thoroughly scolded by the boss, the delay is shorter, but as a rule they are late.

Before going to work they drink their tea. Do you know how we Russians drink tea? It resembles a religious ceremony; one must not hurry, when he drinks his tea.

---

*Frederick Winslow Taylor (1856–1915), a well-known management consultant whose studies of time management and efficiency vastly improved worker productivity. From a management point of view, "Taylorism," as his ideas became known, was a boon; to many in labor, Taylorism was a dehumanizing force in factory life.

After that they would begin to work. Of course, they did not work very quickly. They would take a rest as often as Ivan did in the story. The boss tried to cheer them up at such times. Every day you would hear a nice conversation between administrators and the employed. I must confess that it was not a literary talk, although very flowery; they blamed each other artistically. They would discover so many new and amazing words! Our people are talented, you know.

I must admit that they were always underpaid and had long hours of work. Naturally, they were not interested in "doing their duty." The conditions in our factories were beneath criticism: the choking air, the dirt, and the small working rooms. Nobody, not even the most patient and humble Russian peasant, could stand it without making a protest. And as they were not strong enough to protest openly, they practiced the Italian strike, which became the habit, the second nature of the Russian worker.

The same traditions of delay prevailed in our offices, in our schools, everywhere! We did not appreciate the value of time; or, perhaps, we appreciated it too much to waste it on boring everyday work. It depends on one's point of view.

The same advanced bosses who tried in vain to teach Taylor's system to Russians, attempted to abandon our tradition of delay. In a few offices were established automatic clock machines, to note the time of the worker's arrival. This was instituted in wartime. I remember the big munition factory where that "devilish American invention" appeared for the first time.

The workers held a meeting and found the remedy for defeating the enemy machine.

"I will throw sand in its mouth," said one of the bravest.

So he did. The expensive clock was destroyed by sand and the small stones which were dropped into its mechanism. The tradition "to come a bit later" was saved once more.

Here in America such a thing would be impossible.

I notice, to my great surprise, that not laborers only, but even "professionals," must do their work scrupulously on time, and hurry, hurry, always hurry! How terrible for a genuine Russian greenhorn!

It was a great shock to me when I was called for the first time to an American magazine office, to translate from Russian to English. The editor telephoned to me,—

"Will you kindly undertake that little work? It has to be done pretty soon."

"All right. Please send it to me by mail."

"No!" answered the editor indignantly; "you had better come to the office immediately. We are in a hurry."

It struck me as a shot. He could not wait even a few days, although it was not for a daily paper! It amazed me.

Mechanically I put on my overcoat and went to the office; but all the way I murmured to myself with a deep disapproval, "Why on earth are they in such a hurry?"

I bet you cannot understand my feeling. The poor greenhorn must worry alone: the natives would laugh at her troubles. But I want to describe to you a little scene in the Russian office, so you may see the big gulf between your life and mine. It is difficult for the Russian immigrant to jump across it at once.

The young man comes to the Russian editor. The latter summoned him two days before—by mail, of course, because there is not a telephone in every flat in our cities. The young writer is out of work, but the day before he had a headache and a "rendezvous," so he was too busy to come at once.

The editor begins,—

"How do you do, dear Petr Petrovich? How is everything at home? Take a seat, please."

"Thank you. Mother is preparing a new sort of jam. Do you like the jam made of the rose petals? Come and taste it some time. Mother makes it splendidly."

"Thank you very much. Will you take a glass of tea?" (In Russia we drink it in glasses.) "Ivan, fetch the samovar."

After the third glass of weak tea (the Russians have to drink it weak—another important remark), and a little talk about politics, the editor says,—

"By the way, I have a little work for you. Would you like to translate that section of the English book? Just for quotation, you know."

"Sure! How soon do you need it?"

"Oh, we are in no hurry—a week, or two."

"I have nothing to do now, so I can do it at once."

"So much the better. You will send it next week, then?"

What do you think of such a life, my dear American friends? I am conscience-stricken to have to confess that my comrade greenhorns remember it as lost paradise. Theoretically I always disagree with them. Very often I would talk and write, that our slowness and laziness ruin Russia. Russian writers always used to write about it. The famous Goncharoff's *Oblomoff* is a novel about our national laziness. Our literature, which is called the "conscience" of our nation, was always fighting against that "tradition of rest."

I myself wrote a book, which should have proved by statistics the number of hours we lose daily, weekly, and monthly. There were dreadfully eloquent strings of figures, and they proved to my countrymen, without doubt, that we were always at the tail of every civilized nation, because of our bad habit of delay; and that now we are many centuries behind the time. (It was written before the present revolution.) There was a lot of good advice in my book, and it would have been very helpful to my countrymen; but, I regret to say, it was never printed, owing to a few mathematical mistakes: in some parts of my work there were too many 00000, in others too few of them. You understand, they are such trifles, these 00000; but my publisher (he had a dry heart) said to me,—

"My dear Miss Moravsky, you would do better to continue writing poems and fiction; statistics are not your element."

So my role of social reformer was stopped at the beginning.

But let me drop those disagreeable personal recollections. I will continue more objectively.

My people would never be capable of such a heroic deed as to be at the office on time. Never! Nobody! Even the Bolsheviki, who are in such a hurry and have tried to solve twenty-seven big social reforms daily. I bet you that neither Mr. Trotzky nor Mr. Lenin are on time at their headquarters in the Kremlin. It would be against all their habits. I know the Bolsheviki; I was a Bolshevik myself, when I was fifteen.

I remember the secret meetings of our revolutionary students, belonging to different parties, which were held at night in the University of Odessa. Our president was a Bolshevik.

There was no light in the large hall (we were cautious enough and realized that the light might betray us). A few of us carried small dark lanterns, the speakers talked from the marble table on which the medical students used to chop corpses, and I enjoyed it immensely, because everything recalled to me stories of pirates. (I always had an entirely boyish imagination.)

The seventeenth of the youthful speakers had repeated for the seventeenth time that Tsarism should be overthrown at once, when our watchman came and, approaching the president Bolshevik, said with a slightly trembling voice—

"Comrade president, the police have been told about our meeting. A comrade from the telephone station overheard it; the order to arrest us was given five minutes ago."

There began a little disorder among the conspirators. They stood up, and a few of them moved toward the entrance. But the president Bolshevik said—

"Five minutes ago—hum—we have plenty of time to finish our meeting; our police is slow enough. Please comrade, continue your speech, but keep closer to facts. We all know perfectly well that Tsarism must be overthrown. But state your practical proposition about that newly organized district."

The meeting continued. Half an hour later the second watchman entered and said breathlessly,—

"Comrades, it is high time to flee! The regiment of Cossacks is ordered to seize us."

We began to move again; but the Bolshevik president lifted his hands calmly and commanded,—

"Be still! Say, comrade watchman, where is that regiment of Cossacks located?"

"On the Kulikovo Pole."

"That is a long distance from here, seven or eight versts, and they have to dress themselves and to lead out their horses."

"But the order was given twenty minutes ago!"

"Be quiet, comrades, we have time yet. Don't you know our Cossacks?"

And he knew them well. After nearly half an hour of talking, we left the hall; and after we had parted peacefully, some of us met the Cossacks and gendarmes approaching the university building at full speed. They seemed to realize that they were a bit late!

II

We Russians were used to that kind of slow work, even under the pressure of danger. We never accomplished very much in a short time. But the results depend not always on the quickness of work. On the contrary, it is impossible for people who are always in a hurry to do things thoughtfully and carefully. It is impossible for a political party; it is impossible even for a trade company!

For instance: goods manufactured in America with such tremendous speed are made unskillfully, crudely; they are expensive and yet are not durable. I am talking about the clothes, the toilet articles, and generally about the things which I examined in everyday use. They are far inferior to the French and Russian goods. A pair of Russian shoes could be worn two years, and yet they cost less than American shoes. The delicate hats made in Paris last twice as long as American hats. The good silk dresses from Japan last several years; fur coats from Siberia are handed down from grandmothers to grandchildren as good as new. But here the dainty silken frocks often last no more than five or six months. This is the result of your speedy industries.

If the result of the speed is so bad for the mere goods, how much worse it must be for politics and art! I will not talk about politics—it is wartime, you know. But I think I may safely tell some bitter truths about your current literature, and your theatre.

I made an experiment: I exchanged the ends and the beginnings in some American short stories from the popular magazines—the parts fitted to each other perfectly after that vivisection. Is not that horrible? The stories made to order, made by dozens, like the machine-made shoes!

Of course, America has her great writers, admired by all the world. But their best works were never made in a hurry for the Sunday paper. And many of these writers died in poverty, like Edgar Allan Poe, because they were not suited to your modern speedy civilization.

The American theatre is not a temple, as in Russian, but merely a place of amusement. Can you Americans send your young people to see the modern drama, with the purpose to enrich their souls? No, your theatres, although rich in scenical effects, have not high enough standards. You yourself would laugh if one should call your theatre the school of life. Many of your comedies remind one of ready-made clothes. You have books which teach the beginner how to make a successful drama. But no one book can teach people how to make a good drama. Your writers think too much about quick success and money, and too little about sacred Art.

"Oh, the greenhorn begins to preach!" says the reader. "Is it not too bold for a newcomer to criticize our hospitable country?"

I know it may look too bold. But I criticize America with a loving heart. I do want to see her perfect, because she was the land of my dream, long ago before I came here; and it is so hard to be disappointed with one's long-kept dream!

But the half-disappointed greenhorn loves America in spite of all her faults, and this is the reason she publishes her experiences; perhaps they may be of some use for her American friends.

I always suffer when I see how they spoil, with the best intentions, their art and their goods, their love and their digestion; all because they always hurry so much!

They are especially unkind to their poor stomachs.

A friend of mine, a very stolid and serious person, repeated to me when we happened to dine together,—

"Eat slowly. Sir Gladstone ate slowly. Every healthy great man ate slowly. Don't spoil your stomach." (He was a physician.)

I came almost to hate him. He used to chew his meals as slowly as a whole herd of cows. But now, in America, when I see in the restaurant the crowd of people who devour their lunches with the speed of a first class automobile, and who ruin daily their tired stomachs, because of their habit of hurrying, I recall my doctor friend with a grateful feeling. And I think it would be very helpful to your nation to have hung in every lunch shop a cartoon with these words,—

GLADSTONE ATE SLOWLY

It would be even better, although more expensive, to print the portrait of Sir Gladstone in full and to put below,—

HE ATE SLOWLY!

But I leave the details of my genial proposition to the city father.

The laws of the stomach are violated in America no more often than the laws of the heart.

When I came to America I heard about the enormous percentage of divorces here. I was surprised, and for a short time I formed a bad opinion about American husbands and wives. But I realize, now, that it was a wrong opinion of a greenhorn, who did not get the spirit of the new country. Now I know better; surely American husbands, and especially American wives, are regular people, but the trouble with them is that they hurry too much when marrying.

They are used to hurry all their lives, and it is a dangerous habit, when one must arrange a marriage, which is supposed to be a lifelong business. One must be cautious in such a case, and slow. "Think before marrying" is no less necessary a slogan than "Think before speaking."

Even if an American marriage is a happy one, the couple have not time enough to enjoy their happiness (unless they are millionaires). How many nice women confessed to me here that they can see their husbands just five minutes a day.

"He loves me dearly, you know, but he is so busy! Very often we cannot even dine together, he is always in such a hurry!"

Business before pleasure, business before joy, business before love; one must hurry if one wants to succeed. Don't you think it is a bit cruel, that genuine American creed?

I feel that I begin to talk with bitterness, but I have my personal reasons.

When I was quite a green greenhorn, entirely green, fresh from the steamer, I fell in love with an American.

Oh, it was a terrible experience! I know now how it seems when some one dear to you counts his future appointments, and draws his watch from his pocket every moment when you are happily together. Six days a week belongs to his work, and on Sunday only to you. But Sunday is always such a dull day in America: everybody makes love to his sweetheart on that day, so one feels to be in the general parades of lovers. Every nice eating place is overcrowded, and every cozy bank in the park is inhabited by two or three couples. Even up the Hudson River, even at the Bear Mountains. No, I will never love a businesslike American—never again, thank you.

"Work must be done quickly." Oh, how I hate that heartless sentence! Especially on a sunny spring day, when the only duty of every human being should be, "Sing and love."

How many clerks, shut in dusty offices, would agree with me! How many young girls from shops and factories would shake hands with me on a glorious day of May and say,—

"Oh, you have spoken the very truth: we must not hurry to work now. You are a clever girl, although only a greenhorn."

When the greenhorn in America complains to me of his hard time, when he bemoans loudly about his "lost paradise," his slow work in Russian, I agree with him at times; in spite of my great respect for the business ability of Americans.

In Russia we have often nothing to eat, and the rent is unpaid for a long time. (By the way, we pay rent every month, every three months, or once a year—never for a week, as here. This little fact proves once more that our life is much slower.) We are often out of work, but we have always plenty of time to dream, to love, and to live. The real Russian does not think that work means life: he considers it only a necessary evil. In the depth of his soul he always dreams of a five-minute workday.

Sometimes he can work passionately, however. He would throw all his life to his task. He can write a book night and day, and forget sleep, and food. He can work on his field from twilight to sunset, if it is necessary for having the harvest. He would organize the revolutionary movement, and stand it many years; and be put in jail, and be sent to Siberia, and run away, and start all anew.

He would emigrate to a new country, and overcome thousands of obstacles; but he is incapable of one thing, steady and speedy work.

The steady hours of common, unromantic and hurried work are killing for him. Only in the country, in the forest, and in the field, can he stand it. But you must remember that the country work is not so monotonous as that of the office or factory; the great variety of Nature cannot tire people like always-the-same surroundings of four walls. The spring work and the autumn work is hard, but it is—different. And in the long winter evenings the contemplative soul of the Russian peasant has its long-desired time of dreams. Then he composes songs, poems, stories—probably all the beautiful folk songs were created during the long lazy season of winter.

The Russian peasant can carve amazingly artistic figures of wood; he can paint and make fantastic designs. The hand work of our peasants is appreciated in all Europe! But—that is not a steady, common work, with a foreman behind your back to hurry you up. It is a free creating.

Our artists were always poor pupils in school. Many of the great writers were expelled for laziness; and still they could work passionately. Our vagabonds, exiled to the province near the Black Sea, built many successful towns, as Odessa, our first-class port. The immigrants and criminals of Siberia "lazy people," who could not undertake any steady work in cultured cities, created the new, sane, healthy and wealthy life over there. Our Siberian towns are our pride; their originators were able to work sufficiently, but not as steady machines.

Perhaps Russians, with their blind protest against any kind of steady work, are nearer to the ideal life of humanity. I should think so. I believe that all the work of humanity should be not a hurried job, undertaken for money, but a free, joyous and thoughtfully slow Creation.

(1918)

Songs of Gold Mountain

Anonymous

[Husband: his foolishness is second to none]

Husband: his foolishness is second to none.
Life indeed is tragic for the woman.
Seek a divorce, like an American?
But the Chinese do not work things out
    in that way!
A belly full of resentment,
At the sight of him, eyes burst out in flames.
What evil deed in my previous life made me
    married to you?
Why me? Why did I end up with such a fool?

[Husband: so dumb, second to none]

Husband: so dumb, second to none;
Wife: wounded with deep resentment.
Foolish and naïve, he doesn't know when
    to have fun;
It's a real bore to be with him at any moment.
Alas! is this called fate?
I am disgusted with the family, everyone.
Had I followed the Western practice and
    made my own choice,
Never, never would I have agreed to wed a moron.

[American ways are very extreme]

American ways are very extreme.
This worn writing brush cannot reveal them
    all.
Just let me show you one ridiculous example
    in brief,

And I must warn you, gentlemen, before you
    die of shock from hearing this news:
There was a lawless shrew—
She bullied and humiliated her inept husband;
She divorced him, seized and sold the family
    property;
Then, she openly found and married another man!

Translated by Marlon K. Hom

Unconverted

Bruno Lessing

The Reverend Thomas Gillespie (it may have been William—I am not sure of his first name) noticed a tall old man with fierce brown eyes standing in the front of the crowd. Then a stone struck the Reverend Gillespie in the face. The crowd pressed in upon him, and it would have gone ill with the preacher if the tall, brown-eyed man had not turned upon the crowd and, in a voice that drowned every other sound, cried:

"Touch him not! Stand back!"

The crowd hesitated and halted. The tall man had turned his back upon the Reverend Gillespie, and now stood facing the rough-looking group.

"Touch him not!" he repeated. "He is an honest man. He means us no harm. He is but acting according to his lights. He is only mistaken. Whoever throws another stone is an outcast. 'Before me,' said the Lord, 'there is no difference between Jew and Gentile; he that accomplishes good will I reward accordingly.' Friends, go your way!"

In a few minutes the entire crowd had dispersed; the tall man was helping the clergyman to his feet, and the first "open-air meeting" of the Reverend Gillespie's "Mission to the East Side Jews" had come to an end. The Reverend's cheek was bleeding, and the tall man helped him staunch the flow of blood with the aid of a handkerchief that seemed to have seen patriarchal days.

"Friend," he then said to the clergyman, "can you spare a few moments to accompany me to my home? It is close by, and I would like to speak to you."

The clergyman's head was in a whirl. The happenings of the past few minutes had dazed him. He was a young man and enthusiastic, and this idea of converting the Jews of the East Side to Christianity was all his own idea—all his own undertaking, without pay, without hope of reward. He knew German well, and a little Russian, and it had not taken him long to acquire sufficient proficiency in the jargon to make himself clearly understood. Then began this "open-air meeting," the sudden outburst of derisive cries and hooting before he had uttered a dozen words of the solemn exhortation that he had so carefully planned, then the rush and the stone that had cut his cheek, and—he was only dimly conscious of this—the sudden interference of the tall man. He was glad to accompany his rescuer—glad to do anything that would afford a moment's quiet rest. The Reverend Gillespie wanted to think the situation over.

The tall man led him into a tenement close by, through the hall, and across a filthy court yard into a rear tenement, and then up four foul, weary flights of stairs. He opened a door, and the clergyman found himself in a small dark room that seemed, from its furnishings, as well as from its odors, to serve the purpose of sitting-, sleeping-, dining-room, and kitchen. In one corner stood a couch, upon which lay an old man, apparently asleep. His long, grey beard rose and fell upon the coverlet with his regular breathing; but his cheeks were sunken, and his hands, that clutched the edge of the coverlet, were thin and wasted.

"Rest yourself," said the tall man to the clergyman. "You are worn out."

The clergyman seated himself and drew a long breath of relief. He was really tired, and sitting down acted like a tonic. He began to thank his rescuer. It was the first word he had spoken, and his voice seemed to arouse a sudden fire in the eyes of his rescuer.

"Listen!" he cried, leaning forward, and pointing a long, gaunt finger at the clergyman. "Listen to me. I have brought you here because I think you are an honest man. You are like a man who walks in the midst of light with his eyes shut and declares there is no light. You have come here to preach to Jews, to beseech them to forsake the teachings of the Prophets and to believe that the Messiah has come. But to preach to Jews you must first find your Jews. You were not speaking to Jews. It was not a Jew who threw that stone at you. It is true the Talmud says, 'An Israelite, even when he sins and abandons the faith, is still an Israelite.' But you have not come to convert the sinners against Israel. You have come to convert Jews. And I have brought you here to show you a Jew.

"That old man whom you see there—no, he is not sleeping. He is dying. You are shocked? No, he has no disease. Medical skill can do nothing for him. He is an old man, tired of the struggle of life, worn out, wasting away. Oh, he will open his eyes again, and he will eat food, too, but there is no hope. In a few days he will be no more.

"He is a Jew. We came from Russia together, he and I, and we struggled together, side by side, for nearly a quarter of a century. It did not take me long to forget many of the things the rabbis had taught me, and to become impatient of the restraints of religion. But he remained steadfast, oh, so steadfast! His religion was the breath of life to him; he could no more depart from it than he could accustom himself to live without breathing. It was a bitter struggle, year after year, slaving from break of day until dark, with nothing to save, no headway, no future, no hope. I often became despondent, but he was always cheerful. He had the true faith to sustain him; a smile, a cheerful word, and always some apt quotation from the Talmud to dispel my despondent mood.

"He argued with me, he pleaded with me, he read to me the words of the law, and the interpretations of the learned rabbis, day after day, month after month, year after year—always so kind, so gentle, so patient, so loving. And all the while we struggled for our daily living together and suffered and hungered, and many times were subjected to insult and even injury. And he would always repeat from the Talmud, 'Man should accustom himself to say of everything that God does that it is for the best.'

"Then Fortune smiled upon him. An unexpected piece of luck, a bold enterprise, a few quick, profitable ventures, and he became independent. He made me share his good fortune. We started one of those little banking houses on the East Side, and so great was the confidence that all who knew him possessed in him, that in less than a year we were a well-known, reliable establishment, with prospects that no outsider would ever have dreamed of. Through all the days of prosperity he remained a devout Jew. Not a feast passed unobserved. Not a ceremony went unperformed. Not an act of devotion, of kindness, or of charity prescribed by the Talmud was omitted by my friend.

"Then came the black day—the great panic of six years ago—do you remember it? It came suddenly, on a Friday afternoon, like a huge storm cloud, threatening to burst the next morning.

"They came to him—all his customers—in swarms, to ask him if he would keep his banking place open the next day. 'No!' he said. 'Tomorrow is the Sabbath!' 'You will be ruined!' they cried. 'We will be ruined!' 'Friends,' he said, in his quiet way, 'I have enough money laid aside to guard you against ruin, even if all my establishment be wiped from the face of the earth. But tomorrow is the Sabbath. I have observed the Sabbath for nearly sixty years. I must not fail tomorrow.'

"And when the morrow came the bank failed, and they brought the news to him in the synagogue. But he gave no heed to them; he was listening to the reading of the law. They came to tell him that banks were crashing everywhere, that the bottom had fallen out of the world of business and finance. But he was listening to the words that were spoken by Moses on Sinai.

"And," the narrator's eyes filled, and the tears began to roll down his cheeks, "on the Monday that followed he gave, to every man and to every woman and to every child that had trusted him, every penny that he had saved, and he made me given every penny that I had saved. And when all was gone, and the last creditor had gone away, paid in full, he turned to me and said, 'Man should accustom himself to say of everything that God does that it is for the best!'

"And the next day—yes, the very next day—we applied for work in a sweater's shop, and we have been working there ever since.

"We were too old to begin daring ventures over again. I would have clung to the money we had saved, but he—he was so good, so honest, that the very thought of it filled me with shame. And now he is worn out.

"In a few days he will die, and I will be left to fight on alone.

"But, oh, my friend, there, lying on that couch, you see a Jew!

"Would you convert him? What would you have him believe? To what would you change his faith? Ah, you will say there are not many like him. No! Would to God there were! It would be a happier world.

"But it was faith in Judaism that made him what he was. If I—if all Jews could only believe in the religion of their fathers as he believed—what an example to mankind Israel would be!

"My friend, I thank you. You have come with me—you have listened to my story. I must attend to my friend. May the peace of God be with you!"

The Reverend Thomas Gillespie (although, as I said, it may have been William) bowed, and, without a word, walked slowly out of the room. His lips trembled slightly.

The "second outdoor meeting of the Reverend Gillespie's Mission to the East Side Jews" has never taken place.

(1903)

Kalaun, the Elephant Trainer

Margherita Arlina Hamm

I

Little Nasir stood on a table in the café, dense with the fumes of narghiles and scented cigarettes, and declaimed shrilly, "My Country, 'tis of Thee," which he had just learned in the public school. He was nine years old, but he made brave gestures and pronounced every syllable as it should be.

The swarthy auditors pounded the tables, clapped their hands, and cried out encouragements in the Arabic dialect.

"It is wonderful—wonderful!" said the lean proprietor.

"I could not talk it better," cried the small chinned interpreter from Cairo. "'Mie contree, 'tis of zee, swit land of liberté—he is perfect.'"

"Kalaun Usertesen, thou art a lucky father," declared a pudgy man with black hair and sly eyes who had killed sixteen Turks in Syria.

"Thanks, brothers, thanks! It is my treat. Host, fetch us coffee and brandy and fresh narghiles. Mahabitcum! Good fellowship to all!"

"Mahabitcum!" chorused the men, smacking their lips.

"The lad will be a soldier—a terror to the enemies of the fatherland," voiced the Turk-slayer. "Ah, yes; his fingers are apt for the trigger and the knife."

"Better for the elephant-hook," said another. "He will follow the paternal trade."

"No so!" roared the father, wild with delight. "It is good to be a soldier or to train the elephants, but my son will be a citizen of the great United States. That shall be his trade."

"A member of the government, thou wouldst say?" asked the interpreter.

"How do I know? A citizen of the United States may be what he pleases—anything!"

"Father," piped litter Nasir, "thy speech is neither good Arabic nor good English."

"Hey? Well, thou shalt teach me, O scholar! Thou shalt become wise and instruct thy ignorant sire."

Kalaun leaped up, a bull-necked, short giant with the coppery face, almond eyes, wide nose, high cheekbones, and black hair of the ancient Copt. He extended an arm as massive as the trunk of a tree. The boy straddled it, clutching the big fist, and thus they paraded round the smoky room amid plaudits.

The waiter brought more little cups of coffee, amber-hued and as thick as syrup; brandy in wicker flasks; strange sweetmeats; and live coals at tongs' end to relight the gurgling water pipes, which three men smoked by different stems. The flaring gas jets, eking out the feeble window rays, showed on the dark paneled walls pictures of Abraham Lincoln and fezzed pashas, a battle scene from the Greek war of independence, a print of the desert at night, and a photograph of ruined Karnak.* One of the pashas, probably a tyrant, had a jellied crumb on the tip of his nose.

"'Mie contree, 'tis of zee, swit land of liberté,'" murmured the interpreter, fingering the pieces, like chess pawns, on the dama board. "Wilt thou play a game, Kalaun?"

"No, thanks; that is too much skill. I prefer tavoli, where the dice give chances as in life. But we are going."

He lifted his son on his shoulder, tossed off some brandy amid final "Good fellowships," and went into the street, where it was broad daylight and a smell of salt water and tar came from the adjacent wharves. A yellow horse car jangled through the press of trucks; the sidewalk was held by loafing stevedores and bustling foreigners. At the southern end of the street appeared the greenery of Battery Park and the brownstone Aquarium.

"This is a day of triumph, Nasir," said Kalaun. "Eh, look out for that sign! We will buy some presents for thy exquisite mother, and tonight thou shalt behold my performance with the jungle brothers at the theater."

"I will love to see thee," replied the boy, patting the thick neck. His little brown eyes blinked in the sun.

Nearby, in a street just two blocks long, the center of the Egyptian colony, they entered a shop that had iron-barred windows and contained marvels of every sort. After much haggling and half-jocular threats, a bargain was struck on a red-glass narghile, meerschaum bowl, and silver mouthpiece; also a silk shawl of green pattern, embroidered with gold thread. Kalaun wanted to buy Arabic school books and poems for his son, but learned that this was unsuitable. The shopkeeper tempted Nasir with two colored marbles without price; the boy resolutely chose a bottle of ink instead.

They lived a few doors beyond, on the top floor of a building that overlooked the waterfront masts and the river filled with noisy shipping, beyond which loomed the roofs of railroad stations. It was a cozy home of four rooms, laid with rugs of high color, with silks on the walls; and with the bathtub used as an aquatic garden of papyrus, white lotus, and rose lotus, which bloomed continually and sent out delicate fragrance. What other or better use for a bathtub?

"We bring thee gifts, O princess! beloved Teye!"

The princess examined the offerings coolly, put on one, and began to smoke the other. She permitted herself to be hugged as if it were in the day's work. A swarthy, lithe-bodied little woman, she refused to learn English, cared nothing for free institutions, and could not understand her husband's enthusiasm over the boy's progress in Americanism. Propped up by cushions on the divan,

---

Karnak: ancient temple complex in Egypt.

nibbling sweetmeats with white teeth, she reminded one of a lazy squirrel. She licked her vermilion lips with a dainty tongue.

Kalaun adored her only next to Nasir. He usually asked permission for a kiss, and did not sulk if it was denied.

"Why do you treat your wife so well?" asked a friend one day. "Too much gentleness is not good for women and elephants."

"It may be," he replied; "but I risked my life for Teye; moreover, she is beautiful, and begot *him*."

That night the boy sat in a box at the variety theater, entranced with joy, and joined in the thunderous applause that greeted his father's deeds. Kalaun first came on alone, clad in pink tights and a velvet jacket, and made poses showing his mighty-muscled back and the jutting biceps of his bronze arms. A man in evening dress proclaimed his wonderful history—that he was born of Abyssinian parents, twisted rifle barrels as a baby, had fought Bedouins in the Soudan, been master of the hunt to the Sultan, escaped from a sack thrown into the sea, and held office under the Nawab of Peshawur, in whose dominions he had broken an elephant's back with a blow of the fist. Kalaun grinned, suspecting that the man talked falsehoods, but not feeling responsible for them.

Three great beasts then walked solemnly on the stage, swinging their trunks, and fell on their knees in obeisance. The middle one squealed hoarsely as he was jabbed by the hook for having his back to the audience.

"Hush, brother! Thou art not hurt. Up—up on thy hind legs. Sister, take his arm and march. Do not fear; the platform is solid."

The elephants stood on their leathery foreheads, lay on their backs, with four feet upright like posts, pretended to beat one another with whips, waltzed in large cotton skirts, shot pistols with their trunks, rolled cannonballs under their hoofs, played seesaw, and passed their master loftily through the air. They peeled bananas and drank out of bottles; they stood side by side while Kalaun did gymnastic feats, turning somersaults over their bodies and vaulting over the tallest with one hand. Finally there was a tug-of-war, with a manila cable, between master and animals. They sat on their haunches and pulled lustily, trumpeting; but he seemed to pull better, and they fell forward.

"Brothers," he said to them afterward, as usual, "I apologize to you for this foolish trick, which pleases the public. The wise know which is stronger."

With the advent of summer Kalaun became proprietor of the papier-mâché Streets of Cairo at the seaside, employing many needy countrymen and having a large troupe of elephants and camels. This was a truly glorious life, all in the open. There were silken tents and gay banners, palm trees, turbaned sheiks, dancing girls with rings through their lips, and weird crashing tunes to which the men chanted, "ta-ta—tah—ta—ta-ta." Sometimes Nasir was allowed to ride on the beautifully caparisoned elephants, a vantage whence he spouted, "My Country," with great effect. The interpreter with the small chin, who was employed as barker and professor, would introduce him to visitors, saying:

"Onlee nyan 'ars old. He spik perfect Eengliz as myself."

Teye felt at home here, where everything was familiar and the sun hot. On a divan under a kiosk she lay basking like a princess in gauze and beads and gold anklets, her tiny green slippers having their points curled, her face decently veiled, and part of her shapely stomach visible, as is proper east of Gibraltar. She nibbled sweetmeats, smoked the water pipe, and took little Nasir to the theater, where she could hear again the temple music of her youth.

II

Six years had passed. Father and son were left alone; for Teye, consumed by the chill of Northern winters, had departed silently and gracefully, as she had lived. Kalaun mourned for her, the beautiful princess, whom he hardly dared to kiss when she could refuse no longer; he lay prostrate a day and a night on her grave in the place called Cypress Hills, until the police sent him away. But he found dear consolation in his son, a tall, lithe figure with the paternal snubnose, a student in the highest grade of the public school, a keen-witted young American, who strove to impart knowledge and culture to his father.

"I am stupid, I shall ever be stupid, O Nasir; but I rejoice the more in thy progress."

One or two strange things had happened lately. Kalaun had an offer from the managers of a Western exposition to go to Egypt and collect exhibits. Nasir thought it was a fine chance, his mind inflamed by what he had read of his father's birthplace near Girgeh, — the limitless yellow sands, the pyramids that dwarfed all modern buildings, the gay caravans, date trees and palms and the fruitful Nile, — to hear the grunt of the sacred crocodile, and see the ibis winging the eternal blue sky of the Pharaohs! But, without apparent reason, Kalaun refused the offer, and almost became angry when the boy urged him.

Moreover, on the nights when there was no performance at the theater, Kalaun had the habit of leaving home and being gone for several hours. Where did he go? Not to the café or to any place in the colony. When asked point blank, he replied evasively that it was to get the fresh air. Nasir felt vaguely that these midnight trips were connected with his father's irreligion, since the latter would not attend the church or join the Sunday school where the son found so much profit. Incidentally, Nasir could not make up his mind whether to love the blonde Sunday school teacher with the lisp, or the dark teacher with the curl in the public school. Both were lovely, twice as old as he, and they duly filled him with Western knowledge and religion.

One night Nasir followed his father, but more by chance than design. They went a long way up the waterfront until they came to an open pier that jutted into the river farther than any other. Kalaun sped past the watchman's shanty and disappeared in the gloomy path between mountains of freight. The boy hesitated a moment, fearing many things, then likewise slipped by the watchman. He saw nothing until he came to the very end of the pier.

It was a moonless night; a thousand stars were twinkling against the black velvet of the sky. The dark tide raced swiftly below, reflecting stray gleams of the constellations from oily patches, gurgling and moaning through the piles, rippling and sobbing with multiplied voices. Far across the river shone the electric signs of the railroad stations. No place could have been more solitary and awesome.

Kalaun stood with arm outstretched, his face thrown up to the host of eternal stars. He muttered softly, waved his arms, bowed low with backward steps, fell upon his face in a curious posture, and rose to gaze as before. His guttural whispers mingled with the voice of the dark river.

Not understanding, more frightened than if he had seen his father commit a crime, the boy crept away and regained the street, where he waited under an arc lamp. It was a relief to see usual things going on—a drunken stevedore cuffed by a policeman, and haggling between an all night fruit vendor and his customer. Perhaps the shadows on the pier had deceived vision? It was someone else.

"Ah Nasir; why art thou here? It was wrong to follow."

"I saw thee, father," gasped the boy.

"E-e-everything."

"Well, what does it matter?" replied the other, after some hesitation. "I practice the custom of my ancestors. It is hundreds—aye, thousands—of years established."

"I do not understand."

"Thus we worship the stars. Maybe my ritual is imperfect, there being no priests here and memory uncertain. An aged hermit, wise and holy, who outwardly practiced both the Muslim and the Yesu faith, taught me somewhat of the ancient mystery. This I know—one must prepare for the trial before Osiris in the underworld, passing the lean river horse who guards the gate. The heart is weighed in the scales, and the good ascend to the realm of Aahlu."

He also spoke dimly of the doctrine of mummies and the homeless ghosts of evil folk, the immortality of the soul and its transmigration. Nasir was astonished, confused.

"But thou didst worship formerly in the incense church with my mother."

"No harm. That is a good religion, too. I have always yearned after the ancestral faith, and the elephants behave better when I have worshiped the stars."

"It is a mistake, my father. The books tell that they are like our sun and earth, only a few million miles away."

"The green and yellow are especially beneficent. Have the bookmen eyes better than mine? Can they see more clearly?"

"Yes, with telescopes—cunning instruments."

"My ancestors had instruments also, and studied the sky for thousands of years."

"Come with me to the school and look through the telescope."

"I do not wish it, Nasir. It is not fitting."

"Oh, father, you want me to be an American, but you believe in dead gods, a false religion."

"Only for myself," replied the other, gently. "I desire thee to please thyself with the incense church, which the princess favored. It is the most venerable branch of the Yesu faith, being older than Roman, Armenian, or Greek."

"How can you praise one, yet believe in the other! Is there a temple to the star gods? No; nothing at all."

"If the worshipers are few, my son, the greater are the portions of blessing to be divided among them."

"But the stars are like us. They are dying all the time. They get cold and dark and perish."

"Very well; suppose my gods are dead, utterly. In that case there is no harm to worship them. But if they be alive—"

At home there were more arguments, and the matter gradually became an issue between father and son. Nasir got the opinion of his teachers and cited passages from books; he tried hard to prove to his father that he was superstitious, unscientific, and illogical. But Western bullets of fact invariably glance from the metaphysical armor of Eastern minds. What is truth? How many men have verified the assertions of science? Do not the learned disagree? Who knows the unknown?

However, a new mystery superseded the dispute on religion. Someone in the café reported that a compatriot from Girgeh was coming to the city.

The next day Kalaun made his son promise never to visit the quarter again—on the ground of becoming a thorough American,—and secretly took apartments far uptown. They did not wait to remove all the furniture from the old lodgings, or say farewell to any friends, or even transport the lotus garden that had been kept blooming in the bathtub in memory of the princess. A few days later Kalaun sold his performing elephants and became a tobacconist. The shop was a small, dark one facing a park, and bore no name or sign save the gilt image of an elephant carved out of wood. Few customers were attracted by the taciturn proprietor and his scanty stock of goods displayed on three shelves and in one cracked showcase.

"Have we become poor, father?" said Nasir, troubled. "What has happened?"

"We are not very poor. Thou shalt continue going to school."

"I should like to visit my old teachers sometime."

"Thou didst promise not to, nor to ask why."

"But the selling of the elephants that you were so fond of—"

"Listen. I will tell thee. I have been a wicked man. I feared they would crush me to death,—they know which is stronger,—since I am destined to become an elephant hereafter, in expiation of human sin."

"Why, that is impossible, father!"

"Nevertheless, I have felt it coming on already," said Kalaun, calmly. "Sometimes, when I awake in the night, I feel my arms and legs, which are big, grow bigger still and change to the fore feet and hind feet of the jungle brothers. My skin is thickening. Moreover, I sleep, like them, with one eye open all night."

"The skin thicken—the eye remain open—"

"Precisely. Touch my forehead. And thou canst watch me while I sleep."

Nasir could verify none of the symptoms; he thought long, and came to the conclusion that his father's head was turned by star-worship and grief for Teye. As for saying he was a wicked man, how could that be?

Moody and depressed, quite changed from his former self, Kalaun sat for hours in the dim rear of his shop and puffed at the water pipe, from which curled up fantastic blue jinn. He grudged the entry of infrequent customers. His muscles became flabby; the five-hundred-pound dumbbell was heavy for him; and his face grew pale saffron, marked with lines. Sometimes he was a little cheered after visiting the elephants in the zoo and talking with the keeper about them. The beasts seemed to know him, swinging their trunks in a friendly manner and blinking their tiny eyes. He asked the keeper whether he had any premonition that these sly old devils—forest brothers, to be polite— might some day crush him to death. The Irishman laughed.

Kalaun became yet more strange in his habits, and rarely ventured in the street.

"You are ill," exclaimed the boy, one day. "I will call a doctor."

"Do not, I beg thee, my son! The doctors use evil magic and they cannot avert kismet."

"If you are not ill, tell me what ails you, beloved father."

"It is well. It is time thou didst know."

Sighing, Kalaun told the story of his career. Early in life he left the desert and wandered through the Levant, learning the nature of elephants and how to train them, cultivating his great strength in wrestling and gymnastics. He went back to his native village and fell in love with Teye, the wife of a rich boatman. Not seeing her face, he loved her for her gait and the visible part of her beauty. First he wrestled with the husband and broke his collarbone, then at night he eloped with Teye, going down the Nile in a dahabiyeh. At the coast they took ship for Italy, and he became partner in a circus which showed through the Continent. But the fear of the wronged husband led them on to South America, and the son was born at sea. Again they traveled with the jungle brothers in the Western part of the United States, and finally settled down in New York. Part of the punishment was the death of Teye. She was not happy during the wandering, ever longed for home, and confessed and prayed much at the incense church.

"Father, I know she was as happy as she could be," said the boy, with tears in his eyes. "Thou wast not so much to blame."

Afterward Nasir reflected more deeply on the revelation. It was a weight upon his conscience even more than the star worship. He wished he could enlist the advice of his new teachers. He felt that wrong had been done to many, including himself (though this was a strange, difficult kind he could not grasp), but, personally, he was ready to forgive.

'I see thou hast prepared a judgment," said Kalaun, smiling mournfully, one morning.

"Y-yes, father. Thy conduct was un-American, lawless, and without religion."

"So does the child easily condemn the parent."

"Dear father, forgive me. Wilt thou not confess to a priest and take advice?"

"When the clay is baked the shape does not change."

"At least it will be well to write a letter to the wronged one, asking his forgiveness."

"Our people do not forgive," said Kalaun, shaking his head.

"Not after many years?"

"The soul is immortal, my son. Immortal are its loves and hatreds. But I am an ignorant man."

"Ah, father—"

"If aught happens to me at any time, Nasir, do not trouble the authorities. Thou knowest where our savings are kept."

III

One afternoon the proprietor of the little shop was cleaning up the rubbish of weeks, and thinking it would be better to go away anywhere, to do anything, rather than skulk in this den playing at the occupation of women and feeble fellows. He a shopkeeper! Moreover, there was risk of being discovered. Resolve glowed in the dulled eyes. Flinging down the broom, he sought the keys in order to lock the doors against customers, and laid hands on a stepladder that he might tear down the gilt sign. In imagination he was already free, making a fresh life start with the boy in the spacious West, or perhaps—

A man stood at the counter.

Kalaun was alarmed for a moment, until he saw that it was a friend from the colony.

"Ha, Kalaun! Is it thyself? Strange behavior to leave us without tidings— as if money was owed."

"Thou knowest it was neither that nor lack of good fellowship. How camest to find the place?"

"Chance, which is heavenly and infernal."

"I rejoice to see thee. What news?" The questioner tried to smile.

"There is little. Ah, yes; thy compatriot from Girgeh has arrived," said the friend.

Kalaun hid his agitation. "Has he spoken?"

"He is pleased to learn thou art still pious in the practices of the ancient faith, as rumor tells."

"He wished to see me?"

"Naturally, being a childhood friend."

"Perchance thou art his messenger."

"What? Is it a riddle? Thy gaze is strange—"

"A wandering of the mind," stammered the other.

At midnight Kalaun went to the pier to seek the aid of the stars in deciding his future course. He had not been there in a long time, and this was to be the last. But a mist hung over the river and dark clouds veiled the sky. He gazed upward, and found nothing to worship, no beacons of solace or aid in the murky heavens. A dank, salt smell came from the water moaning and gurgling through the piles. All was bleak and terribly desolate.

He turned to go, shuddering. Out of the deeper gloom between masses of freight came a figure that might have been his son repeating the earlier espionage. It was not. The stranger leaped upon him, binding his arms to his waist. Neither uttered a sound. Why call out when it is useless? The shock animated Kalaun; he felt surging back the mighty strength of which he had lately been bereft. Everything seemed possible, even to balk kismet that played this scurvy trick in place of the apprehended elephant-crushing. He tore himself from the stranger's grasp, seized him by the throat, choked him, and by an old wrestling device prepared to fling him over shoulder into the river. The assailant's tongue hung out, and he was almost limp; his legs dangled without support on the planks; he made a low gurgling sound like the water. Yet he drew a curved kungair, sharp enough to split hairs, and twisted it in the athlete's bosom. A sighing, a groan—Lo, a herd of jungle brothers danced gleefully around and bowed to the stars—the princess lay on a magnificent divan—was that the bellowing of the river horse?—the audience kept applauding—Nasir stood on the café table—they put her under the earth—the lotus flowers— The great muscles fell lax as the heart's blood gushed forth. Rolling the body into the river and tossing the knife after, the stranger departed.

In the colony it was said, with lifted eyebrows, that the man from Girgeh had gone home quickly after attending to his affairs.

(1905)

The Tooth of Antar

Lucille Baldwin Van Slyke

Of the many trials of Nazileh Sewaya's strange new life, the Dutch baker lady's daughter was perhaps the most bothersome. To be sure, the chubby Geraldine was really only a part of the bewildering ordeal of going to public school when one longed ardently to go back to the classes in Father Shiskim's little basement church. In public school the little Americans laughed impudently at one's halting, prettily guttural English; they did not know how hard it was to talk English when one still thought in a hybrid Arabic Syrian. In public school one's bitterest enemies "cheesemadic" (schismatic) Syrians, made noses at one unrebuked.* But Father Shiskim said he could not go on teaching one little nine-year-old, when twenty were clamoring for her place, that they too might learn to speak "Ameercan En'leesch," and so Nazileh could only sigh and endure.

The Dutch baker lady's daughter had a maddening way of teasing her all the way home from school. And she wore huge bows on flaxen hair, a stiffly starched apron, shiny boots, and *the hat!* On top of the gorgeous ribbons, the red-and-yellow hat!

Nazileh hid her own curly braid with its "elasteeck" band under her shabby old coat, and pulled the brown veil tightly over her ears. The comparison was altogether too painful; she couldn't pretend not to care.

"Why do you not mit the other dagos walk?" asked her tormentor. "Why do they not talk mit you at recess?"

"They ees cheesemads; me, I ees oth'dox," explained Nazileh politely. "Eet ees nod good thad I should walk weeth cheesemads!"

"But they is dagos, chust the same like you, aind't they?" persisted Geraldine.

"They ees nod dag-go; no mor' ees I a dag-go," Nazileh protested, lifting her darkly fringed eyes to the insipidness of Geraldine's blue orbs. "Oxcuse, but you nod onde'stan'. Een Syreeah, een Beirut, the dag-go do nod leeve; the dag-go leeve een Etalee. Me, I—"

"Mein papa, he says you is all dagos," interrupted Geraldine stolidly, "und he knows."

Nazileh shook her curly head; her thick lips pouted mournfully.

"The cheesemads ees cheesemadic," she explained slowly. "They ees of a truth ver' bad, those ones. Once, las' year, some cheesemads they ees keel my

*Of the modern Syrian Christian religions in Van Slyke's story, significant distinctions are drawn between the Schismatic Syrians, or Jacobites, and Syria's various versions of Catholic Christianity.

fathaire! They ees nod oth'dox like me—they go nod to Fathaire Shiskim's choorch; but, like me, they have leeve before een Syreeah, een Beirut."

Against this Oriental persistence even Teutonic stubbornness had to give way.

"Maybe it makes like some folks call me Dutch und I is Cherman," Geraldine suggested.

Nazileh paled under her lovely, dusky skin.

"A ger-rm like teecha tells—a ger-rm! A diszees ger-rm!" she gasped. "*Aie!* Gee-ral-deen, you ees nod! They ees small, those ones. Eef thad we eat them, they geeve us scarlat fev'an' black deeth an'—"

Geraldine stood still and laughed until her pink cheeks looked like a ripe pomegranate.

"A Cherman!" she snickered; "I said a Cherman! They aind't the same like a cherm."

Nazileh gave it up in despair. It was one of those things one could not understand, this germ business. One could not feel them, one could not see them; one simply had to accept them, like the evil eye.

"Mein mama," boasted Geraldine, skipping elaborately over the sidewalk cracks, "she makes it today a lofely birthday cake mit five lights for a rich lady's little boy's birthday that is five years old."

"Ees he yust got hees tooth?" asked Nazileh, in amazement. "An' feeve year?"

"Tooth?" demanded Geraldine. "Course he's got lots of teeth! This is his birthday und his party."

"Een Beirut," said Nazileh, "eet ees nod of a beerthday we makes a par-rty for leedle boy; we makes eet a par-rty when thad he attain hees tooth."

Geraldine, for once, was tremendously impressed.

"Honest?" she asked. "What for? What kind of a party?"

"Hones'," said Nazileh solemnly; "weeth *sneinatt*, an' weeth *baklawa*, an' weeth *pilau*—"

"Don't talk dago," objected Geraldine; "I don't know what you say."

"Thad ees nod dag-go," the little Syrian answered; "thad ees theengs to eat— eet ees cake an' meat." Her dark eyes were shining with delight, and her words tumbled awkwardly in her eagerness to tell. "Eet ees put een all the bowls, an' all the people thad one know, they geets a bowl of *sneinatt*; they say, 'Blessin' on hees tooth!' An' when they eat thad cake, then they take thad bowl 'ome to thad babee's mothaire, weeth some othaire cakes for thad babe!"

"Are you going to have some when your baby gets a tooth?" demanded Geraldine. "Will you give us a piece?"

The joyous light died in Nazileh's eyes; she sighed deeply. In this strange land of Brooklyn, where one's mother only wept and made endless yards of lace, would one ever see *sneinatt*?

"He nod got thad tooth now," she answered cautiously; "he too leedle now."

"Going to get him out?" asked Geraldine. "I'm going to get mine out."

The dark eyes shone again. In the matter of brothers Nazileh felt entirely superior to the Dutch lady's daughter. For Antar—darling, dimpled, dusky

Antar—was the pride of her heart; the Dutch baby was as nothing beside him.

Did the Dutch baby have a glorious red-and-green seater, a wonderful red tasseled cap, or altogether amazing yellow shoes? Of a truth, that Dutch baby possessed nothing but silly white clothes that even a schismatic baby would scorn. At the very thought of her heart's treasure Nazileh entirely forgot the Dutch lady's daughter, and scuttled down the street in her eagerness to embrace the beloved Antar.

He was lying on his rug, crying lustily.

"Soon thou wilt laugh!" she murmured in Syrian, as she bent over him. "Soon thou wilt laugh with me! I take him out," she explained to her mother, who was bending over the lace; "I take him out now."

Her mother shrugged her shoulders. "It makes nothing if you do," she answered wearily; "he howls like a jackal all day."

"He howls for me," insisted Nazileh proudly; "now that I come, he does not howl."

Antar had undoubtedly ceased his wailing for a moment, though the tears still flowed from his great brown eyes and his mouth quivered weakly. He only whimpered fretfully while Nazileh pulled the wonderful sweater over his queer little acorn-shaped head.

But out on the sidewalk, in spite of the numerous attractions of Dix Street, he resumed his lusty cries with fresh vigor.

Nazileh cradled him in her thin arms and sat on the curbing to rock him.

"*Aie— aie—aie!*" she sang in strong, nasal tones to the tuneless tune that her people have intoned for generations, that uncanny little tune that may mean joy or sorrow, love or hate. She crooned a strange medley of Syrian and American words.

"Hush, oh, hush, my little heart!" she sang in Syrian; and, when he would not hush, she tried the American lullaby she had learned in public school.

> Sail, babe, sail,
>   Out upon leefe's sea;
> Only don' forget to sail
>   Back again to me!

But Antar would not be comforted. He howled and howled until his swarthy little face assumed a queer garnet hue. He beat his thick red lips with his chubby fists; the sound of his wailing rose about the strident clamor of the street.

Nazileh grew pale with terror. Had Antar swallowed a "diszees ger-rm"? In Beirut there had been no dreadful germs, but, in this strange land of Brooklyn, who could tell? With sudden inspiration, she got up and lugged the heavy baby across the street to the priest's house. Umn Salim, who kept house for Father Shiskim, she knew all things; she would know what to do it Antar had swallowed a "diszees ger-rm."

The priest's house was very imposing outside, it quite overshadowed the little basement church that stood next door, which, save for its modest cross above the low doorway, might have been almost anything but a church. But Father Shiskim lived in back rooms on the top floor of the great house, and the stairs seemed endless to Nazileh, with the heavy baby in her arms. Once she stumbled in the darkness on the ragged oilcloth, and a savage-looking woman opened a door and sharply bade her to stop crying.

"Eet ees nod I," Nazileh explained patiently; "eet ees these babee thad cries—I take heem to Umn Salim."

The woman only grunted, but she held the door open carefully until Nazileh reached the top, so that the last flight was not nearly so bad.

Umn Salim herself opened the door. She was very old, was Umn Salim, and the curly tendrils that escaped from her gaudy headkerchief were snowy white; her deep-sunken eyes flashed good humoredly, and she laughed with much shaking of her fat cheeks.

"Leetle Ameercan ge-url," she teased. "No more Syreean, now thad she goes ad thad poobleeck school."

She stooped to take the baby from Nazileh's tired arms.

"He deed nod like thad dar-rk stair," she said, pushing a chair toward the little girl; "thad dar-rk make heem cry."

"He cry nod of the stair," panted Nazileh; "he cry an' cry. Me, I theenk he deed eat a diszees ger-rm. Whad you theenk?"

Umn Salim was swaying her fat self in a way that soothed the whimpering baby, for he dropped his head on the cushiony shoulder with a long sigh of relief, and his wailing died away in a petulant "yah-yah-yah" as he gnashed his aching gums together.

"Whad mighd thad be?" asked Umn Salim. "Whad ees thad?"

Nazileh explained anxiously.

"Oh ho!" chuckled Umn Salim. "Me, I theenk thad yust fooleesch! Thad too seelly! Me, I am old—I nevaire eat such a one!" She touched the little string of beads at Antar's throat.

"*Mashallah*!" she murmured. "Eef thad diszees ger-rm came, would eet nod be scare off, like the evil eye, by these beads?"

Nazileh put her hand to her own beads swiftly. Long ago, in Beirut, her grandmother had placed them around her neck to ward off the evil eye of envy that brings sickness; and the little girl herself had divided her chain with her wee brother, that he too might be safe.

"Teecha say," she answered doubtfully, "thad the waxnate keep off the black deeth, an' thad the evil eye ees nod so." She sighed wonderingly. "Once thad teecha say, 'Pr-retty beads! I geeve you feefty cen's on those beads!'"

Umn Salim sat down on the sofa and laid the fretful baby across her knees.

"*Schut*!" she sputtered softly. "Why she geeve thad feefty cen's eef thad she nod know they keep off thad evil eye? She craftee, thad one; don' you let her fool you!"

"But Antar! They nod keep thad seeckness off Antar!" began Nazileh doubtfully.

Umn Salim ceased jogging her knees, and regarded the baby thoughtfully. She poked his red cheeks, she felt of his hot, dirty fists, and nodded wisely. Then she leaned over and tucked her forefinger into his mouth.

And Antar bit!

"*Wullah!*" cried Umn Salim. "He 'owls of a tooth, thad one!"

Nazileh knelt swiftly and pushed her thumb between the moist lips.

"Eet ees!" she cried delightedly; "but eet shows nod! Why does eet show nod?"

"Eet ees nod yet all come," said Umn Salim sagely; "eet ees like the bud an' the flower. The theengs like thad come when thad eet ees time—when thad Allah decide!"

Nazileh sat back on her ankles in an anxious little heap. The baby's eyelids drooped heavily; he drew a long, sighing breath, and fell asleep.

"Umn Salim," whispered the child, "eef thad tooth comes, weel my mothaire make *sneinatt?*"

The old woman shook her head doubtfully.

"Little one," she answered in Syrian, "thou shalt not learn too soon that in this land of Brooklyn things are not as they are in Syria. And, of a truth, thy mother is too sad for rejoicing." She sighed and looked out of the window into the dingy court below.

"Een thees land," she went on, speaking swiftly again in English, her voice growing sharp with the vehemence of her feeling, "we laugh nod; we remember onlee the sad theengs—we forgeet the pr-retty theengs of our fathaires." She got up abruptly and put the baby on the sofa. In spite of her flesh and her age, she moved rapidly across the room and swept back tempestuously to put a heavy hand on Nazileh's sholder.

"Twelve year I leeve een thees land," she said passionately; "een all thad time my neighbors breeng me nod *sneinatt*. They care nod, those laz-ee ones! They weel nod boil thad whead—they weel nod cut those feegs—they ees shame to carry *sneinatt* as they deed een the land of Syreeah!"

Nazileh jumped up with her eyes glistening.

"Me—I ees nod shame!" she cried eagerly. "I weel carry sneinatt—"

They were so intent that neither of them was aware, until his hearty guttural voice rang out, that Father Shiskim had come into the room. Then they stood, with eyes downcast, while they made the pretty Syrian obeisance, with their right hands touching lightly their hearts, their lips, and their foreheads in one swift, graceful gesture.

Father Shiskim seemed very big indeed, standing there in the center of the shabby, low ceilinged room. Even when he had handed Umn Salim his beloved silk hat, and tucked his biretta over his closely cropped curls, Nazileh was still awed by his bigness. He went into the little room beyond to don his tightly buttoned cassock, with its thin purple sash, and came back smiling from the depths of his great curly beard.

"Oh, ho!" he laughed, when he saw Antar. "Thad one mighd break thad sofa eef thad he nod be careful."

"Come!" he said, when he was comfortably settled in his armchair. "Come, leetle one, an' say thad En'leesch thad you learn een poobleeck."

"I nod learn En'leesch," Nazileh sighed; "I learn 'reethmedeecs, an' spellin', an' thad pheeseeck cult, an' thad chog-raphy—thad ver' hard, thad one!"

Father Shiskim laughed.

"Well, Antar, he learn good En'leesch yet?" he teased.

Nazileh forgot her timidity. Her dark eyes shone with fun. "Thad's nod to laugh now," she said merrily; "thad Antar—whad you s'pose? Thad Antar mos' nearlee got hees tooth!"

"Oh, ho!" breathed Father Shiskim, "I am fairlee terreefy!"

Nazileh smiled happily. Then she stooped to lift the sleeping boy.

"Me, I theenk I go 'ome," she murmured politely. "Goo'by."

The big priest got up suddenly, and lifted the baby tenderly. Then he held out his hand to the little girl.

"I go down to geet some air," he said cheerfully, "while thad laz-ee woman geet my sooper—eh?"

"Oxcuse!" protested Nazileh. "Thad one, he too heavy for you!" But she clung gratefully to the big, comfortable hand all the way down the dark stairway, and she sighed happily as she trudged homeward.

"Thad Fathaire Shiskim," she murmured dreamily, "he can haf me, all righd!"

"Antar—hees tooth ees nearlee een!" she announced joyously to her mother.

Umn Antar did not look up from the lace that grew so swiftly in her nimble fingers.

Nazileh put the baby on his rug, and knelt gently before the busy woman.

"Wilt thou make *sneinatt?* she asked shyly, in her prettiest Syrian.

The mother's eye lifted dully from the lace.

"*Sneinatt?*" she asked blankly. "What have we to do with feasting? *Aie*—geet sooper," she added sharply, in English.

Nazileh sighed and obeyed. Her mother did not seem to see her; she did not speak at all. She ate her supper, fed the baby, and then sat down again to her lace. When it grew darker, she lighted the lamp, stared out into the street an instant, and then sat down, with a curious twist of her thick lips.

Nazileh left Antar wrapped closely in his rug, and slipped out again into the noise of Dix Street. She fingered her beads nervously as she crossed the roadway and ran breathlessly down the side street toward the public school. Teacher lived around the corner from the great brick building, Nazileh knew, for once she had proudly carried a message for her; but her heart thumped madly when she rang the bell.

"Please, teecha!" she stammered pitifully, when the maid had brought Miss Graham to the door, "I like thad you geeve me those feefty cen's for those beads!"

The teacher smiled down at the little maid.

"Why, it's Nazileh. Come in, dear!" She held the door to the sitting room open. "Now tell me what it is you want."

The dark fringed eyes dropped bashfully.

"I like that you geeve me those feefty cen's—"

"Oh, you do want to sell your beads," said the smiling lady. "Then just wait until I get my purse!"

Nazileh stood, trying to choke back the frightened sobs, fingering the beloved beads with her dirty, slender little hands. Teacher came back with another lady—a tall, stern looking lady, who stared at the little girl through formidable eyeglasses.

The tall lady watched teacher unfasten the beads with very evident disgust.

"You do the craziest things, Pris," she said languidly; "those things are worth about ten cents, I should say, and they are probably covered with germs."

Nazileh lifted horror-stricken eyes to her.

"They ees the evil-eye beads!" she stammered.

"They look it," said the tall lady dryly.

But the teacher held the pretty trinket in the light, where the colors shone gaily.

"Just you wait, Madge," she laughed. "When they are cleaned and have a new clasp, you won't know them. Here's your money, kiddy, and a shiny penny for a peppermint stick, besides, so run along."

Nazileh did run along; she ran as if the evil eye pursued her. Now that the mysterious protection of the beads was gone, danger seemed to lurk in every step. She scudded along under the street lamps with terror in her fast-beating heart. It seemed to her that she would never get back to the blessed familiarity of Dix Street.

Outside the shop of Abu Nageeb, she paused, and sobbed convulsively. The money was tight in her hot little hand, and she sat down on the step and opened her fingers slowly to stare down at it.

Abu Negeeb's shop was quite wonderful. All the delectable dainties of the East were to be found in his shining glass jars—pistachio nuts, pine seeds, figs stewed with annis, the round cakes of *baklawa*, and the queer little slabs of conserves made from what Umn Nageeb alone could tell.

Nazileh's voice quivered with emotion as she stood before him.

"I like to buy those ones thad make *sneinatt*—thad whead an' thad feeg an' thad nut," she faltered.

Abu Nageeb stared at her in amazement. His swarthy hands clutched his apron.

"*Sneinatt?*" he asked, his lips parted in glistening wonder. "Thad's funnee—nobudee makes *sneinatt* in thees land!"

"I make eet!" answered Nazileh staunchly; "I make eet for my brothaire Antar."

Abu Nageeb smiled dreamily, and stared across the shelves at the gaily wrapped packages of dates. Then he sighed.

"Thad's long time ago thad I carry *sneinatt* for my brothaire—my leedle brothaire." He put his hand to his throat and coughed.

He weighed out the wheat and the nuts like one in a dream.

"Blessings on thy brother's tooth," he murmured in Arabic, as he handed her the packages.

The excitement of handling the bundles took away the great fright that had possessed her. She reached the top of the stairs quite breathless. But she stepped into the room slyly, holding the packages behind her until she could drop them quietly on the oilcloth-covered table.

Her mother did not look up; she was still bending over the lace, under the flickering light of the carelessly trimmed lamp; her fingers never seemed to stop their restless twisting of the shining hooks.

Nazileh went over and stood at her shoulder.

"Now wilt thou make *sneinatt?*" she asked bravely. "I have brought the wheat, all cracked, and the figs, and the nuts."

The woman dropped her lace in amazement, and stared at her daughter. She was no longer pretty, this tired little mother of Nazileh and Antar; her dusky hair had lost its lovely gleam, and her eyes were heavy with weariness and weeping. In the first days of her widowhood she had clung to her children like a wild creature, but of late a dull resentment that they existed had possessed her. The burden of caring for them stupefied her; she was sinking into a fright-ful apathy that deadened her to every feeling except that of unutterable weari-ness. She stared at the girl like one suddenly roused from sleep.

"Wilt thou?" pleaded Nazileh, her dark eyes shining softly. "Wilt thou make *sneinatt*, little mother of my heart? And I will take it to Father Shiskim and Umn Salim and Abu Nageeb and"—she broke into English with a swift little burst of giggles—"an' to the Dootch ladee's funnee daughter—eh?"

She ran across the room, caught up the parcels, and came back quickly to put them in her mother's lap.

"Ah!" she sniffed delightedly; "thad smell mos' nice like anytheeng!"

The woman fingered them oddly.

"Who gave thee these?" she asked curiously.

Nazileh stirred uneasily.

"I haf bought them een the shop of Abu Nageeb," she said slowly.

"But thad monee?" demanded her mother. "Where deed you geet thad monee?"

Nazileh trembled.

"Now thad I ees waxnate,"—her voice faltered, but she began again coura-geously: "Now thad I ees waxnate, the evil eye an' the black deeth may come nod. Thad nice teecha—she make thad she like those leedle beads; she geeve me—"

"*Mashallah!*" exclaimed the woman, in horror. "You haf sell your beads!"

The child nodded dumbly.

"For *sneinatt*—for Antar!" she whispered.

The lamplight shone on Nazileh's frightened face; she stretched out her up-turned hands pleadingly.

"Now welt thou make eet?" she beseeched. "Umn Salim—she say we do too mooch forgeet to do like we do een Syreeah—the theengs of our fathaires we do forgeet—an' eef we make *sneinatt*, thad weel be like they do een Syreeah—an' thad Antar, he mos' bes' babe we got, my mothaire!"

The night wind blew in from the bay, where the gleaming lights of the ferry boats shone softly; from the street below them the Babel of voices sounded faint and far away.

Something stirred in the heart of the woman, something that seemed to lift the weight of poverty and woe. She nodded her head slowly.

"On the morrow, little one," she said softly.

Then suddenly she stretched out her arms, mutely, and gathered her daughter to her breast.

"Thou art a little fool!" she murmured, her lips against the soft curls, "a little fool!"

Nazileh snuggled happily against her shoulder.

"Thad's whad you say long ago een Syreeah," she giggled merrily—"een Syreeah—een Beirut—on the 'ousetop. My fatheraire, he too deed laugh; thad's thad time I was scare of a leezard—do you remember?"

Her head drooped heavily now; she was very tired, was Nazileh.

"Thad's one good theeng—we nod leeve where thad leezard could scare Antar," she murmured drowsily. "But thad Syreeah—thad's mos' bes' land I know—we mus' nod forgeet—"

Umn Antar's tears flowed swiftly, yet a strange peace filled her soul.

"We nod forgeet," she whispered, hugging Nazileh closer; "we nod forgeet, my heart of hearts!"

(1911)

H.R.H. The Prince of Hester Street

Myra Kelly

"It will be difficult," said Miss Bailey, gently insubordinate, "very difficult. I have already a register of fifty-eight and seats for only fifty. It is late in the term, too; the children read and write quite easily. And you say this new boy has never been at school?"

"Never," admitted the Principal. "His people are rather distrustful of us. Some religious prejudice, I believe. They are the strictest of the strict. The grandfather is a rabbi and has been educating the boy—an only child, by the way."

"Put him in the kindergarten," Miss Bailey interjected hopefully.

"No," answered the Principal. "He's too old for that."

"Then let him wait until he can enter with the beginners in September. He will be really unhappy when he finds himself so far behind the others here."

"I'm afraid I must ask you to take him now," the Principal persisted. "His father, the Assemblyman for this district, sees some advantage in sending his boy to school with the children of his supporters. But, of course, I sha'nt expect you to bring the child up to the grade. Just let him stay here and be happy. If you will send your roll book to my office I shall have him entered."

And so it chanced, on an afternoon of early March, that the name of Isaac Borrachsohn was added—all unalphabetically—at the end of the roll call of the First Reader Class.

A writing lesson was in progress on the next morning when the new boy arrived. Miss Bailey, during her six months' reign over Room 18, had witnessed many first appearances, but never had charge of hers been borne into court on such a swelling tide of female relatives. The rather diminutive Teacher was engulfed in black-jetted capes, twinkling earrings, befeathered hats, warmly gleaming faces, and many flounced skirts, while the devoted eyes of the First Reader Class caught but fleeting glimpses of its sovereign between the red roses rising, quite without visible support, above agitated bonnets.

Against his background Isaac glowed like a bird of paradise. The writing lesson halted. Bluntly pointed pencils paused in mid-air or between surprise-parted lips, and the First Reader Class drew deep breaths of awe and of admiration: for the new boy wore the brightest and tightest of red velvet Fauntleroy suits, the most bouffant of underlying shirts, the deepest of lace collars, the most straightly cut of Anglo-Saxon coiffures, the most far reaching of sailor hats. Sadie Gonorowsky, the haughty Sadie, paused open-eyed in her distribution of writing papers. Morris Mogilewsky, the gentle Morris, abstractedly bit off and swallowed a piece of the gold fish food. Isidore

Belchatosky, the exquisite Isidore, passed a stealthy hand over his closely cropped red head and knew that his reign was over.

Miss Bailey determined, in view of the frightened expression in the newcomer's eyes, to forgive his inopportune enlistment. At her cordial words of welcome the alarm spread from his wide eyes to his trembling lips, and Teacher turned to the relatives to ask: "Doesn't he speak English?"

There ensued much babbling and gesticulation. Issac was volubly reproved and then one of the younger and befeathered aunts made answer.

"Sure does he. Only he was bashful, and when he should get sooner over it he English just like you speaks. Just like you he speaks. He is a goot boy. Where is he goin' to sit? Where's his place?"

Miss Bailey reflected with dismay that there was not an unassigned desk in the room. Fortunately, however, Patrick Brennan was absent on that morning—he was "making the mission" at St. Mary's church with his mother—and his queer assortment of string, buttons, pencil stumps, and a mute and battered mouth organ, were swept into a drawer of Teacher's desk. Isaac was installed in this hastily created vacancy, the gratified relatives withdrew, and the writing lesson was resumed.

When Isaac found himself cut entirely away from the maternal apron strings, his impulse was towards the relief of tears, until his wandering gaze encountered the admiring eyes of Eva Gonorowsky and an aimless hand came in contact with the hidden store of chewing gum with which the absent Patrick was wont to refresh himself. It was lightly attached to the undersurface of the chair, and Isaac promptly applied it to the soothing of his spirits, deciding that a school which furnished such dark and curly-locked neighbors and such delectable sustenance was a pleasant place. So he accepted a long pencil from Sarah Schrodsky, and a sheet of paper from Sadie Gonorowsky, and fell to copying the writing on the board.

While he labored—quite unsuccessfully, since all his grandsire's instructions had been in Hebrew—Miss Bailey passed from desk to desk on a tour of inspection and exhortation, slightly annoyed and surprised to find that the excitement consequent upon Isaac Borrachsohn's introduction had not yet subsided. Eva Gonorowsky was flagrantly inattentive, and Teacher paused to point an accusing finger at the very erratic markings which she had achieved.

"Eva," said she, "why do you keep your writing so very far from the line?"

"I ain't so big," Eva responded meekly, "und so I makes mistakes. I tells you scuse."

"Honey," responded Miss Bailey, her wrath turned away by this soft answer, "you could do beautifully if you would only look at the board instead of staring at the new boy."

"Yiss ma'an," acquiesced Eva. "But, oh, Teacher, Missis Bailey, ain't he the sweet dude!"

"Do you think so? Well, you need not stop writing to look at him, because you will be seeing him every day."

"In this class? Oh, ain't that fine!" Eva whispered. "My, *ain't* his mamma put him on nice mit red-from-plush suits and stylish haircuts!"

"Well, Isidore Belchatosky has a velvet suit," said the gentle hearted Miss Bailey, as she noted the miserable eyes of the deposed beau traveling from his own frayed sleeve to the scarlet splendor across the aisle.

"But it's black," sneered the small coquette, and Teacher was only just in time to snatch Isidore's faultless writing from the deluge of his bitter tears.

When the First Reader Class filed down the yard for recess, Miss Bailey was disgusted to find that Isaac Borrachsohn's admiring audience increased, until it included every boy in the school young enough to be granted these twenty minutes of relaxation during the long morning. He was led away to a distant corner; there to receive tribute of deference—marbles, candy, tops, and political badges. But he spoke no word. Silently and gravely he held court. Gravely and silently he suffered himself to be led back to Room 18. Still silently and still gravely he went home at twelve o'clock.

At a quarter before one on that day, while Morris Mogilewsky and Nathan Spiderwitz, monitors of gold fish and window boxes, were waiting dejectedly for the opening of the school doors and reflecting that they must inevitably find themselves supplanted in their sovereign's regard—for Teacher, though an angel, was still a woman, and therefore sure to prefer gorgeously arrayed ministers—there entered to them Patrick Brennan, fortified by the morning's devotion and reacting sharply against the morning's restraint.

"Fellars," he began jubilantly; "I know where we can hook a banana. And the Ginney's asleep! Come on!"

His colleagues looked at him with lackluster eyes. "I don't need no bananas," said Morris dispiritedly. "They ain't so awful healthy fer me."

"Me too," Nathan agreed. "I et six once und they made me a sickness."

"Bananas!" urged Patrick. "Bananas, an' the man asleep! What's the matter with ye anyway?"

"There's a new boy in our class," Morris answered. "Und he's a dude. Und Teacher's lovin' mit him."

"Und he sets in your place," added Nathan.

"I'll break his face if he tries it again," cried Patrick hotly. "Who let him sit there?"

"Teacher," wailed Morris. "Ain't I tell you how she's lovin' mit him?"

"And where's all *my* things?" Patrick demanded with pardonable curiosity. "Where am I to sit?"

"She makes you should set by her side," Morris reassured him. "Und keep your pencil in her desk. It could be awful nice fer you. You sets right by her."

"I'll try it for a day or two," said Patrick grandly. "I'll see how I like it."

For the first hour he liked it very well. It was fun to sit beside Miss Bailey, to read from her reader, to write at her desk, to look grandly down upon his fellows, and to smile with condescension upon Eva Gonorowsky. But when Teacher opened her book of Fairy Tales and led the way to the land of magic,

Patrick discovered that the chewing gum, with which he was accustomed to refresh himself on these journeys, was gone. Automatically he swept his hand across the under surface of his chair. It was not there. He searched the drawer in which his treasures had been bestowed. Nor there. He glanced that the usurper in his rightful place, and saw that the jaws of Isaac moved rhythmically and placidly. Hot anger seized Patrick. He rose deliberately upon his sturdy legs and slapped the face of that sweet dude so exactly and with such force that the sound broke on the quiet air like the crack of a revolver. Teacher, followed by the First Reader Class, rushed back from Fairy Land, and the next few minutes were devoted to separating the enraged Patrick from the terrified Isaac, who, in the excitement of the onslaught, had choked upon the casus belli, and could make neither restitution nor explanation. When Isaac was reduced, at the cost of much time and petting on Miss Bailey's part, to that stage of consolation in which departing grief takes the form of loud sobs, closely resembling hiccoughs and as surprising to the sufferer as to his sympathizers, Patrick found himself in universal disfavor. The eyes of the boys, always so loyal, were cold. The eyes of the girls, always so admiring, were reproachful. The eyes of Miss Bailey, always so loving, were hard and angry. Teacher professed herself too grieved and surprised to continue the interrupted story, and Patrick was held responsible for the substitution of a brisk mental arithmetic test in which he was easily distanced by every boy and girl in the room. But Isaac was still silent. No halcyon suggestion beginning, "Suppose I were to give you a dollar and you spent half of it for candy," no imaginary shopping orgie, could tempt him into speech.

It was nearly three o'clock when at last he found his voice. In an idle inspection of his new desk he came upon one of those combinations of a pen, a pencil, and an eraser, which gladden the young and aggravate the old. It was one of Patrick's greatest treasures, and had long been Eva's envious desire, and now Patrick, chained to the side of his indignant Teacher, saw this precious, delicate, and stubborn mechanism at the mercy of his clumsy successor. Isaac wrenched and twisted without avail; Patrick's wrath grew dark; Eva shyly proffered assistance; Patrick's jealousy flamed hot. And then, before Patrick's enraged eyes, Eva and Isaac tore the combination of writing implements to fragments in their endeavor to make it yield a point. Patrick darted upon the surprised Isaac like an avenging whirlwind, and drove a knotty little fist into the center of the Fauntleroy costume. And then, quite suddenly, Isaac lifted up his voice:

"Don't you dast to touch me," he yelled, "you —— —— Krisht fool."

Miss Bailey sprang to her feet, but before she could reach the offender he had warmed to his work and was rolling off excerpts from remarks which he had heard at his father's club rooms. These were, of course, in Hebrew, but after much hissing and many gutturals he arrived, breathless, at the phrase as Anglo-Saxon as his hair:

"You be ——! Go to ——!"

Of all Miss Bailey's rules for the government of her kingdom the most stringent were against blasphemy. Never had her subjects seen their gentle lady so instinct with wrath as she was when holding the wriggling arm of Patrick with one hand and the red plush shoulder of Isaac with the other. She resumed her place in the chair of authority. She leaned forward until her eyes, angry and determined, were looking close into Patrick's, and began:

"You first. You commenced this thing. Now listen. If you ever touch that boy again—I don't care for what reason—I will whip you. Here, before the whole class, I shall spank you. Do you understand?"

"Yes," said Patrick.

"And now you." turning quickly to Isaac. "If you ever again dare to say bad words in this room I shall wash out the mouth you soil in saying them. Do you understand?"

Isaac was silent.

"Do you understand?" repeated Miss Bailey.

Isaac spoke no word; gave no sign of comprehension.

"Morris," called Teacher, "come and tell him that in Jewish for me," and Morris, with many halts and shy recoilings, whispered a few words into the ear of Isaac, who remonstrated volubly.

"He says he ain't said no bad word," the interpreter explained. "His papa says like that on his mamma, and his mamma says like that on his papa. Fer him, that ain't no bad word."

"It is a bad word here," said Teacher inexorably. "Tell him I'll wash out his mouth if he says it again."

Miss Bailey was so ruffled and disgusted by the course of events that she allowed only the Monitor of the Gold Fish Bowl to stay with her after school that afternoon. When readers were counted and put upon the shelves, charts furled, paint brushes washed, pencils sharpened, and blackboards cleaned, Morris pressed close to this lady and whispered:

"Say, Teacher, I should tell you somethings."

"Well, then, old man, tell it."

"Teacher, it's like this; I ain't tell Ikey, out of Jewish, how you say, you should wash out his mouth."

"You didn't tell him? And why not, pray?"

"Well," and Morris's tone, though apologetic, was self-righteous, "I guess you don't know 'bout Ikey Borrachsohn."

"I know he said two very bad things. Of course, I did not understand the Jewish part. What did he say? Did you know?"

"Sure did I, on'y I wouldn't to tell it out. It ain't fer you. It ain't no fer—fer ladies."

Miss Bailey patted her small knight's hand. "Thank you, Morris," she said simply. "And so it was bad?"

"Fierce."

"Very well; I shall ask some other boy to tell him that I shall wash out his mouth."

"Well," Morris began as before, "I guess you don't know 'bout Isaac Borrachsohn. You dassen't to wash out his mouth, 'cause his grandpa's a Rabbi."

"I know he is. Is that any reason for Isaac's swearing?"

"His papa," Morris began, in an awed whisper; "his papa's the King of Hester Street."

"Well," responded Teacher calmly, "that makes no difference to me. No one may swear in this room. And now, Morris, you must run home. Your mother will be wondering where you are."

Three minutes later Morris's dark head reappeared. His air was deeply confidential. "Teacher, Missis Bailey," he began, "I tells you 'scuse."

"Well, dear, what is it?" asked Miss Bailey with divided interest, as she adjusted a very large hat with the guidance of a very small looking glass. "What do you want?"

Again Morris hesitated. "I guess," he faltered; "I guess you don't know 'bout Isaac Borrachsohn."

"What has happened to him? Is he hurt?"

"It's his papa. Ain't I told you he's the King of Hester Street und he's got dancing balls. My mamma und all the ladies on our block they puts them on stylish und goes on the ball. Und ain't you see how he's got a stylish mamma mit di'monds on the hair?"

"Yes," admitted Miss Bailey, "I saw the diamonds." Not to have seen the paste buckle which menaced Mrs. Borrachsohn's left eye would have been to be blind indeed.

"Und extra, you says you should wash out his mouth," Morris remonstrated. "I guess, maybe, you fools."

"You'll see," said Miss Bailey blithely. "And now trot along, my dear. Good afternoon."

Teacher hurried into her jacket and was buttoning her gloves when the Monitor of the Gold Fish Bowl looked timidly in.

"What now?" asked Teacher.

"Well," said Morris, and he breathed hard, "I guess you don't know 'bout Isaac Borrachsohn."

Miss Bailey fell away into helpless laughter. "That would not be your fault, honey, even if it were true," she said. "But what has he been doing since I saw you?"

"It's his papa," answered Morris. "His papa's got p'rades."

"He has what?"

"P'rades."

"And are they very bad? I never heard of them."

"You don't know what is p'rades?" cried Morris. "Won't your mamma leave you see them?"

"What are they?" asked Teacher. "Did you ever see them?"

"Sure I seen p'rades. My papa he takes me in his hand und I stands by the curb und looks on the p'rade. It goes by night. Comes mans und comes cops und comes George Wash'ton und comes Ikey Borrachsohn's papa, mit proud looks—he makes polite bows mit his head on all the peoples, und comes Teddy Rosenfelt. Und comes cows und comes more cops und ladies und el-fints, und comes Cap Dreyfus and Terry McGovern. Und comes mans, und mans, und mans—a great big all of mans—und they says: 'What's the matter mit Ikey Borrachsohn's papa?'—he ain't got no sickness, Miss Bailey, on'y it's polite you says like that on p'rade. Und more mans they says: 'Nothings is mit him! He's all right!' That is what is p'rades. Ikey's papa's got them, und so you dassen't to wash out his mouth."

"One more bad word," was Teacher's ultimatum; "one more and then I'll do it."

Miss Bailey's commands were not lightly disregarded, and Patrick Brennan spent the ensuing week in vain endeavor to reconcile himself to a condition of things in which he, the first born of the policeman on the beat, and therefore by right of heredity a person of importance in the realm, should tamely submit to usurpation and insult on the part of this mushroom sprig of moneyed aristocracy, this sissy kid in velvet pants, this long-haired dummy of an Isaac Borrachsohn. Teacher could not have meant to cut him off from all hope of vengeance. If she had—then she must be shown that the honor of the house of Brennan was a thing beyond even her jurisdiction. A Brennan had been insulted in his person and in his property. Of course, he must have satisfaction.

If Morris could have known that Patrick, of whom he was so fond, was plotting evil against the heir-apparent to the throne of Hester Street, he might have persuaded that scion of the royal house of Munster to stay his hand. But the advice of Patrick *père* had always been: "Lay low until you see a good chanst an' then sock it to him good and plenty." So Patrick *fils* bided his time and continued to "make the mission" with his pious mother.

After his initial speech in his English, "so like Miss Bailey's," Isaac Borrachsohn resumed his cloak of silence and spoke no more the language of the land. Even in his own tongue he was far from garrulous, and yet his prestige continued to increase, his costumes grew ever more gorgeous, and his slaves—both male and female—daily more numerous. In reading and in "Memory Gems" his progress was, under his veil of speechlessness, imperceptible, but in writing and in all the prescribed branches of Manual Training he acquired a proficiency which made it impossible to return him to his royal sire. Gradually it was borne in upon Miss Bailey that she had met her Waterloo—a child who would have none of her. All her attempts at friendliness were met by the same stolid silence, the same impersonal regard, until in desperation she essayed a small store of German phrases, relics of her sophomore days. Six faulty sentences, with only the most remote bearing upon the subject in hand, were more efficacious than volumes of applied psychology, and the reserve of Isaac Borrachsohn vanished before the rising conviction that Teacher belonged to his own race. How otherwise, he demanded, could she speak such beautiful Hebrew? When Morris translated this tribute to Patrick, a flame of anger and of hope lit up that Celtic soul. Such an accusation brought against Miss Bailey, whom he had heard his noble father describe as "one of ourselves, God bless her!" was bitter to hear, but the Knight of Munster comforted himself with the conviction that Teacher would no longer shield the sissy from the retribution he had now doubly earned. But it should be a retribution fitted to the offender and in proportion to the offense. Long experience of Jewish playfellows had taught Patrick a revenge more fiendish than a beating, a ducking, a persecution by "de gang," or a confiscation of goods and treasures. All of these were possible and hard to bear, but for Isaac's case something worse was needed. He should be branded with a cross!

Fortune, after weeks of frowning, was with Patrick on that warm April afternoon. Isaac was attired in a white linen costume so short of stocking and of knickerbockers as to exhibit surprising area of fat leg, so fashionable in its *tout ensemble* as to cause Isidore Belchatosky to weep aloud, so spotless as to prompt Miss Bailey to shield it with her own "from silk" apron when the painting lesson commenced. Patrick Brennan had obeyed his father's injunction to "lay low" so carefully that Teacher granted a smiling assent to his plea to be allowed to occupy the desk, which chanced to be empty, immediately behind Isaac's.

On each little desk Miss Bailey, assisted by her whole corps of monitors, placed a sheet of drawing paper, a little pan containing India ink dissolved in water, and a fat Japanese paint brush. The class was delighted, for, with the possible exception of singing, there was no more popular occupation. Briskly the First Reader Class fell to work. Carefully they dipped brushes in ink. Bravely they commenced to draw. Teacher passed from desk to desk encouraging the timid, restraining the rash.

Patrick dug his brush deep down into his ink, lifted it all wet and dripping, cast a furtive glance at Teacher's averted head, and set stealthily work at the bent and defenseless back of Isaac Borrachsohn's spotless suit. From shoulder to shoulder he drew a thick black mark. Then another from straight cropped hair to patent leather belt. Mrs. Borrachsohn belonged to the school of mothers who believe in winter underwear until the first of June, and Isaac felt nothing. But Eva Gonorowsky saw and shuddered, hiding her eyes from the symbol and the desecration. Patrick glowered at her, filled his brush again, bent quickly down, and branded the bare and mottled legs of his enemy with two neatly cross strokes.

In an instant the room was in an uproar. Patrick, his face and hands daubed with ink, was executing a triumphant war dance around Isaac who, livid and inarticulate with rage, was alternately struggling for words and making wondrous Delsartean attempts to see his outraged back.

"I socked it to you good and plenty!" chanted Patrick in shrill victory. "Look at your back! Look at your leg! It's ink! It won't come off! It will never come off! Look at your back!"

Miss Bailey clanged the bell, caught Patrick by the waistline, thrust him under her desk, fenced him in with a chair, and turned to Isaac who had only just realized the full horror of his plight. Isidore Belchatosky and Eva Gonorowsky had torn off the white tunic—thereby disclosing quantities of red flannel—and exhibited its desecrated back. And speech, English speech, returned to the Prince of Hester Street. Haltingly at first but with growing fluency he cursed and swore and blasphemed; using words of whose existence Teacher had never heard or known and at whose meaning she could but faintly guess. Eva began to whimper; Nathan lifted shocked eyes to Teacher; Patrick kicked away the barricading chair and, still armed with the inky brush, sprang into the arena, and it was not until five minutes later that gentle peace settled down on Room 18.

Miss Bailey had received full parental authority from the policeman on the beat and she felt that the time for its exercise had come.

"Patrick," she commanded. "Position!" And the Leader of the Line stood forth stripped of his rank and his followers, but not of his dauntless bearing.

Teacher with a heavy heart, selected the longest and lightest of her rulers and the review continued.

"Hips firm!" was the next command, and Patrick's grimy hands sprang to his hips.

"Trunk forward—bend!" Patrick doubled like a jackknife and Miss Bailey did her duty.

When it was over she was more distressed than was her victim. "Patrick, I'm so sorry that this happened," said she. "But you remember that I warned you that I should whip you if you touched Isaac. Well, you did and I did. You know—all the children know—that I always keep my word."

"Yiss ma'an," murmured the frightened First Reader Class.

"Always?" asked Patrick.

"Always," said Miss Bailey.

"Then wash out his mouth," said Patrick, pointing to the gloating Isaac, who promptly ceased from gloating.

"Oh, that reminds me," cried Teacher, "of something I want you to do. Will you tell Isaac you are sorry for spoiling his new suit?"

"Sure," answered Patrick readily. "Say, Isaac, I'm sorry. Come an' git your mouth washed."

"Well," and Miss Bailey temporized, "his clothes are ruined. Don't you think you could forgive him without the washing?"

"Sure," answered Patrick again. "Ain't it too bad that you can't too! But you said it, and now you've got to do it. Like you did about me, you know. Where's the basin? I'll fill it."

Teacher was fairly trapped, but, remembering that Isaac's provocation had been great, she determined to make the ordeal as bearable as possible. She sent for some water, selected a piece of appetizing rose pink soap, a relic of her Christmas store, and called Isaac, who, when he guessed the portent of all these preliminaries, suffered a shocking relapse into English. Nerved by this latest exhibition, Miss Bailey was deaf to the wails of Isaac and unyielding to the prayers and warning of Morris and to the frantic sympathy of Eva Gonorowsky.

"Soap ain't fer us," Morris cried. "It ain't fer us. We don't ever make like you makes mit soap!"

"I noticed that," said Teacher dryly. "I really think you are afraid of soap and water. When I finish with Isaac you will all see how good it is for boys and girls to be washed."

"But not in the mouth! Oh, Missis Bailey, soap in the mouth ain't fer us."

"Nonsense, honey," answered Teacher; "it will only clean his teeth and help him to remember not to say nasty words." And all unaware of the laws of "kosher" and of "traef," the distinctions between clean and unclean, quite as rigorous as, and much more complicated than, her own, Constance Bailey washed out the mouth of her royal charge, and, it being then three o'clock, dismissed her awed subjects and went serenely home.

On his progress towards the palace of his sire, Isaac Borrachsohn, with Christian symbols printed large upon his person, alienated nine loyal Hebrew votes from his father's party and collected a following of small boys which nearly blocked the narrow streets. The crosses were bad enough, but when it was made clear that the contamination, in the form of bright pink soap, had penetrated to the innermost recesses of the heir of the Borrachsohns, the aunts, in frozen horror, turned for succor and advice to the venerable rabbi. But he could only confirm their worst fears. "Soap," said he, "is from the fat of pigs. Our boy is defiled. Tomorrow he must be purified at the synagogue. I told you it was a Christian school."

Then did the Assemblyman quail before the reproach of his women. Then did he bite his nails in indecision and remorse and swear to be revenged upon the woman who had dared so to pollute his son. Then did Isaac weep continuously, noisily, but ineffectually for, on the morrow, to the synagogue he went.

Miss Bailey, when she saw that he was absent, was mildly self-reproachful and uneasy. If she could have known of the long and complicated rites and services which she had brought upon the boy who had been entrusted to her to be kept happy and out of mischief, she might not have listened so serenely to the janitor's announcement two days later.

"Borrachsohn and a whole push of women, and an old bird with a beard, are waitin' for you in the boys' yard," he whispered with great *empressement*. "I sent them there," he explained, "because they wouldn't fit anywhere else. There's about a hundred of them."

Mr. Borrachsohn's opening remark showed that the force of Isaac's speech was hereditary. "Are you the —— —— young woman who's been playing such fool tricks with my son? You'll wish you minded your —— business before I get done with you."

The belligerent attitude was reflected by the phalanx of female relatives, whose red roses waved in defiance now, as they had nodded in amity a few short weeks before. For an instant Teacher did not grasp the full meaning of Mr. Borrachsohn's greeting. Then suddenly she realized that this man, this trafficker in the blood and the honor of his people, had dared to swear at her, Constance Bailey. When her eyes met those of the Assemblyman he started slightly, and placed Isaac between him and this alarming young person who seemed not at all to realize that he could "break her" with a word.

"Is this your child?" she demanded. And he found himself answering meekly:

"Yes ma'an."

"Then take him away," she commanded. "He is not fit to be with decent children. I refuse to teach him."

"You can't refuse," said Mr. Borrachsohn. "It is the law—"

"Law!" repeated Teacher. "What is the law to you?" She was an open-eyed young person; she had spent some months in Mr. Borrachsohn's district; she had a nasty energy of phrase; and the King of Hester Street has never translated the ensuing remarks to the wife of his bosom nor to the gentle-eyed old rabbi who watched, greatly puzzled by his ideal of a Christian persecutor and this very different reality. Gradually the relatives saw that the accuser had become the accused, but they were hardly prepared to see him supplicating and even unsuccessfully.

"No, I won't take him. I tell you his language is awful. I can't let the other children hear him."

"But I shall see that he swears no more. We taught him for a joke. I'll stop him."

"I'm afraid you can't."

"Well, you try him. Try him for two weeks. He is a good boy; he will swear no more."

"Very well," was Teacher's ungracious acquiescence; "I shall try him again. And if he should swear—"

"You will not wash out his mouth—"

"I shall, and this time I shall use hot water and sapolio and washing soda."

Mr. Borrachsohn smiled blandly and turned to explain this dictum to his clan. And the dazed Miss Bailey saw the anger and antagonism die out of the faces before her and the roses above them, heard Mr. Borrachsohn's gentle, "We would be much obliged if you will so much accommodate us," saw the rabbi lift grateful eyes to the ceiling and clasp his hands, saw Mrs. Borrachsohn brush away a tear of joy, and felt Isaac's soft and damp little palm placed within her own by the hand of his royal sire, saw the jetted capes, the flounced skirts and befeathered hats follow the blue and brass buttons of the janitor, the broadcloth of the Assemblyman and the alpaca of the rabbi, heard the door close with a triumphant bang, saw the beaming face of the returning janitor, and heard his speech of congratulation:

"I heard it all; I was afraid to leave you alone with them. Will you excuse me, Miss Bailey, if I just pass the remark that you're a living wonder?"

Still densely puzzled and pondering as to whether she could hope ever to understand these people, she sought the Principal and told him the whole story. "And now why," she asked, "did he make such a fuss about the washing only to yield without a struggle at the end?"

The Principal laughed. "You are mistaken," said he. "Mr. Borrachsohn gained his point and you most gracefully capitulated."

"I," cried Teacher; "I yield to that horrid man! Never! I said I should use soda and sapolio—"

"Precisely," the Principal acquiesced. "And both soda and sapolio are kosher—lawful, clean. Miss Bailey, oh, Miss Bailey, you can never be haughty and lofty again, for you met 'that horrid man' in open battle and went weakly down before him."

(1904)

SOURCES

Abdullah, Achmed. "A Simple Act of Piety." In *The Best Short Stories of 1918*, edited by Edward J. O'Brien. Boston: Small Maynard, 1919. First published in *All-Story Weekly* 83 (April 20, 1918): 216–226.

Aldrich, Thomas Bailey. "Unguarded Gates." In *Unguarded Gates and Other Poems*. Boston: Houghton Mifflin, 1895. First published in *Atlantic Monthly* 70 (July 1892): 57

Anonymous. ["American ways are very extreme"]. In Hom, 126.

———. ["At a moment of tremendous opportunity"]. In Hom, 189.

———. ["Being idle in the wooden building"]. In Lai, Lim, and Yung, 88.

———. "Crude Poem Inspired by the Landscape." In Lai, Lim, and Yung, 128.

———. ["For one month, I was imprisoned"]. In Lai, Lim, and Yung, 130.

———. ["Four days before the Qiqiao Festival"]. In Lai, Lim, and Yung, 36.

———. ["Husband: his foolishness is second to none"]. In Hom, 114.

———. ["Husband: so dumb, second to none"]. In Hom, 115.

———. ["Instead of remaining a citizen of China"]. In Lai, Lim, and Yung, 40.

———. ["Since I left South China"]. In Hom, 206.

———. ["Spring returns to the continent"]. In Hom, 209

———. ["The young children do not yet know worry"]. In Lai, Lim, and Yung, 106.

——— "Twelve Hundred More." In *Songs of the American West,* edited by Richard E. Lingenfelter, Richard A. Dwyer, and David Cohen. Berkeley: University of California Press, 1968. First published in *The Blue and Gray Songster*, San Francisco: S. S. Green, 1877.

Antin, Mary. "The Lie." *Atlantic Monthly* 112 (August 1913): 177–190.

Beer, Morris Abel. "Moses" and "Old China." *Poetry* 10 (July 1917): 191.

Bourne, Randolph. "Trans-National America." *Atlantic Monthly* 118 (July 1916): 86–97.

Cahan, Abraham. "The Apostate of Chego-Chegg." *Century* 59 (November 1899): 94–104.

Chesnutt, Charles W. "Uncle Wellington's Wives." In *The Wife of His Youth and Other Stories of the Color Line*. Boston: Houghton Mifflin, 1889.

Chew, Lee. "The Biography of a Chinaman." *The Independent* 15 (February 19, 1903): 417–423.

Connolly, James B. "The Americanization of Roll-Down Joe." *Scribner's* 41 (May 1907): 575–583.

Converse, Florence. "Maggie's Minstrel." *Century* 67 (November 1914): 106–116.

Dailey, Jeanette. "Sweet Burning Incense." *Overland Monthly* 77 (January–February 1921): 9–14.

Day, Caspar. "Veronika and the Angelinos." *McClure's* 32 (January 1909): 277–284.

Dudley, Dorothy. "Paderewski." *Poetry* 10 (July 1917): 189.

Fuller, Henry Blake. "The Alien." In *Lines Long and Short: Biographical Sketches in Various Rhythms*. Boston: Houghton Mifflin, 1917.

Gates, Eleanor. "A Yellow Man and a White." *Scribner's* 37 (June 1905): 727–737.

Gibran, Kahlil. "Dead Are My People (Written in exile during the famine in Syria)." In *The Treasury of Kahlil Gibran*, edited by Martin L. Wolf, translated by Anthony Rizcallah Ferris. New York: Citadel, 1951.

Gilman, Charlotte Perkins. "The Melting Pot." In *The Late Poetry of Charlotte Perkins Gilman*, edited by Denise D. Knight. Newark: University of Delaware Press, 1996.

Hamm, Margherita Arlina. "Kalaun, the Elephant Trainer." *Century* 47 (February 1905): 502–511.

Haskin, Frederick J. "The Alien in the Melting Pot." Appendix E in *The Melting Pot: Drama in Four Acts*, by Israel Zangwill. Rev. ed. New York: Macmillan, 1924.

Hoier, Thomas, and Jimmie Morgan. "Don't Bite the Hand That's Feeding You." New York: Leo. Feist, 1915.

Hom, Marlon K., ed. *Songs of Gold Mountain: Cantonese Rhymes from San Francisco Chinatown*. Berkeley: University of California Press, 1987.

Kallen, Horace M. "Democracy Versus the Melting-Pot: A Study of American Nationality." *The Nation* (February 18–25, 1915).

Kelly, Myra. "H.R.H. The Prince of Hester Street." In *Little Citizens: The Humours of School Life*. New York: Grosset & Dunlap, 1904. First published in *McClure's* 23 (May 1904): 103–112.

Lai, Him Mark, Genny Lim, and Judy Yung, eds. *Island: Poetry and History of Chinese Immigrants on Angel Island, 1910–1940*. Seattle: University of Washington Press, 1991.

Lazarus, Emma. "The New Colossus." In *The Poems of Emma Lazarus*. Vol. 1. Boston: Houghton Mifflin, 1889.

Lessing, Bruno. "Unconverted." In *Children of Men*. New York: McClure, 1903.

Lowell, Amy. "The Foreigner." *Poetry* 4 (April 1914): 2–5.

MacBrayne, Lewis E. "The Promised Land." *McClure's* 20 (November 1902): 66–74.

McKay, Claude. "America." *Literary Digest* 75 (October 28, 1922): 33. First published in *Liberator* 4 (December 1921): 9.

Michelson, Max. "A Polish Girl." *Poetry* 9 (March 1917): 299.

Moravsky, Maria. "The Greenhorn in America." *Atlantic Monthly* 122 (November 1918): 663–669.

Páez, Catalina. "The Old Lamp." *Scribner's* 45 (May 1909): 560–569.

Poole, Ernest. "Salvatore Schneider." *Current Literature* 45 (August 1908): 228–233.

Price, C. A. "Ellis Island." *Scribner's* 41 (March 1907): 370.

Rihani, Ameen. "I Dreamt I Was a Donkey-Boy Again." In *The Book of Khalid*. New York: Dodd, Mead, and Company, 1911.

Roosevelt, Theodore. "True Americanism." In *American Ideals and Other Essays, Social and Political*. New York: G.P. Putnam, 1900. First published as "What 'Americanism' Means." *Forum* 17 (April 1894): 196–206.

Ruotolo, Onorio. "Mother America." Papers. Immigration History Research Center. University of Minnesota.

Sandburg, Carl. "Happiness." In *Chicago Poems*. New York: Henry Holt, 1916.

Schauffler, Robert Haven. "The Island of Desire." *Outlook* 100 (March 23, 1912): 666–673.

Spadoni, Adriana. "A Great Man." *Outlook* 104 (July 26, 1913): 685–691.

Steiner, Edward A. "A Slavic Oklahoman." In *The Broken Wall: Stories of the Mingling Folk*. New York: Fleming H. Revell, 1911.

Štýbr, Joseph. "Americanization." *The Czechoslovak Review* (June 1919): 153–154.

Sui Sin Far. "The Wisdom of the New." In *Mrs. Spring Fragrance*. Chicago: A. C. McClurg, 1912.

Swanstrom, Arthur M., and Carey Morgan. "The Argentines, the Portuguese, and the Greeks." New York: Joseph W. Stern, 1920.

Syrian, Ajan. "Alma Mater." *Poetry* 6 (June 1915): 110–111.

Tsiang, H. T. "Chinaman, Laundryman" and "Rickshaw Boy." In *Quiet Fire: A Historical Anthology of Asian American Poetry, 1892–1970*, edited by Juliana Chang. New York: Asian American Writers Workshop, 1996. First published in *Poems of the Chinese Revolution* (Privately printed, 1929.)

Twain, Mark. "John Chinaman in New York." In *Sketches Old and New*. New York: P. F. Collier, 1917. First published in *Galaxy* 10 (September 1870): 426.

Van Slyke, Lucille Baldwin. "The Tooth of Antar." In *Eve's Other Children*. New York: Frederick A. Stokes, 1912. First published in *McClure's* 36 (March 1911): 578–586.

Walrond, Eric. "On Being Black." *New Republic* 32 (November 1922): 244–246.

Willsie, Honoré. "What is an American? The Suicide of the Anglo-American." *Collier's* 50 (November 9, 1912): 13–14, 42.

Zakharchuk, Dmytro. Introduction to his second book of poems and "Foreign Country." Papers. Immigration History Research Center. University of Minnesota.

ABOUT THE EDITORS

Tim Prchal has published essays on late nineteenth- and early twentieth-century immigrant experience in *Studies in American Fiction* and *MELUS* and has presented papers on the subject at numerous academic conferences. Prchal's other published essays range from explorations of William Wells Brown to F. Scott Fitzgerald and from mystery fiction to American realism. He teaches American literature and writing at Oklahoma State University.

Tony Trigilio is the author of two books of criticism, most recently *Allen Ginsberg's Buddhist Poetics* (Southern Illinois University Press, 2007), and the book of poems, *The Lama's English Lessons* (Three Candles Press, 2006). His essays and reviews have been published in *American Literature, Tulsa Studies in Women's Literature*, and *Modern Language Studies*. He is an associate professor of English and director of the creative writing–poetry program at Columbia College, Chicago.